DATE DUE

LIBRARY OF
MONEY AND BANKING
HISTORY

THE FISCAL HISTORY OF TEXAS

Also Published In

Reprints of Economic Classics

By **WILLIAM M. GOUGE**

A SHORT HISTORY OF PAPER MONEY
& BANKING IN THE UNITED STATES [1833]

THE

FISCAL HISTORY OF TEXAS

EMBRACING AN ACCOUNT OF ITS

REVENUES, DEBTS & CURRENCY

FROM

THE COMMENCEMENT OF THE REVOLUTION
IN 1834 TO 1851-1852

WITH

REMARKS ON AMERICAN DEBTS

BY

WILLIAM M. GOUGE

[1852]

REPRINTS OF ECONOMIC CLASSICS

Augustus M. Kelley · Publishers
NEW YORK 1968

First Edition 1852

(Philadelphia: Lippincott, Grambo & Company, 1852)

Reprinted 1968 by

AUGUSTUS M. KELLEY · PUBLISHERS

New York   New York   10010

Library of Congress Catalogue Card Number

68 - 18226

PRINTED IN THE UNITED STATES OF AMERICA
by SENTRY PRESS, NEW YORK, N. Y. 10019

THE

FISCAL HISTORY OF TEXAS.

EMBRACING AN ACCOUNT OF ITS

REVENUES, DEBTS, AND CURRENCY,

FROM

THE COMMENCEMENT OF THE REVOLUTION IN 1834 TO 1851–52.

WITH

REMARKS ON AMERICAN DEBTS.

BY

WILLIAM M. GOUGE,

AUTHOR OF "A SHORT HISTORY OF PAPER-MONEY AND BANKING
IN THE UNITED STATES."

PHILADELPHIA:
LIPPINCOTT, GRAMBO, AND CO.
1852.

PREFACE.

In 1833 the author of this work published "A Short History of Paper-Money and Banking in the United States," the reception of which by the public was far more favorable than he anticipated. He has been for some time collecting materials for a continuation of that history; and a visit to the capital of Texas, in the early part of 1852, afforded him as good an opportunity as he could desire of making himself acquainted with whatever was most important in the currency concerns of that distant region. A rise in the waters of the rivers, which put an end to ordinary travelling, left him at leisure to extend his inquiries further than he originally intended. As he proceeded, he found the materials far more important than he had supposed them to be, and the result is the volume now presented to the public. It embraces much that could not with propriety be introduced into a continuation of "A History of Paper-Money and Banking in the United States," as most of the important events it records occurred before Texas became a member of the Union.

In the conduct of this work, the want of a good general history of Texas has been much felt—that by Kennedy extending no further than to 1839–1840. The general historian ought to have prepared the way for the inquirer into the fiscal concerns of the Republic; but he has had to prepare the way for the general historian.

Other difficulties have been encountered through the loss, by fire, of part of the records of the Republic. But free access to all that remained was courteously granted by the Texan authorities, and whenever the record was deficient, they kindly supplied what was wanted by oral information. Especially are the thanks of the author due to P. Hansboro' Bell, the   Governor, James

B. Shaw, Comptroller, John M. Swisher, Auditor, James H. Raymond, Treasurer; to W. D. Miller the former, and Thomas S. Duvall the present, Secretary of State; and also to Mr. Brewster, the editor of the Texas State Gazette, and Mr. De Cordova, the editor of the South-Western American.

The extracts, when of any length, are given in distinct type. This gives the volume all the advantages of a documentary history, and will enable the reader to distinguish at a glance what is said by the author from what is 'said by others. It will also afford those who have not leisure or inclination to read the whole work, facilities in selecting the passages in which they may be most interested.

If the book is not as amusing as the last new novel, the writer cannot help it. He has done the best he could, in the short time allowed him, with the dry and stubborn materials he had to handle. He comforts himself with the hope that, as he does not write for boarding-school misses, such dryness as necessarily arises from the nature of the subject will be pardoned. Some of the details may be interesting to few but citizens of Texas, and creditors of Texas; but the principles involved are highly important, not only to those whose political position requires them to study finance as a science, but to all who are in any way interested in the preservation of the public faith when pledged for the payment of public debts.

November, 1852.

INTRODUCTION.

IT may appear to some quite unnecessary to devote a whole volume to the fiscal concerns of a people, who, at the beginning, numbered but twenty thousand; who, when they were annexed to the United States, did not exceed one hundred thousand; and who, according to the census returns of 1850, were then less than two hundred thousand. But history is of importance only as it illustrates principles; and principles may be as strikingly illustrated in the small communities of Rhode Island, Delaware, or Texas, as in the larger ones of New York, Massachusetts, or Virginia.

The founders of the Republic of Texas were quite as bold and quite as brave as the founders of ancient Rome; and, in all probability, quite as good. At all events, they did not invite their neighbors of Arkansas and Louisiana to a camp-meeting, and then steal their wives and daughters from them.

In the short period of seven months, they achieved the independence of a country larger than Great Britain and Ireland, and for ten years, without direct aid from any foreign government, they sustained this independence, in defiance of all the attempts which a nation of ten millions made to reduce them to subjection.

The history of such a people cannot be without interest. As we proceed, it will be found that all the fiscal faults which the great nations of Europe and America have committed on a large scale, the Texans have committed on a small.

Owing to the connections which this people have since entered into with the United States, interesting questions arise to the publicist. Texas is the first region that has been annexed to our Union, by the free consent of both parties, without purchase and without conquest; but it will not probably be the last. It is important that we should know what liabilities, in regard to the public debts of communities so annexed, are thus brought on the United States.

But in points even more important than these does the fiscal history of Texas command attention.

The paper-money disease is hereditary with us Americans. If it is subdued in one form, it breaks out in another. To the old provincial paper-money, succeeded State paper-money and continental money. Then, brought almost to death's door by the violence of our complaint, we searched for a remedy, and thought we had found one in that provision of the U. S. Constitution which declares that "no State shall emit bills of credit." The disease, however, soon made its appearance with new vigor; the States evading the principles of the Constitution by establishing corporations to do that which they have not the power to do themselves.

Do the banks suspend specie payments? This only increases the amount of paper issues, and the number of paper issuers. The corporations of cities and towns, turnpike companies, bridge companies, railroad companies, and individuals in all the private walks of life immediately commence the issue of notes for dollars and the fractional parts of dollars. A new term is not then introduced into the language, but a new application is made of an old term, and "shin-plasters" mean in America what "shin-plasters" mean nowhere else.

Does the United States Government want money? Instead of borrowing gold and silver, it borrows paper from the banks, or resorts to the issue of treasury notes, and makes them receivable for duties. In the only very important war we have had since the War of Independence, it kept on with the issue of these notes till they were depreciated far below par; and the contrivances resorted to in the times of Van Buren and Polk to throw into circulation treasury notes bearing no interest, or only nominal interest, show that even those statesmen from whose professed principles better things might be looked for are themselves deeply infected with the hereditary disease of the nation. If such slight fiscal embarrassments as were felt in the times of Polk and Van Buren could induce them to sanction or connive at the issue of treasury notes bearing no interest, or only nominal interest, there is every reason to believe that, in a period of real exigency, they would have resorted to the issue of treasury notes of such small denominations as would have driven gold and silver out of circulation.

Do we wish to get rid of a Bank of the United States? We proceed in such a way that, in putting down one bank, we put up five hundred.

Does the deep experience of the evils we have suffered under both a national bank and a league of "pet banks" incline us to separate bank and State? Our sub-treasury system is so imperfectly framed that disbursing officers must, of necessity, use banks as depositories; and then, though the revenues of government are collected in gold and silver, they are paid out in paper.

Is one form of paper banking found not to answer? We then resort to another. To acts incorporating each bank separately, succeed general banking laws, by which they are incorporated altogether.

Does a "safety fund" afford evidence, by its own action, that there is no safety in it? Then we resort to "free banking," and require, from the issuers of notes, deposits of mortgages and stocks by way of security. This system does very well in fair weather, and we inquire no further.

Do the States want money? They perhaps, like Pennsylvania, resort to a pitiful evasion of the organic law of the Union, and issue "relief notes;" or it may be, like Indiana, more boldly violate the Federal Constitution, by emitting small bills of credit, and calling them treasury notes.

Do the banks throughout the country suspend specie payments? Then we have a good opportunity of getting rid of the whole concern. But we embrace it not. We re-establish the system by *coercing* a return to specie payments—a measure which inflicts twice as much evil on the community as would be produced by gradually winding up the suspended institution. We will do anything, we will suffer anything, rather than give up our paper-money.

Occasionally, in particular parts of the country, suffering intensely under our hereditary malady, we resort to severe legal and even constitutional provisions to prevent further issues of paper. But the power that makes State constitutions and State laws can also unmake them; and we hardly become convalescent before we relapse into our old disease.

Texas, though it, from 1835 to 1845, formed no part of the

American Union, was yet an American State. It was a State *without* the Union. The people were Americans by birth, thought, habits, feeling. Their political institutions distinguished them in one particular only from the States *within* the Union. They had within them that disease which taints all American blood, the paper-money disease, inherited from their ancestors. This, "the original sin" of Americans, had never been washed away by any baptism of sufferings. It is interesting to trace the manner in which this hereditary corruption displayed itself under the peculiar circumstances in which the Texans were placed, free from the restraints imposed by the United States Constitution. In this point of view, the history of currency and finance in Texas becomes more important than it would be if it were simply the history of currency and finance in a small community of 20,000 to 100,000 persons, distinguished in no way from the communities surrounding it.

Closely connected with the subject of paper-money, is that of public debt. Where there is the first, there will be the last. And it is no small objection to paper-money that it, in some instances, involves governments in debt that would otherwise be exempt from such burdens ; and that it, in other instances, where public debts would be small, increases them to such an amount as to make them intolerable.

Our own views on this subject are, in the main, as follows :—

1. A public debt is a public evil.

2. Nevertheless, it is sometimes necessary to incur public debts in order to secure the liberty and independence of a nation. In such cases, we submit to one evil in order to avoid a greater.

3. In other cases, it seems expedient to incur public debts, even when they are not absolutely necessary. The benefits resulting from them may more than compensate for the evils.

4. Great caution should be had in incurring public debts, because there is not naturally the same checks on them as on private debts. The private man who incurs a debt has to depend on himself alone for the payment of both principal and interest. The public men who create debts throw all the burden of paying them on others. They may incur these debts for their own special benefit, and the community will have to pay them. Even when the selfish interests of the lawgivers are not advanced in this way, great caution ought to be had in incurring public debts, as too great facility in borrow-

ing always leads to profusion in expenses. In addition to this, there is an important check on private debts which does not apply to public debts. A private man, when he incurs a debt, knows that he must not only pay the interest punctually, but that he will sooner or later be called on for the principal. But if a government only pays the interest punctually, the principal may remain unpaid forever.

5. Nothing but violations of constitution, and violations of law, or gross frauds in the negotiation of public debts, will justify a repudiation of them. No matter how unwise it may have been to borrow it, and no matter how foolishly it may have been expended, if the money has been borrowed according to law and constitution, it ought to be paid.

6. There is no force in the observation that one generation is not bound by the debts of another. The property created by the industry of one generation passes to that which succeeds it, and so on in perpetuity. The State never dies. The individuals that compose the State are always changing, just as the atoms of the human body are changing; and it is impossible to mark the succession of individuals that compose a State in such a way as to say that one class of them shall not be responsible for the debts incurred in the times of their predecessors. The benefits that may arise from incurring a public debt may extend through many generations. If the wars of William Pitt were really necessary to preserve the independence of Great Britain, it is just and right for the English people of the present day to pay the interest on the debt incurred in the prosecution of these wars. The Americans of the present generation have done no more than justice in paying off the debt of the Revolution, for they are in the full enjoyment of the blessings of the Revolution.

7. After a government has once made a regular audit of a claim against it, and issued a negotiable acknowledgment of the same, it has no right in after years to reopen that audit. A negotiable evidence of public debt, no matter what its form may be, transfers all the rights of the original holder to the final possessor. This point was very clearly set forth by Mr. Sedgwick, of Massachusetts, in the debate in Congress, in February, 1790, on the funding of the revolutionary debt.

" Whenever a voluntary engagement is made for a valuable consideration for property advanced, or services rendered, and the terms of the contract are understood, if *no fraud* or *imposition* is practised, the party engaging is bound to the performance, according to the literal meaning of the words in which it is expressed. Such contracts, whether of a government or an individual, may either be transferable or not transferable. The latter species of contract receives an additional value from its capacity of being transferred, if the circumstances of the possessor should render the sale of it either necessary or convenient to him. To render the transferable quality of such evidences of contract in any degree advantageous to the possessor, it is necessary to consider, in case of sale, the alience possessed of all the property of the original holder; and, indeed, it is highly absurd, and even contradictory, to say, that such evidences of debt are transferable, and at the same time to say that there is in them a kind of property which the holder could not convey by *bona fide* contract.

"This is the construction which has invariably been given to these contracts, whether formed by government or by individuals."

These are the views which we, and the great majority of our readers, have held from our youth upwards. But, in opposition to these sentiments, Texas maintains, through her authorities, that a State, in the times of her prosperity, is not bound to fulfil the engagements she entered into in the times of her adversity, but is at liberty to modify them to such extent as to herself may seem equitable.

These views are very distinctly set forth in a message which Governor Bell sent to the Legislature, on the 12th of November, 1851.*

" The Republic of Texas having executed her bonds and other evidences of debt *in an exceedingly dark and gloomy period of her history*, it became *necessary* to issue them for nominal amounts, bearing no sort of proportion to the amount actually received, and to pledge her resources, arising mainly at that time from her revenue, for their redemption. These securities, generally speaking, were concentrated at very low rates in the hands of moneyed speculators, who had contributed nothing to the achievement of her independence, or to the relief of her actual necessities in the administration of the government at the time they were issued. This *consideration*, well understood and appreciated, induced an inquiry in respect to the mode of redeeming these securities, *as no one could entertain the opinion, for a moment, that the government was under any obligation, either in justice or morality, to redeem them by paying the amount expressed on their face;* and that inquiry resulted in the passage of the act of the State Legislature of March 20, 1848, 'to provide for ascertaining the debt of

* The reader must not hold Governor Bell personally responsible for these sentiments, but regard him as the exponent of a community in which these principles have so long been taken for granted, that it is supposed to be unreasonable to doubt their correctness.

the late Republic of Texas,' which act required the auditor and comptroller of the State to reduce all claims presented for liquidation to the actual par value which was realized by the Republic at the time of their issue. The evident meaning and contemplation of that act was, that the holders should be paid in accordance with that amount thus ascertained by the auditorial board, subject to the revision of the Legislature; and the amounts so ascertained were considered all that was actually due from the State to her several creditors.

" That the Legislature had the right to pass this law, there can be no question; and that individuals holding the bonds or other evidences against the late Republic were bound by it, there can be as little."

If these principles be true, they ought to be universally adopted; for what is right in Texas, cannot be wrong in Virginia, Pennsylvania, or Ohio.

If these principles be true, they will prove a great relief to necessitous governments; for, according to the doctrine above laid down, the stronger the necessity a State is under, in times of adversity, of entering into contracts for supplies of money, the stronger the reason for setting aside such contracts in the days of her prosperity. The greater the necessities of a government, the less favorable, of course, the terms on which it can borrow; but it will lose nothing in the long run by that, for neither "morality nor religion" requires it ever to pay more than it has received. More especially is this true, if the evidences of public debt pass into the hands of moneyed men; and as the great mass of the evidences of public debt always pass into such hands, the State is thereby relieved from its engagements. It is quite enough if it pays one-half, one-quarter, or one-fifth of what it has promised to pay. That the Legislature has a right to pass such a law as this, there can be no question; and as little question that the creditors are bound by it!

Such are the principles of the authorities of Texas. If they be true, they ought, as already remarked, to be universally adopted. If they be not true, they ought to be promptly rejected. With nearly all our States and cities, and many of our counties, running into debt, it is of great importance that the nature of the obligation which public debt imposes should be correctly understood. Public opinion is, to a very great extent, the practical rule of morality; and if a wrong public opinion prevails in one State, it will be apt to spread into others. Ours is, moreover, a family of

States; and if one member of a family does ill, all the other members will suffer in reputation.

If sovereign States are not bound by their contracts, neither are railroad, nor canal companies, nor individuals; for there cannot be one rule of justice and morality for men in public, and another for men in private life.

There is already too much indifference in this country about the payment of debts. The public authorities ought not to increase the evil by setting the people a bad example. But if the States, to whom men look up for the administration of justice, become lax in the fulfilment of their public obligations, private men will be very apt to become equally lax in the discharge of their individual liabilities.

We can assure our friends in Texas that nothing was further from our intention, when we visited them, than to make a book about them. We were much pleased with their beautiful country, and much pleased with the people, a few only excepted. But the people with all their intelligence and enterprise, and their country with all its advantages, will never be duly appreciated by the rest of the world, till they review the decision to which they have come respecting the debt incurred in achieving and sustaining their independence. In our pages, we have carefully brought together all the facts necessary for such review, together with whatever else is interesting in the history of finance and currency in Texas. If we have erred, it has not been from selfish interests, for we have never been an owner of one dollar's worth of Texan securities.

CONTENTS.

CHAPTER I.

PROCEEDINGS UNDER THE GENERAL CONSULTATION.

Meeting of the Consultation, October 16, 1835—Reassembling of the same, November 3—Report on supplies sent to the army, and on money in the treasury—Glance at military operations—Extracts from the speech of Mr. Branch Tanner Archer— Money received from Mr. Thomas F. McKinney and from citizens of New Orleans —The land-offices closed—Grants of land to settlers and soldiers

CHAPTER II.

LEGISLATIVE PROCEEDINGS UNDER THE PROVISIONAL GOVERNMENT.

Ordinances to raise an army and navy, and to supply them with necessaries—Provision for auditing claims—Duties on imports and tonnage—Collectors of public dues—Act to authorize a temporary loan of one hundred thousand, and a permanent loan of one million dollars—Other ways and means—Liberal grants of land to soldiers

CHAPTER III.

EXECUTIVE PROCEEDINGS OF THE PROVISIONAL GOVERNMENT. FIRST PERIOD: NOVEMBER 14, 1835, TO JANUARY 2, 1836.

Comprehensive proceedings in four months—Pecuniary affairs of the General Council—A treasurer appointed—First report of Committee on Finance—Donation of Mr. Hutchins, of Natchez—Proceedings in relation to a United States Bank note— Plan for raising a revenue—Gov. Smith's objections to the way in which money-matters were conducted—Small costs of the campaign—Loan from Mr. Brookfield, of New Orleans

CHAPTER IV.

PROCEEDINGS UNDER THE PROVISIONAL GOVERNMENT IN RELATION TO THE PUBLIC LANDS.

The Commissioner of the Nashville Colony arraigned for contumacy—Great difficulties with the land-speculators in the Department of Nacogdoches—Indignation of Governor Smith—Determined action of the Council

CHAPTER XXXIV.

PRESENT CONDITION OF TEXAS.

APPENDIX.

THE FISCAL HISTORY OF TEXAS.

CHAPTER I.

PROCEEDINGS UNDER THE GENERAL CONSULTATION.

Meeting of the Consultation, October 16, 1835—Reassembling of the same, November 3—Report on supplies sent to the army, and on money in the treasury—Glance at military operations—Extracts from the speech of Mr. Branch Tanner Archer— Money received from Mr. Thomas F. McKinney and from citizens of New Orleans —The land-offices closed—Grants of land to settlers and soldiers.

IT is no part of our plan to give a particular view of the considerations that induced the Texans to dissolve their connection with Mexico. Suffice it to say that land-speculations and antipathy of race appear to have been the main causes of the revolution, the incidents connected with which we propose to narrate so far only as connected with the debts thereby incurred.

On the 15th of August, 1835, the citizens of the town of Columbia held a meeting, appointed a Committee of Safety and Correspondence, and resolved "that a Consultation of all Texas, through her representatives, was indispensable."

On the 16th of October following, between thirty and forty representatives, from eight different municipalities, assembled in General Consultation at San Felipe de Austin; but adjourned on the next day to the 1st of November, because "there was not a sufficient number to form a quorum, owing to the members being absent in the army." Before adjourning, they authorized such of their number as could not join the army to unite with a General Council, which had been instituted on the 11th. Of this Council, Mr. R. R. Royal was President.

On the 1st of November, the General Consultation reassembled ;.

but they were not able to form a quorum till the 3d.   They then elected Branch Tanner Archer President; and on the same day, the Council, of which Mr. Royal was President, resigned their powers.

In their report to the Consultation, they say :—

"On the 14th of October, Mr. Lewis Hall was commissioned as contractor for the army, from whose reports there are reasons to believe that upwards of one hundred beeves and a considerable quantity of corn-meal are on the way or repairing to head-quarters; and as connected with this subject, we will also inform you that supplies of sugar, coffee, bacon, blankets, shoes, tents, clothes, &c. have been forwarded from Columbia, Brazoria, and Matagorda.

"We have reason to believe that one eighteen-pounder and a twelve-pounder of artillery are on the way, with a fair proportion of powder and ball.

"The Council has made provisions for the collection of the public dues.

"We authorized a contract for a loan of one hundred thousand dollars of the citizens of New Orleans, and appointed T. F. McKinney an agent to repair to New Orleans, and to carry it into effect.

"Our finances arising from the receipt of dues for lands, as will appear on file in Mr. Gail Borden's report, marked F, which were in his hands, are fifty-eight dollars and thirty cents.   This money has been exhausted, and an advance by the President of the Council of thirty-six dollars.   There were also several hundred dollars in the hands of Mr. Money, the alcalde of the municipality of Austin.   Upon this money several advances have been made by Mr. Cochran, and probably will nearly cover the amount of the money in the alcalde's hands; as such, you may consider that at this moment the Council is out of funds."

"Despise not the day of small things."   As we proceed, we shall find the Government of Texas running in debt to the amount of millions, and, what is more, acquiring the ability to pay all it owes.   Even now we find all the germs of an extended fiscal system—contracts for purchases—measures for the collection of public dues—and authority to negotiate a loan.   Besides this, the Council suspended the proceedings of the land-offices, issued letters of marque and reprisal, established a mail route, and authorized the raising of three companies of volunteer rangers, amounting in all to eighty-five men, "*promising* each volunteer one dollar and twenty-five cents a day."

Even before the Consultation assembled, the miniature armies of Texas were active in the field.   Hostilities may be said to have commenced on the 20th of September, when a detachment of about two hundred Mexican cavalry from Bexar arrived on the western bank of the Guadaloupe, and attempted the passage of the river; but were repulsed by eighteen men under Captain Albert Martin, the whole of the available force then at Gonzales. (*Kennedy*, vol. i. p. 107.) On the 1st of October, under the command of Colonel Moore, they put to route the Mexicans under General Castonado; and on the 8th, under Captain Collinsworth, they attacked and captured the fort of Goliad, containing stores to the amount of ten thousand dollars, with two brass cannon and three hundred stand of arms. A still more important encounter was that of the 28th of October, near the mission of the Conception, when ninety-two Texans, under the command of Colonel Bowie and Captain Fannin, met a detachment of the Mexicans, consisting of about four hundred men, and obtained a complete victory over them.

But the glories of the field we must leave to more ambitious historians. The humble subject of dollars and cents engages our attention. We cannot, therefore, stop to tell how, on the 3d of November, a detachment of fifty men from Goliad, under Adjutant Westover, attacked and entered Lipantitlan, near San Patricio, the garrison of which (in number twenty-one) surrendered, and were dismissed on their parole on condition of not serving again against Texas during the war. Neither can we give the particulars of the " Grass Fight," in which five Mexicans were killed and several wounded, while the Texans escaped with only one man wounded. It is enough to say that, on the 3d of November, when the General Consultation was reorganized, the only place of any importance in Texas Proper, in possession of the Mexicans, was San Antonio de Bexar.

On taking the chair, Mr. Archer, the President elect, made an address, in which he suggested the propriety of establishing a provisional government, to consist of a governor, lieutenant-governor, and council, who should be clothed with both legislative and executive powers. Adverting to financial affairs, he said :—

" It will be necessary to procure funds in order to establish the contemplated government, and to carry on the war in which we are now engaged : it will, therefore, be our duty to elect agents to procure those funds. Without funds, however heroically your armies may fight, however wisely your councils may legislate, they will erect but a baseless fabric that will fall of its own weight."

The soundness of these principles will not be contested by the reader. In times of war, he who stays at home and works renders just as much service to his country as he who goes out to fight. If everybody should go out to fight, everybody would starve. Without money, wisdom and valor avail nothing. The Rothschilds and the Barings are just as much entitled to the glory that results from successful battles as are the Napoleons and the Wellingtons.

To illustrate this by the case now before us : If Mr. Gail Borden had not paid over the public money then in his hands, amounting to fifty-eight dollars and thirty cents; if Mr. President Royal had not advanced thirty-six dollars; and if Mr. James Cochran had not made " several advances," amounting in all to " several hundred dollars," how could supplies have been sent to the army ? And if supplies had not been sent to the army, the glorious battle of the Conception might never have adorned the annals of Texas. The captures of Goliad and Lipantitlan did, indeed, occur before the fiscal system of the Council was fully matured ; but the reader will agree with us that, without supplies obtained from some quarter, it is as impossible to capture cities as it is to fight pitched battles.

" Great events from little causes spring." " The rights and liberties of thousands of freemen are in your hands," said Mr. Archer, in his opening address to the Consultation ; " and millions yet unborn may be affected by your decisions." Yes ; and the rights and liberties of these thousands and millions, born and unborn, may be more dependent on Mr. Gail Borden's fifty-eight dollars and thirty cents, Mr. Royal's thirty-six dollars, and Mr. Cochran's " several hundred dollars," than perhaps any one of these gentlemen has imagined.

But a truce to reflections. We must resume our narrative. On the 6th, in the morning, it was resolved " that a committee of five be appointed to provide for the necessities of our army and troops on the road generally, with authority to borrow money, or originate other debts for that purpose ;" and on the afternoon of the same day, the committee made report as follows :—

"The committee, to whom was referred the subject of providing for the necessities of the army, beg leave to report that they have received of Thomas F. McKinney, by the hands of Dr. C. B. Stewart, a loan of five hundred dollars, of which they have expended, in payment of drafts on the authorities, the sum of two hundred and thirty-eight dollars, as will appear by the accompanying account, which leaves a balance in the hands of Dr.

Stewart of one hundred and sixty-two dollars, and one hundred left with Messrs. Robert Mills & Co., of Brazoria, leaving a balance in hand, in all, of two hundred and sixty-two dollars. Paid to express twenty, after making out the account, leaves two hundred and fifty-two dollars."

Here we find the national debt increasing, but not in such a way as to cause regret, as it increased the national means. And these means were further increased by subscriptions by the citizens of New Orleans, which, as was formally announced to the Consultation on the 8th, amounted to seven thousand dollars, when the agent, Mr. E. Hall, left that city, and were then probably augmented to ten or fifteen thousand dollars.

The Consultation expressed its sense of the obligation conferred in a letter of thanks, and made Captain Hall a present of a league of land, 4428 American acres. On the 9th, it made the captain an agent to purchase military stores at New Orleans. On the 11th, it adopted the plan of a provisional government. On the 12th, it elected Henry Smith Governor, J. W. Robinson Lieutenant-Governor, and chose a Council of thirteen members. On the same day, it elected Messrs. B. T. Archer, W. H. Wharton, and S. F. Austin, commissioners to proceed to the United States. On the 13th, the plan of the Provisional Government was enrolled; and, on the 14th, the Consultation adjourned to meet on the 1st of March, 1836, unless sooner called by the Governor and Council.

All the proceedings of the General Council, and of the Consultation, appear to have given satisfaction, except an order issued by the first on the 27th of October, and afterwards strengthened by the Consultation, to close the land-offices, and to forbid all further surveys. It was not free from objection, inasmuch as prudent men are not willing either to purchase land, or to expend labor and capital in its improvement, till the title is fully secured. But, as Mr. Barret said, in a report from a select committee on November 13 : "The land-offices have been closed, that no advantage should be taken over the soldier in the field, in making his selections of lands."

From the beginning, the Texan leaders regarded the land as the chief means of defraying the expenses of the war. Thus, Mr. Archer said, in his opening speech :—

"Some of our brethren of the United States of the North, hearing of our difficulties, have generously come to our aid ; many more ere long will be with us ; services such as they will render should never be forgotten. It will be proper for this Convention to secure them the rights and privileges of citizens, and to secure to them their land in 'head-rights,' and place them on the same footing with those of our citizens who have not yet obtained their lands.

"Some fraudulent sales or grants of land, by the late Government of Coahuila and Texas, will require your attention."

In like spirit, the Consultation said, in their letter of November 4, to the citizens of New Orleans:—

"Any who embark in our cause, in the army or navy, shall be liberally rewarded in land and money, and in the blessings of a grateful and redeemed people."

And the policy of Texas was then fixed, as far as it could be by Article XIV., in the plan of the Provisional Government, requiring all persons, "in any way concerned in the location of lands, forthwith to cease their operations during the agitated and unsettled state of the country, and until the land-office can be properly systematized," and also by the following articles in addition :—

"Article XV. All persons now in Texas and performing the duties of citizens, who have not acquired their quantum of lands, shall be entitled to the benefit of the laws on colonization, under which they emigrated ; and all persons who may emigrate to Texas during her conflict for constitutional liberty, and perform the duties of citizens, shall also receive the benefits of the laws under which they emigrated.

"Article XVIII. All grants, sales, and conveyances of land, illegally and fraudulently made by the legislature of the State of Coahuila and Texas, located or to be located within the limits of Texas, are hereby solemnly declared null, void, and of no effect.

"Article XIX. All persons who leave the country in its present crisis, with a view to avoid a participation in its present struggle, without permission from the alcalde or judge of their municipality, shall forfeit all or any lands they may hold or may have a claim to, for the benefit of the government : Provided, nevertheless, that widows and minors are not included in this provision."

As the colonization laws of Texas granted a league and "labor" of land, equal to 4604 American acres, to each settler who was the head of a family, and the one-third of a league, 1476 acres, to each single man, the bounty thus granted was sufficient to induce residents of other countries to remove to Texas, and identify themselves with her interests.

CHAPTER II.

LEGISLATIVE PROCEEDINGS UNDER THE PROVISIONAL GOVERNMENT.

Ordinances to raise an army and navy, and to supply them with necessaries—Provision for auditing claims—Duties on imports and tonnage—Collectors of public dues—Act to authorize a temporary loan of one hundred thousand, and a permanent loan of one million dollars—Other ways and means—Liberal grants of land to soldiers.

ACCORDING to the recommendation of Mr. Archer, the Provisional Government was endowed with both legislative and executive powers, and it began to act almost immediately in its double capacity.

It passed ordinances (November 26) " to raise a regular army" of 1120 men, and " to organize a corps of rangers" of 178 men, including officers; (December 8–12), to accept the services of at least 5000 volunteers; (December 18), to create a legion of cavalry, 380 strong; and (June 7) to raise an army to be called " the Army of Reserve for the Protection of the Liberties of Texas," to consist of 1145 men, officers included.

Not content with these formidable preparations on land, it turned its attention to the sea, and (November 27) passed " an ordinance and decree to establish a navy"—"to consist of two schooners of twelve guns each, and two schooners of six guns each."

Armies and navies must be fed, paid, and clothed. And, accordingly, the Provisional Government passed an ordinance (November 19) to purchase provisions for the army; two other ordinances (November 30) to purchase munitions of war, provisions, arms, &c.; a resolution (December 6) to purchase articles for the volunteers; " an ordinance and decree (November 27) for advancing the sum of fifteen hundred dollars for the benefit of the volunteer army of the people, under the command of General Stephen F. Austin ;" and another (December 2) " for supplying the army of the people, now before Bexar, with money."

That these duties might be properly performed, an ordinance

was passed (November 30) "for appointing a commissary, and defining his duties;" another (January 22), appointing a sutler; and another (December 22), "creating the office of commissary-general, and regulating the offices of paymaster and quarter-master-general."

Nor was the Provisional Government insensible to the importance of having claims properly audited, accounts regularly kept, and of those various checks and guards which are necessary in the disbursement of public funds. For a time, the General Council itself seems to have performed all these functions, governed solely by its own discretion; but (November 26) an ordinance was passed " prescribing the manner and form of settling the accounts of the volunteer army of Texas;" and, on the same day, another "for appointing a treasurer, a secretary to the executive, and two chief clerks, and defining their several duties." This was followed by another (December 2–12), "altering and changing the manner of drawing drafts on the treasurer;" by another (December 29), " creating the offices of auditor and controller;" by another (January 7), " prescribing the manner in which all claims by volunteers shall be presented for payment, and also to prevent frauds and impositions on the government;" and, finally, by a resolution (January 17), for appointing a committee of finance to act in the place of the General Council when it could not form a quorum.

But where the use of all this apparatus of treasurer, controller, and auditor, if there was neither money to keep nor money to disburse? The members of the Provisional Government were men of too much sense not to see this. They turned their attention to the ways and means which other governments have resorted to in times of exigency. They found that they might all be resolved into taxing, borrowing, begging, selling, and (if it be permitted to use such rough words), robbing and cheating, and they appear to have determined to try all six.

Their first act for raising a revenue by taxation was passed December 12, and was entitled "An ordinance and decree establishing duties on imports and tonnage, and for other purposes." It imposed duties of ten and twenty per cent. on foreign goods; but made free sundry articles. This was followed by a supplement (December 15), imposing a tonnage-duty of one dollar and twenty-five cents per ton, and establishing a duty of twelve and a half cents a gallon on whiskey, American gin, rum, and brandy. But hardly had this act time to reach the seaports, when (December 27), with worse than American instability in tariff matters, another act was passed raising the duties to fifteen and twenty-five per cent. *ad valorem*, and embracing a new list of non-dutiable articles.

This was followed (December 30) by an ordinance and decree appointing collectors of public dues, *i. e.* on lands granted or sold, an ordinance which amounted to nothing, so far as effective revenue was concerned, inasmuch as it provided that " duly audited treasury orders" should be received in payment. A supplemental ordinance was passed on the same day, and another January 15. This last was intended to obviate the inconvenience those persons sustained whose audited drafts exceeded the amount they had to pay for land dues. In such cases, the collector was authorized to indorse on the back the amount the public debtor had paid in, and he could apply the balance of the draft to other purposes.

The chief reliance of the Provisional Government was, however, on loans, and it passed several acts with a view of effecting this object. The first of these (November 24) authorized and empowered Thomas F. McKinney, of Velasco, to borrow one hundred thousand dollars for a period of not less than one year, at a rate not exceeding ten per cent. per annum. Another act, explanatory of this, passed Jan. 10, 1836, authorized Thomas F. McKinney and Samuel M. Williams to execute the bonds; to borrow part of one hundred thousand dollars, if they could not borrow the whole; and made the bonds (in six months from the date of their issue) receivable at par value in payment of any debts due to Texas for lands or other revenues.

This was designed to secure a temporary loan. Another act, passed December 4, " *created* a loan of one million dollars ;" instructed Messrs. Austin, Archer, and Wharton to negotiate the same at a rate not exceeding ten per cent. per annum; and directed the Governor to cause the bonds to be made out for one hundred thousand dollars each, for a period of not less than five nor more than ten years, payable in the city of New York, or any other city of the United States, as the case might require. By another act (December 5), the commissioners were instructed

" To pledge or hypothecate the public lands of Texas, and to pledge the public faith of Texas, in such manner, and with such restrictions as shall best comport with the honor and dignity of the State, and give effect to the pledges: *Provided, also,* that the said commissioners shall be authorized and instructed to create a stock or funded debt, upon such pledges as may be agreed upon, to be sold in shares on terms such as will not exceed the rate per cent. ordained in the ordinance authorizing a loan for Texas: *And be it also further provided,* that such part or parts of the public revenues of the country may be pledged as shall be sufficient to pay the annual interest upon any and all loans effected under the restrictions hereinbefore stated."

Thus the act gave the commissioners power to pledge the public faith, the public lands, the public revenues—everything that Texas possessed.

The government tried to sell, offering land script in great abundance, but found few willing to buy.

Begging is a mode of raising ways and means which the Kings of England frequently resorted to in old times. But the Government of Texas did nothing more in this way than pass a resolution (December 8) authorizing its foreign agents to receive all moneys and donations of any kind that might be given or presented to Texas, by citizens of the country which they might visit. There was no impropriety in this, as many citizens of the United States had shown a disposition to contribute before being solicited.

Robbing is another governmental mode of raising revenue. The Provisional Government tried its hand at this in two ways; at least we find it difficult to give any other interpretation to a resolution adopted January 17, 1836, in the words following, to wit:—

" SECTION I. Whereas, the troops garrisoned at Bexar being without the necessary provisions and clothing for their support and comfort, and the probability of its being some time yet before the necessary supplies from our agents in the United States, for the support, subsistence, and use of the army, will be received; and it being absolutely necessary to make immediate provisions for the sustenance and support of these troops at Bexar; *and it being impossible to drive beeves and procure provisions for their use, without horses:"* Therefore

" *Be it resolved,* by the General Council of the Provisional Government of Texas, that Lieutenant-Colonel Neill, commandant at Bexar, be, and is hereby authorized and empowered to employ as many Mexicans, or other citizens, for the purpose of driving up beeves, and procuring provisions for the troops under his command, as may be required for that purpose."

This, however, may have been regarded as only reprisal. Much of the war between the Mexicans and Texans was of a predatory character, and such will always be the character of war between nations whose wealth consists principally in cattle, whether they be Arabs, Tartars, Texans, or Mexicans.

The second way in which the Provisional Government tried its hand at robbing was in granting letters of marque and reprisal. It passed two acts with this object, by the first of which (Nov. 27) it was provided that twenty per cent. of the proceeds of the prizes should be paid into the treasury.; by the second (Nov. 30), the amount was reduced to ten per cent. In thus authorizing individuals to fit out privateers, it could plead the precedents of the best-established and most righteous governments.

But its greatest and best stroke of financial policy the Provisional Government reserved for the last. This was embodied in an act passed Jan. 7, 1836, but not approved of by the acting Governor till the 20th, by which it was ordained and decreed—

"That the Treasurer shall immediately cause to be printed in a neat form, and shall issue in discharge of claims against the government and drafts on the treasury, the amount of one hundred and fifty thousand dollars in treasury notes, varying in specified value from one dollar to one hundred dollars, specifying on the face thereof that they will be received in payment for lands and other public dues, or be redeemed with any moneys in the treasury not otherwise appropriated."

Thus, in theory at least, the Provisional Government completed the financial circle of taxing, borrowing, begging, selling, robbing, and cheating, for governmental paper money always degenerates into an instrument of fraud and oppression.

For the officers on the civil list the Provisional Government made moderate but decent allowances.

To the army it was more liberal. They were placed on the same footing, in regard to pay and rations, as the army of the United States.

The public lands the Provisional Government bestowed very freely. By one act (Nov. 24), it gave 640 acres to each soldier of the regular army. By another, of Dec. 8, 640 acres were granted to each volunteer who should enlist for the war, and 320 to those who should enlist for three months. By an act of Dec. 12, it was provided that 640 acres should be given to the representatives of each volunteer who should be killed in battle or die in the service.

This seemed very liberal; but the cash value of the article bestowed was very small. Land, to him who has neither capital to stock it nor skill to cultivate it, is worth only what others are willing to give for it. The charges of the Mexican Government for a league of land were less than four cents an acre. The amounts, then, bestowed by the Provisional Government were equivalent only to cash bounties of twelve and twenty-five dollars.

The offer, however, drew volunteers from the United States, as they were more or less governed in estimating the value of the bounty by the price which land,bore in their own neighborhoods.

After they got their titles, they found they had to pay twelve dollars for surveying 640 acres, and one dollar for the record, thus reducing the bounty to the equivalent of about twelve dollars. The result was that land was at a very low price, or at no price.

For a time, indeed, after the battle of San Jacinto, when certificates were first issued, Nov. 1836, land-claims occasionally sold as high as $200 or $300 for 640 acres. But they subsequently sold as low as ten dollars for 640 acres, or at a fraction more than one cent and a half an acre.

CHAPTER III.

EXECUTIVE PROCEEDINGS OF THE PROVISIONAL GOVERNMENT.   FIRST
PERIOD: NOVEMBER 14, 1835, TO JANUARY 2, 1836.

Comprehensive proceedings in four months—Pecuniary affairs of the General Council—A treasurer appointed—First report of Committee on Finance—Donation of
Mr. Hutchins, of Natchez—Proceedings in relation to a United States Bank note—
Plan for raising a revenue—Gov. Smith's objections to the way in which money-
matters were conducted—Small costs of the campaign—Loan from Mr. Brookfield, of New Orleans.

" THE North Americans are the only people who, in defiance
of all obstacles, have struck the roots of civilization deep into the
soil of Texas.   Even as I trace these lines, I reflect upon their
progress with renewed wonder and admiration.   They are, indeed,
the organized conquerors of the wild, uniting in themselves the
threefold attributes of husbandmen, lawgivers, and soldiers."

Thus speaks Kennedy, an Englishman, the historian of Texas.
And he does our countrymen no more than justice.   Let twenty
thousand unquiet spirits roll over into Tamaulipas, Chihuhua,
Sinaloa, Sonora, or any other neighboring territory, and they will,
in two months' time, do precisely what was done by the Provisional
Government of Texas.   They will substitute the common for the
civil law (with necessary modifications); establish trial by jury
and the writ of *habeas corpus;* Anglicize and Americanize everything.   It matters not from what part of the Union you take them.
The forms of legislation are so familiar to all that, in any twenty
thousand, you will find men who can enact laws as numerous at
least as those of Solon or Lycurgus, and, perhaps, quite as just
and as wise.

The Provisional Government was four months in power, but in
two months it passed all the laws we have mentioned, besides many
others which it is not our province to record.   The next question is
as to how it performed its executive duties; and to answer this, we
must refer to the journals.

The General Council met, and was organized, Nov. 14, 1835. Nov. 15, "accounts ' 1' and ' 2' were presented, and ordered to lie on the table till to-morrow." Thus early did fiscal concerns engage its attention.

Nov. 16, Mr. Barret, from the select committee to whom had been committed the duty to make extracts from sundry communications from the United States and elsewhere, made a report, from which, among other things, it appeared—

"That, at San Augustine, thirteen horses and four hundred dollars cash had been subscribed since Sunday last, which, added to former subscriptions for the support of the country, made in the aggregate a considerable amount; and that much larger sums would be advanced if necessary; that about eight hundred dollars had been subscribed at Natchitoches, Louisiana, and two thousand at Mobile, Alabama; that if money was wanted, Mr. Thomas F. McKinney would accept small drafts, five or six hundred dollars at a time, till a loan could be effected in the United States; and that the receivers of public moneys of the Department of Nacogdoches, having a considerable amount of funds on hand, had surrendered them to the Provisional Government, and they would be in a few days in the treasury."

All this was very encouraging, and on the same day a fiscal committee, consisting of Messrs. Millard, Wilson, and Clements, was appointed to attend to these important matters.

On the next day, Mr. Barret, from the Committee on the Affairs of State and Judiciary, made a report, in which it was made a leading paragraph—

"That the immediate appointment of a treasurer to the Provisional Government, whose duty shall be clearly defined, is now devolving upon this body. Receipts and disbursements of the public moneys have been hitherto carried on without system; consequently, without any other responsibilities to the public than that high sense of moral feeling which so eminently distinguishes the free sons of that country in revolutionary times from which our citizens have descended."

It was not till ten days afterwards that an ordinance was passed for appointing a treasurer; and the oath prescribed by the organic law was not administered to Joshua Fletcher, Esq., Treasurer *pro tem.*, till the 28th of November. On the 5th of December, all was made right by his being regularly elected treasurer.

Previous to this, however, on the 18th of November, the fiscal committee made a report; and this, as the first financial document of a government which, in little more than a month from date, was to have complete control of a territory larger than the kingdom of France, deserves to be handed down to posterity.

" Mr. Millard, from the Committee on Finance, made the following report :—

" Your Committee on Finance, to whom were referred the accounts of Thomas Bray and Madison M. Stevens, beg leave to report :—

" That the accounts so submitted against the Government of Texas are, in their present form, unreasonable, and ought not to be paid.

" The account marked ' 6,' that of Thomas Bray, for furnishing Cole's company of wagoners with one hundred and seven pounds of bread, at twenty-five cents per pound, amounting to twenty-six dollars and seventy-five cents, should be reduced to fourteen cents per pound ; and he be allowed fifteen dollars and seventy-eight cents in full for the amount of his account. And further, the account of Madison M. Stevens, for carrying one express to Nacogdoches, that he be allowed compensation for ten days' service, at two dollars and fifty cents per day, amounting to twenty-five dollars, and that the amount of his expenses already paid be deducted from the same, leaving a balance due him of ten dollars and fifty cents.

" The above, in the opinion of this committee, would be paying the above-named individuals full compensation for articles furnished and services rendered.

HENRY MILLARD,
Chairman.

CHARLES WILSON, }
J. D. CLEMENTS, } *Committee.*

" The foregoing report, having been read, was ordered to lie on the table."

What powerful influence Messrs. Bray and Stevens brought to bear on the watchful guardians of the public treasury, we know not ; but nearly a month afterwards the committee made a report, in which it was recommended that their demands should be paid in full.

So, in reports from the Committee of Finance, and the Committee of Public Accounts, eighty-four accounts, amounting in all to $7,764 78, besides a few others, the amounts of which are not distinctly stated, appear to have been passed and allowed up to January 25, 1836. Some ten or more were rejected for want of sufficient vouchers ; six were laid over for further consideration ; and six referred to the House for its special action.

The following extracts from the Journal are characteristic of the times :—

" November 30. By leave, General Houston presented to the Council one hundred dollars, a donation from John Hutchins, of Natchez, Mississippi, to the Provisional Government, for the use of Texas in her present struggle for liberty.

" Mr. Millard presented the following resolution, which was adopted unanimously :—

"*Resolved*, That the thanks of the General Council of the Provisional Government of Texas be, and they are hereby presented to John Hutchins, of Natchez, Mississippi, for the interest and zeal he has evinced in the cause of Texas, and particularly for his liberal donation to this government of one hundred dollars, to defray the expenses of this government, and to assist their efforts, for the security and establishment of their constitutional liberty, against the tyranny and oppression of the government of the usurper, Santa Anna.

" Mr. Millard moved that a copy of the foregoing resolution, signed by the President and Secretary, be forwarded to Mr. Hutchins, which was agreed to.

" December 1. The President stated to the Council that he had paid over to the Treasurer the one hundred dollars presented by John Hutchins, of Natchez, Mississippi, and taken the Treasurer's receipt, which was ordered to be deposited in the executive office."

This is the last event of any importance in the fiscal history of Texas previous to the 10th of December, the day on which Cos and Utargechea capitulated, which ended the campaign.

Some time afterwards, December 16, we find nearly a page of the Journal devoted to a report and resolution of the Committee of Finance on a branch post-note of the United States Bank for one thousand dollars. And it was resolved that—

" The Treasurer be authorized to pass the said note to Mr. Thomas Gay, or any other person, in exchange for cash or smaller notes; and that, if the said note for one thousand dollars should prove to be spurious, the Treasurer should be bound to refund the amount to Thomas Gay, or whoever shall have changed the same, with interest, at the rate of ten per cent., from the time he may lay out of the use of his money."

The reader will be gratified to learn that this thousand dollar bill, the sum of the contributions of some people in the United States, and the only bank-note that appears ever to have reached the treasury of Texas, proved to be genuine.

Previous to this, however, and even previous to the receipt of the hundred dollars from Mr. Hutchins, of Natchez, namely, on the 27th of November, the Committee of Finance made a report, in which, after dwelling for some time on the immense natural resources of Texas, greater than those of New York, Pennsylvania, Virginia, and Ohio, all put together, they proceeded to develop a plan for raising a revenue. The portion of the land granted to individuals or settlers, they estimated at ten millions of acres, a direct tax on which of one cent an acre would produce one hundred thousand dollars per annum. The United States Government having, from the sales of its public lands, derived a revenue of a million per annum, the committee suppose that Texas may derive from this source a quarter of a million a year, though not immediately. As a means more readily available, they recommend a tonnage duty of two dollars and twelve and a half cents a ton, and, believing the export of cotton to amount to sixty thousand bales, they suppose "the amount derived from this branch of the revenue (*i. e.* the tonnage duties) could be fairly estimated at 125,000 dollars."

"Another sure and certain source of available revenue presents itself to the consideration of your committee, viz., an export duty on cotton, which it would not be deemed high to place at one quarter of a cent per pound. The ease and facility with which this duty can be collected, and the near approach of the season for the exportation of the article, must necessarily render this subject of impost, in the opinion of your committee, the first in the list of available means. Your committee, therefore, recommend a duty of one quarter of a cent per pound for every pound of cotton exported out of Texas. Assuming the amount of bales exported as correct in the preceding item on tonnage, the revenue would be increased by this item of impost about 60,000 dollars."

The committee also proposed duties of fifteen and thirty per cent. on imports, but offered no estimate of the amount they would yield to the treasury.

Thus easy is it to cipher out a revenue on paper. But as our concern is not now with the revenues of Texas *in posse*, but *in esse*, we 'must return to the consideration of the management of the means which the Provisional Government actually possessed, consisting of a few thousand dollars (somewhere between $3,000 and $10,000), found in the coffers of the Mexican Government it had superseded, and the contributions of its own citizens, and those of the United States.

For a short time, all orders on the Treasurer, after having been passed by the General Council, were signed by the Governor and Secretary; but, on the 2d of December, an ordinance was passed making the signature of the chairman of the Committee of Finance all-sufficient.

This did not please Governor Smith, who was something of a precisian.

"I object to the bill for the following reasons: First. The Committee on Finance, with whom the whole discretion of appropriating money and drafting on the treasury is vested, is, like all other committees belonging to your body, liable to change and shift its members; as such, indiscreet appropriations might be made, and money drawn for improper uses. A bare report to the Council of what has been done, in order that it be noted in your journals, would afford no check to the acts of the committee, because the appropriations and drafts on the treasury would be made prior to the report of the committee; and, as such, they would be left without check or corrective.

"Secondly. I consider that no appropriation of money should be made, except by law; that no committee, or separate authority, should be privileged to make appropriations, or draw money from the treasury, without the necessary forms being complied with. Acting without the proper functionaries of secretary, comptroller, &c., it would be well to incorporate in our plan as many checks and balances as would be consistent, without producing complexity."

Governor Smith was clearly right. According to the established principles of American polity, the legislature should make appropriations; a board, or an officer, specially appointed for the purpose, should audit all claims; and the treasurer should pay them. The General Council was betrayed into some improprieties by its acting in both a legislative and executive capacity, and, on the 12th of December, by a vote of twelve to two, it passed the bill in defiance of the Governor's veto.

Struck, however, as it would seem, with the force of the Governor's observations, they previously, on the 11th of December, resolved—

"That there should be appointed by the President a Standing Committee of Public Accounts, to consist of one member from each of the principal standing committees, except the Committee of Finance, and that it should be the duty of said committee to receive, audit, and register said accounts, entering in a book, to be purchased for that purpose, the title and amount of said accounts, in such a manner as to show their situation at any particular time, whether passed, rejected, or under consideration, and report upon the same to the Council, as often as twice every week, say Wednesday and Saturday."

Thus, everything was not left to the Finance Committee, and, while one committee audited the accounts, another committee (such accounts being first approved by the Council) ordered them to be paid.

Soon afterwards, a regular system of account-keeping was introduced, by the appointment of an auditor and comptroller.

All this may seem like very trifling in a government, the immediate means of which were so insignificant as were those of the Provisional Government of Texas. But all that a government with an empty treasury can do, is to promptly audit accounts, carefully register them, reject such as are not supported by sufficient vouchers, and give to creditors, whose claims are justly founded, some acknowledgment of the same. All this did the Provisional Government of Texas; and some of its principles of polity, especially that of *promptly* auditing accounts, might be adopted with advantage by the United States Government, and perhaps by some of the States.

The actual doings, in a financial way, of the Provisional Government contrast most ludicrously with its magnificent enactments for raising revenue and negotiating loans; and yet be it remembered that, during the period specially treated of in this chapter, a region twice as large as Great Britain and Ireland was cleared of its Mexican foes.

How was this effected? The pecuniary means of the government were, as we have seen, very small. But everybody fought, and everybody contributed. What was wanted for the use of the army was, according to the custom of war, forcibly seized, if it could not otherwise be got possession of; but the rule was always to give an acknowledgment, making the government responsible for the value of what was thus taken.

"Deficient in all the resources requisite for war, except moral energy and courage, the colonists themselves contributed, from their private means, whatever was calculated to be of use to the troops. Leaden water-pipes and clock-weights were melted down for ammunition, and even the women cheerfully assisted in moulding bullets and making cartridges."—*Kennedy*, vol. ii. p. 115.

The actual cost of the campaign we have been curious to know, but cannot tell. Others appear to have had a like curiosity, for the first Congress under the Republic called for a report of the transactions of the treasury under the Provisional Government, but the desired report does not appear to have been made. Subsequently to this, the Congress of Texas—in humble imitation of the Congress of the United States—keeping its public records in combustible buildings, suffered the loss of part of those in the Treasurer's office from fire. The world must, therefore, for the present, at least, be content with such account of receipts and expenditures, under the Consultation and under the Provisional Government, up to January 2, 1836, as we have been able to gather from the journals.

Before concluding the history of this year, we ought to state that a loan was effected; not a very large one, indeed, but yet such as was deemed worthy of the following insertion in the journals:—

"December 29. Mr. Harris presented to the House the receipts of E. Hall, our agent at New Orleans, for eleven hundred dollars—received of William Brookfield, money loaned for the use of Texas, to purchase arms, ammunition, &c.

"On motion of Mr. Royall,

"*Resolved*—That the thanks of the General Council be presented to Mr. Brookfield for his generous and patriotic conduct in loaning eleven hundred dollars to E. Hall, our agent at New Orleans, for the purpose of procuring and forwarding arms, ammunition, &c., and that the receipt of Mr. Hall for the same be entered on the journals of the Council, the original to remain on file among the papers of the Council, and a copy to be given to Mr. Brookfield, as evidence of his claim, to be adjusted at some future period.

"The following is a copy of the receipt:—

"Received, New Orleans, December 7, 1835, from Mr. William Brookfield, eleven hundred dollars as a loan for the service of Texas.

"$1100.   EDWARD HALL,

                              "*Agent for the Government.*

"Approved by F. Thorn and A. C. Allen."

Thus grateful were the Texans, in those times, for the smallest aid afforded them, and thus particular were they in acknowledging the obligation.

CHAPTER IV.

PROCEEDINGS UNDER THE PROVISIONAL GOVERNMENT IN RELATION TO THE PUBLIC LANDS.

The Commissioner of the Nashville Colony arraigned for contumacy—Great diffi-culties with the land-speculators in the Department of Nacogdoches—Indig-nation of Governor Smith—Determined action of the Council.

THESE proceedings were of so much importance that we must devote to them a distinct chapter.

It has already been mentioned that the order to close the land-offices and to stop all surveys had given dissatisfaction in some quarters.

December 1, Mr. Barret, from a select committee to whom the subject had been referred, made the following report:—

" Your committee, to whom was referred the report of the commissioners appointed for securing the papers and documents of the several land-offices of the Department of the Brazos, agreeably to the 14th section of the Pro-visional Government of Texas, passed by the Consultation of the chosen delegates of all Texas, in general convention assembled, on the 13th of November, 1835, report:—

" That they have duly considered the conduct of Wm. H. Steele, the commissioner of the colony of the Nashville Company, in refusing to recog-nize the authority of the commissioners, &c., and condemning the proceed-ings and orders of the delegates of the people of Texas, assembled in general convention, and in refusing to obey, and treating with contempt the man-dates of the Provisional Government, organized by the people's representa-tives; and are unanimous in advising that the General Council should take prompt and efficient means to enforce obedience to the laws of the country. To this end your committee advise the adoption of the following ordinance."

So indignant was the Council, that its common rule was sus-pended; the ordinance read a first, second, and third time; and passed immediately. In the body of it was distinctly set forth "the contumely and contempt" with which Wm. H. Steele had treated the people's representatives; and the Governor was re-quested to issue a special commission, " with a writ of assistance, to command, in the name of the people, all officers, whether civil or military, and all good citizens, to give aid, and be aiding and assist-ing" in bringing the contumacious Wm. H. Steele before the General Council.

As this was a point on which the Governor and Council were agreed, any attempt at resistance on the part of Mr. Steele would have been extreme folly. But he had no disposition to resist. On the 15th of December, as appears from the Jour-nal, he came voluntarily before the Council, and stated

" That the warrant to arrest him had not been served upon him, but hear-ing that one had been issued, he appeared for the purpose of explaining the reasons of his refusal. That the citizens of Viesca did not understand that their delegates were clothed with conventional powers, but that they generally approved of the doings of the Convention, so far as they were in-formed of them. That he lived at a great distance from the seat of govern-ment, from which communications were very uncertain. That the refusal was made through misunderstanding, and in the moment of excitement, and not from any disrespect to the government or its authorities."

On motion of Mr. Royall, the Council resolved that it was satis-fied with this explanation; and not long afterwards (December 27), Mr. Steele gave unquestionable proof of his patriotism by making a conditional purchase from them of one hundred and fifty-three sheets of stamped paper (see printed Journal, page 229)—no trifling aid to the treasury in that time of trouble.

Far greater difficulties had the Council to contend with in the extensive Department of Nacogdoches, where the people generally seemed to have little disposition to obey the order to close the land-offices and stop the surveys. This appears from the Report of the Committee on State Affairs (December 4), in which, after giving a view of the reasons that led to the issue of the order, and of the authority by which it had been issued, they conclude with expressing a belief that "the good citizens of the Nacogdoches Department, in view of all these facts and necessities, will sub-mit, and yield obedience, especially when convinced that resistance will not only be vain, but subject them to heavy penalties."

But "the good citizens" of the Department of Nacogdoches were not so complaisant. There was hardly one of them, perhaps, who had not at that time more land than he could make a proper use of. But they were far removed from the seat of war; and while their brethren of western Texas had all the lively excitement of fighting the Mexicans, they could not see why they might not divert themselves with the minor excitement of land-speculations.

The next notice of this subject which we find in the Journal is contained in a letter of Governor Smith, dated December 7 :—

"I hasten to lay before your honorable body an official communication from Dr. S. H. Everitt, one of your commissioners appointed to take charge of the archives of the land-offices of the Department of Nacogdoches, &c. You will see by his communication what has been done, and will, I hope, take such immediate steps as will be calculated to carry the decree into effect with the least possible delay. I make this a separate communication, touching no other subject-matter, in order that it receive the prompt and undivided attention of your body."

Dr. Everitt's letter not being printed in connection with the Governor's message, we are left in ignorance of the exact doings that called for the prompt and undivided attention of the Council. But, on the next day, December 8, the Committee on State Affairs made a report, in which they reaffirm what had been stated in their report of the 4th, and then proceed as follows:—

"Therefore, that this House cannot legally pass any ordinance granting the power of making titles in any way until the said 14th article is complied with, at least so far as that the papers and documents are under the control of the officers of the Provisional Government. When this shall have been effected, your committee have no further hesitation in advising that the several legal commissioners of each land-office, or some other person specially appointed, be authorized to proceed in completing all titles to land made for settlers on surveys, returned before the passage of the said 14th section. But in doing this, all proper guarantees against injustice or fraud should be carefully incorporated in the decree for such purpose.

"In the mean time, your committee have confidence in assuring this Council, and the people at large, that neither the orders of the Convention nor decrees of the Provisional Government have any other object or effect than of securing an equal and fair opportunity for all our citizens to obtain their landed rights; and although the time of perfecting titles may be extended, no acquired right or privilege either is or can be affected. The right exists unimpaired, while the bare legal form remains to be executed."

Here let us stop to do justice to the Texans. However dark their prospects, or however desperate their condition, they never seem to have lost sight of the admirable advantages their country affords for land-speculations. This is a credit due to them without distinction of party, and to the Western Texans as well as the Eastern. All the Provisional Government wanted was that "all should start fair," and herein, we think, the Provisional Government was decidedly right.

The next record in the Journal relating to the troubles in the Department of Nacogdoches, is contained in a letter from the Governor, dated December 26. Some extracts follow:—

"Mr. Forbes incloses back a commission which had been previously sent to him. * * * And furthermore says that, owing to the combined and active opposition of some six or eight speculators, sustained by individuals from the States, who employ them to engross the lands that are properly the public domain, the intentions of the government, and its acts relating to the public lands, and even its judicial acts, have been delayed and interrupted, greatly to the injury of the public.

*   *   *   *   *   *   *

"Your honorable body will plainly see, from the foregoing, the situation of the land-offices to the east, and that the acts of the Convention have not been carried into effect; nor does it appear that they can be, short of a military force; and whether such a course would be calculated to produce any salutary effect, is for your honorable body to determine. That some kind of effort should be made by us to sustain and protect the public interest must be obvious to all. While we are contending with a powerful foe, even for our very existence, that we should find men among us capable of committing piracies both on sea and land, is, I must admit, rather discouraging; but permit me to say to you that every opposition has a powerful tendency to stimulate me to greater exertion, and I hope will have the same effect on your honorable body. Opposition, strong, vigilant, and persevering, by me was anticipated; hence I am never taken by surprise, or deceived in the persons who stir it up. They never consider the public good, but seek their own private interests; hence they are ever vigilant and on the wing. It is made our duty to guard and protect that which they wish to destroy. They dread organization as a great evil, because honest investigation follows as a matter of course, which they dread, preferring darkness to light, because their deeds have been evil.

"These men have their unprincipled hirelings and satellites to operate, and endeavor to keep themselves behind the screen. They may not be generally known to your body, and as such will, no doubt, often attempt to practise fraud upon you by their insinuating approaches. Me, they seldom approach. They may overpower, but never can deceive."

In a report, dated December 28, a committee of the Council took occasion to inform the Governor that they were as little liable to be imposed on by these men as he was himself. This will appear from the following extracts:—

"Your Committee on State and Judiciary, to whom was referred the Governor's message of the 26th instant, and various letters and documents from Nacogdoches, respectfully report—

"That, from the general information contained in the Governor's message, and letters from S. H. Everitt, Esq., the only acting commissioner under the 14th section of the organic law, in the Department of Nacogdoches, and the other documents referred, your committee are unwillingly convinced of the prevalence of a spirit of disorganization in some parts of that country, which, in a more limited degree, also, exists else-where in Texas; and that this spirit is the natural consequence of the revolutionary state of our country, a change in its form of government, a mixed population coming from various parts of the world, strangers to each other, and unassimilated in character or habit.　But your committee are well convinced, from their knowledge of the Anglo-American character, which constitutes the greater part of Texas citizens, that the intelligence and moral feeling of the mass of the people, ever reflective, would have, ere this, led them to consistency of conduct and respect for the existing authorities, created by their own representatives from the present necessity, however crude in organization, yet giving order and affording protection for the time, were it not for ambitious demagogues, designing and sinister speculators, equally destitute of patriotism and regardless of the people's rights, and every other consideration that obstructs the gratification of their own private ends.　Such men, even in a settled and well-regulated community, often distract the minds of the honest and undesigning, and disturb the harmony of society, until, by a severe rebuke from the people themselves, or by the strong arm of the law, their career of wickedness is checked, and they become objects of contempt and infamy.　That the good people are troubled by such men among them, is by no means unexpected.　To guard against the consequences of their evil machinations is our first duty, and involving immense responsibility upon all the officers of the Provisional Government; and we cannot hope to effect this, unless union, prudence, justice, and firmness, are the governing motives of all our conduct throughout all our councils.

" Your committee most cordially respond to the principles of action re-commended to this Council, as necessary to the very existence of order and respect for the laws; and are fully aware of the magnitude of the evil, and deep injury to the country consequent upon the intrigues, frauds, and un-controlled ravages of the daring and unprincipled land-speculators who infest the country, agitating the public mind with base falsehoods, and keeping up discord, distrust, and disrepute, to their own and only source of present protection, and last barrier against anarchy and internal war, the Provisional Government of Texas.　Your committee confidently assure his excellency that the General Council know these men too well to be deceived by them, and while acting under the influence of principles hitherto governing the conduct of this body, feel that the virtue and intelligence of the people will sustain their acts."

The report was adopted.　On the 31st of December, an address was voted to the people, giving the reasons for closing the land-offices.　New commissioners were appointed to take possession of the archives of the land-offices in the Department of Nacog-doches, and the land-speculators' rebellion was subdued without bloodshed.

CHAPTER V.

EXECUTIVE PROCEEDINGS UNDER THE PROVISIONAL GOVERNMENT.
SECOND PERIOD: JANUARY 2 TO MARCH 13, 1836.

Condition of affairs at the beginning of 1836—Two vessels of war procured—Prospect of loans in New Orleans—Conflicts of Governor Smith and the Council—Mr. Smith superseded, and Mr. Robinson made acting governor.

WITH the beginning of 1836 commenced a new era in the fiscal history of Texas. Its bills for raising a revenue and negotiating loans had been passed, and its commissioners were on the way to the United States, or had actually arrived there. Governor Smith's rigid notions of correctness were no longer shocked by a single committee appropriating money, auditing claims, and drawing drafts on the treasury. Texas had now her auditor and controller; and, so far as regards account-keeping, everything was as regularly conducted as in the best-established dynasties. It is true that there was no money in the treasury, and claims were daily accumulating against it; but this is the natural order of things in revolutionary periods.

Nor did all the legislative acts of the General Council prove ineffective. Early in January, two schooners, the "William Robbins," (afterwards the "Liberty,") and the "Invincible," were purchased from McKinney and Williams; but whether they had or had not the formidable armament of six and twelve guns, provided for in the "Ordinance for Establishing a Navy," is a point on which history is silent.

"Communications," says Kennedy, "were received, in the beginning of January, from Stephen Austin, who was then at New Orleans, where he had obtained a loan for 200,000 dollars, and expected to procure another for 40,000 or 50,000 dollars."

The whole amount was not realized, as we shall hereafter have occasion to show. No notice of it appears on the Journal of the Council, but there is no doubt that the news was received, and it was very encouraging.

That a nation of twenty thousand should successfully contend with a nation of eight or ten millions, is certainly a remarkable event in this world's history. Some have attributed it to the factions which existed among the Mexicans, and which prevented their bringing all their forces to bear on the revolted province. No doubt this had its effect. But the Texans also had their factions, as is evident from what we have already recorded, and the difference in the character of the two nations is shown by the fact that the factions among the Texans, violent as they were, did not prevent their making an effectual resistance to the common enemy.

From the beginning, there appears to have been little harmony between Governor Smith and the Council. He had a due sense of his dignity, as chief magistrate of a country twice as large as Great Britain and Ireland, and judged of his powers by analogy with those of the President of the United States. He claimed the right of making appointments to office. The Council contended that it was his duty to commission whomsoever they might appoint. They passed bills, and he vetoed them; and they, by constitutional majorities, passed the bills again in defiance of the vetoes. He was a precisian in treasury matters; they were somewhat latitudinarian.

They differed also on points of policy. The Mexican revolutionist, General Mexia, had planned a descent on Tampico, and some of the Texans were for making an attack on Matamoras. Both of these projects had the sanction of a part, if not of the majority of the Council, and both were pointedly disapproved of by the Governor; the last, as subsequently appeared, from his having a private plot of his own for capturing that city of the Mexicans.

On returning to the Council a bill they had passed, " authorizing persons to be appointed to make provisions for General Mexia," he said :—

" I have no confidence in General Mexia's co-operating in our favor. That his intention is to make a descent on the seaports west of us, for the purpose of robbing, to recuperate his own desperate fortune, I have no doubt, but can see no possible advantage it would be to Texas. What his designs or intentions are, I have no right to know, but really think it would be unwise to run this government to the expense necessary to fit him out without having any guarantee or control over him or his conduct.

Furthermore, as the bill runs, it would seem that the outfit would be made before this government would be advised of his plans.   Besides, I consider it bad policy to fit out or trust Mexicans in any matter connected with our government, as I am well satisfied that we will in the end find them inimical and treacherous.   For these, and many other reasons not enumerated, I cannot sign the bill."

This was December 9 ; and, on the next day, Mr. Harris presented the following resolution, which was adopted :—

" Whereas, the Provisional Government of Texas have received information, of which there is no doubt, that the enemy have large reinforcements on the road to our frontiers, *with whom there are forty thousand dollars in money*, and if the same is not cut off or prevented from uniting with the force now at Bexar, our small but patriotic army will be compelled to retire, being overpowered by four times their number: *Therefore be it resolved, by the General Council of the Provisional Government of Texas*, That General Mexia be, and he is hereby invited, together with the brave officers and men under his command, to repair immediately to Bexar by the way of Goliad, and there co-operate with the volunteer army of the people.

" *Resolved,* That an express be dispatched immediately to General Mexia, with a copy of this resolution."

Colonel Powers tendered his services to repair immediately to Velasco, or any other point, to wait on General Mexia; but the Mexican declined co-operating, and Bexar was captured by the Texans without his aid or assistance.

In few things, except hatred of the Nacogdoches land-speculators, do the Governor and Council appear to have been agreed ; but they did not come to an open rupture till January 9, 1836. Then Governor Smith sent them a message, which, for peculiarity of diction, is unmatched by any North American state paper, though it is hardly equal to some of the effusions of that great European orator, Daniel O'Connel.

We give some extracts from it, premising that the contemplated expeditions against Tampico and Matamoras were what had specially excited the Governor's wrath, the more so as they had drawn away part of the forces necessary for the defence of the important post of Bexar.

"To the Honorable the President and Members of the General Council :—

" GENTLEMEN : I herewith transmit to your body the returns and correspondence of Colonel Neill, Lieutenant-Colonel Commandant of the post at Bexar.

" You will in that correspondence find the situation of that garrison. You will there find a detail of facts calculated to call forth the indignant feelings of every honest man. Can your body say that they have not been cognizant of, and connived at this predatory expedition? Are you not daily holding conference and planning co-operation both by sea and land? Acts speak louder than words; they are now before me, authorizing a generalissimo, with plenary powers, to plan expeditions on the faith, the credit, and I may justly say the ruin, of the country. You urge me by resolutions to make appointments, fit out vessels as government vessels, registering them as such, appointing landsmen to command a naval expedition, by making representations urgent in their nature, and for what? I see no reason, but to carry into effect, by the hurried and improvident acts of my department, the views of your favorite object, by getting my sanction to an act disorganizing in its nature, and ruinous in its effects. Instead of acting as becomes the counsellors and guardians of a free people, you resolve yourselves into low, intriguing, caucussing parties; pass resolutions without a quorum, predicated on false premises; and endeavor to ruin the country by countenancing, aiding, and abetting marauding parties; and if you could only deceive me enough, you would join with it a piratical co-operation. You have acted in bad faith, and seem determined by your acts to destroy the very constitution which you are pledged and sworn to support. I have been placed on the political watch-tower. I feel the weight of responsibility devolving upon me, and I confidently hope I will be able to prove a faithful sentinel. You have also been posted as sentinels; but you have permitted the enemy to cross the lines, and, Mexican-like, you are ready to sacrifice your country at the shrine of plunder. Mr. President, I speak collectively, as you all form one whole, though at the same time I do not mean all. I know you have honest men there, and of sterling worth and integrity; but you have Judas in the camp—corruption, base corruption, has crept into your councils—men who, if possible, would deceive their God.

"Notwithstanding their deep-laid plans and intrigues, I have not been asleep; they have long been anticipated, forestalled, and counteracted. They will find themselves circumvented in every tack. I am now tired of watching scoundrels abroad and scoundrels at home, and as such I am now prepared to drop the curtain. * * * * * *

"Look around upon your flock: your discernment will easily detect the scoundrels. The complaint: contraction of the eyes; the gape of the mouth; the vacant stare; the hung head; the restless, fidgety disposition; the sneaking, sycophantic look; a natural meanness of countenance; an unguarded shrug of the shoulders; a sympathetic tickling and contraction of the muscles of the neck, anticipating the rope; a restless uneasiness to adjourn, dreading to face the storm themselves have raised.

"Let the honest and indignant part of your Council drive the wolves out of the fold; for, by low intrigue and management of this kind, they have been imposed upon, and duped into gross error and palpable absurdities. Some of them have been thrown out of folds equally sacred, and should be denied the society of civilized man.

"They are parricides, piercing their devoted country, already bleeding at every pore. But, thanks be to my God, there is balm in Texas, and a physician near. Our agents have gone abroad; our army has been organized; our general is in the field. A convention has been called, which will afford a sovereign remedy to the vile machinations of a conspiring, intriguing, and corrupt Council. I now tell you that the course here pointed out shall be rigidly and strictly pursued, and, unless your body will make the necessary acknowledgments to the world of your error, and forthwith proceed, and with the same facility and publicity (by issuing a circular), and furnishing expresses, to give circulation and publicity, in a manner calculated to counteract its baleful effects, that, after twelve o'clock to-morrow, all communication between the two departments shall cease, and your body will stand adjourned until the first of March next, unless, from the emergencies of the country, you should be convened by proclamation at an earlier period.

"I consider, as the devisers of ways and means, you have done all contemplated by the organic law, and that your services are now no longer needed. Until the Convention meets, I will continue to discharge my duties as commander-in-chief of the army and navy, and see that the laws are executed.

"The foregoing you will receive as notice from my department, which will be rigidly carried into effect. You are further notified that audience will not be given to any member or special committee other than in writing. I will immediately proceed to publish all the correspondence between the two departments by proclamation to the world, and assign the reasons why I have pursued this course, and the causes which have impelled me to do it.

"I am, gentlemen, your obedient servant,

"HENRY SMITH, *Governor*."

"*January* 9, 1836."

Where the analogy of the United States Government failed him, Governor Smith had recourse to that of Great Britain in determining the extent of his power. The King or Queen of Great Britain has power to prorogue Parliament; but the President of the United States has not power to prorogue Congress. Our Texan Oliver Cromwell had become tired of his "Long Parliament," and was for dissolving it by a process as summary as that adopted by his English prototype, and with apparently much the same feelings.

The men who composed the General Council were not the men to yield quietly to such a usurpation. If the "Praise God Barebones Parliament" had surrendered to one tyrant, that was no reason why free and independent Americans should tamely submit to another. They received the Governor's communication, January 11, and referred it to a committee, who forthwith made report—

"That they are unable to express any other views to this House than indignation at language so repulsive to every moral feeling of an honorable man, and astonishment that this community should have been so miserably deceived in selecting, for the high office of Governor, a man whose language and conduct prove his early habits of association to have been vulgar and depraved, and his present disposition that of a tyrant.   That they repel the infamous charges preferred against this Council and its members as false and unfounded in every part; and contemn the style and language as low, blackguard, and vindictive, and every way unworthy of and disgraceful to the office whence it emanated, and as an outrageous libel on the body to whom it is addressed, and therefore advise the return of the paper, accompanied with the following resolutions."

This report was unanimously adopted, together with resolutions, declaring that the members of the Council were the immediate representatives of the Sovereign People—that they would sustain the dignity of the government—that Henry Smith be ordered forthwith to cease the functions of his office, and answer certain charges and specifications preferred against him, &c. &c.

On the next day, they issued an address to the people, in which they repelled the charges brought against them in "that impudential document," as they called the Governor's message, and brought very serious charges against His Excellency himself.   A single paragraph will serve to show the character of the address:—

"All these acts of stubbornness and perverseness were not sufficient to gratify his thirst for sole dominion and arbitrary sway of the land.   His dignity was insulted at the idea of the existence of the co-ordinate branch of the Government, to curb his acts and check his usurpation.   He became more and more restless, until, enraged at the presumption of the Council, in the exercise of a constitutional right, and in conformity with the true interests of the country, to pass an ordinance and decree, by a constitutional majority, after it had been vetoed by ' His Excellency,' he ignites: his fury, in a blaze, consumes his prudence (what he had) ; he orders the Council to disperse, shuts the door of communication between the two departments, and proclaims himself the government."

Governor Smith appears to have been astonished by this act of the Council, and sought to reconcile matters by sending them, on the 12th, a kind of half apology.   After confessing that he had used "much asperity of language," but which he considered was called for by what he deemed "imprudent acts" of the Council, and much "intrigue and duplicity," he concluded as follows:—

"If, therefore, your body should think proper to acknowledge their error by an immediate correction of it, which I consider would only be their reasonable duty, all difference between the two departments shall cease, and, so far as I am concerned, be forever buried in oblivion; and that friendly and harmonious intercourse resumed which should ever exist between the different branches of the government.   I suggest and solicit this from the purest motives, believing the public good would thereby be advanced.   Believing the rules of Christian charity require us to bear and forbear, and as far as possible to overlook the errors and foibles of each other, in this case I may not have exercised towards your body that degree of forbearance which was probably your due. If so, I have been laboring under error, and, as such, hope you will have the magnanimity to extend it to me, and the two branches again harmonize to the promotion of the true interests of the country."

Gov. Smith's "Christian charity" came too late. The Council refused to revoke its acts. But the Governor refused to be tried by them, held on to his seals of office, and on one occasion (Feb. 3), sending to demand some papers, thus instructed his messenger:—

"You will further notify them that, if these things are not promptly complied with, and they immediately desist from their injurious and disorganizing operations, I will immediately order their arrest and transmission to the post of Bexar, to be tried by court-martial."

"Every inch a king" was Henry Smith—or would have been if he could have been. But the members of Council were sovereigns also, not only by right of election, but by right of descent from the heroes of 1776. From the 10th of January, Lieut.-Gov. Robinson became, under their sanction, the acting governor. It was by him the act was signed authorizing the issue of treasury notes. Governor Smith would, if he could have found no other reason, have vetoed it from the mere principle of contrariety.

CHAPTER VI.

PROCEEDINGS UNDER THE GOVERNMENT AD INTERIM, 1836.

Movements of Santa Anna—His capture by the Texans—David G. Burnett, President *ad interim*—Gloomy condition of affairs as set forth in his message to the first Congress—Small cost of the war to Sept. 1836—Small revenue of Provisional Government—Loans of Messrs. Erwin, Triplett, and their associates.

WHILE Governor Smith and the Council were contending for prerogatives, the Mexicans were preparing to reinvade the country. On the 12th of February, 1836, Santa Anna reached the Rio Grande at the head of a powerful army, and swept rapidly along, marking his course with the most horrible massacres, recapturing from the Texans, in less than two months' time, a country larger than all England, and spreading devastation in every direction.

Fortunately for the people in this emergency, political power passed from the hands of the Provisional Government, and its contending factions, into the hands of a Convention, which assembled on the 1st of March at the town of Washington, on the Brazos. In this, the darkest period of their history, the Texans made (March 2) a declaration of independence, adopted a constitution (March 17) as an independent republic, and (March 16) established a government *ad interim* to act till the constitution could be brought into full operation.

On the 21st of April, the battle of San Jacinto was fought. On the next day, the Mexican President, Santa Anna, surrendered himself a prisoner of war; and thus, in seven months after the commencement of hostilities, was achieved the independence of a government which *claimed* territorial limits more extensive than those of our thirteen original States from Maine to Georgia included.*

---

* The area of the territory claimed by the Texan Government was 379,054 square miles. The Atlantic States, from Maine to Georgia, have, including Vermont, a surface of 378,402 square miles; without Vermont, 268,290. The area of the British Isles is 122,185. That of France, 202,125. That of Austria, 260,000. Texas has, within her *reduced* limits, 274,366 square miles.

The government *ad interim,* appointed by the Convention, had simply executive powers.   David G. Burnett was made President, and Baily Hardiman, Secretary of the Treasury.

Its fiscal doings are summed up in President Burnett's message to the First Congress of the Republic (Oct. 4, 1836), and in the accompanying report of the auditor and comptroller.

After mentioning that the movements of the enemy had, a few days after its organization, compelled the government *ad interim* to remove from Washington to Harrisburg, he says:—

"At this gloomy period, the financial affairs of the country were in a condition more deplorable than its military equipments.   The Commissioners, Messrs. Austin, Archer, and Wharton, appointed by the late Provisional Government, had negotiated a loan for two hundred thousand dollars, and another for fifty thousand, with sundry individuals in the city of New Orleans.   It was doubtless the best arrangement that could be made at that period.   Mr. Robert Triplett, a principal subscriber to each of the above loans, presented himself to the government at Harrisburg.   Twenty thousand dollars had been paid on the first loan, and the whole of the second was advanced.   The ratification of these loans had been submitted to the Convention, and by them was referred to the Executive Government.   On inspecting the terms of the loans, some of the conditions were considered inadmissible.   The exclusive right to an immediate location of the script was a privilege which, it was believed, would cause infinite dissatisfaction in the country, and be especially obnoxious to the volunteers of the army, the nature of whose services would seem to preclude any right of priority of location in others.   For no species of public service is considered more onerous or more entitled to recompense than that which is rendered on the field of battle.   Under these impressions, we proposed to Mr. Triplett a modification of the loans, and agreed to reduce the price of the lands, or rather to make a donation of thirty-two leagues of land, to be distributed *pro rata* among the stockholders, in consideration of the relinquishment of the right of priority of location, conceded to them by the original terms of the contract.   The modification was accepted by Mr. Triplett, for himself.   He was not vested with authority to bind his co-lenders, but he expressed an opinion that they would also accede to it.   From the first loan, the government confidently anticipated a fiscal aid of some importance in the then pressing emergency, but as the sequel will disclose they were unhappily disappointed.   Mr. Triplett, on his return to the United States, presented his modified contract to his associate stockholders, and to our surprise they unanimously voted against its reception, and declined advancing the residuum of the loan.

"Some disappointment resulted from this decision of the lenders, and the government felt the inconvenience of an illusory anticipation.   A new proposition has been made to the lenders to adjust the amounts advanced on the principles of the modified contract, but no definite answer has been had to that overture.   The presumption is that it will not be accepted, and that the settlement of the whole transaction will devolve on Congress, for I have long since determined to submit the whole matter to your consideration.

" The result of this negotiation afforded conclusive evidence of the impracticability of anticipating the wants of the country by ordinary loans. Some other course was necessary, and the government resolved to issue script for land, considering the public domain as the most available and the least objectionable source of public revenue. Accordingly, the agent appointed, in New Orleans, Thomas Toby, Esq., a gentleman who had already made considerable advances on the account of the government, and had manifested a warm sympathy in our behalf, was authorized to issue script to the amount of five hundred thousand acres of land, to be located on the public domain of Texas, and to dispose of it at the established minimum price of fifty cents per acre: he has subsequently been empowered to extend his issues to one million of acres.   *   *   *

" A number of patriotic citizens have voluntarily executed their bonds for various sums, and tendered them to the government, with a view to relieve the present exigencies of the country. These bonds, amounting in the aggregate to one hundred and twenty thousand dollars, have been transmitted to the agents, Messrs. T. Toby & Brother, by the quartermaster-general, and the hope is entertained that they will prove a present convenience.   *   *   *

" The recent and much lamented decease of the Honorable Baily Hardiman, whose devoted patriotism and inflexible integrity are well known, and who has been with me through all the vicissitudes of the times, deprives me of the pleasure of presenting you with a regular report from the Treasury Department. The principal intelligence in my power to convey, you will find in the auditor's *exposé*, herewith transmitted.   *   *   *

" It will be recollected that the powers conferred on the government *ad interim* were extraordinary; that they comprised the plenal attributes of sovereignty, the legislative and judicial functions excepted. The circumstances under which that government has been administered have been equally extraordinary.

" Sometimes, when Texas was a moving mass of fugitives, they have been without 'a local habitation,' and scattered to the cardinal points; again, they have been on Galveston Island without a shelter and almost without subsistence; and never have they been in circumstances of comfort and convenience suitable to the orderly conducting of the grave and momentous business committed to their charge. That errors should have been committed under such circumstances will not surprise those who have an honest consciousness of their own fallibilities. But that those extraordinary powers have not been perverted to any sinister purpose, to the damage of the country, to personal aggrandizement, or to the creation or advancement of a party, or to the success of a speculation, I assert with a modest, but firm and assured confidence."

The auditor and comptroller say, in their report—

" The whole amount of claims audited and paid by treasury orders from the 1st of January last, at which time our offices were established, up to the 27th of September inclusive, is as follows :—

Military claims,	. . . . .	$225,154 20
Naval,	. . . .	27,364 73
Civil,	. . . .	8,587 92
Contingent,	. . . . . .	6,427 84
Total,	. . . .	$267,534 69

" In cases where cash has been advanced and for supplies furnished by merchants previous to the 1st of March last, the orders have been drawn bearing an interest of eight per cent. per annum. The amount of orders of this description is fifty-nine thousand four hundred and sixty-eight dollars and forty-three cents.

" The account of Bryan & Hall, late agents of the government at New Orleans, have been submitted to this office, and are now under consideration. The whole amount of their liabilities [claims] is seventy-seven thousand four hundred and sixty-eight dollars and seventy-six cents, of which the sum of fifty-three thousand four hundred and sixty-eight dollars and seventy-six cents was due previous to the 1st of September instant."

As this report brings up accounts to a date five months later than the battle of San Jacinto, it shows at how little expense to the government the independence of the country was achieved. If it had been possible for the Texans to be hard-money men and prompt-payment men, the expense would have been much less than is above stated.

These claims were all paid by drafts on an empty treasury. They were receivable for back dues on the public lands, but there was little or no demand for them for this purpose, and they sank much in value.

Something might have been derived from the duty on imports, but the majority of the merchants so arranged their business as to anticipate the operation of the act. McKinney and Williams afterwards brought one or two vessels into port, but the Provisional Government, taking into consideration the great aid these gentlemen had rendered to the cause, passed an ordinance (January 4, 1836) exempting these importations from duties, in order to place them on a level with the other merchants.

In a subsequent report from the Treasury Department, there is an allusion to a sum of about nine hundred and fifteen dollars received for customs under the first customs act; but whether is thereby meant the first customs act under the Provisional Government or under the Republic, we cannot tell.

In the Report of the Secretary of the Treasury of April 18,

1837, it is stated that of the audited claims there had been redeemed

" By J. Fletcher, Treasurer of the Provisional Government, as per his account filed in this department, ... $664 08
" By B. Hardiman, Secretary of Treasury of government *ad interim,* . . . . $80 00."

But in what manner these enormous amounts were redeemed, we are left to conjecture.

The sixty-five thousand dollars borrowed at New Orleans was the only efficient revenue the government *ad interim* possessed. And be it remembered that the loan from Triplett and others, and the loan from Erwin and others, were both honorably paid.

The exact amount of the Triplett loan was twenty thousand and seventy dollars, which was liquidated by granting to the parties forty thousand acres of land for the principal, with an addition of one hundred and thirteen thousand three hundred and fifty-seven acres by way of bonus.

The amount received from the Erwin loan was forty-five thousand eight hundred and twenty dollars, which, with interest added, six thousand one hundred and seventy dollars and forty-four cents, was liquidated by a grant of land of one hundred and three thousand three hundred and eighty-one acres, with eighteen thousand two hundred and eight acres additional by way of bonus. A balance of about five thousand dollars which remained due was paid in money to the representatives of this firm in February, 1852.

CHAPTER VII.

PROCEEDINGS UNDER THE REPUBLIC.   FIRST SESSION OF FIRST
CONGRESS : OCTOBER 3 TO DECEMBER, 1836.

Gen. Houston installed as President—Deplorable condition of the navy—Contributions of Gen. Thos. J. Green—Acts relating to the military establishment—High
salaries of officers on the civil list—New tariff, and sale of Galveston town-plot—
"A public debt a public blessing"—Unsuccessful effort to negotiate a loan of
twenty thousand dollars—Act to establish a general land-office—Questions whether
foreign volunteers should be allowed to sell their land-certificates to aliens, and
whether aliens should be allowed to hòld lands in Texas—Recognition of decree
for establishing the Agricultural and Commercial Bank—Act to incorporate the
Texas Railroad, Navigation, and Banking Company—Proceedings under this act.

THE first Congress commenced its first session, at the town of
Columbia, on the 3d of October, 1836 ; and on the 22d, Gen.
Samuel Houston, who had been duly elected by the people, was
formally installed as President of the Republic.

On the 26th, Mr. Fisher, chairman of the Committee on Naval
Affairs, made a report, showing the deplorable condition of the
navy :—

" Your Committee on Naval Affairs, to whom was referred the report of
the acting Secretary of the Navy, and a resolution calling for an increase of
the same, have instructed me tó submit the following report, and the bill
accompanying it, from the report of the acting Secretary of the Navy.

" That arm of the national defence appears to be in a most deplorable
and crippled condition. The 'Brutus' and 'Invincible' are both in New York,
in a situation which prevents their services from being immediately available ; and the 'Liberty' is detained in New Orleans.   Thus, while momen-
tarily in expectation of a blockade from the enemy, our whole line of sea-
coast is defended by but one national vessel, the 'Independence,' mounting
seven guns, and four small privateers, each pursuing its own prey, and not
immediately subject to the orders of government.   While our navy remains
in this condition, it is in the power of the enemy, at his pleasure, to cut off
our supplies, and seize upon our seaports.   It appears to your committee
that the error which has produced the present bad condition of our navy has
been radical, and coexistent with its first formation.   In order to raise a naval
force sufficient to co-operate with that of the enemy, the government was
forced to purchase such vessels as could most easily be procured.   These were
vessels either originally unfit for the purpose intended, or worn out in the

merchant service. The consequence has been that these vessels demanded daily repairs, and were seldom in a situation for actual service. So far, in our struggle with Mexico, our navy has proved adequate to the protection of our sea-coast, and to the annoyance of the enemy. But the navy of the enemy has lately been increased by the addition of several vessels of the most splendid description ; it therefore becomes imperiously necessary that our navy should be increased in the same ratio.

" Your committee, therefore, suggest the immediate building or purchase of the following description of vessels :—

" One sloop-of-war, 600 tons, mounting 24 guns; probable cost, ...	$60,000
" One steam-vessel, mounting 10 guns, . . .	45,000
"Two schooners, 200 tons, mounting 11 guns, .	30,000
	$135,000"

On a subsequent page of the Journal, we find it recorded that Gen. Thos. J. Green " had voluntarily sold and sacrificed some, and mortgaged other of his property in the United States (to the amount in all of $20,333 04), for the purpose of procuring men, munitions, provisions, &c., for our army, and also to release two of our national vessels, then in New Orleans, under arrest for debt, and upon a charge of piracy."

The bill reported for the increase of the navy was passed (November 18), with an amendment providing that there should be two steam-vessels, instead of one, and each capable of transporting seven hundred and fifty men and provisions.

Besides this act, the first Congress, at its first session, passed an act, December 20, to fix the military establishment of Texas at one regiment of cavalry, one of artillery, and four regiments of infantry, amounting, officers included, and including the corps of engineers and ordnance, and the staff, to 3,587 men ; December 5, an act to protect the frontier, by raising a battalion of 280 mounted riflemen ; and, December 22, a joint resolution, " authorizing the President to receive *forty thousand* volunteers."

December 9, an act was passed to compensate the officers on the civil list. The President's salary was fixed at ten thousand dollars a year; that of each of the members of his cabinet at three thousand five hundred; and a long list of civil officers in proportion. A State government would have been content to allow its chief magistrate a salary of one thousand, or fifteen hundred dollars ; but Texas was an independent republic, and had to support its imperial dignity among the nations of the earth. Mr. Branch

Tanner Archer maintained that the President ought to have as much salary as the President of the United States, and contended for this with great zeal, for two or three days in succession.

That such precisians as ex-Governor Smith might have no cause of complaint, an act was passed, December 15, appropriating $150,000 to defray the expenses of the navy ; $700,000 for those of the army ; and $150,000 for those of executive and civil departments—in all, a round million.

" To raise a revenue by imposts," an act was passed, December 20, imposing *ad valorem* duties of various rates, from one to fifty per cent., and a tonnage-duty of $1 25 per ton ; but it defeated itself by one of its provisions making audited drafts on the treasury receivable for such duties.

An act, relinquishing to Michael B. Menard and others a league (4444 acres) and "labor" (*i. e.* a lot of 177 acres) on the east end of Galveston Island (the town-plot of Galveston), was passed December 9, on condition of their paying for it $50,000, in approved acceptances on New Orleans. And acts and resolutions were also passed authorizing land-script to the amount of 500,000 acres to be issued to Thomas Toby, of New Orleans, to be sold by him at fifty cents an acre; making David White, of Mobile, an agent to sell script at the same rate, to the amount of $100,000 ; and providing for the relief of Wm. Bryan, of New Orleans, by granting him land-script, by the sale of which he might pay himself what was due to him by the Republic.

But the chief dependence of the Congress of Texas was on loans from abroad. True disciples, in this respect, of Alexander Hamilton, they, or at least a part of them, regarded a public debt as a public blessing. This is evident from a report made by a select committee, December 16, Mr. Chenoweth, chairman :—

"At present, our indebtedness is small, and our liabilities almost entirely to private individuals, whose claims, your committee are of opinion, may properly be merged and cancelled by the creation of substantial loans. An outstanding national debt may, in many respects, be looked upon as beneficial, by a community isolated and dependent as Texas, if the creditors, as such, can afford us substantial patronage. And until we can stand immutable among the nations of the earth, your committee would advise that the pecuniary interests of our creditors will excite for us the sympathies and protection of mankind."

A public debt was not an evil, but an inconvenience was felt in

its being due to the citizens of Texas, instead of "to foreigners,"
i. e. the citizens of the United States. Therefore, leaving unrepealed the acts of the Provisional Government authorizing the
million loan, and the hundred thousand dollar loan, an act was
passed, November 18, "to authorize the President to negotiate
a loan or loans on the bonds of the government, not exceeding five
million dollars," at a rate of interest not exceeding ten per cent.
per annum ; and due provision was made that two commissioners
should proceed immediately to the United States, for the purpose
of negotiating said bonds, and subsequently to Europe, if that
should be necessary. To raise immediate means, another act
was passed, December 10, authorizing the President to borrow
twenty thousand dollars, and empowering him to stipulate "for
such an amount of interest" as he could best contract for ; that is,
empowering him to borrow at the rate of twenty or thirty per
cent., or more, if he could not borrow the money for less.

The act of most importance in its practical bearings, passed at
this session, was that to open the land-offices, or, as it was entitled, "An act to establish a General Land-Office for the Republic
of Texas." This, besides one general, established eleven district
offices, and provided—

"That surveys should be made at the expense of those holding warrants,
but, when they held 'land-script,' at the expense of the government. That
grantees should pay, as a government fee, the price as fixed by the colonization laws of Coahuila and Texas in force at the time they emigrated to
this country. That no person should, by virtue of an improvement, have a
right to claim more than one league and 'labor' of land. That the land-
offices should open on the 1st of June, 1837, for all those citizens who
were in the country when independence was declared (March 2, 1836),
and for those who served a term as volunteers previous to that time, and
remain open six months for their exclusive benefit. That every free white
person, head of a family, who should arrive in the Republic from and after
January 1, 1837, should be entitled to 1280 acres of land, and every single
white free man 640 acres, to be increased to 1280 acres in case of his
marriage, but patents not to be granted till after they had been three years
resident."

As this bill gave land to almost everybody that was in the
country, and almost everybody that was to come into the country,
it served to diminish still more the value of soldiers' certificates.

It was, however, of benefit to those who were on the spot, and
who had the means wherewith to purchase soldiers' certificates
and settlers' "head-rights."

At one time it seems to have been mooted whether the soldiers should not be restricted to selling their certificates to actual residents of Texas. Nay, the question, "Is it expedient to authorize by law foreign volunteers to sell their bounty land to aliens?" was formally referred to a select committee, which, through Mr. Baker, its chairman, made a report, November 29, 1838, in which they said—

"'Is it expedient to authorize by law foreign volunteers to sell their bounty land to aliens?' The heart of every true friend of Texas must answer, 'Yes; it is expedient;' and justice and gratitude demand that they should have the right to sell it to whomsoever and wheresoever they can. That they should not be compelled to sell it alone to Texan speculators, but that the defenders of Texan liberty should have all the rights and all the benefits this government can confer."

In a report extending through nine or ten pages, the committee gave equally satisfactory answers to the questions—

"Is it expedient to authorize by law those aliens who have aided Texas in her struggle for independence, to hold lands in Texas, by paying a bonus to the government for the same?"

"Is it expedient to authorize by law the citizens of Texas to sell lands to aliens, upon condition that the purchaser pay a bonus to the government for the same?"

The answer to all these questions was, substantially, "Yes; it will be best for the country, and best for the land-speculators we have among ourselves." That so formal a report should have been made on this subject is proof how rife the spirit of land-speculation was in Texas at a time, indeed, when her independence had been effected, but when it was not known that it could be sustained.

The act to open the land-offices was vetoed by President Houston, because it was

"Evidently impracticable, without opening a wide door for confusion, to commence a new system of surveys and of granting lands, until some definite rules or principles are established to ascertain what land is held by valid titles and what is vacant." Because, it would be "doing a great injustice to the army, and to those who are entitled to bounty land, to open the land-offices until such rules are established, as to the selection and location of bounty lands, as will place them on a just equality with others." And, lastly, because the bill, "if published now, will only serve to distract the public mind, and divert the public attention from the defence of the country against the common enemy, and direct it almost exclusively to the location of land-script, and to land-speculation."

"*L'état! c'est* MOI," said Louis XIV. "*Je suis l'état.*" "The State! that is *me.* I am the State." From some things we have heard, we have been led to believe that, as Louis XIV. was "the State," in the kingdom of France, so Samuel Houston was "the State," in the Republic of Texas. But, when a question about land-speculations arose, all his power and influence was a mere nullity. On the 22d of December, both House and Senate passed the bill, by constitutional majorities, and it became a law in defiance of the President.

At the period of which we are now speaking, the last quarter of 1836, paper-money banking had reached its culminating point in our Federal Union. Men who had made the subject their especial study saw that an explosion must occur. But the Congress of the United States was blind to the evils about to ensue, and so was the Congress of Texas.

On the 30th of April, 1835, nearly six months before the commencement of hostilities, the State of Coahuila and Texas passed a decree, making Samuel M. Williams, of the firm of McKinney and Williams, the *empresario*—that is, the contractor, or, more literally, the undertaker—to establish a bank in the Department of Brazos, to be called the "Commercial and Agricultural Bank." The said bank was to have a capital not exceeding one million dollars, divided into shares of one hundred dollars each. As soon as three hundred thousand dollars were subscribed, a meeting was to be called, and directors chosen. The bank was to continue for twenty years, and to have the privilege of establishing branches anywhere and everywhere. It might receive eight per cent. per annum, on loans not exceeding six months, and ten per cent. on loans exceeding that time; and only the capital of the bank was to be responsible for the notes it issued. It was a most liberal charter throughout, and especially as it provided that the subscribers should "adequately secure the value of their shares with real estate in the Republic." Or, if there was anything illiberal in it, it was contained in a single clause, which provided that, "as soon as one hundred thousand dollars, at least, have entered the vaults of the bank, it may commence operations; a commissioner, to be appointed by the executive, previously intervening, who shall, furthermore, examine every year the state of the concerns of the association."

Construed according to the common principles of bank interpretation, we do not know that even this clause can be considered as illiberal, for it does not say "one hundred thousand dollars *in specie;*" and, whatever the word "dollars" may mean in Coahuila, it means, in Texas and the United States, whatever people choose to make it mean.

By an act passed December 10, 1836, "for the relief of McKinney and Williams," the President was required to appoint a commissioner "for the purpose contemplated in the tenth article of the charter of the Bank of Agriculture and Commerce, granted to Samuel M. Williams by the Legislature of the State of Coahuila and Texas, in April, 1835, in order that the parties may exercise and enjoy their privileges under said act."

That the Congress of Texas looked upon this as only the commencement of a system, is evident from the next section, which authorized and empowered the Secretary of the Treasury "to negotiate a loan, from *any bank or banks that may be established in this Republic*, of sufficient amount for the payment of all just claims held by McKinney and Williams against this government."

If there is any doubt on this subject in the mind of the reader, it will be removed when we inform him that only six days afterwards, or on the 16th of December, an act was passed " to incorporate the Texas Railroad, Navigation, and Banking Company," with a capital stock of five millions, to be increased, if desirable, to ten millions, and with the right of connecting the waters of the Rio Grande and the Sabine by means of internal navigation, together with the privilege of making branch canals and branch railroads in every direction.

It was the day of magnificent schemes; but admiration ought not to be withheld from this, especially when it is considered that, at this very moment, when a line of artificial navigation of five hundred miles was projected, the Texans had not the means of defending their coast from the insults of a single Mexican sloop-of-war.

In every respect but two, the charter was of the most liberal description. It provided that the bank should not go into operation until it had " a *specie* capital of one million dollars paid in," and that the charter should be forfeited unless a bonus of twenty-five thousand dollars should be paid in gold and silver, within eighteen months of the date of the act.

The necessary amount of stock, five millions, was subscribed by eight individuals and firms; and, within the period prescribed by the charter, the bonus was tendered in Texas treasury notes, which by law were then receivable for all public dues. The Treasurer refused to receive them, but gave a written acknowledgment that the tender had been made. And, if it were not for the provision requiring a "million dollars to be paid *in specie* before the bank can commence operations," the charter might be worth looking after by Northern speculators.

Even as it was, some people made money out of the scheme. None of them, as we have learned from one of the number, paid anything in; but one of them sold out his interest to a gentleman of New York for thirty thousand dollars, and received his pay in store goods. The successful salesman then bought out the interest of another of the subscribers for ten thousand dollars. And another one of the gentlemen concerned disposed of his interest for three leagues of land, which he has since sold at two dollars and a half an acre. Thus this ten million scheme enabled three of the parties to realize a net profit of about sixty thousand dollars.

The rest of the subscribers retain their original shares to this day.

Of the operations of the Commercial and Agricultural Bank, we shall have occasion to speak hereafter.

CHAPTER VIII.

SECOND SESSION OF THE FIRST CONGRESS: MAY 1 TO JUNE, 1837.

Pecuniary destitution of the Government of the Republic—Recognition of its independence by the United States—Statement by President Houston of the insufficiency of the navy—Governor Smith made Secretary of the Treasury—Proceedings
of the agencies at Mobile and New Orleans—The Secretary of the Treasury reports a plan for raising a revenue, and funding the outstanding debt—Acts passed
accordingly—Government liabilities worth only fifteen cents in the dollar—Projects
for additional banks—Deplorable condition of the treasury—First effective act for
the issue of treasury notes.

THE first Congress met, by adjournment, on the 1st of May,
1837, at the town of Houston, about eighty miles inland, by the
post-route, from Galveston. Its loan acts had produced nothing.
Its customs act had produced nothing. And its acts for the sale of
land-script had produced little or nothing.

The "land-dues" were the only branch of the revenue that was
at all productive. Mr. Gail Borden, who has already figured
largely in our history on account of the fifty-eight dollars and thirty
cents he paid into the treasury of the Consultation, made himself
still more illustrious in this year by paying into the treasury of the
Republic the sum of $7,346 37. It is true that this amount was
in "land-script," and, therefore, not available as efficient revenue.
But Mr. Gail Borden paid over what he had received.

Yet there was cause for pride and exultation. The independence of Texas had been acknowledged by the Government of the
United States. "We now," said the President, "occupy the proud
attitude of a sovereign and independent republic, which will impose
upon us the obligation of evincing to the world that we are worthy
to be free. This only will be accomplished by wise legislation, the
maintenance of our integrity, *and the faithful and just redemption
of our plighted faith wherever it has been pledged.*"

.When the President went to announce this and other matters to
Congress, he was received with a pomp and ceremony which may
cause the reader to fear that the Texans had, by living under

Mexican rule, lost something of their republican simplicity. Our extract is from the House Journal, of May 5, 1837 :—

"The Senate then entered the hall, preceded by their sergeant-at-arms; the President *pro tem.* took his seat on the right hand of the Speaker, and presided jointly with him.

"The Senators were provided with seats in front of the chair, and the officers of the two Houses associated in their several duties at their respective stations.

"At twelve o'clock, His Excellency, the President, entered the hall, accompanied by the heads of the several departments, and other officers of the government, and also by Joseph Tucker Crawford, Esq., His Britannic Majesty's Consul, at Tampico, and Commissioner from the British Government to this Republic, and preceded by the joint committee of the two Houses. The President was received by the members of the two Houses standing uncovered, and was conducted to a seat between the President *pro tem.* of the Senate, and the Speaker of the House.

"The heads of the departments, the British commissioner, and the other attendants of His Excellency, were accommodated with seats on the right hand of the chair.

"The members having resumed their seats, after a short pause, His Excellency rose, and read the following communication :—

[Here follows a communication, which fills eight pages of the printed Journal.]

"His Excellency, having concluded, retired from the hall, conducted and accompanied as on his entrance."

In this communication, the President gave, substantially, such a view of the finances as is contained in the initial paragraph of this chapter, renewed his objections to opening the land-offices, and, speaking of the subject of maritime defence, said:—

"The insufficiency of our navy must be a subject of serious consideration. When the constitutional government assumed its functions, the armed vessels, 'Brutus' and 'Invincible,' were in the port of New York, and remained there until a few weeks past, when they returned, but without either crews or provisions for a cruise.

"The 'Independence,' having not more than two weeks' provisions, was taken to New Orleans some months since, where she has been detained, and has not yet been reported to this government for service.

"At an early day, a confidential officer was dispatched to the United States, for the purpose of purchasing such vessels as would enable us to keep the command of the Gulf from our enemy. He has reported to the proper department, and his arrival is daily expected with one or more fine vessels, in preparation to defend our commerce, and make reprisals on the enemy.

"Our commerce has suffered to some extent, and a small portion of our supplies for the army has been captured, and taken into Mexican ports."

Before the close of the session, the "Independence" was captured by the enemy, and the navy reduced to the "Brutus" and the "Invincible."

The reader's old friend and acquaintance, ex-Governor Henry Smith, was now Secretary of the Treasury, and he, in anticipation of the meeting of Congress, had, on the 18th of April, presented a report to the President. It was made up chiefly of complaints of the Toby agency at New Orleans, and the White agency at Mobile. The former would render no account of its transactions to the department, and dishonored all the drafts drawn upon it. Mr. Thomas Toby had, moreover, "pursued the unwarrantable course of selling the script at one, two; and three years' credit."

Mr. David White gave no better satisfaction. In addition to land-script, commercial acceptances for fifty thousand dollars, being the amount that had been paid in for the purchase of the town-plot of Galveston, had been put into his hands. "Many drafts have been drawn on this agency, and but few paid. If any portion of the fifty thousand dollar acceptances have been paid, it is unknown to this department; and of the few which have been paid, it is believed they were generally paid in land-script, for which the agent claims his commission of 7½ per cent."

We suspect that, if the agents had had an opportunity, they too would have had complaints to make. The simple truth was, that they were appointed to sell what, in time of peace, had little commercial value even in Texas, and what in time of war had hardly any.

So wrathful was the President that he ordered that no further sales should be made by these agents, and that they should pass over to a special agent, appointed for the purpose, such land-script as remained in their possession.

The whole amount of audited claims, from January 1, 1836, to April 18, 1837, was stated by the auditor at $604,985 43, of which only $1,569 34 had been redeemed by receiving the evidence of them in payment of public dues.

In conformity with a resolution passed at the first session, the Secretary of the Treasury made another report, on the 12th of May, containing a plan of revenue and finance. In this, he suggested a new tariff, which, he supposed, would yield two hundred thousand dollars per annum : Direct taxes on lands, and all other property, which, at one-half per cent. *ad valorem*, would yield one hundred and twenty-five thousand dollars. And besides these, license taxes on wholesale and retail dealers, taverns, public shows, and billiard-tables, the produce of which would probably amount to ten thousand dollars. Add to these, forty thousand dollars for "present supposed dues on granted lands, and the Republic would have an annual revenue of three hundred and seventy-five thousand dollars."

With these projects of taxation, Governor Smith combined a plan for funding, which consisted in issuing certificates of stock, redeemable in not less than five, nor more than ten years, and bearing an interest of ten per cent., the said certificates to be issued in exchange for audited drafts and other outstanding evidences of the public debt.

Speaking on this point, the Governor says:—

"It appears clear to me, under the present depreciated state of the government liabilities, that, if this plan be adopted, the public creditors will soon feel relief, and the claims against the government, in the form of auditor's warrants, now possessing but a nominal value, say fifteen cents in the dollar, would soon approach their par value. If the banking institutions of the country should go into operation, as contemplated, this stock, then secured, would be deemed good security for bank accommodations, and, I have no doubt, would soon gain a similar credit in the United States, and the public credit, if not entirely restored, would become greatly assisted and benefited."

Here we find Governor Smith suggesting that Texan bonds should be made a foundation for Texan banks. But whether he therein anticipated or borrowed the wisdom of the founders of the New York free banking system, must be left to the decision of the reader.

An act for funding the public debt was passed June 7; and acts to create a revenue by import duties and direct taxes were passed June 12.

Thus far all was according to the recommendations of the Secretary of the Treasury. But on the 9th, only two days after the passage of the funding act, and three days before the passage of the acts imposing import duties and direct taxes, another act was passed authorizing the issue of promissory notes of government, to the amount of five hundred thousand dollars, and making them receivable for all public dues. This was not according to Governor Smith's recommendation, and gave rise to serious difficulties between him and the Congress.

June 12, an act was passed supplementary to the act to establish a general land-office. By one section of this, it was provided that the opening of the land-offices should be further postponed till the 1st of October; and by another it was enacted—

"That, after the first day of October next, no individual arriving in the country shall be entitled to land as an emigrant; and from this time forward no more bounty land shall be given as an inducement to any one to enter into service in the army of Texas."

It was quite time that some provision like this should be adopted; for, if lands should be given to every emigrant, it would be difficult for those who had bought up soldiers' certificates and old settlers' "head-rights" to find purchasers.

President Houston vetoed this bill; but, like that to which it was a supplement, it was passed in defiance of him.

It was thought that the Commercial and Agricultural Bank, and the Texas Railroad, Navigation, and Banking Company, with their capitals (that were to be) of six to eleven millions, would not afford sufficient banking facilities to a population of somewhere between twenty and fifty thousand. Therefore, projects were brought forward for the incorporation of a "Joint-Stock Company for the Erection of a Hotel and Bath-house at Velasco, with Banking Privileges;" for another of like kind at Houston; for the incorporation of the "Internal Improvement and Banking Company of Texas;" for the incorporation of the "Red River and Aransaso Bay, Railroad, Navigation, and Banking Company," embracing a scheme hardly less magnificent than that of the "Texas Railroad, Navigation, and Banking Company;" and, finally, for establishing a bank on the faith of the government.

All these projects were favorably received. But, before the necessary laws could be passed, news was received of the grand explosion of the banks in the United States, and they were suffered to die a natural death.

The fact that, at the commencement of this session, audited drafts, the only Texan "promises to pay" which were then afloat, were worth but fifteen cents in the dollar, must have convinced the reader that the finances of Texas were in a deplorable condition. If he supposes there was any improvement before the Congress adjourned, the following message from the President will dispel his illusion:—

"EXECUTIVE DEPARTMENT, CITY OF HOUSTON, *June* 6, 1837.

"Gentlemen of the Senate and House of Representatives :—

"I cannot forbear calling your attention to the condition of the subsistence and quartermaster's department of this government. The inclosed document will exhibit the amount of liabilities that must be immediately met, or the credit of the government will be entirely destroyed.

"I would have laid the subject before your honorable body at an earlier day, had it been in my power to have acquired the information desirable. Without the interposition of Congress, the situation of the country must be truly deplorable.

"The government was unable, upon its own credit, to obtain the supplies absolutely necessary to the emergencies of the army. The Executive has been compelled to give his individual obligation for supplies for the army, indorsed by some of the honorable members of your body. This was done at a time when a part of the army was in an actual state of mutiny, from want of every kind of provisions. Galveston Island would have been deserted, had not this course been pursued.

"Since the commencement of the constitutional government, no public officer has received any salary. Their personal expenses are great, from the fact of their having to pay an exorbitant price for board. Their individual means are quite exhausted. They have tendered me resignations from time to time, induced by their actual necessities, intending to pursue some other course that they might obtain the means of subsistence. The Executive, since he has come into office, has received into the treasury and disbursed only five hundred dollars for provisions for the troops. Under these circumstances, your honorable body must be aware of the absolute necessity of some provision being made to sustain the country ; and the aid which it is in your power to give is most sincerely and earnestly invoked.

"SAMUEL HOUSTON."

The message was referred to the Committee of Ways and Means, and on the next day that committee reported a bill for the issue of five hundred thousand dollars in promissory notes; but the whole of these, it was provided, should be issued and paid out alone for, and on account of, the expenses of the civil department of the government, except one hundred thousand dollars for the purchase of horses and munitions to be used by the rangers and mounted gun-men in a war against the Indians.

CHAPTER IX.

"CALLED SESSION" OF THE SECOND CONGRESS: SEPTEMBER 25 TO NOVEMBER 4, 1837.

The opening of the land-offices postponed—Differences of opinion of the Secretary of the Treasury and Congress on the subject of treasury notes—Reasons for not issuing land-script to the soldiers—Low price of land-script at New Orleans—Act for augmenting the navy.

NOVEMBER 6th was the time appointed by law for the Second Congress to assemble; but the President, by proclamation, called them together on the 25th of September. In his opening message, he gave, as his reasons, that preparations were making to run the boundary-line between the United States and Texas, and that this might conflict with the law of the last session for opening the land-offices—

"Inasmuch as some of the districts would necessarily fall within that section of country over which the United States have, for some years, exercised civil jurisdiction; but over which, there is no doubt, the Government of Texas, so soon as the limits of each country are defined, will be manifestly entitled to the civil, as well as the political, jurisdiction."

Without any unnecessary delay, a joint resolution was adopted "to suspend the operations of the land-offices until the further action of Congress." Thus, a measure which was to have been consummated on the 1st of June, 1837, and which was afterwards deferred to the 1st of October, was now indefinitely postponed, greatly to the satisfaction of President Houston, and greatly to the chagrin of some of his opponents.

The act, passed at the last session for funding the public debt, had not been carried into effect; and neither had that for the issue of promissory notes. For this, the Secretary of the Treasury was called to account. He replied, October 13th, that the two laws were incompatible; and that the act of June 9th, requiring promissory notes to be issued, appeared to be superseded in its chief provision by an act of subsequent date, or of June 12th, for imposing duties on imports, which last act required that all such duties should be paid "in gold and silver, or such current bank-notes as the government might direct." If the duties were received in treasury notes, as directed by the act of June 9th, it would be folly to fund the outstanding audited drafts, inasmuch as the government could then comply with its promise to pay interest only by giving to the fundholder other paper promises. Therefore, he had waited for the further action of the Congress.

Governor Smith's plan was a very plausible one. It rested, in fact, on sound principles, but on principles which could not be carried out in the existing condition of things in Texas.

In a long report, the Secretary of the Treasury explained his views; but his reasons were not satisfactory to the lawgivers of the Republic. They were resolved that a government paper-money should be issued in the form of promissory notes, or treasury bills. But here a new difficulty arose. The President was, by law, required to subscribe the bills, and it would be a work of great labor to sign so many. How could he do it? He was still suffering under a wound, received at the battle of San Jacinto, and was otherwise indisposed. Either compassionating the condition of the President, or else resolved that their favorite measure should not be defeated by any pretext, however plausible, Congress passed a joint resolution, October 23d, "authorizing William G. Cooke to sign the name of the President to the promissory notes of the government," in the preamble to which due prominence was given "to the disabled situation of His Excellency's right arm from a former wound, aggravated by his present sickness." It was added that "the necessary and pressing wants of the country require that the issue of such notes should immediately commence."

The Secretary of War was also called to account for not having issued land-warrants to the soldiers, as had been ordered; and the President answered for him:—

"It (the law containing the order) was not thought to be imperative as to its immediate execution. Had the Executive approved its immediate execution, or the Secretary of War performed it, nothing appeared more ruinous to the country. Our army was numerous; it was destitute of clothing; it was without ten days' provisions; it had not five hundred efficient arms; it was wofully defective in ammunition (and, I regret to say, that the country is without any at this time): we had to look abroad for our supplies: general discontent prevailed in the army.

"Our only reliance, for the remedy of these evils, was upon the script which had been sent to agents of the government in the United States, to be disposed of.   Unless that scheme should prove successful, the army must remain destitute, which would soon have led to anarchy and its dissolution.

"Under the directions of the government *ad interim*, the acting pay-master-general had issued upwards of thirty thousand acres of land-certificates for discharged soldiers.   They immediately sailed for New Orleans; and, on their arrival there, finding themselves destitute of means, they found persons there always ready to purchase at a great sacrifice.   It was sold at twenty cents per acre, and under that price.   Speculators soon availed themselves of these facts.

"When the script of the government was brought into market at fifty cents per acre, there were always persons who had purchased the soldiers' certificates for a mere nominal amount, who were prepared to speculate upon it at a price from twenty-five to thirty cents per acre, alleging that it emanated from the government, and that it was equally as good as the script sent there by the government.   This, at once, depreciated the script of the government, and rendered it impossible to vend it for cash, or to purchase supplies for the army, without paying from one to two hundred per cent. advance for them."

This reasoning did not convince the Texan Congress.   They, in defiance of the President's veto, passed a joint resolution to require the Secretary of War to issue land-warrants to the soldiers. If they did this with a view of buying them up themselves, at a low price, the journals do not disclose the fact.

At this session, an act was passed for augmenting the navy.   It authorized

"The buying or building, arming and equipping 'of one ship or brig, of about five hundred tons burden, to mount eighteen guns; two barks or brigs, about three hundred tons burden, mounting twelve guns each; and three schooners, about one hundred and thirty tons burden, mounting five or seven guns each.'   It was further enacted 'that the sum of two hundred and eighty thousand dollars is hereby appropriated for the purpose' aforesaid, 'and that the public faith is *solemnly* pledged for its payment.' "

Under this act sundry vessels were purchased, of which we shall have occasion to speak hereafter.

CHAPTER X.

FIRST REGULAR SESSION OF SECOND CONGRESS: NOVEMBER 6 TO DECEMBER, 1837.

Issues of treasury notes commenced November 1, 1837—New difficulties between the Secretary of the Treasury and Congress—Want of money and want of credit —"Boundless revenue" expected from the opening of the land-offices—The navy almost extinct—Moderate amount of public expenses up to November, 1837—A new tariff—Authority for the issue of more treasury notes—Distinction between original holders and assignees of Texan securities—The agent sent to the United States to sell land-script recalled—Unreasonable expectations of the Texan Government in relation to its public lands—New act for opening the land-offices.

ONLY one day elapsed between the close of the "called" and the commencement of the regular session, and that was a Sunday.

The Secretary of the Treasury was again called to account. The issue of treasury notes commenced on or about the 1st of November, but on the 5th he addressed a letter to the collectors of customs, forbidding them to take such notes in payment of duties; and, on the 13th, he, by order of the President, addressed another letter directing them to receive the said notes as cash.

In his report to Congress on this subject, the Secretary says :—

" In issuing the inhibitory order, I conscientiously believe I was right, and acting in the lawful discharge of my duty. And, in issuing the countermand which immediately followed, I also considered I was right, as it was ordered by my superior, who assumed the responsibility."

In a good many respects, the Government of Texas appears to have been imperial rather than republican. And if Henry Smith, when in one position, knew how to command, he here gave evidence that, when placed in another, he knew how to obey.

Again was the Secretary of the Treasury called to account. He had done nothing towards funding the floating debt. Why had he neglected this important duty ?

He replied:—

" In two previous communications to your House, I have adverted to the substantial reasons which have induced me to delay its execution, in

terms, as I conceived, too plain to be misunderstood. Ever willing, however, to account for any seeming neglect of official duty on my part, I give
the following as the last, though not the least reason, why that law has
been delayed in its execution : Two different bills have been sent up to
New Orleans for suitable and necessary stationery to be used for that and
other public purposes, neither of which, however, have been filled, for reasons which it is easy to imagine."

A plain-spoken man was Henry Smith; but here he resorts to
a euphuism. It was too much even for him to say that the
government had neither cash nor credit wherewith to purchase
pen, ink, and paper.

On the 21st, the President, having been before prevented by
sickness, delivered his message.

In it he said :—

" The finances of our country, since the commencement of the revolution
up to this time, have been in a more embarrassed situation, doubtless, than
any other nation ever experienced.   Since the commencement of the present administration, during the first year, there was at the disposition of
the Executive, or in the treasury, but five hundred dollars in cash.   The
several amounts that had been appropriated for specific or general purposes
depended on the sale of script, and *that*, by acts of Congress, was placed in
the hands of foreign agents, who were irresponsible to the Executive. * *
This imaginary and unfortunate expedient is now at end, and has left the
government in a situation to afford the most ample redemption of all her
pledges and responsibilities.

" A boundless revenue to the country will accrue from the opening of
the land-offices, and so soon as that can take place consistently with the
positive provisions of the constitution, and regulated by such enactments as
will guard the public interest against fraud and imposition, it will meet the
desire of the Executive, and promote the public tranquillity."

As will be seen hereafter, this " boundless revenue" was all an
illusion, and even less was derived from the opening of the land-
offices than from the sale of land-script.

" Owing," he continued, " to the financial derangements of the United
States, from which our currency was almost entirely derived, and where, it
was hoped, that this country could obtain a negotiation for five millions of
dollars, our expectations have not been realized.   By the last advices from
our agents of the loan, they had not succeeded, but regarded the prospect
of success greater than had been at any previous time."

Here was another illusion of the Texans, even greater and more
permanent than that founded on the sale of land-script, or that
resting on the opening of the land-offices.

Of the treasury note system, the President gave a qualified approval ; *provided* the issues were not of a greater amount than " would meet the actual necessities of a circulating medium."

The report of the Secretary of the Navy was very gloomy :—

" While the country has been gradually rising from the effects of the revolution, our navy has become almost extinct. The embarrassed situation of our financial affairs has heretofore rendered it impossible to make the necessary appropriations for keeping it up ; and we now have but one small vessel afloat to guard a coast of more than six hundred miles in length. While our navy is in this shattered condition, and entirely unable to afford the necessary protection to our commerce, the Mexicans have found means to make such additions to their own naval strength as will enable them to hold an entire control of the Gulf."

On the 30th of November, the Secretary of the Treasury made a report ; from one of the documents appended to which, we learn that the amount of claims audited up to 17th of November was—

Military	.	.	.	.	$903,720 85
Civil	.	.	.	.	142,902 59
Naval	.	.	.	.	56,850 65
Contingent	.	.	.		23,334 35
Total	.	.	.	.	$1,126,808 44

" From which should be deducted drafts taken in for public dues, &c., $34,824 79, leaving outstanding $1,090,984 45."

Here we find that even two years after the commencement of the war, the public debt, so far as ascertained, was but little more than a million ; not because the government had any objection to running in debt to a greater amount, but because few would trust it, except such as could not well avoid so doing.

Six months having elapsed since the passage (June 12) of the last act for raising a revenue by a duty on imports, it was now (December 18) deemed high time to pass another, and accordingly another was passed, giving a new list of free articles, and modifying the *ad valorem* rates on some of the articles that remained dutiable. Another act was passed to give efficiency to the law licensing billiard-tables, retailers of liquor, &c.

So good a purpose did the treasury notes appear to answer, that an act was passed (December 14) authorizing an increase of the issues in the amount of $150,000, and the invidious distinction in the act of June 9, in which it was provided that treasury notes should be issued only to defray the expenses of the civil department, and those of the gun-men and mounted rangers was done away with. A liberal appropriation of them was now made for the pay of the officers of the army and navy. But it was provided that any soldier or sailor, who should present his drafts to the Treasurer, to be exchanged for treasury notes, should take *an oath* "that said draft or drafts had originally been issued to him, that he had not sold them, alienated, or pledged them to any person, and that he was then the *bona fide* and sole owner of it or them."

This making of a distinction between the original holders of public obligations, and those into whose hands they might pass, was a cardinal principle of Texan policy. But it only injured those it was professedly intended to serve. The more the restrictions that are imposed on the passage of public obligations from hand to hand, the more is their value diminished. By this law, the soldier or sailor, who was at the seat of government, could exchange his drafts for treasury notes, which were receivable for all public dues; while he that was at a distance was obliged to sell his drafts for what they would bring, and as they were receivable only for land-dues and direct taxes, they were of less value than treasury notes.

Texan regulations in regard to the different evidences of public debt were so various, and changed so often, that it seems as if it must have been necessary for a man to fee a lawyer to ascertain the exact value of the different securities he held in his hands.

By way of giving a little variety to the currency, a resolution was passed (Dec. 14th) authorizing the Treasurer to issue "change notes" of the denominations of one, two, and three dollars, in exchange for notes of larger denominations. On the same day, an act was passed "to prevent the issuing of individual printed or lithographed notes;" and the train of currency measures for the session was completed by another act passed on the same day, and entitled "An act to Sustain the Currency of the Country." This declared that "nothing but gold and silver, or promissory notes of this government, should be received in payment of duties on goods imported, nor shall any bank-notes be received in payment of any dues to the Government of Texas."

This left audited drafts receivable for dues on lands, and direct taxes, but they were in a form so ill adapted to circulation that but few of them found their way into Eastern Texas, the best-settled and wealthiest portion of the country, and where alone the people had much ability to pay taxes; and as these people had not audited drafts on hand, they, as a general rule, paid no taxes at all.

To the soldiers, this Congress was very liberal, so far as grants of land were concerned. As there was much difficulty in reconciling the various conflicting laws, and as the allowance did not bear an equal proportion, in many cases, to the services rendered, an act was passed, Dec. 4th, granting to all those who had served in the army three months, three hundred and twenty acres; to those who had served six months, six hundred and forty; to those who had served nine months, nine hundred and sixty; and to those who had served twelve months or upwards, twelve hundred and eighty. By an act of Dec. 21st, a bounty of six hundred and forty acres was bestowed on each man who had been in the battle of San Jacinto. And by another, passed Dec. 18th, a league of land was bestowed on each and every person who had been "permanently disabled by loss of eye, arm, or limb, or such other bodily injury as would incapacitate him for bodily labor, by wounds received in the service of Texas."

The agent who had been sent to itinerate in the United States to sell land-script, Mr. J. K. Allen, having been as unsuccessful as the local agents at New Orleans and Mobile, an act was passed, Dec. 14th, peremptorily recalling him, and requiring him, within four months from January 1st, to surrender to the Secretary of the Treasury all the land-script in his possession, or else be considered guilty of a high misdemeanor.

There is something exceedingly amusing in the wrath of the Texan authorities towards those who were appointed to sell their land-script. They sent men abroad to sell that which had little or no value at home. That they might make these sales, they sent them into the United States—a country, the people of which had, in one or two years, bought as much wild land from their own government as they could bring into cultivation in ten or twenty years. Had the effort been made in the height of the banking infatuation, some success might have crowned it, for men could then have been found who would have bought lands in Patagonia, if any there had been offered for sale. But when the Texan land-agents made their appearance in the market, everything was top-

pling, and everything soon tumbled over. Then the most fertile
lands could, in many places, be bought " for a mere song." Yet,
when there was no sale for lands in a country in which there was
a well-established government, and in which an orderly state of
society prevailed, the Texan authorities attempted to sell land in
a country which was then little better than a military commonwealth, which was still contending for its independence, and in
but few parts of which was good order established. They looked
upon their land-script as " a cash article," charged their agents
with it as if it had been so much money, and then drew upon them
for such amounts as their necessities required.

Speaking of the agency at Mobile, Henry Smith, Secretary of
the Treasury, said, in his report of April 18th, 1837:—

"All the drafts made on that agency were drawn contingently, and
agreeably to the principles of commercial transactions, not liable to protest,
unless specially made so by the act of the agent. Why that agency has
caused so many drafts to be protested, contrary to their tenor, and contrary
to special and positive instruction, is as unaccountable to this department
as it is injurious to the faith and credit of the government. And, inasmuch
as the agencies spoken of have not only cramped our energies and created
distrust at home, but paralyzed and ruined our credit abroad, I deem it
high time that the government should institute an investigation into their
conduct, and withdraw their misplaced confidence. Notwithstanding these
agencies ·must have greatly over half a million of government means in
their hands, counting the land-script only at the minimum price, still these
means, instead of being made available to the government, seem to be tied
up in speculation, and entirely beyond their control."

Equal plainness of speech did Henry Smith use in speaking of
the Toby Agency at New Orleans, and Samuel Houston, President of the Republic, in his message of Nov. 21st, after saying of
them what we have already quoted (page 72), added something
about their " having given no security so as to insure accounta-
bility, and furthermore [were] placed beyond the jurisdiction of
ourselves"—i. e. "irresponsible to the Executive."

What summary punishment President Houston would have in-
flicted, if he had had these agents within his jurisdiction, must be
left to conjecture. But the most severe penalties would not have
enabled them to sell the land-script. The wonder is, not that they
sold so little, but that they sold any. The probability is that,
when they did sell, it was not for money, but for articles needful
to the army and navy of Texas; and if they got in this way ten

cents an acre (specie value), they got the full value of the commodity in a foreign country.

The grand act of the session was, after all, " the act to reduce into one act, and to amend the several acts relating to the establishment of a general land-office." It filled more than fourteen pages ; and provided for the opening of the land-offices for first-class claimants—that is, for old settlers and soldiers—on the first Thursday of February, 1838, and for others in six months afterwards.

President Houston, as usual, vetoed the bill, and the Congress, as usual in measures that promised to afford opportunities for land-speculation, passed it on the 14th of December, in defiance of his veto ; the Senate unanimously, and the House by a vote of 26 to 2.

CHAPTER XI.

ADJOURNED SESSION OF SECOND CONGRESS: APRIL 9, 1838, TO MAY 24, 1838.

Treasury notes at par—Reasons for this—New issues authorized—The loan act modified—Increase of public expenditures.

WHEN the adjourned session of the Second Congress commenced, treasury notes had been about six months in circulation. For a time they were at par with specie, or nearly at par. This may surprise the reader. Audited drafts, which were as much pledges of the faith of the government as were treasury notes, had been afloat for months. They were receivable for dues on the public lands, for direct taxes, and for a time for customs. Yet so far were they from becoming a currency, that they did not even become a regular vendible commodity. They were not quoted in the prices current as flour, bacon, and cotton were quoted. In May, 1837, when Governor Smith proposed to fund them, they "possessed but a nominal value, say fifteen cents in the dollar." By the 1st of November, the amount of these outstanding audited drafts was increased to about a million, a measure which we may be sure did not tend to raise their market value.

Yet the government then resolved to add another half million to
the public debt, and treasury notes, the evidences of this new debt,
were for a time of equal or nearly equal value with silver !

For this several reasons may be assigned :—

1. The treasury notes were for round sums, and for amounts
which made them convenient for circulation, namely, from one
dollar to one hundred dollars. Audited drafts were for whatever
the claim of the public creditor might amount to; frequently for
large sums, and generally for odd numbers of dollars and cents.
To pass them from hand to hand required a calculation which
they who had them to pay or receive did not find it always easy
to make.

2. These treasury notes were in the form of bank-notes, a form
of money with which most of the people of Texas had been familiar
from infancy; and, indeed, the only form of money with which
some of them were much conversant.

3. They bore a rate of interest which was easily calculated, and
a rate (ten per cent.) which was sufficient to cause them to be
hoarded by such as had faith in their ultimate redemption. Some
of the audited drafts bore interest, but the rate of them was only
eight per cent.

4. Texas was at this time flooded with the notes of the banks of
the South-Western States, many of which were at ruinous rates of
depreciation; and which rates were, moreover, always fluctuating.
The want of some medium that would regulate prices was much
felt. One kind of irredeemable paper is much to be preferred to
many kinds.

5. About this time the laws for raising a revenue from customs
began to be effective. In the quarter ending September 30, the
gross amount that had accrued was about sixty thousand dollars,
which was at the rate of two hundred and forty thousand dollars
a year. This increase of revenue would have sustained the value
of audited drafts if they had been still receivable for duties on
imports; but by one of those frequent changes of public tenders
which disgrace the fiscal history of Texas, they were no longer so
receivable. The whole revenue from customs was applied to
sustain the credit of treasury notes.

6. A market was found for these treasury notes in the United
States. An American is very careful how he parts with his silver

dollars or his gold eagles, especially if the bonds offered in exchange be in such large amounts as one thousand dollars. But reduce the denominations of the public securities to one hundred dollars or less, and at the same time afford him an opportunity of making what he regards as a good sale for his commodities, and the temptation is too strong for him to resist it. By issuing notes of as low a denomination as one dollar, the Texan Government afforded to all—down to the very negroes in the New Orleans markets—opportunities for speculating in Texan securities. In this indirect way, the Government of Texas obtained supplies for the army and navy, and the merchants of Texas replenished their warehouses.

Admirable would this system have been if it could only have been sustained. But it contained in itself the principles of its own destruction. The notes soon began to depreciate; and even after the depreciation was as great as fifty per cent. at New Orleans,* a bill was reported authorizing an additional issue of one hundred and fifty thousand.

This bill, which was modestly entitled "an Act to Define and Limit the Issue of Promissory Notes," was passed in the House by a vote of twenty-four to seven, and in the Senate, where the amount was increased to one million, without a formal division.

The President refused to sign it, and gave his reasons, on the 12th of May, in a message which filled six pages. In it he says:—

"When the (treasury note) currency was projected, both the government and the country were without resources. National existence, and freedom, and imperishable glory had been achieved, but the struggle had left us destitute and naked. There were no banks! there was no money! our lands could not be sold, and the public credit was of doubtful character!

"To avoid the absolute dissolution of the government, it became necessary to resort to some expedient that might furnish temporary relief. This could be only effected by creating a currency that should command some degree of credit abroad.

"It was hoped and believed, that if a small issue of government paper was made with specific means of redemption pointed out, which appeared to be ample and well guaranteed, and the government should evince a prudent and discreet judgment in its management, it would command such articles in the market of the United States as were indispensable to the country.

"The result has justified the expectation."

* According to General Hunt, the notes passed at this time at eighty-five to sixty-five cents in the dollar in Texas.

Here we find that it was calculated from the beginning that the means of the citizens of the United States would be drawn from them through the instrumentality of these treasury notes.

"The government will never be able, by all the issues it can make, to satisfy the demands of private speculation and interest. The vast issue of all the banks in the United States, in their most extended condition, failed to attain this object. * * *

"There has not probably been in circulation at any time more than a half million of dollars. The present bill requires the Secretary of the Treasury to increase the issue to a million. No time or discretion is allowed to that officer. The circulation of the country is to be doubled in as little time as is required to issue the paper."

A bill was then reported "to authorize the President to *reissue* the promissory notes of the government." After having been bandied about for some time between the House and the Senate, it was finally, May 18, approved by the President.

It authorized and required him "to have reissued, and continue to have reissued" the said promissory notes as they returned into the treasury, until all the appropriations made by government should be satisfied ; and he was authorized to increase the issues to an amount not exceeding one million dollars, if in his opinion the situation of the Republic should be such as to require it. The bill further appropriated one hundred and fifty thousand dollars in promissory notes for the payment of civil list claims, two hundred thousand for military claims, and one hundred thousand for naval claims. But it required all those who presented military and naval claims to take an oath that they were the original holders thereof. Thus absurdly did the law draw a line of distinction between different classes of public claimants.

A bill was also passed, May 16, "authorizing the payment of the interest of the funded debt" in other evidences of debt, *i. e.* in treasury notes. And another, May 24, opening the land-offices, from and after the first Thursday of August, 1838, to holders of land-script. Also an act, May 15, to raise a corps of cavalry two hundred and eighty strong, and appropriating fifty thousand dollars for their use; thus completing the appropriation of the additional five hundred thousand dollars the President was authorized to issue.

All the efforts to borrow money under the five million act having proved ineffective, another was passed this session, May 16, modifying some of its provisions.

By one section power was given to the commissioners " to sell the bonds for the notes of any bank or banks whose paper shall be at par with the best bank paper in the city of New York or Philadelphia ; and further, to stipulate that the notes of such bank or banks, purchasing such bonds to the amount of $100,000, should be received in payment of all public dues, so long as said bank or banks should, in the judgment of the Government of Texas, be of good character, and worthy of confidence."

The reader will see the bearing of this, when he calls to mind the fact that the banks of Philadelphia had not then resumed specie payments.

By another section, it was made " the duty of the commissioners to contract with the Bank of the United States of Pennsylvania (if practicable), if not, with the Manhattan Bank of New York, or the Union Bank of Louisiana, to áct as fiscal agent of the Republic of Texas."

The Secretary of the Treasury, Mr. Smith, sent the project of this law to the House, requested that it might be adopted without amendment or alteration, and appears to have been therein gratified.

The Secretary further informed the House that the engraved notes had arrived, and would be substituted for the printed notes, which had thus far, from necessity, been exclusively used.

Col. J. K. Allen, the itinerant agent for vending land script in the United States, appeared at the treasury within the time stipulated by law, and thus escaped the severe penalties with which he was threatened in case of disobedience.

The First Auditor made a report, in which he stated that, from the 18th of November, 1837, to the 13th of April, 1838, he had audited military claims to the amount of $586,988 97. From this, it appears that, in five months, the audited claims for a single branch of the service, were equal to one half of the amount audited in the two previous years for all branches of the service, and these the years of most active hostility. But we need not dwell on this point. The reader knows that issues of government paper-money always increase government expenditures.

CHAPTER XII.

THIRD CONGRESS: FROM NOVEMBER 5 TO DECEMBER 11, 1838.

Fraudulent land claims—The navy totally destroyed—Extensive entries of lands—
Income and expenses—Sanguine expectations of revenue—Imports and exports—
Plan for creating a creditor interest in the United States friendly to Texas.

THE third Congress assembled at Houston November 5, 1838. The Secretary of War stated, in his report, that 2,990,000 acres of bounty land had been issued up to the 15th of October :—

" The numerous and varied claims for land due to discharged soldiers, has occupied almost exclusively the attention of the department, and the adoption of some rules for its guidance has met with much recrimination ; but unquestionably has resulted in the correction of frauds attempted on the government. In consequence of the defect in the laws regulating bounty lands, the soldier has, in many instances, claimed the amount twice, say for six months, or two terms of service ; that is, if enlisted for a definite period, he obtains his discharge and receives his land, and by re-enlisting for another period, claims the same amount again."

From the report of the Secretary of the Navy, it appeared that this branch of the national defence had been totally destroyed ; one of the vessels composing it " being wrecked in coming into port, and the other destroyed by the October gale of 1837." " The officers and men attached to the navy were disbanded, agreeably to your Excellency's order, retaining the number specified." Speaking of prize-money, the Secretary says : " The sailors of this Republic have received that boon in but one instance ; the portion of each not amounting to more than seven dollars and seventy-six cents."

The Commissioner-General of the Land-Office reported that the number of certificates issued by the several boards of land commissioners, and recorded up to November 1, was 10,890, amounting to 26,242,199 acres. According to this statement, the land entries that had been made in the nine months that had elapsed since the opening of the land-offices, covered an area larger than the whole State of Ohio. These entries did, indeed, include many of the grants of the old settlers, but it must still be admitted to be a pretty extensive land business for a Republic that had then, according to computation, a population of no more than fifty thousand to sixty thousand souls.

On the 3d of November, the Secretary of the Treasury, Henry Smith, made his report.

After speaking of the agents for the sale of land script, of whom he had nothing particularly good to say, he mentioned that the whole amount of issues of land script was 2,193,000 acres, of which 870,400 had been returned by the agents, and 60,800 funded, " leaving 1,260,800 acres to the credit of this account."

The total amount of audited claims, not for the year, but from the beginning of the government, up to September 30, 1838, he stated, was :—

Civil list,	. . . . . .	$326,959 68
Contingent,	. . . . .	170,589 79
Naval,	. . . .	137,169 42
Military,	. . . . . .	1,426,895 81
Total,	. . . . . .	$2,061,614 70

The customs that had accrued (besides those for one quarter at Matagorda), amounted, up to September 30, to $335,955 83 ; leaving, after deducting $57,821 27 for expenses of collection, a net revenue of $278,134 56. This, it should be remembered, was not for the year, but for a period of about fifteen months, counting from the time in which the custom-house had been brought into successful operation.

On paper, the finances of Texas began to appear to flourish; but he who knew that all these dollars were mere treasury note dollars, depreciated many per cent. below par, was the victim of no illusion.

In relation to the public debt, he remarked that military script to the amount of $396,800, and land script to the amount of $30,400, making, together, $427,200, had been funded in ten per cent. stocks.

Of the direct taxes, the Secretary could give no satisfactory account ; but, said he, " the probable amount, however, will not, in my opinion, fall short of $500,000 for the year 1837–1838."

The land dues, it was admitted, had not proved as lucrative as had been hoped for, only a very trifling amount having been received since the opening of the land-offices, but it was confidently expected that this one branch of the revenue would yield, in a short time, $237,200.

The treasurer, in his report, presented a very respectable-looking sheet; total receipts, $1,023,071 48; total disbursements, $825,-699 14. But the receipts, when analyzed, were found to consist of $875,739 53 from the Secretary of the Treasury in treasury notes; some $8,000 or $9,000 from other public officers; only $133,649 98 from customs; $1,500 from sales of lot on Galveston Island; $3,195 54 from prize-money; and from land-dues and direct taxes, nothing. It is unnecessary, we presume, to remind the reader that what revenue was received, was in the government's own paper.

Appended to this report, we have an abstract, showing the amount of imports and exports, up to September 30, 1838:—

" Total amount of goods imported, . . $1,740,376 87
" " " exported, . . 183,323 00
" Balance of trade against the Republic, . 1,557,053 87"

Balance of trade against the Republic! The Texans had been carrying on a most profitable trade. They had been exporting their land script and their treasury notes, and receiving in exchange for them, from " aliens," i. e. citizens of the United States, the necessaries and comforts of life, and the munitions of war. If Texas could only have made this trade a permanent one, she would have been under no necessity of cultivating either her cotton fields, or her sugar lands.

On the 13th, a resolution was adopted requesting the Secretary of the Treasury to give his views on the propriety of increasing the issues of promissory notes; on the effects which the abolition of the tariff would have on the credit of the currency; and on other financial topics.

On the 29th, the Secretary made a long reply, in which he began with complaining that the Texan Congress had not received his suggestions with that deferential respect which the British Parliament is accustomed to pay to the suggestions of the Chancellor of the Exchequer.

" As the head of the Treasury Department, I have ever considered it my duty to devise and recommend the best ways and means to create a competent revenue for the support of the government, and in a manner which would, in my opinion, be the least burdensome, and as such the least objectionable to the governed. In assuming this position, though the Congress have not thought proper to pass any law defining the duties of my department, yet, by implication and analogy, I am bound to arrive at that conclusion. It is a matter well understood that our civil institutions are based on the same principles as those of the United States of the north, who have, in a great measure, copied after Great Britain, their ancestors, which is going far enough back for my present purposes. By reference to the laws and statistics of England, it will be found the Minister of Finance is required to lay before Parliament the state of the funds in exact detail, and to suggest such measures as he may deem necessary concerning them; and should they object to any of his views, they must refer the necessary amendments again to him, in order to have his views on the amendments, for the purpose of preventing any injurious clashing of laws and acts with some other branch of the finance. In consequence of the strict adherence to this concert of action, notwithstanding the immense and apparently overwhelming debt of that nation, by strictly and carefully maintaining the rights of individuals sacred, the stocks of Great Britain are constantly at or above par. [A mistake.] This courtesy has, however, not been heretofore extended to me, nor have I, with all my exertions, been able to succeed, except partially, in any project which I have introduced to Congress."

Mr. Smith then reproaches the Congress for having thwarted his favorite plan for funding the outstanding audited drafts. After this he denounces the treasury note issues, not because he had any objections to such kind of medium, either in the abstract or the concrete, for he was not a hard-money man, but because these notes being receivable for all public dues, left him without gold and silver to pay the interest on the funded debt, and because they had been issued in such a way as to make an invidious distinction between the public creditors. In the existing state of things he thought that the best that could be done was to fund all the outstanding claims of every description, including the treasury notes bearing interest, and issue others bearing no interest.

" The stock created as above recited would float off to the United States, and even to Europe, and fall into the hands of bankers and capitalists, thereby increasing a foreign interest in our favor; for it is with governments as with individuals, and I presume it is a matter well understood in banking transactions, that banking institutions will not permit a firm or an individual to fail who has become largely indebted to them, so long as it is possible to sustain them, or at least till they can be thrown off on some other institution; for the ties of interest are as a threefold cord, and not easily broken."

From this, it is evident that Mr. Smith had in his composition a spice of " the wisdom that is of this world," and the result affords an additional confirmation that "the children of this world are in their generation wiser than the children of light." Just as he predicted, the stock floated off to the United States, and an interest was thereby created which yielded important aid to the Texans in their favorite measure of annexation, and aid not less important when the question arose about the settlement of the boundary line between Texas and New Mexico. By these measures, taken together, the value of Texan lands has been increased many fold; and neither of these measures could have been carried at the time and in the manner in which they were carried, if there had not been persons in the United States who had a deep interest in Texan securities.

Mr. Smith objected to an abolition of the tariff, and even to any immediate modification of it. "All laws calculated to alter or modify the tariff should not go into effective operation for at least one year after the date of their passage, by which time the people, both at home and abroad, would be prepared to meet them, without sustaining any very serious loss or damage."

He then proceeded to cipher out a revenue for the Texan government, to wit:—

1837.	Old land dues	. . .	$300,000	
	New land dues	. . .	312,659	
	Direct taxes	. . .	185,506	798,165
1838.	Direct taxes	. . .	200,000	
	Revenue from imports	.	335,955	535,955
1839.	Direct taxes	. . .	250,000	
	Import duties	. . .	400,000	650,000

Making a snug little revenue for the three years of $1,984,120; and so neatly did he arrange his figure work as to persuade himself that, on the 30th of September, 1839, there would be a balance in the treasury of $6,372 34, after redeeming all the promissory notes then in circulation. "Most of the foregoing estimates are made from correct data, and the balance is by no means overrated."

On the 16th of November, 1838, an act was passed requiring the President to issue one hundred thousand dollars, in the promissory notes already authorized for the defence of the frontier, and to quell the insurrection then existing among the Indians and Mexicans in the Nacogdoches Department; and this was the last fiscal act of any importance signed by Samuel Houston, during his first presidential term.

CHAPTER XIII.

THIRD CONGRESS: FROM DECEMBER 10, 1838, TO JAN. 26, 1839.

President Lamar's views of exchequer bills and treasury notes—He recommends a national bank, founded on the credit and resources of the Government of Texas —Government banking the worst form of banking—Refusal to make treasury notes a legal tender for private debts—Authority given to raise additional troops— The steam-vessel "Zavalla" purchased—A contract for the purchase of other vessels of war recognized by law—Stock books again opened for funding the floating debt—Act to establish a sinking fund—Officers of government required to receive their dues in treasury notes.

MIRABEAU B. LAMAR, who succeeded General Houston as President, sent to the two Houses, December 24, a message which filled more than twenty-eight pages; about eleven of these were devoted to banking, and its kindred topics.

"The exchequer bills of England," said the new President, "the assignats of France, and the treasury bills of the United States, furnish memorable examples of the inability of the most powerful and opulent governments to establish a good practical circulating medium on their own credit alone, without the facilities of prompt redemption." He then denounced corporate banks "as having been productive of more evil than good, and as having exerted a pernicious influence on society." After this followed plaudits of the United States Bank, such as none but the most prejudiced partisan could utter, and an excuse for which, on the part of Mr. Lamar, is to be found only in his ignorance of the history of that institution. So complete was this, that he supposed that the bank was established "at the commencement of the last war between the United States and Great Britain," when the fact was, that it did not commence operations till three years after the close of the war.

President Lamar then gave his own plan, which was that of a national bank, founded exclusively on the credit and resources of the government, and the control of which should be exclusively in the government; the directors to be elected by joint ballot of the two Houses, and the president and cashier to be appointed by the President of the Republic, by and with the advice and consent of the Senate. This bank was to be, at one and the same time, a fiscal agent for government, an exchange regulator for those who had exchanges to make, an office of deposit for those who had surplus cash on hand, a loan office for planters, a bank of discount for merchants, and a paper money manufactory for the benefit of all together. " The bank would, of course, be extended by branches established at every convenient and suitable part of the Republic."

As the Republic of Texas had already converted itself into a bank of issue, by emitting promissory notes, one would think that this might have satisfied President Lamar; but it did not. His views are explained in the following extract :—

" An admixture of private interests would embarrass its operations, without bringing equivalent advantages to the institution. Such a bank, incorporated for a suitable term of years, founded on a specific hypothecation of a competent portion of the public domain, which should be immediately appropriated to that purpose, with the additional guarantee of the plighted faith of the nation, and an adequate deposit of specie in its vaults, would, it is confidently believed, confer many eminent and continued blessings upon the country. It would furnish an immediate and complete remedy for the existing pecuniary difficulties, which result entirely from the insufficiency and depreciation of our present circulating medium. A well digested project of such an institution, when fully propounded to, and understood by the people, cannot fail to propitiate a very general approbation, and to enlist the national pride of a large majority of our fellow-citizens. And an institution having all the elements of usefulness and prosperity in itself, and sustained by the confidence and affections of an enlightened people, can scarcely be supposed capable of degenerating into an instrument of fraud or of oppression, or failing to realize the benefits expected from it. The triple security it would offer to its creditors, is of the highest character, and of the most indubitable responsibility; for it is an approved maxim, that real estate affords the best possible guarantee for the ultimate payment of a debt. The pledge of a nation's faith will give peculiar solemnity and increased confidence to its obligations, and a competent deposit of specie will always be present, or presently attainable, to answer the contingent and occasional demands for that article. It is indeed true that real estate is not sufficiently commutable or transitive to answer the ordinary and daily purposes of commerce and exchange. These can be accomplished only by specie itself, or by that active and undoubted credit, of which a known and sufficient deposit of the metals, or something equivalent to them, is the proper basis. It is believed that the proposed bank would be amply furnished with that equivalent, and to all necessary extent with the actual deposit itself. It is evident that a bank so constituted, the exclusive property of a stable and popular government, and combining the three guarantees of land, specie, and the public faith, would not require to retain in its vaults as large a proportion of the dormant capital as is acknowledged to be indispensable to the safe conduct of a private institution."

In supposing land to be a proper basis for banking operations, President Lamar had been anticipated by John Law, the author of the Mississippi Scheme, and by the distinguished founders of the New York Free Banking system. They, too, found that "real estate was not sufficiently *commutable* or *transitive* to answer the ordinary and daily purposes of commerce and exchange;" and, therefore, proposed that people should be allowed to coin their broad acres into pieces of paper. Two of the three articles that formed President Lamar's "triple security," namely, the public faith and the public lands, having been already pretty well used up by the Republic of Texas, as a bank of issue, and a bank for borrowing, it is to be regretted that he did not state where the third, that is, "the adequate deposit of specie," was to come from. Equally is it to be regretted that he did not distinctly explain what he meant by the "something equivalent" which was to serve as so admirable a substitute for the specie itself. Everything that can be bought and sold is the equivalent of specie. Old furniture and old clothing are included in this category, as any one may prove who will make trial with the Jew brokers in Chatham street, New York; and so, also, are corn-husks, and cotton seed. But the probability is, that President Lamar did not mean any of these, or anything else possessing intrinsic value. Neither did he mean Texan securities, either public or private. But, taking into view the measures that were then in train to bring about a close connection between the Republic and the Pennsylvania Bank of the United States, we are led to the conclusion, that "that equivalent with which the proposed bank would be amply furnished," was to consist of that "active and undoubted credit" which the Bank of the United States was, on all occasions, so ready to supply.

Towards the close of his communication, Mr. Lamar made some observations which it may not be amiss to quote.

"The control of the circulating medium of a country is as necessary to its salutary administration, as is that of any other department of its interests. If banking powers be valuable in promoting an equal and safe circulation, then it is obvious that it belongs to the government to direct and superintend the distribution and exercise of these powers. It is a portion, and one of peculiar interest too, of the sovereign authority, and to surrender it into the hands of a few private, and, in a political sense, irresponsible individuals, would be as repugnant to the true spirit of our institutions, as to subject the management of the war and navy departments to such partial and unpledged hands. Private corporations, or private individuals, may have interests diverse and incompatible with the nation's, and have as little right to be made the fiduciary agents of the government. If it be proper to extend franchise to one class of our fellow-citizens, comprehending generally but few in number, why may they not be claimed by all; and why throw impediments in the way of a man participating in them. If a few men may become bankers, and throw their equivocal and precarious paper currency on the community, why not let every man be a banker, and abandon your circulating medium to the illimitable cupidity of private speculation. The planter, the mechanic, and the laborer, are as much entitled to the immunities and privileges of the government, as the speculator or the money-dealer. Let all rights be equal. Let all trades be free. The Constitution has so ordained it, and so let us carry it into practice. The fostering hand of legislation should be extended to all classes of society.

" Each individual of a patriotic people cherishes, supports, and defends the government, and none have an exclusive claim to reward or privileges in the exercise of their industry. If banking be profitable, let that profit enure to the government. If the people must pay an interest for the use of money to facilitate their legitimate operations, let them bestow their sacrifices, not upon the mercenary, but where it will promote the public welfare, and in process of time revert to their own advantage."

Truths misunderstood or misapplied may do much harm.

The regulation of money is one of the attributes of sovereignty ; but this is sufficiently provided for in the Federal Constitution, wherein it is declared that Congress shall have power to coin money, regulate the weight and value thereof, and adequately punish counterfeiters. This is all the regulation metallic money requires, and we should have none other.

The State governments have the power to establish banks of deposit, discount, and exchange ; but they have no constitutional authority to establish banks of issue, inasmuch as the Constitution of the United States expressly forbids them to issue " bills of credit," and what they have not power to do themselves they have not power to delegate to others.

The business of banking, properly so called, that is, the business of receiving deposits, making discounts, and dealing in exchanges, should be thrown open to all, individuals and copartnerships, and on precisely the same principle that the business of brewing is thrown open to all. No more privileges should be bestowed or restrictions imposed on bankers than are bestowed or imposed on bakers, brewers, or butchers. But no individual, copartnership, corporation, or government should be suffered to issue paper money.

From corporate banking, we have suffered more in the United States than from all other causes of evil put together, and yet there is one evil that is worse than even corporate paper-money banking.

It is government banking as proposed by General Lamar.

Where corporate banking prevails, there is a power above it—the government—by which, occasionally, at least, its excesses may be checked. But substitute for this government paper-money banking, and we have the evil without any checks.

The money power and political power will then be in the same hands. The demagogues who now control the elections will then control the money market also; and woe to the people who are subject to this double despotism.

Excesses in issue it would be impossible to avoid, because those who have the management of public affairs would no longer have those checks on expenditure which the necessity of raising revenue by taxation or by negotiating loans, now imposes. Before the people could well understand the operation of the system, they would find the nation deeply involved in debt which they would have to pay by new taxation. They would, moreover, be exposed to all the evils of an uncertain currency; less fluctuating, perhaps, than corporate bank currency, but its constant tendency would be to depreciation, and the honest fulfilment of contracts would be almost impossible.

The present modes of bribery and corruption might then be all safely dispensed with, because all that would then be necessary would be to give a man a *douceur* in the form of a loan from the government bank, with an understanding that it was not to be repaid till convenient.

Let the Whigs suppose such a bank under the management of the Democrats, and let the Democrats suppose it to be under the control of the Whigs, and each party will come to a just conclusion of the evils it would produce.

Some people delight to speak of the constitutional treasury system as a government bank. If it be so, then everybody who keeps his own money has a bank in his own pocket. This is an application which may be made of the word, but it is an unusual one ; and when it is used by opponents of the constitutional system seems intended to confound, in the minds of their hearers, things that are different. So long as the government confines itself to keeping its own money, and issues no drafts except such as are, dollar for dollar, representatives of gold or silver actually in deposit, its bank (if any will still call it by that name) will do much good and no harm. But let it to these functions add issues of notes resting on the same basis that bank issues now rest, and to these let it add the receipt of private deposits, discount of notes, and dealings in private exchanges, and it will be just such a bank as President Lamar wished to establish, all the evils of which no pen can portray.

A bill to incorporate the Bank of the Republic of Texas, reported in conformity with the views of the President, was read a second time, January 21, 1839, and then laid on the table by a vote of sixteen to fourteen.

A committee, to whom the subject had been referred, reported that a repeal of the duties on imports would be utterly destructive of revenue and of credit.

A committee, to whom a bill had been referred " for a stay of execution for a twelvemonth unless promissory notes were taken in payment," reported that such a measure would be destructive of credit and confidence, and a violation of the obligation of contracts.

In justice to the Texans, it must be said, that they never made their government paper a legal tender in the payment of private debts. Neither did they (fond as a portion of them unfortunately were of Lynch law), ever do violence to a man because he was unwilling to receive their paper for more than its market value. Hence their government paper-money did, in many respects, much less evil than did "the continental money" of our revolutionary Congress.

December 21, 1838, an act was passed exempting from direct taxation for one year the inhabitants of certain counties infested by the Mexicans and Indians.

It was ordered, by an act of the same day, that a regiment of eight hundred and forty men be raised for the protection of the northern and western frontier, and that three hundred thousand dollars in treasury notes be appropriated to pay the expenses of the same. Provision was made, December 29, for adding to these eight companies of mounted volunteers, in all, four hundred and seventy-two men; and January 1 and 10, 1839, two companies of rangers, one hundred and twelve men; and again, January 23, three companies of mounted volunteers, one hundred and seventy-seven men. On the 24th of January an act was passed appropriating one million dollars for the protection of the frontier and for military purposes in general. January 26, two more companies of rangers (one hundred and twelve men) were ordered to be raised.

The troubles which caused the raising of most of these forces do not appear to have been of long duration, as, January 26, an act was passed "to appoint commissioners to take charge of the property of those engaged in the *late* rebellion in the County of Nacogdoches."

On the 4th of January an act was passed allowing to each head of a family six hundred and forty acres, and to each single man three hundred and twenty acres, who had arrived in the Republic since the 1st of October, 1837, or who might arrive by the 1st of January, 1840, with the intention of settling therein. To each permanent resident citizen who had, or who might arrive at the age of seventeen years, was also made a conditional grant of three hundred and twenty acres of land. Appropriations of land were also made for the benefit of those officers and soldiers whose families were then in the country or might arrive by the 1st of January, 1840.

January 10, an act was passed sanctioning the contract, made by certain agents of the Republic with Gen. James Hamilton, of South Carolina, for the purchase of the steam-vessel "Charleston," (afterwards the "Zavalla,") for the price of $120,000.

January 26, an act was passed, the preamble to which declared that, whereas the agent of the Republic had made a contract for the purchase of one ship, of eighteen guns; two brigs, of twelve guns each; and three schooners, of six guns each; and,

"Whereas, It has become indispensably necessary, in order to repair and keep in service the said vessels, as well for the protection of the coasts and harbors of Texas, as for the protection of the commerce thereof, that an appropriation be made : *Be it enacted*, That the sum of $250,000 in treasury notes, in the promissory notes of the government, be appropriated for the naval service of the year 1839."

Most fortunate were the Texans in making these purchases, for, as we have seen, their little navy had been totally destroyed. It would be anticipating the course of our narrative if we should say that neither the " Zavalla," nor any of the other vessels have, to this day, been paid for.

January 19, an act was passed requiring the stock-books to be again opened, and to remain open till the first of January, 1840, for the purpose of funding the government liabilities. By one section of this act, it was provided that no promissory note hereafter issued or paid out should bear interest; but the holders of said notes should be allowed to fund them in the ten per cent. stock of the government.

January 22, an act, supplementary to the five million loan act, was passed, strengthening the pledges of faith and revenue, and declaring that, as soon as the government should deem it expedient to sell the public lands, $300,000 a year of the proceeds thereof should be set aside as a sinking fund, for the ultimate redemption of the five million loan.

On the same day, an act was passed authorizing the President to issue bonds to an amount not exceeding one million, at eight per cent. per annum. Except in relation to the rate of interest, the terms and conditions were similar to those of the five million act without the supplement.

January 23, all officers of government, district judges and the chief justice excepted, were prohibited from demanding for the dues or appurtenances of their office, or appointment other than the promissory notes of the Republic.

CHAPTER XIV.

FROM THE CLOSE OF THE THIRD TO THE CLOSE OF THE FOURTH CONGRESS: FEBRUARY, 1839, TO OCTOBER, 1840.

Loan from the Commercial and Railroad Bank of Vicksburg frustrated—Encouraging prospects of a loan in Europe—Hopes of a large revenue from customs, and other taxes—Joy on hearing of a loan from the United States Bank—Removal of seat of government to Austin—Extracts from President Lamar's message to fourth Congress—Deficiency of revenue—New revenue act—Act to provide for more certain operation of the sinking fund—For issue of treasury bonds—For funding the floating debt in eight and ten per cent. stocks—Low price of treasury notes, and gloomy condition of affairs.

IT may have struck the reader as strange that the Texan Government, with all its loan acts, and all its different commissioners in Europe and America, and all its pledges of faith, and land, and revenues, and everything else it possessed, should have been able to borrow, in a direct way, not even one hundred thousand dollars. Prudent capitalists would, indeed, be very cautious about lending to a revolutionary government. But there were many banks in the United States in that day living by expedients, and it might be supposed that they could not but be benefited by issuing their notes in exchange for Texan securities.

Something like this was attempted in the spring of 1839, and the only wonder with us is, that it was not attempted before. The tale is thus told in the *Houston Morning Star* of April 10, 1839:—

" It appears that arrangements had been made with one of the agents of the Commercial and Railroad Bank, at Vicksburg, Mississippi, to negotiate a loan for eight hundred thousand dollars, for which he was to receive the moderate compensation of fifty thousand dollars! The president of the bank, without consulting the directors, and even without the knowledge of the cashier, agreed to make the loan, which, with a deduction of three hundred thousand dollars of the funded debt of Texas, owned by the above-mentioned agent, was to be paid over to our commissioner. To cap the climax, in a day or two the bank suspended specie payment. Fortunately for us, Mr. Robbins, the cashier, put his veto upon the loan, and thus relieved our country from being deluged with a quantity of shin-plasters, not worth, in reality, half as much as our own currency."

But, if no loan could be obtained in Mississippi, it did not thence follow that none could be negotiated in London. And, on the 9th, the editor of the *Morning Star* announced that he had been favored with the perusal of a letter from a gentleman of high standing, who had recently visited Europe, in which was the following passage :—

" The loan of five millions can be easily obtained in London. I learn that Gen. Hamilton is appointed commissioner with Mr. Burnley, to negotiate the same, at which I really rejoice. Gen. Hamilton is well known and much respected in London. The house of Horseley, Palmer, & Co., stands ready to take the loan."

Ten days afterwards, the editor gave a long article, in which he expressed doubts if any great advantage would, after all, result from the success of the commissioners :—

" If Texas had no liabilities to meet, and no notes to redeem, the judicious application of five millions of dollars to the promotion of internal improvements, might give an impetus to the zeal and energy of the inhabitants.   *   *   *   But the notes have been bought up, and by persons of the United States. This being the case, the money, instead of remaining in the country, will find its way back again."

The editor then complains of extravagance in public expenditures :—

" We have an army of trifling extent, and have nearly as many staff officers as they have in the United States.   *   *   It is stretching the truth but very little to say that we have an army and naval officer for almost every soldier and seaman in the service."

Soon after this, the *Morning Star* had a controversy with the *Houston Intelligencer* about the public revenue for the year. The *Morning Star* supposed the total would be $1,079,000 ; but the *Intelligencer* put down the customs at $954,000, the direct taxes at $564,000, the receipts for the sale of city lots at $1,000,000, and swelled the whole revenue to $3,018,000. The *Civilian* reduced the amount to $2,200,000.

A correspondent of the *Star*, in an article that appeared on the 8th of May, advised the people, in every section of the Republic, to hold meetings and pass resolutions to receive nothing but gold and silver, and treasury notes. This would drive the notes of the banks of the States out of circulation, and treasury notes, which would take their place, would thereby be raised in value. " The faith of the Republic is pledged for their redemption, and time alone is requisite to allow the government to give dollar for dollar in specie for its notes. They could be cancelled in two years by a direct tax, but such a course is contrary to sound policy."

Here is more proof that running into debt, and keeping in debt, was matter of principle with the Texans.

On the 24th of June, the *Star* said :—

"Our promissory notes are now so much depreciated that they are almost worthless. Everything in the country is immensely high, and still the government goes on recklessly throwing out its pictured bits of paper, regardless of the fact that every one they put out depreciates the value of the rest. Were the expenditures necessary and beneficial, so much objection could not be made ; but such is by no means the case."

It was not long before the editor of the *Star* began to think that a loan would not be so bad a thing after all; at least this is our inference from the leading article in his paper of July 11:—

"GOLDEN NEWS!!!

"A letter was received in this city yesterday afternoon, brought by the 'Emblem,' from Col. Barnard E. Bee, dated New Orleans, July 4, conveying to us the gratifying intelligence that General Hamilton had, before leaving the United States for Europe, negotiated a loan for $500,000, under the law authorizing one million to be raised, and that Lynch Hamilton, a son of our commissioner, would be on, in the next boat from New Orleans, *with the money.*"

This joy did not seem soon to expire, for, on the 23d, the editor exclaims—

"Everybody is on the tiptoe of expectation for the report of the cannon which shall announce the arrival of the steamboat from Columbia, because $500,000 are expected. We assure the gentleman who may be so fortunate as to be the bearer of the money, that he will be welcome as the flowers of May."

But the money never came to Houston, and the cannon were not fired. It was deposited in a bank in New Orleans, and consisted of United States Bank post-notes, to turn which into ready means the government had to pay seven and a half per cent. discount. The whole amount, moreover, was overrated.

The government now removed to the new city of Austin, at the foot of the Cordilleras, and on the very borders of the Indian hunting-grounds. The removal, at this moment, was an act of folly, as it increased the expenditures of both the governors and the governed ; but it afforded an opportunity of speculating on the sale of lots in the new metropolis, and it invited speculations to lands in the interior; and these two motives combined were too strong to be resisted. Some months afterwards, the Indians stealthily entered the town, killed two men, and stole a number of horses. Such was the spot selected for the assembly of the legislative and executive wisdom of all Texas.

Here the fourth Congress convened on Monday, November 11, 1839; and, on the 12th, President Lamar sent them a very long message.

The passages which follow embrace the points of most interest to the reader:—

" Our foreign relations are daily assuming a more pleasing aspect, and afford us at the present moment the strongest assurance that our national character will ere long be recognized by the most important governments of the earth."

" I regard the prospect of obtaining a loan of five millions of dollars, authorized by an act of the last session, as cheering and satisfactory. The commissioners appointed to negotiate that loan, after obtaining an advance of $280,000 upon the eventual success, proceeded to Europe, with a view to its final consummation; and I am assured by communications from one of them, that nothing but the peculiarly embarrassed condition of the money market in England, growing out of some recent and heavy exportations of bullion to the Continent, has prevented a sale of our bonds before this time; and upon terms which, it is believed, will secure to us in cash the nominal amount, at least, for which they were issued. These embarrassments, however, were considered temporary in their nature, and are said to be already yielding to a more healthful and settled state in the monetary affairs of the country; and we may now look, with confidence, to an early realization of the hopes which have been so long entertained in reference to this subject, and upon the fulfilment of which so much of our national prosperity depends. The $280,000 obtained by the commissioners have been almost exclusively devoted to the purchasing of public arms and ammunition, the enlistment of a regular force, and to the equipment of the navy for efficient operations."

This was part of a loan of some $400,000 obtained from the Pennsylvania Bank of the United States.

The new Secretary of the Treasury, Mr. James H. Starr, made his report on the 3d of November.

The reader will recollect that the late Secretary had offered an estimate, according to which there was to be a small balance in the treasury on the 30th September, 1839. Alas for human hopes!—the amount of outstanding liabilities was greatly increased.

Mr. Smith supposed that the income of the year from customs, direct taxes, and other branches of revenue would be upwards of a million; the editor of the *Civilian*, that they would be $2,200,000; and the editor of the *Intelligencer*, that they would be upwards of $3,000 000.

The total amount actually received into the treasury was $302,166 90, and all that in the government's own inconvertible paper!

While the receipts fell short of, the expenditures greatly exceeded Mr. Smith's estimate. He had forgotten to allow anything for military and naval expenses, and sundry other things too numerous to mention. The expenditures amounted to $1,606,-654 33, without counting new treasury notes issued in exchange for old ones.

The public debt, which was, September 30, 1838, $1,887,526. 82, was now swelled to $3,102,083 35, without counting the million of liabilities incurred for the purchase of vessels of war.

President Lamar, his Cabinet, and the Congress were not the men to be frightened by such an exposition as this. They were too brave for that; and so they immediately set about passing new revenue laws, one of which filled nineteen, and another, with its supplements, twenty-one pages.

There is no use, however, in raising money, unless it be spent, and the Texan Congress provided for this by several acts, one of which, passed February 3d, and entitled an " Act making Appropriations for the Support of the Government for the year 1840," filled more than six closely printed pages. Either from prudential or other considerations, the Congress did not state on the face of the bill the whole amount appropriated.

" It is estimated," said the Secretary, " that the receipts at the treasury during the ensuing year, under the proposed system for collecting the revenue, will be as follows, viz. :—

From customs,	$400,000
Taxes and land-dues,	500,000
Sales of lots in the cities of Austin and Calhoun,	400,000
	$1,300,000

Referring to this estimate, in a communication dated November 14, he remarked:—

" Under the present system of the laws, however, owing to their great defects in prescribing the manner of assessing and collecting the direct tax, and the inability of this department to compel the receivers of public moneys to pay them into the treasury, it is believed that not one-fourth of that sum would be realized to the government."

But the fourth Congress did not content itself simply with new modes of raising revenue, and new modes of spending; it also devised new modes of borrowing. As some of our readers may have still in possession some of the new-fashioned securities that were uttered under its auspices, we must be more particular in describing the laws which authorized them, than we have been in relation to others passed this session.

January 14, an act was passed "to provide for the more certain operation of the sinking fund to extinguish the five millions loan." It filled sixteen sections. Omitting details which need not be introduced here, its chief provisions were :—

"1st. In case it shall be deemed inexpedient to bring the public lands into the market on or before January 1, 1842, or that, when so brought forward, it should be deemed inexpedient to sell them, it is hereby declared to be then and after that period the duty of the Secretary of the Treasury to provide from other sources the said three hundred thousand dollars a year."

From what source the Secretary was to get the three hundred thousand dollars a year, the bill did not mention.

The next important provision was :—

"Should the market price of said bonds [in London, Paris, Amsterdam, or wherever the said loan should be negotiated] reach fifty per cent. premium beyond the par value of the same, the holders of said bonds shall be required, on the application of said agents, to surrender and cancel the same on the payment of said par value and said premium."

This was prudent foresight. Texan securities might rise in foreign markets to $180, or perhaps to $200, for $100 paid. To provide for such a contingency, the Congress reserved to itself the privilege of buying them in, as soon as they should reach $150.

The 15th section we will give in full :—

"Be it further enacted, That for the redemption of all loans negotiated by the authority of the Republic of Texas, independently of the reservation of the sinking fund, the proceeds of the public lands generally, its revenues and public faith, are solemnly pledged."

Thus, in addition to the particular pledges for each loan, Texas gave another for all together.

February 5, an act was passed "for creating funds for the support of government for the year 1840."

Section 1 provided that blank forms of bonds for 100, 500, and 1000 dollars, should be prepared, bearing an interest of eight per cent. per annum, payable half yearly in gold and silver.

Section 2 provided for the issue of these bonds to the amount of $1,500,000.

Section 3 declared that these bonds should be received in payment of customs and direct taxes.

Section 4 set apart the revenue from the license tax, and the tax on personal property, as a fund for the payment of interest on these bonds.

Section 5 provided that the bonds should have coupons attached to them.

These are what are known as Texas treasury bonds, and they differed from the treasury notes of the first and second issues, only in being of larger denominations. The second section provided for their "issue as circumstances may require in payment of appropriations, for the support of government for the year 1840."

These bonds soon sunk to twenty cents in the dollar.

February 1. An act was passed to authorize the commissioners of the five million loan " to pledge a portion of the bonds, in order to enable them to raise money by an advance on the bonds, which may be made on the credit of eventual success in negotiating the loan."

On the same day that it passed the act for the issue of treasury bonds, February 5, the Congress passed another " to provide for the redemption of the promissory notes of the government now in circulation, and for funding other liabilities of the government."

Section 1 required the Secretary of the Treasury to procure certificates in blank, for sums of one hundred, five hundred, and one thousand dollars, to be transferable by simple indorsement.

Section 2 provided that these certificates should be issued to the holders of such of the promissory notes of the government as should present them to the stock commissioner before the first of July ensuing; and, that the said certificates should bear an annual interest of ten per cent., payable semi-annually in gold and silver.

Section 3 provided that the said certificates should be issued in exchange for all other liabilities of the government which may have been properly and regularly audited.

Section 4 provided that for such promissory notes as should not be presented for funding till after July 1, certificates should be issued bearing only eight per cent. interest.

Thus, the government provided for its fiscal emergencies : first, by making provision for funding, at eight and ten per cent. interest, all such of its outstanding liabilities as bore no interest ; and secondly, by authorizing the issue of a new batch of treasury notes, of large denominations, to be called treasury bonds, and to bear eight per cent. interest.

The fourth Congress adjourned on the 5th of February, and did not hold a second session.

Lamar's administration did not give general satisfaction. "Apart from politics, and as a private citizen," said the *Austin City Gazette*, March 13, 1840, "we shall ever respect him for his literary acquirements, his amiable disposition, and unassuming manners; but, as President of the Republic, we must, in common with a large portion of our fellow-citizens, condemn many, very many of his acts; not that we blame the heart so much as the easy disposition of the man. It is there that the mischief lies: he allows others to think—to act for him."

The following view of the state of public affairs, we extract from a communication published in the *Austin City Gazette*, October 21, 1840 :—

"Texas promissory notes are worth about fifteen cents upon the dollar— there is little prospect of a loan—the taxes are not promptly paid; and if they were, would only return to the treasury, at par, that which was issued for less than one-sixth of the amount. The continual issue of this sort of currency can have but one tendency now, and that is, to depreciate it still further. In this exigency, what are we to do? All the officers of government, from high to low, have been required to receive its issues at par, in payment of their salaries. This has not raised it: but it has impoverished them; and now an ordinary day-laborer receives more of it per diem than any civil officer under the establishment. * * * *

"We are at the lowest round of the ladder. Congress will soon convene, and the pay of its members will not purchase their food. The members cannot long live upon patriotism; and many of them have nothing else but that and their pay to live upon."

CHAPTER XV.

PROCEEDINGS UNDER THE FIFTH CONGRESS: NOVEMBER, 1840, TO NOVEMBER, 1841.

Various devices for borrowing—Remarks of the new Speaker of the House of Representatives—Smallness of the revenues—Great increase of the public debt—Project of invading Mexico—Repeal of act for funding treasury notes—Retrenchment of public expenses—Annunciation that a loan had been negotiated in Europe—Effect of this news on the public mind, and on the price of Texan securities—Mr. Horseley Palmer, ex-Governor of the Bank of England, plans a national bank for Texas, to be presided over by Mr. Jaudon, ex-cashier of the United States Bank—News of the negotiation of the loan confirmed—Doubts subsequently arise—Mr. Bullock and his pigs—Difficulties with M. de Saligny, the Minister of France to Texas.

BEFORE we proceed further, we beg to solicit the reader's admiration for the various devices to which the Texan Government had recourse, to meet the various tastes and fancies of those with whom it had dealings, or wished to have dealings.

Did a man wish to lend money to it? He had the choice of four loans: namely, the one hundred thousand dollar loan act, and the million dollar loan act of the Provisional Government (both of which remained unrepealed); and the million and the five million loan acts of the Republic.

Was the Republic indebted to him? He received an audited draft. This he might keep if he chose, or pay it in for land-dues. Did not this satisfy him? He could exchange his audited draft for treasury notes, which were receivable for all public dues. Was not this satisfactory? Then he could receive in exchange for it treasury bonds bearing eight per cent. interest. If he chose to keep them, the interest would be constantly accumulating; and if he should have immediate use for them, they were receivable everywhere in public payments. Did not even this satisfy him? Then he could fund his draft in ten per cent. stock, the interest on which was payable semiannually "in gold and silver."

This was the state of affairs when the fifth Congress assembled at Austin, on the 2d of November, 1840.

Mr. Kauffman, the Speaker of the House of Representatives, made, in his opening address, the following remarks:—

"But *seven* members of the last House have been deputed by the people to join in the labors of this! The destinies of Texas have been committed to other, and, I earnestly trust, abler hands. What has produced this extraordinary revolution? We cannot believe that our predecessors were dishonest or incapable; but we *know* that they failed to satisfy the expectations of an anxious and confiding people. What was their error? The voice of the nation answers: They increased, instead of diminishing, *the national expenditures.* Let us, then, gentlemen, with one accord, resolve to avoid the rock on which they split."

In his message, President Lamar said: "The settlements have been extended on various parts of the frontiers." But he did not add that this was the cause of new difficulties with the Indians.

He regretted that it was not in his power to give satisfactory information as to the operations of the loan commissioners. They were trying the markets of France, England, and Holland, with varying prospects of success.

He thought the complaints some made of the burden of taxation were very unreasonable; for, though the duties on imports were nominally fifteen per cent., they amounted in reality to no more than three per cent., inasmuch as they were paid in the depreciated paper of the government.

The acting Secretary of the Treasury, Mr. William Sevey, in his report of October 15, 1840, and in the supplement thereto, gave no distinct account of the revenue for the year; but stated that the total revenue collected, from the organization of the government up to September 30, 1840, was $903,052 01; or, including the amount in the hands of, and supposed to be in the hands of, collecting and receiving officers, $1,486,235 67.

The revenue officers of Texas took delight, from the very beginning, in deceiving themselves by the supposition that there were large amounts of revenue on the way to the treasury. So well as we can ascertain, from a collation of various documents, the actual receipts into the treasury were, during the year ending September 30, 1840, as follows—rejecting repayments, promissory notes received from the Secretary, and the proceeds of the loan from the United States Bank:—

Customs, ...	$166,821 12
Land-dues, licenses, and direct taxes, . .	123,224 66
Austin lots, ...	158,974 81
Galveston lots, ...	9,822 71
Fines, ...	25 00
Donations, ...	51 56
	$458,919 86

This was but little more than one-third the amount Mr. Secretary Starr had estimated, and this was received in government paper, which, at twenty cents in the dollar, would be equal to only ninety-two thousand dollars in specie.

The chief support of the government in this year was from the proceeds of the loan from the United States Bank, on which drafts were drawn to the amount of one hundred and fifty-eight thousand four hundred and ninety-five dollars and ninety-eight cents. During the whole of President Houston's first term, twenty-five thousand dollars in par funds were all he could command. President Lamar was highly favored in having in one year such funds to the amount of nearly one hundred and sixty thousand dollars.

The audited drafts and certificates issued during this period are admitted to have been two millions two hundred and fifty-eight thousand one hundred and four dollars and sixty-two cents, or nearly ten times as much as the gross revenue.

The acting Secretary made the public debt four millions eight hundred and twenty-two thousand three hundred and eighteen dollars and sixty-two cents; but if the audited drafts and treasury notes which he *supposed* were in the hands of collecting officers be added, it was five millions four hundred and eighty-five thousand five hundred and two dollars and twenty-eight cents, without counting the liabilities incurred for the purchase of and fitting out of the navy. The increase of debt in one year exceeded two million three hundred thousand dollars.

While things were in this position, the Mexicans threatened another invasion of the country. But the Texans were not disheartened. Mr. Burnet, who was now, owing to the indisposition of General Lamar, the acting President, said, in a message of December 16—

" Our overtures have been rejected. * * * Let us not forget that a resort to the sword cancels all previous pledges, and opens the way to a new adjustment. Texas proper is bounded by the Rio Grande. Texas, as defined by the sword, may comprehend the Sierra del Madre. Let the sword do its proper work."

A joint committee responded cordially to these sentiments on the 18th of December; and still more plainly on the 12th of January, 1841.

"Your committee are fully aware that it is a fact well known and long established that money is the sinews of war; without that, no force can long be kept together in the field. That we have neither money at home nor credit to any extent abroad is an undeniable fact, how humiliating soever may be the acknowledgment. How, then, are we to sustain an army in the field? Where are the means to come from? For defensive measures, your committee know not—for offensive measures, they answer, from the coffers of the enemy, wrested from him with a strong hand.

"Your committee are of opinion that it would be much easier to sustain an army beyond the Rio Grande than within our own territory; that there the war would be made to support the war; and the captures and contributions, the proceeds of which, in accordance with the law of nations and the usages of war, would come into the military chest, would, if well, managed, defray all the expenses that could be incurred by an army in the enemy's country."

Several changes were made in the revenue laws with the view of increasing the income of government. And

February 4, an act was passed declaring that, from and after its passage, so much of a certain act as provided "for the bonding or funding of the promissory notes or liabilities of the government, be repealed." This deprived the holders of "red backs" of even a promise to pay interest on their demands.

At the close of the session, February 5, 1841, the Speaker made an address to the House, in which were the following remarks:—

"We are a nation comparatively without means, and our legislation has to be based upon a *depreciated* and *depreciating* credit. I believe, however, I may safely say, that we have accomplished much for the permanence and prosperity of this country. The regular army has been *virtually* disbanded; the navy has been laid up in ordinary; superfluous offices have been abolished; and our appropriation bill this year is not more than one-third as large as that of the last."

Dark and gloomy, indeed, were prospects when the Congress adjourned; but the horizon was soon to become bright, as will be evident from the following extract from the *Austin City Gazette* of April 21, 1841:—

"THE LOAN.

"PARIS, *February* 4, 1840.

"To the Editor of the *New York Times and Star.*

"SIR : As the commissioners of loans of the Republic of Texas were instructed by His Excellency, President Lamar, in the event of their effecting a negotiation of the loan for that Republic, to make a public announcement of the fact, that meritorious holders of the securities of the government, who may have aided the country in the hour of its necessity, may not be the victims of the speculation of those acting under secret information, I will thank you to state in your paper that I have this day concluded in this city a contract with the Bank of Messrs. J. Lafitte & Co. for the Texan loan. * * *

"J. HAMILTON."

In a few days afterwards, April 28, the good news was confirmed.

"It is said the bonds have been taken by the house of Lafitte & Co. at 90 cents in the dollar. The French Government have guaranteed their punctual redemption. *The whole loan is negotiated.*"

The effect this produced will be evident from what was said by a Texan, writing from New Orleans under date of April 10 :—

"Our notes and bonds have now all sorts of prices. * * * I am informed by pretty good authority that Captain Wright, of New York, has had a letter from a broker in New York, offering him fifty cents for all in hand from thirty to sixty thousand, and that he will not sell."

"The news of the negotiation of a loan for Texas," said the *N. O. Bulletin,* "has a most beneficial effect. Texan securities have experienced a sudden elevation in the market, and the process may be expected to go on until they obtain to the par quotation."

Further particulars are given in the *Austin City Gazette* of May 5 :—

"Private letters from New Orleans of the 21st ult. quote Texas ten per cent. bonds at forty cents; eight per cent. bonds at thirty-five; promissory notes at thirty ; and furthermore state that Texas money is in demand, and looking up."

The same paper, of May 19, extracts from the *Charleston Patriot* of April 24 a long letter dated London, March 9. In this, it is said that the loan had been negotiated on such terms that, if the guarantee of the French Government were procured, the bonds, to the amount of seven millions of dollars, would be brought out at ninety-five ; but, if the guarantee could not be procured, at fifty-five. Among other things, this writer says :—

"It is, moreover, understood that Mr. John Horseley Palmer, the late able head of the Bank of England (certainly one of the first practical financiers in Great Britain), is engaged in preparing for General Hamilton the plan of a national bank for the Republic of Texas, which is to constitute a reservoir to hold, save, and distribute through a sound circulation the benefits of the loan as soon as it is realized. In case this bank is chartered, which it unquestionably will be by Texas, it is said, in circles which entitle the report to no small credit, that General Hamilton is making offers to Mr. Jaudon, the late able and distinguished agent of the Bank of the United States in London, to go out to Texas in the autumn to take charge of this financial organ of the Texan Government. Should Mr. Jaudon accept this situation, the progress which Texas would make in five years would transcend in value twenty years of successful military conquests in Mexico. She cannot pay too high a salary for such a man, who unites to great practical efficiency in business, accurate and comprehensive views of finance, an admirable temper, and great firmness and decision of character."

When we presented to the reader the first fiscal report of the Provisional Government of Texas, we told him to "despise not the day of small things." By this time, we hope he is convinced both of the wisdom of the apostolic injunction and of its special applicability to the subject selected for his particular meditation. Here we find the Government of Texas, less than six years having elapsed, already in debt to the amount of six or seven millions; proposing to run in debt to the amount of seven millions more; an ex-Governor of the Bank of England preparing a plan of a national bank for the Republic; and Mr. Jaudon, ex-cashier of the Bank of the United States, preparing to remove to Texas, to perform for that Republic all those functions which he and Mr. Biddle together had performed for the United States.

Some time afterwards, unfavorable reports having been circulated, the following official notice was issued:—

"TREASURY DEPARTMENT, CITY OF AUSTIN, *June* 29, 1841.

"To quiet all apprehension, and to remove the doubts that have been created by recent newspaper publications, it is thought proper to give this public and official notice to all whom it may concern, that official information has been received by the Executive of the positive sale of our bonds by our loan commissioner at Paris; the proceeds of which will, it is confidently expected, be realized in the city of New York in the course of the month of August next.

"JOHN G. CHALMERS,
Secretary of Treasury."

July 7, the editor says,

"*The Loan.*—Dispatches were received by the Hon. Secretary of the Treasury, on Monday last, from our loan commissioner, confirmatory of the information published in our last. The loan is obtained, the contracts are signed, and the specie will be forthcoming in due season. *We have seen the documents.*"

Various were the suggestions made in the Texan papers as to the proper disposition of the money, and Alexander Hamilton's Report on a National Bank was republished to aid the Texans in coming to a proper conclusion.

July 14, the *Austin City Gazette* contained a letter from the loan commissioner, General Hamilton, dated London, May 18, a part of which we must quote:—

"Since my last respects, I have completed my contract with J. Lafitte & Co. for the Texan loan; in conformity to which, he issued the inclosed prospectus and explanatory notice. After, in writing with M. Guizot, and in verbal conference with the king and Minister of Finance, I had assured myself, as I supposed, of the favorable disposition and protection of the French Government for the negotiation of the loan in France. After, however, the prospectus was issued, and I had left Paris, to superintend the subscriptions in England, the *Journal des Débats*, the special organ of the court, came out with a strong article against the loan, dissuading the French citizens from going into it; and in the *Messager* and *Moniteur*, M. Humann, the Minister of Finance, by a sort of semi-official, took a similar course."

Messrs. Lafitte & Co. then postponed opening the books for receiving subscriptions. The residue of Gen. Hamilton's letter gives the ground of his strong hope and expectation that this difficulty would be adjusted.

In the success of the commissioner, the Texans did not lightly abandon their hopes, as will appear from the following extract from the *Austin City Gazette* of August 11:—

"Rumors having been rife about town, for the last few days, prejudicial to the loan, we made all necessary inquiries at head-quarters respecting their truth, and, as we expected, they prove to be without foundation. So far from any unfavorable accounts having been received, the latest information from Hamilton is altogether of a favorable character. He states that the difficulties between M. Lafitte and the Minister of Finance are amicably adjusted. He adds, in a letter to the Hon. B. E. Bee: 'The books will be opened with all the power and influence of the House (Lafitte & Co.) on the 30th of June. *M. Lafitte has resolved to carry matters through triumphantly.*'"

But while Gen. Hamilton was exerting all his financial and diplomatic powers in Paris, there were proceedings going on at Austin, of which he was not aware, and which were destined to thwart all his movements. They appear to have commenced early in the year; but full revelation was not made of them till September 1, when an account was given of them in the *Austin City Gazette*, so much of which as is necessary we shall transcribe, as we cannot trust ourselves to tell so important a story in our own words.

After alluding to a statement in another paper, in which the difficulties between the French minister to Texas and the high officers of the Republic were attributed to " British intrigue," the editor proceeds to say :—

" The difficulties were in the first instance altogether of a private and personal character between M. de Saligny and Mr. Bullock, and were lamented by the friends of both parties; the difficulties were increased by the killing of Mr. B.'s pigs by one of M. de S.'s servants, whereupon Mr. B. assaulted the servant, and the minister made his complaint to the government. The district attorney, under the instruction of the government, had Mr. Bullock arrested to answer for said assault, and the District Court not being in session at the time, Mr. B. was bound in heavy recognizances to appear before said court to answer the charge. Thus that matter stands until the next session of the court in November next. As might naturally be expected, this occurrence still further embittered the feelings of both parties to such an extent that, in April last, Mr. Bullock, who keeps a public hotel in this city, meeting M. de Saligny on his premises, ordered him off. M. de Saligny immediately made a second complaint, and insisted on the immediate punishment of Mr. Bullock; on this, Mr. B. was again handed over to the judiciary, and bound over, as in the former case, to answer the charge at the term of the District Court. A long and warm discussion took place between the French minister and the Texan Secretary of State, and the whole matter has been referred to the French Government.

*   *   *   *   *   *   *

" In conclusion, we would remark that M. de Saligny, who is brother-in-law of M. Humann, the Minister of Finance of France, is expected at his residence in this city, in the course of the present month, when, it is hoped, everything will be amicably settled. *   *   *   The connection thus existing between M. de Saligny and a member of the French Cabinet accounts for all the obstacles thrown by that government in the way of Messrs. Lafitte & Co.'s fulfilment of their contract for the Texan loan."

The *Texas Centinel*, of May 6—a paper of politics opposite to those of the *Austin City Gazette*—says:—

" We are authorized in saying that our government has sent on a request to the French Government for the recall of M. de Saligny."

On the 10th of June, the editor devotes more than a column to the subject :—

" Our columns will not permit us at present to enter into a full detail of the ex-official conduct of this foreign functionary. *   *   *   Can that great and wise head (Louis Philippe) of one of the mightiest nations of the earth look for an instant with approbation upon the conduct of M. Saligny, in *knowingly* passing counterfeit money upon obscure and honest citizens of this country—in refusing to pay his tavern bills—in wantonly destroying the property of our citizens—in smuggling into our country a large amount of merchandise for commercial speculation, under the cloak of his diplomatic privilege, as provisions?" &c. &c.

Mr. Bullock's pigs were the aggressors. The Texan editors, with an amiable partiality for everything belonging to their own country, conceal the fact; but we have been on the spot, and inquired into the particulars. M. de Saligny had a number of horses which were fed with corn. Mr. Bullock's pigs intruded into the stables to pick up the corn the horses suffered to fall to the ground. One of M. de Saligny's servants killed some of the pigs. Mr. Bullock whipped the servant. This enraged M. de Saligny; he influenced his brother-in-law, M. Humann, the Minister of Finance at Paris, and Gen. Hamilton's loan was defeated.

We have had occasion to observe before that, however the Texans might quarrel among themselves, they would always unite against the common enemy, the Mexicans. So it was on this occasion. All Texas stood by Mr. Bullock and his pigs. Houstonites and Anti-Houstonites were of one accord. Nor will it be too much to say that, as Rome was saved by the cackling of geese, so Texas was saved by the squeaking of pigs. If the loan had been obtained, it would have been used in establishing a national bank, by which every dollar would have been made to look like ten. The result would have been that the debt of Texas, instead of being twelve millions, would have been twenty-five, thirty, perhaps forty millions. The most intelligent Texans agree in opinion that this would have been the result. All honor, then, to Mr. Bullock and his pigs; and this heretofore much despised animal must be regarded hereafter as possessed of classic interest. If his figure, carved in marble, should be placed over the entrance of the treasury of Texas, it would serve as a memento to future ages of his having been the salvation of the Republic, and teach Mr. Branch Tanner Archer's " thousands and millions, born and unborn," that the humblest of agents may be instrumental in producing consequences of the utmost importance.

CHAPTER XVI.

PROCEEDINGS UNDER THE SIXTH CONGRESS: NOVEMBER, 1841.

Connection of events, great and small—The loan defeated—Increased confusion in
finances—The Secretary of the Treasury suggests that all debts of the government
be funded in a stock bearing two and a half per cent. interest—This the first
suggestion of scaling or repudiation in Texas—Contrast of financial affairs at the
beginning and close of President Lamar's administration.

SIR WILLIAM MOLESWORTH, in a speech in Parliament, spoke
of the loss of an axe as the cause of one war between the Caffres
and the British in South Africa, and the stealing of a goat as the
cause of another.   The present war raging in that region is said
to have had its origin in a cause as trivial as the stealing of a
hog.   One chain connects together all events, both great and
small.   But it is not always that we can trace the connection link
by link, as we can in the defeat of the Texas loan commissioner in
Paris, and the assault on Mr. Bullock's pigs at Austin.

Did the Texans anticipate this result ?   We believe not.   They
were very anxious to obtain the loan, and did not estimate properly
the effects of offending the French minister at Austin, and of
getting, through him, the ill-will of his brother-in-law, the Minister
of Finance at Paris.   More conciliatory measures would, no doubt,
have been adopted, if they had properly appreciated the personal
influence of these two functionaries.   But .so far were they from
trying to conciliate M. de Saligny, that they, from the beginning,
put him at defiance.   When Mr. Bullock was arrested, Mr. Chalmers, the Secretary of the Treasury, went bail for his appearance,
thus identifying the Texan Government with the aggressive tavern-
keeper.   The government, also, as we have seen, went so far·as to
demand the recall of M. de Saligny, and yet it did not give up all
hopes of the loan.   This is evident from the message which President Lamar sent to the sixth Congress, soon after the commencement of its session at Austin, November 1, 1841, and in which he

expressed his regret " that no certain and positive intelligence had yet been received from our loan commissioners in Europe."

Certainly something was desirable for the recuperation of the finances of the Republic, for they were becoming most deplorable. The disbursements for the year amounted to $1,176,288 72, as stated in the report of the Secretary of the Treasury of October, 1841, while the receipts amounted to only $442,604 67. And as both receipts and disbursements were (except $4,776 of the latter), in the inconvertible paper of the government, the revenue was of no avail either to the government or its creditors.

The debt was admitted to be $5,782,798 81, without counting the naval debt, and a number of unliquidated claims. These latter were becoming very embarrassing, as will be seen by the following extracts from the report of the Secretary of the Treasury :—

" The amount of floating, unliquidated debt cannot be ascertained ; there was no appropriation to meet it, and the department was compelled, from necessity, to refuse to issue auditor's certificates to satisfy such claims, inasmuch as they were receivable for a great part of the public revenue, and would, in all probability, have absorbed that part for which they were receivable. A half million would be amply sufficient to cover all claims of that description, which would swell the public debt to $7,800,000, including the naval debt in the total."

Here we find the public debt becoming so embarrassing that the government was compelled to decline issuing the proper evidences of the amount due to the public claimants, and now, for the first time, we find any reference in Texan documents to the subject of scaling or repudiation. In this point of view, the following extracts from the report of the Secretary of the Treasury become interesting :—

" The question arises, what plan should be adopted to extinguish this debt, and meet the current expenses of the government? The subject is one of much difficulty and embarrassment, and involves so much conflict between the rights of the creditors and the interests and necessities of the government, that there is but little prospect of suggesting such a plan as will meet the wishes or satisfy the expectations of all parties interested. To repudiate the public debt altogether, as suggested by many, would justly stigmatize us as a people in the eyes of all enlightened foreign nations. To meet all engagements fully and promptly, is entirely out of our power. Necessity compels, therefore, in some measure, to do violence to our sense of justice, as well as to the rights of our creditors, in adopting a compromise which shall guard their rights, as far as we can consistently with the successful administration of the government. While public faith, which should be held sacred, if possible, at all times, would seem to require the payment of our engagements 'to the uttermost farthing,' still, it should be borne in mind, that we have not received full consideration for our liabilities ; and if, under the imperious circumstances of our situation, we can only afford a liberal reimbursement to our creditors of their investment, strict justice will have been obtained."

No such language as this was held as long as it was possible to borrow. Up to this date, the Government and the people of Texas had always maintained, that what they promised to pay they intended to pay. They had never said, Though we promise to pay one hundred cents on the dollar, we mean to pay only fifty cents, or thirty cents, or twenty cents, or as much as to ourselves may seem just and equitable. If they had said so, they would never have been able to borrow one dollar, or to give currency to their treasury notes. After they had, however, borrowed as much as they possibly could, in every possible form—after they had completely exhausted their credit—then first they began to speak of departing from the letter of the contract.

There is little hope that the "right of creditors" will be much respected when those rights come in collision with "the interests and necessities" of government. The moment that a necessitous government finds its credit so completely exhausted that it can borrow no more, in that moment it has no interest in keeping further terms with its creditors. To this condition of things was the Government of Texas reduced at the close of President Lamar's administration.

Still, it is interesting to see with what apparent reluctance ideas, which involve a violation of natural justice, are at first promulgated; even by statesmen connected with the administration of necessitous governments. Mr. Secretary Chalmers, it will be observed, expresses his great regret that Texas could not fully comply with her engagements. "Necessity *compels*, in some measure, to do violence to our own sense of justice, as well as to the rights of our creditors, in adopting a compromise." Then he makes an attempt to palliate the injustice : "While public faith, which should be held sacred, *if possible*, at all times, would seem to require the payment of our engagements to the uttermost farthing, still, it should be borne in mind that we have not received full consideration for our liabilities."

Afterwards he goes a little further. He had commenced by

admitting that "public faith should be held sacred." Then he adduced "necessity" as a reason for its violation. Then he proceeds to palliate this violation by affirming that Texas had not received as much as she had promised to pay. Finally, he persuades himself that, if Texas cuts down the amount of her engagements one-quarter, or one-half, "strict justice will be obtained."

Thus it is with individuals, and thus it is with nations, whenever they depart from the strict rule of right. Ideas of laxity in complying with engagements, at first received with reluctance, are afterwards tolerated, and finally sanctioned as being all that strict justice requires. The succession of ideas contained in this paragraph of Mr. Chalmers's report became afterwards the history of the public mind in Texas.

He then proposed that the whole public debt should be merged in one consolidated fund, payable in twenty years, and bearing an interest of two and a half per cent. per annum. It would have been well for the creditors if such a project could have been carried into execution. But, as Texas had no revenue except her own worthless paper, it was just as impossible for her to pay two and a half per cent. as to pay ten per cent. All, therefore, that Mr. Chalmers did, by his elaborate treatment of the subject, was to prepare the public mind in Texas for practical repudiation.

But let not more blame be attached to this gentleman than he deserves. All he proposed was to reduce the interest: he did not suggest the scaling of the principal. The guilt of calling in accounts which had been regularly audited, and the negotiable acknowledgments of which had been many years in circulation, must be ascribed to those who followed him.

Thus ended the unfortunate administration of President Lamar. When he entered into office in November, 1838, the treasury notes, and other obligations of the government, were at from sixty-five to eighty-five cents in the dollar. When he left office in November, 1841, the same securities were worth no more than fifteen to twenty cents. (See General Hunt's Address, pp. 4–6.) During his three years of service, the public debt was increased, as nearly as can be ascertained, from $1,887,526 32 to $7,300,000. This was not owing to any increased necessity the Texans had for defending themselves against the Mexicans. It was owing to the profusion and extravagance with which everything was conducted under the administration of this amiable but misguided man; which extravagance and profusion were, in no small degree, fostered by the hopes which were entertained of the negotiation of a loan in Europe.

CHAPTER XVII.

PROCEEDINGS UNDER THE SIXTH CONGRESS, IN CONTINUATION: NOVEMBER, 1841, TO NOVEMBER, 1842.

General Hunt's view of financial affairs at the commencement of President Houston's second term—Exchequer bills issued—Treasury notes no longer received for customs and direct taxes—Extra session of sixth Congress—Exchequer bills below par—Act making them receivable for public dues at only their market rates—The preliminaries for a loan of one million dollars entered into with Mr. Bourgeois.

WHILE the sixth Congress was in session (December, 1841), General Samuel Houston entered upon his second term as President of the Republic. Of the fiscal embarrassments he had to encounter, an adequate idea may be obtained from the preceding chapter, taken in connection with the following extract from General Memucan Hunt's Address:—

"The small loan, obtained by the loan commissioner at Philadelphia, had long been exhausted, and the issues of the government had very greatly exceeded the means of payment from incomes of import duties and direct taxation. Indeed, treasury notes were down to fifteen or twenty cents in the dollar. This state of things forced the government to financial acts neither creditable to the Republic nor agreeable to its citizens; but it could not be avoided. Without some relief to the currency, the wheels of government must have stopped. No officers, except the chief justice and the district judges, all of whom, at the time, were creditors of the government, and some of them for considerable sums, received salaries sufficient to support them. In this state of things, Congress passed a law, January 18, 1842, repealing the act of 19th January, 1839, requiring all officers (the chief justice and judges excepted) to receive, as compensation, the treasury notes of the government, and passed what is familiarly known as the 'Exchequer Bill' on the 19th of January, 1842.

"The provisions of this law were, mainly, that, after the first day of February, 1842, it would not be lawful for any collector of the customs to receive anything but gold or silver, or the 'exchequer bills' of the government, in payment for imposts or duties; and that it was not lawful for sheriffs, or collectors of direct and license tax, to receive anything in payment of taxes, except gold and silver, or the 'exchequer bills' of the government. President Houston was authorized to issue exchequer bills, payable on demand, and receivable in payment of all public dues to an amount not exceeding two hundred thousand dollars, and exchequer bills were to be paid out for no other purpose than to carry out the objects of the general appropriation act of Congress. A further provision authorized all land-dues (except land-tax) and all payments for patents to be made, as heretofore, receivable in the liabilities of the government. This law then adds that all laws and parts of laws previously passed, authorizing the issue and re-issue of promissory notes, and their reception in payment of duties or taxes thereafter to be assessed, be repealed."

As this law made treasury notes no longer receivable (except for arrears of duties and taxes), it deprived them of nearly all the little value they had left. They fell from fifteen and twenty cents in the dollar, which was their value at the close of Lamar's administration, to ten cents, to five, to four, to two cents in the dollar. Finally, they sunk so low that no price at all could be obtained for them in many parts of Texas.

One gentleman has told us that he gave fifteen dollars in treasury bills "for three glasses of brandy and water *without sugar.*" We have heard of one instance in which a fifty dollar treasury note was used to light a cigar; and perhaps some were applied to still more ignoble purposes.

The issue of exchequer bills then commenced. These were, in reality, only treasury notes under a new name. Like the "red backs," they were promises to pay what the government had not the ability to pay; and, like the same "red backs," they were receivable for public dues. But as the Congress of Texas had, by act of 1842, declared that treasury notes should no longer be received in payment of duties or taxes, no one could tell but the Congress would, in 1843, pass a similar act in respect to exchequer bills. It will, therefore, occasion no surprise to the reader, when he is told that there was difficulty in giving currency to this new emission. The merchants refused to receive them, except when they could get nothing else; and when they did receive them, they paid them in immediately for customs. The consequence was that the exchequer bills sunk rapidly, in value, to thirty-three cents, and before the end of the year, to even twenty-five cents in the dollar.

This was not owing to the extent of the issues, for they were, in reality, very moderate, there being seldom so many as fifty thousand dollars in exchequer bills in circulation at one time. It was owing to the bad fiscal management of the Texan Government, and its frequent violations of public faith, depriving it of all confidence both at home and abroad. When the issue of the "printed treasury notes" commenced, in the fall of 1837, though they were less adequately secured, the government found it possible to throw about half a million into circulation, and keep them nearly on a par with specie, for a period of several months. Even after the issues were swelled to nearly a million, by the addition of engraved treasury notes, the depreciation was so gradual that, by the end of the year, or in November, 1838, the notes were at eighty cents in the dollar. But in 1842, the public, both at home and abroad, had begun to regard Texan faith, in money matters, as very like Punic faith, and a small emission of only forty thousand had the effect of sinking their value to the extent already stated.

The fears that exchequer bills would run the same course as treasury notes were soon realized. "An extra session of the sixth Congress was convened by the President, June 27, 1842; and on the 23d of July, a law was passed requiring the collectors of customs, sheriffs, clerks, and postmasters, throughout the Republic, to receive the exchequer bills only at the current rates at which such bills were sold in the market."

Thus, in less than six months after the law was passed for the issue of exchequer bills, was violated the pledge of faith that they should be received, at their face value, in payment. We can readily believe General Hunt, when he says:—

"This act of Congress, and of President Houston, gave great dissatisfaction to many citizens of the Republic. It was looked upon as an act of bad faith without justification, as the whole amount of exchequer bills which the President was authorized to issue could not exceed two hundred thousand dollars, all of which could have been cancelled for customs and direct taxes in a year.

"Had the government, at the extra session of Congress, in 1842, increased the rates of import duties to an amount double or treble what they were, and the direct taxes in the same ratio, to pay the officers' salaries, and other expenditures, in currency, or exchequer bills worth par, it appears to me it would have been better and more satisfactory than the repudiation of a part of the amount for which the exchequer bills promised to be worth on their face, and the consequent injury it did to the credit and reputation of the Republic."

So long as the exchequer bills were worth but thirty-three cents in the dollar, the receipt of them in public payments at their full value operated as a practical reduction of the burdens of the tax-payers. But the act, requiring that they should be received for customs and other public dues, at their market rates, instead of the amount expressed on their face, did not cause them to rise greatly in value. To this fact President Houston bears testimony, in his message of December 1, 1842:—

"The exchequer bills being thus left dependent alone on import duties for their redemption, no other demand existing for them, depreciated, and at one time were worth in market but twenty-five cents in the dollar, though the whole amount issued up to this time is only one hundred and twenty-five thousand dollars, and the amount now in circulation cannot by possibility exceed thirty thousand."

He confirms this testimony in another message, dated January 7, 1843:—

"The Honorable House will also recall to their recollection the fact that the money has been depreciated to a scale never above fifty cents, and for a great part of the year was worth but thirty cents in the dollar."

When the independence of Texas was unacknowledged, when the enemy was at her door, when the issue of the struggle was doubtful, but *before* she had violated her public faith, she could issue treasury notes to the amount of half a million, and keep them in circulation for months without any sensible depreciation. She could even, as we have seen, increase the issue to a million, and they would still be worth eighty cents on the dollar. But, in four years after her independence had been achieved, and when it was recognized by France, Britain, Holland, and the United States, she could not keep in circulation, at one time, fifty thousand dollars in exchequer bills, without their depreciating to fifty, thirty-three, and even twenty-five cents in the dollar.

Strange as it may seem, at this very time negotiations were carried on for a new foreign loan, and with encouraging prospects of success, as appears from the following passage in the report of the Secretary of the Treasury, November 1, 1842:—

"On the 14th day of June last, a contract was signed in New Orleans, between the Hon. Commission on the part of the government, and Mr. Alexander Bourgeois (d'Orivanne) for a loan to Texas of one million of dollars; the first instalment, as per contract, to be paid within six months from date of same. The powerful interest which Mr. Bourgeois can command, and which will be exerted in favor of the loan, induces the belief and expectation that the proceeds will soon be available to our government."

The loan was not effected; but for what reason is not stated. But the sentiments avowed by Mr. Chalmers, as Secretary of the Treasury, in his official report, ought of themselves to have defeated all attempts to borrow. When the highest financial functionary of a government declares that such a government has a right arbitrarily to modify its contracts, nobody ought to be willing to lend to it. The French Government was very anxious to establish close commercial, if not political connections with Texas. In the prosecution of this object, it was even willing to overlook the insult to its minister, M. de Saligny. But there would have been gross impropriety in its guaranteeing a loan to a government which avowed its intention of departing from the letter of the contract, whenever that contract, either expressly or by implication, provided for the payment of a premium on the money borrowed.

CHAPTER XVIII.

PROCEEDINGS UNDER THE SEVENTH CONGRESS: NOVEMBER, 1842, TO NOVEMBER, 1843.

Gloomy condition of public affairs as depicted in President Houston's message—The removal of the archives of the Land-Office forcibly resisted—Exchequer bills of small denominations issued.

THE seventh Congress convened at Washington, on the Brazos, November 14th, 1842. On the first of December, President Houston made an address to them in person, in which he gave the following statement of the condition of public affairs :—

"Since the commencement of legislation in Texas, as a separate and independent power, we find the proceedings of Congress but too frequently paralyzed by acts of selfishness and partiality. The public good has been too often disregarded, and the national interests left out of view; and thus, without establishing any general principle or system of legislation, temporary expediency has been substituted for a due consideration of the national good. Under this state of things, it is but too true that the nation has been gradually declining. Instead of deriving facilities and advantages from the lapse of time, its decline, since the year 1838, to its present point of depression, has been more regular and more rapid than perhaps that of any other country on the globe possessing the same natural advantages."

Fiscal embarrassments are closely connected with, and in part at least the causes of, national decline. The continued prosperity of the United States has been owing, in no small degree, to the easy condition (a few years only excepted) of the finances of the Federal Government. If the Government of Mexico had only an adequate revenue, it would be easy for it to restore order in its different provinces. The rapid decline of the Texans as a nation was owing chiefly, if not solely, to the wrong manner in which their financial affairs were conducted. After the battle of San Jacinto, they never had any serious conflict with the enemy. Their troubles were of their own creating, and to be traced to their bad management of the pecuniary concerns of the Republic.

The President then adverted to the low rate at which exchequer bills had passed in the market, although but a very small amount had been issued; after which he proceeded to speak of some acts of insubordination, which will be best described in his own language:—

"In the month of March last, during the incursion of the enemy, under the provisions of the constitution, the President felt it his imperative duty to order the removal of the archives and heads of department from the city of Austin to a place of safety. * * * Resistance, however, has been offered, and continued up to the present time. Acts of the most seditious and unauthorized character have been perpetrated by persons styling themselves the 'Active Committee.'"

Of the proceedings of this committee, we have a further account, in another address of the President, delivered on the 4th of January, 1843:—

"When the last command was sent to Austin for the removal of the archives, the Executive contemplated a sufficient force to have effected that object. The circumstances attending this failure are reported to be that the command, twenty in number, arrived at Austin on the 30th of December, and on the same day placed in three wagons the boxes containing the most important land-papers, furnished them by the Commissioner of the General Land-Office. The mob of resistance increased in number from the time that the object of the visit was known; and before the wagons left the avenue, the arsenal was broken open, and the artillery, charged with grape and canister, was brought up and fired on the wagons and teams. No damage, however, was done to them; and only two shot are reported to have entered the General Land-Office. The company who were authorized to take the archives in charge continued their march until they arrived at Kinney's, eleven miles from Austin, on their way to Caldwell on the Brazos. They encamped at Kinney's for the remainder of the night, and in the morning found that the malcontents had placed the artillery in advance of them, and represented their numbers as ninety-nine men. Those in charge of the archives not having sufficient force, left them and returned to their homes—reporting that Capt. Joseph Daniel, attached to the General Land-Office, had been shot at several times, but had escaped, leaving his family in Austin. What injury he sustained, is unknown. The malcontents also declared to those employed in bringing away the archives that, on their return to Austin, they would put the Commissioner of the General Land-Office, Col. Thomas William Ward, to death; and further declared that, if the President had been taken and given up to them, they would freely have surrendered the archives. They are represented to have been in a state of intoxication, and unreserved in their threats of violence against the person and life of the chief magistrate of the country."

Acts of rebellion, which threatened the very existence of the government, could add nothing to the value of Texan securities. They had, however, with the exception of exchequer bills, sunk so low already that it was not possible for them to sink much lower. And with a view of sustaining the credit of these bills, an act was passed, January 6, requiring the Secretary of the Treasury so to pay them out as never to have, at any one time, more than fifty thousand dollars in circulation. Notwithstanding the restriction on the amount, exchequer bills were, during the year, at various stages of depreciation.

The original act had required the issue of notes of the denominations of one hundred, fifty, twenty, ten, and five dollars. This new act made it the duty of the Secretary of the Treasury " to issue the bills in the denominations, one, two, three, five, ten, and twenty dollars, issuing as many of the smaller denominations as practicable."

Exchequer bills were subsequently issued for seventy-five cents, fifty cents, twenty-five cents, and twelve and a half cents. Every effort was made to adapt them to the uses of the community; yet the whole amount issued up to December 4, 1843, was, as will be seen by reference to Appendix J, only one hundred and thirty-seven thousand two hundred and eighty-one dollars and seventy-one cents. Of this amount, never more than fifty thousand were in circulation at one time. The amount was generally much less. The whole amount in circulation, in the beginning of December, 1843, was, by estimate, less than fourteen thousand dollars ; yet, in October of that year, exchequer bills were, as will be seen by reference to Appendix J, worth, in most parts of Texas, no more than sixty cents in a dollar.

CHAPTER XIX.

PROCEEDINGS UNDER THE EIGHTH CONGRESS: 1843-44.

Repudiation denounced by President Houston—The negotiation for a loan with Mr. Bourgeois unsuccessful—Commencement of hard-money policy—Low rate of exchequer bills—Objections to paper issues receivable for public dues.

THE eighth Congress assembled at Washington December 4, 1843. The President, in his message of December 12, gave a gloomy view of affairs. Referring to a particular topic, he said:—

"It may be as well to allude to a fact which has greatly prejudiced the nation. The charge that we had repudiated our government liabilities has been industriously urged, not only abroad but at home, as a cause of distrust and an accusation of bad faith. Other governments of high respectability have done so. Texas never has, and, I trust, never will."

Through nearly two pages the President proceeded in the same strain. But so low was the credit of the Texan Government, through repeated violations of public faith, and through long-continued financial mismanagement, that nothing could raise it.

On the 17th of January, 1844, it was announced that nothing had been realized from the contract with Mr. Bourgeois. And, on the 27th of the same month, means were even taken to prevent any such negotiations in future, by enacting "that all laws authorizing the President to negotiate a loan or loans, upon either the public faith or the hypothecation of the public lands, be and the same are hereby repealed." A previous Congress had annulled the five million loan act: this abrogated the million.

January 17, an act was passed declaring that

"All bonds, obligations, or recognizances, *hereafter* made payable to the Republic, or the President of the same, or any of the counties, shall be held and deemed as payable and recoverable in gold and silver only: and all fines, *hereafter* assessed or incurred, shall be paid in gold, or silver, or exchequer bills, any law to the contrary notwithstanding."

Thus, as far as circumstances would admit, did Texas now adopt a hard-money policy.

February 5, an act was passed declaring that, after the first of

March ensuing, no more exchequer bills should be issued until the amount in circulation should be reduced to twenty thousand dollars; after which, that amount might be kept in circulation, but no more.

If the reader will turn to Appendix J, he will find that, though the issue of exchequer bills was reduced so low, yet in but few parts of Texas, and at but few times, from January to July 31, 1844, were they at par. The most of the quotations are at sixty, seventy, seventy-five, and eighty cents in the dollar; and in one month, at Galveston, the chief seat of commerce and customs, they ranged from fifty to one hundred.

This may excite surprise, when it is considered that the net revenue from customs, during the year ending July 31, 1844, was nearly one hundred and seventy-eight thousand dollars. But it should be recollected that, as they were receivable at the custom-house, not at the amount expressed on their face, but at the rate they bore in the market, the merchants had no more interest in paying them in than in paying in gold or silver. Hence it will be seen that the payments "in par funds," by which, it is to be presumed, is meant metallic money or its equivalent, nearly equalled the payments in exchequer bills.

This fact, in connection with others, shows how difficult it is to keep up the value of even a small amount of paper-money supported solely by government revenue. It is not the annual, but the monthly, and, in some circumstances, even the semi-monthly, amount of revenue that determines the amount of such paper that can be safely issued.

Our banks do, indeed, keep a large amount of notes in circulation, but it is only by redeeming the average amount, twelve times or oftener in each year, that they maintain those notes on a par with specie. Government must do likewise, if it uses a paper currency intended to serve as a substitute for coin, especially if it makes its issues in a country already saturated with bank paper. All the amount of circulating notes which a government, with a revenue of twenty-four millions a year, could safely issue, would be two or three millions. It might, indeed, issue twenty or thirty millions, and keep it in circulation for a time on a par with specie. But such issues would, sooner or later, be sure to return upon it in greater amounts than the monthly revenue could absorb, and then the public credit would sustain serious injury.

It is to be hoped that these truths will be remembered by the fiscal authorities of the United States the next time they are tempted to issue treasury notes of small denominations intended to circulate as money. But two or three millions of such paper are all, as has been shown, that a government, with a revenue of twenty-four millions, can safely issue. Now, two millions of surplus revenue will pay the interest on forty millions of stock loans at five per cent., and on thirty-three millions at six per cent. To so much greater extent can government borrow, by means of the funding system, than by resorting to issues of circulating paper.

The serious embarrassments of the United States Government in the war of 1812–14 were, in part, owing to disregard of these principles. It issued treasury notes, and received them in payment of public dues, whereby it left itself without the means of paying interest on stock loans.

Such issues do, indeed, afford an easy way of relieving the immediate wants of a necessitous government; but the very facility with which ways and means can thus be raised is no small objection to them. They often cause the postponement of those efficient measures which ought to be at once adopted.

It must also be admitted that loans made, in the first instance, by means of treasury notes, seem, in some respects, more eligible than loans of gold and silver. By their means government borrows, from day to day, just such sums as it wants, and just where it wants, and has no large amount of money lying dead on hand. In this way, also, it avoids deranging the operations of the banks, as may be done by large stock loans of gold and silver taking from them, though temporarily, their specie basis. But all these advantages may be secured, and the evils above spoken of be avoided, by issuing notes, *not* receivable for duties, but bearing a moderate rate of interest, and, if not paid by a certain day, *fundable* in a stock loan, bearing a higher rate of interest.

Treasury notes, *receivable for public dues*, should never be used, unless it be to relieve a *temporary* embarrassment, and when it is reduced almost to a certainty that government will, in a few months, have a *surplus* revenue sufficient to redeem them.

The difference of one or two per cent., which treasury notes, receivable for public dues, would bring in the market over treasury notes simply *fundable*, ought to be regarded as of little account, so very important is it that government should always have a revenue in something else than its own paper.

CHAPTER XX.

PROCEEDINGS UNDER THE NINTH CONGRESS : 1844-45.

The finances somewhat improved—Contrast of expenditures in Lamar's and Houston's second terms—Idem of imports and exports—Sound views of President Jones—The further issue prohibited of exchequer bills, and other paper intended to pass as money—The receipt of paper for public dues forbidden.

THE ninth Congress assembled at Washington December 2, 1844. In a message delivered to them, a few days afterwards, December 7th, President Houston said :—

"It is believed the receipts from the various sources of revenue will, at least, equal the expenditure—perhaps leave a small surplus in the treasury."

This state of affairs was very different from that of former years, and shows what can be done by persevering economy.

In the three years of President Lamar's administration, from December, 1838, to December, 1841, the public debt was swelled from less than two millions to more than seven millions.

In the three years of President Houston's administration, from December, 1841, to December, 1844, no additions appear to have been made to the debt, except by increments of interest, and by the bringing in of back accounts.

In the three years of President Lamar's administration, the Treasurer's payments were, according to the best accounts that can be gathered, as follows :—

" Year ending September 30, 1839,	.	.	$1,504,173 58
"	"	" 1840, .	.	2,174,752 74
"	"	" 1841, .	.	1,176,288 72

$4,855,215 04

" Average amount per annum, $1,618,405."

In the three years of President Houston's second term these payments were, besides $17,907 30 on account of the mail service and collecting of taxes, as follows :—

"Disbursed for appropriations of 1842, . . $198,051 00
  "   "   1843, . . 147,274 38
  "   "   1844, . . 147,850 32

                                                $493,175 70
"Average amount per annum, including mail service, and collection of taxes, $170,361."

This difference is owing, in part, only to differences in the character of the men who presided over the government. President Lamar, as a paper-money man, was profuse on principle. He knew of no limit on expenditure but the limit of credit. President Houston, as somewhat of a hard-money man, was more inclined to economy. But if Houston had been Chief Magistrate from 1838-39 to 1841-42, he could have restricted but in part the extravagant expenditures of these years. And if Lamar had succeeded him, he would have been compelled, from the force of circumstances (however contrary it might have been to his nature), to be in some degree economical.

If it had been possible for the Texans to be hard-money and prompt-payment men, they might have achieved their independence, and defrayed all the expenses of the Republic, at a cost of two hundred thousand dollars a year. This may seem a small amount, but neither nations nor individuals know how little is necessary to sustain them till necessity forces them to make the experiment. The disbursements in the last term of President Houston show that our estimate is within bounds. During Lamar's administration, the Mexicans only threatened. During Houston's second term, they made an incursion into the country.

But the Texans never became economical till constrained by necessity. So long as there was any hope of negotiating a loan in Europe, and so long as they could borrow from the citizens of the United States, by new issues of treasury notes, their extravagant expenditures were continued.

When they were reduced to such straits that they could borrow no longer, except from themselves, and then only to a limited amount, in anticipating the revenue by issues of exchequer bills, then they became saving.

We have not the means of instituting such a comparison of the commerce of the country as is desirable, for we have not been able to find any account of the imports and exports for part of the time; but the following items prove that its foreign commerce was much greater during part of Lamar's than during part of Houston's second term:—

	Imports.	Exports.
Year ending Sept. 1, 1839,	$1,506,897 67	$274,518 09
" " 1840,	1,378,568 98	220,401 15
	2,885,466 65	494,919 24
Average per annum,	$1,442,733 32½	$247,459 62
Year ending July 31, 1843,	$471,205 32	$415,768 75
" " 1844,	686,503 03	615,119 34
	1,157,708 35	1,030,888 09
Average per annum,	$578,854 17	$506,444 04

These tables show how effective excess of paper currency is in encouraging imports, and discouraging exports. The imports, in two years of Lamar's administration, when treasury notes were the circulating medium, were nearly six times as great as the exports. On the contrary, in two years of Houston's second term, when such notes were no longer current, the exports nearly equalled the imports.

These tables show more. They show to what extent contributions were levied on citizens of the United States, in Lamar's time, by means of Texan promises to pay, for nine-tenths of the imports were from the United States, and were paid for, if paid at all, in Texan treasury notes, and other evidences of Texan debts. In these two years, the imports exceeded the exports in the aggregate sum of $2,390,547 41. All this was a levy on citizens of the United States; for Texan securities had no market in Europe.

Dr. Anson Jones, who succeeded Gen. Houston as President of the Republic, delivered his inaugural address on the 9th of December, 1844. Prominent points in it were:—

"The maintenance of the public credit, and the preservation of the national faith, both as it regards individuals and nations.

"The entire abolishment of paper-money issues by government, corporations, or individuals, and the consequent introduction of an exclusive hard-money currency."

In a message dated December 16, he expatiated somewhat at length on these points:—

"Circumspect as was the preceding administration in holding the reins in the emission of exchequer money, it created a sort of illusion as to the fiscal ability of government, which was made manifest in the extraordinary amounts of private appropriations by the different sessions of Congress. These appropriations, it is true, were in a great measure arrested, but only by the exercise of that power vested in the Executive which is always used with great reluctance.

"The urgent necessity which three years since required of the government a resort to the issue of exchequer bills, has now ceased to exist, and the continuance of the system is no longer justified.

"The fallacy and the danger of a factitious paper currency have been demonstrated by every civilized nation upon the earth, and Texas, having once participated in this demonstration, should now, when she is able to do so, abandon the experiment, and resort in time to what the experience of the past has conclusively shown to be the only safe expedient for governments—a hard-money currency, as a circulating medium. As a commercial convenience, recourse may be had to a system of treasury drafts, drawn against specie in actual deposit."

In conformity with this recommendation, an act was passed February 3, 1845, repealing the law authorizing the issue of exchequer bills, and forbidding the Secretary of the Treasury, or any other officer of the government, to issue any bonds, notes, bills, or other description of paper representing money, intended for circulation, or to be received in payment of any class of revenue, and requiring the Secretary to cause to be destroyed all the exchequer bills received at the treasury department. This law further provided that, after the receipt of the whole amount of exchequer bills in circulation, and such other paper liabilities of the government as were in circulation, and were receivable by law for dues to the government, nothing but gold and silver should be received, except for land-patents, and other land-office dues, which might, as before, be received in the liabilities of the government.

So much of this law as prohibited the receipt of Texas government paper in payment of public dues was a violation of the oft-plighted faith of the Republic. But it put an end, for the present, to the paper-money system of Texas. And at the request of President Jones, we make a special record of the fact that his signature was never affixed to a paper bill of credit.

CHAPTER XXI.

PROCEEDINGS UNDER THE NINTH CONGRESS, CONTINUED: 1845.

The Congress of the United States pass a resolution for annexing Texas to the Union—The people of Texas, in convention, assent to the terms, and adopt a constitution for the State of Texas—Provisions in relation to public debt and government paper-money—Extract from report of Commissioner of General Land-Office—Great extent of land held by individuals—View of public lands as a means of paying public debts.

BETTER times for Texas were at hand. On the 1st of March, 1845, the President of the United States approved of a joint resolution of the Senate and House of Representatives for annexing Texas to the Union. In this resolution, it was, among other things, declared that—

" Said State * * * shall also retain all the vacant and unappropriated lands lying within its limits, to be applied to the payment of the debts and liabilities of Texas, and the residue of said lands, after discharging said debts and liabilities, to be disposed of as said State may direct; but in no event are said debts and liabilities to become a charge upon the Government of the United States."

Thus was provision sought to be made that Texas should retain all her lands, and at the same time pay all her debts—the said lands to be set aside as a special fund for the payment of the debts, and only the *residue* thereof, after the debts should be discharged, to be applied to such other purposes as the State might direct.

June 16, 1845, an extra session of the ninth Congress was convened at Washington, on the Brazos, to take into consideration the resolution of annexation. This body approved of the proclamation of the President of Texas, of May 5, authorizing an election for delegates to meet in convention, July 4, 1845, for the purpose of acquiescing in the annexation of Texas to the Union, and adopting a constitution for the State.

On the 4th of July, 1845, the Convention met accordingly, in the city of Austin, and in the name of the people of the Republic of Texas, assented to the annexation of Texas to the United States, on the condition and guarantees of the said joint resolution of the Congress of the United States. In the ordinance then adopted, the first paragraph, after reciting the joint resolution for annexing Texas to the United States, declares that—

"In order to manifest the assent of the people of this Republic, as required in the above-recited portions of the said resolution, we, the deputies of the people of Texas, in convention assembled, in their name, and by their authority, do ordain and declare that we assent to, and accept the proposals, conditions, and guarantees contained in the first and second sections of the resolution of the Congress of the United States aforesaid."

Thus did the people of Texas, in convention assembled, acknowledge the obligation of the debts incurred by the government of the Republic. Thus did they guarantee the United States against all claims on account of said debts. And thus did they consent that "all the vacant and unappropriated lands lying within the limits of Texas should be applied to the payment of the debts and liabilities of Texas;" and that only the *residue* of said lands, after discharging such debts and liabilities, should be disposed of as said State might direct.

Its view of the evils of government paper-money and of public debt, the Convention embodied in the following provisions of the constitution:—

"Art. VII. Sec. 8. And in no case shall the legislature have the power to issue treasury warrants, treasury notes, or paper of any description intended to circulate as money.

"Art. VII. Sec. 33. The aggregate amount of debts hereafter contracted by the legislature shall never exceed the sum of one hundred thousand dollars, except in case of war, to repel invasions, or suppress insurrections."

The provision to prohibit the issue of treasury notes and treasury warrants was adopted by a vote of forty-five yeas to thirteen nays.

August 5, the Commissioner of the General Land-Office made a report, a part of which it is proper to introduce here. Inasmuch as the customs, the chief source of Texan revenue, were to be transferred to the United States, little would remain but the public lands wherewith to pay the debts incurred under the government of the Republic.

"Superficial extent of Texas, as comprised within the limits defined by statute of first Texan Congress, page 133, 379,319 square miles; or, 254,284,160 acres.

"Total amount of land issued by the various boards of land commissioners, 43,543,970 acres.

"Total amount recommended from the above, as good and lawful claims, by the committee appointed to detect fraudulent certificates, 19,212,206 acres.

"Total amount issued by Department of War as bounty and donation claims, 6,300,000 acres.

"Total amount of land-script sold by the government of the late Republic of Texas, 368,787 acres.

"Total amount of legal claims to land issued by the authorities of Texas, 25,880,993 acres.

"Total amount issued by various boards of land commissioners, and supposed to be fraudulent, 24,331,764 acres.

"Total amount of land issued by the authorities of Mexico, a portion of which is supposed to be invalid, 22,080,000 acres.

"Total amount of public domain subject to location and unsurveyed, 181,991,403 acres."

To enable the reader to form some idea of the quantities above set forth, it is proper to state that the amount issued by the Department of War as bounty and donation claims (six million acres) was more than double the area of the State of Connecticut, exceeded the territorial surface of either New Jersey or New Hampshire, and was greater than that of Massachusetts and Rhode Island put together. The total amount of issues by the Mexican Government (twenty-two million acres) exceeded the whole of New England, exclusive of Maine. The issues under Texan boards of commissioners, supposed to be fraudulent (twenty-four million acres), were nearly equal in extent to the State of Ohio. The whole amount appropriated by both the Texan and Mexican authorities (seventy-two million acres) exceeded what is contained in the States of New York, New Jersey, Pennsylvania, Maryland, and the District of Columbia. Texas, with a population of about one hundred thousand, had more land appropriated for individual use than is to be found in the four central States above mentioned, having an aggregate population of six millions and a half. If nothing else will, this fact ought to convince the reader of the magnificent scale on which land-speculations have been carried on in Texas; and in these land-speculations he will find the key to all important events in Texan history.

But great as was the amount of land claimed by individual owners, it was less than one-third of all the land in the country. The amount of public domain still subject to location, and remaining unsurveyed (one hundred and eighty-one million acres), was equal in extent to the States of Virginia, North Carolina, South Carolina, Georgia, Kentucky, and Tennessee. Compared with the North-Western States, it greatly exceeded in extent Ohio, Indiana, Michigan, Illinois, and Missouri.

August 27, a committee made report that 236,803 square miles of the surface of Texas were appropriated, leaving 160,516 unappropriated. Referring to sales of the public lands, as a means of paying the public debt, and supposing the sales to be continued for thirty-seven years, the committee say:—

" If .it can be sold at that time (1882) for $1 25 per acre, the public domain of Texas will be worth, in the year 1882, $128,462,400.

" If the accounts of traders and travellers are entitled to credit, one-half of this country is suitable for the occupancy of the agriculturist. Deducting, then, one-half for sterile wastes and mountain ranges, the present worth of this fund, at 6 per cent., will not meet the public debt of Texas."

According to the report of the Commissioner of the General Land-Office, " the amount of public land subject to location, and unsurveyed," was 181,991,403. If to this be added " the amount issued by various boards of land commissioners and supposed to be fraudulent," 24,331,764 acres, the sum will be 206,323,167 acres; and some addition should be made from the " total amount issued by the authorities of Mexico, 22,080,000 acres, a portion of which was supposed to be invalid." Suppose one-half of these invalid, and we have a grand total of 217,363,167 acres.

Such was the land-fund at the disposal of the government of Texas, according to the report of the Commissioner of the General Land-Office. But the committee of the Convention reduced it to 102,730,240 acres. In so doing, they seem to have taken into the account all the " head-rights" or settlers' claims, and soldiers' rights, not yet " located," and also the enormous grants made by the united State of Coahuila and Texas, which the independent government of Texas had steadily refused to acknowledge. The commissioner gives the extent of land " subject to location, and unsurveyed." The committee give the amount " unappropriated."

Even this reduced amount is but little inferior to the territorial surface of all our States on the seaboard, from Maine to Pennsylvania inclusive. Yet the committee state that, supposing one-half of these lands to be waste, the residue, 56,365,125 acres, will not, by the year 1882, if sold at $1 25 an acre, discharge the public debt of Texas, then less than twelve millions of dollars.

The committee may be right, supposing the debt to go on accumulating till the year 1882, at compound interest, at the rate of 6 per cent. per annum, and supposing no sales of land to be effected till that year. But, supposing the sales to commence immediately, and only enough to be sold in each year to pay the interest on the debt, and reduce the principal a few hundred thousand dollars, the whole would be liquidated in much less time than is stated in the report by the committee.

But her lands were not all that Texas had pledged to her public creditors. In addition thereto, she had pledged her custom revenues, her direct taxes, her license taxes, and, what is more than all, her public faith, which amounted to a pledge of everything she possessed, or might hereafter possess. If she transferred any of these pledged revenues, the customs for example, to a third party, she was bound, on principles of equity, to make good the deficit from some other source.

Here we cannot help observing that the principles on which the committee proceeded in estimating the public lands of Texas, as a fund wherewith to pay her public debt, were very different from those commonly adopted by American statesmen. They seem generally to suppose that the lands are worth intrinsically $1 25 an acre; but that, as they have cost nothing, or next to nothing, they cannot be too lavish in giving them away.

The truth is, the public lands of the United States have never repaid the original cost, including therein the sums paid the Indians, the cost of the Indian wars they have occasioned, the cost of surveys and management, and interest on the whole. The richest man in the world would have been ruined if he had held our public lands as a commercial speculation.

Even now the fee simple of all the public lands in the United States is not worth more than fifty to one hundred millions, taking into consideration the amount they annually yield and the expenses of management. Yet they might, if properly guarded, have proved a valuable resource to government, as a fund for borrowing on in times of exigency. And Congress has no more right to give them away than it has to give away the public ships, the public buildings, or the money in the public treasury.

CHAPTER XXII.

GENERAL VIEW OF THE FISCAL POLICY OF TEXAS.

Comparison of powers of the Continental and of the Texan Congress—Comparative
view of continental money and of Texan promissory notes—The Texan promissory notes more effective as governmental means, but yet productive of great
evil—Illusion of the Texan authorities in regard to loans and lands—Frequent
changes of revenue laws, and of public tenders—Evils of government issues.

SOME time elapsed after the meeting of the Convention, before
the revenue and other laws of the United States were extended
over Texas, and we will take advantage of this *quasi interregnum*,
to state some facts, and make some reflections, which could not
before be introduced without breaking the thread of our narrative.

In many respects, the Texan Congress had more efficient powers
than were possessed by our Congress of 1776. The latter was a
mere consulting body, and, in so far as raising a revenue was concerned, it could do little more than make suggestions to the States,
which suggestions the States might attend to, or not, as they saw
fit. It had to depend on the action of the States to give currency
to its continental paper. It had power (or assumed power) to
borrow, but it had no power to raise money to pay what it borrowed, or even interest on the same. The Texan Congress united
in itself all the powers which both the Continental Congress and
our State revolutionary assemblies possessed. It was sovereign
and supreme. It depended on no other political power to carry
its measures into effect. The county, city, and town governments
were of its own creation, and directly subordinate to it. There
were great advantages, in a fiscal point of view, in this unity of
power.

The coincidences in the history of our own revolutionary paper
currency and that of Texas are many and striking, but the points
in which they differed are not unworthy of notice.

1. Our revolutionary paper-money emanated from various sources.
In addition to the issues of the Continental Congress, we had

those of all, or nearly all, the thirteen State governments. The relative value of these was always changing, giving occasion for great speculation, and causing great confusion in exchanges. The Texan paper-money, though various in form, all emanated from one source ; and thus had a uniformity which our revolutionary paper-money did not possess.

2. The continental issues amounted, in all, to about three hundred and fifty-seven millions. According to the Hon. Samuel Breck, of Philadelphia, the burden this imposed on the people, and, consequently, the advantage the Congress derived therefrom, was equal to about fifteen millions in specie.* This is at the rate of a little more than four and a half cents in the dollar. The treasury notes of Texas never, according to the report of the auditor and comptroller, netted less to the government than twelve and a half cents in the dollar. For the whole of the first issues, or "printed notes," par was received. From the commencement to the close, the government received, for all its securities, on an average, fifty cents in the dollar. Thus, the revolutionary government of Texas did much better with its paper-money than did our Continental Congress.

3. An effort was made to support the credit of our continental currency by acts of compulsion. When it was but five months old, on the 11th of January, 1776, Congress, says an eye-witness, resolved—

"That whosoever should refuse to receive in payment continental bills should be declared and treated as an enemy of the country, and be precluded from intercourse with its inhabitants, *i. e.* outlawed. This ruinous principle was continued in practice for five successive years, and appeared in all shapes and forms, *i. e.* in tender-acts, in limitations of prices, in awful and threatening declarations, in penal laws, with dreadful and ruinous punishments, and in every other way that could be devised, and all executed by a relentless severity by the highest authorities then in being, viz., by Congress, by assemblies, and conventions of the States, and by committees of inspection, whose powers in those days were nearly sovereign, and even by military force."

Honor to whom honor is due. The Texans resorted to no such means to sustain their paper-money. It never was made a legal tender for debts due to individuals. An act was, indeed, passed to require the officers of government to receive their fees in this

---

* See an article on this subject, by this gentleman, in Fisher's *National Magazine* for June, 1845. As Mr. Breck thinks there was sound policy in making these issues, he could have had no disposition to underrate the advantages thence derived.

paper-money; but, if they thought this a hardship, they were at liberty to resign. Fond as a portion of the Texans, unfortunately, are, or at least were, of Lynch law, they never resorted to this summary mode of proceeding to force any man to receive their government paper for more than it was worth. The result was that, when "red backs" were almost the exclusive circulating medium, specie was the standard of ultimate reference. If a man bought an article on credit, for, say one hundred dollars, he gave a note promising to pay one hundred dollars in silver, or so many treasury notes, as should, when the note fell due, be worth one hundred dollars in silver.

From the superior moderation and the superior wisdom the Texan Congress and the Texan people herein displayed over their revolutionary grandsires of 1776; the reader will, perhaps, indulge the hope that the race is improving—that the hereditary taint, of which we have elsewhere spoken, is becoming weaker. We shall be happy if future events prove this hope to be well founded.

4. Texas treasury notes ceased to be a circulating medium after they sunk to eight for one, that is, after eight dollars in paper were worth but one in silver. "The depreciation of continental money;" says an author, whom we have already quoted, "never stopped the circulation of it."

"As long as it retained any value, it passed quick enough; and would purchase hard-money, or anything else, as readily as ever, when the exchange was two hundred for one, and when every hope, or even idea of its being ultimately redeemed at its nominal value, had entirely vanished."

In another place, he remarks: "Its circulation was never more brisk than when it was five hundred for one."

5. The losses sustained by the successive depreciation and ultimate non-redemption of continental money fell exclusively on the people of the old thirteen States. It never was exported. Great part of the treasury notes of Texas were sent to the United States, and much of the loss sustained by their successive depreciation had to be borne by people not immediately interested in this revolutionary struggle. The great surplus of imports over exports, in some years of Texan history, cannot be accounted for, except on the supposition that Texan securities were exchanged in the United States for arms, provisions, and other necessaries. In this way supplies were obtained which were essential to the suc-

cess of the Texan revolution. As a fiscal machine, government paper-money yielded more aid to the Texan than to our Continental Congress. By its means, the Continental Congress made levies on the American people alone; while, by similar means, the Texan Congress made levies on the people of what was then a foreign country.

Still, it is matter of regret that these issues were ever made. With how little expense the whole revolutionary struggle might otherwise have been conducted, is proved by the small cost of achieving Texan independence, and the small cost with which it was sustained during the three years of General Houston's last presidential term. We pretend not to say that a people, situated as the Texans were, could have carried through the conflict without running into debt. All that could be expected in the way of taxation, from so small a community, was revenue enough to defray the expenses of their civil establishment, and that placed on the most economic scale. To carry on such hostile operations as were indispensable, it was necessary to borrow in some form or other. But the Texans selected the very worst mode of borrowing. From the very beginning their debt took a wrong form.

They began by issuing drafts on the treasury. This would all have been well if there had been any money in the treasury. But, as there was none, these drafts, on the principles of common law and of common sense, became "set-offs" against sums due to the treasury; and, as they greatly exceeded in amount the sums due for customs and other taxes, they prevented the government from realizing even so much efficient revenue as was necessary to defray the expenses of the civil establishment.

These drafts sunk in value to fifteen cents in the dollar. Then recourse was had to the issue of treasury notes. But as these, like the treasury drafts, were receivable for customs and other taxes, they became, like them, "set-offs" against the amounts due the treasury.

The result was that the Texan Government had no efficient revenue, or none worth speaking of. All it did, by all its apparatus of custom-house officers and tax-gatherers, was to redeem part of its outstanding liabilities. This would have been very well if borrowing from day to day, or from month to month, could have met all fiscal exigencies; but in time of war governments require something more than merely temporary loans to carry on operations.

All that could reasonably have been expected from a government, under such circumstances as was that of Texas, was a fair settlement with its creditors for supplies furnished and services rendered, and giving them evidences of the same, bearing interest, to be discharged immediately, in lands; or, *after* the close of the war, either in lands or in money, out of such revenue as might then arise. It was folly to attempt to pay during the war any debt that might be incurred in its prosecution out of any revenue that could then be raised.

The extravagance with which everything was conducted was owing partly to the facilities of running in debt which these paper issues afforded; partly to the character of the men at the head of affairs, who knew nothing about economy in either private life or public; and partly to other causes.

"The large appropriations and issues of treasury notes under President Lamar's administration were," says General Hunt, "made in anticipation of the sale of the five million of bonds which were authorized by one law, and the one million·authorized by another, and the sanguine assurances from time to time of General Hamilton that he certainly expected to succeed in the sale of the five million bonds which he and Mr. Burnley were empowered to sell."

These sanguine expectations were common among the Texans, but on what ground they rested it is difficult to imagine. A government's ability to pay interest is the measure of its ability to borrow; and its ability to pay interest is determined by the amount in which its ordinary revenue exceeds its ordinary expenses. The revenue of Texas fell far below what was necessary for the support of even its civil establishment. To be sure, it had lands, and a prospective ability to pay, after peace should be made with Mexico; but the experience of British capitalists in the Greek, the Chilian, the Peruvian, the Mexican, and other foreign loans, had taught them that it was not safe to rely on the prospective ability of revolutionary governments. The American Congress of 1776 effected no loans abroad from private capitalists, or none but such as were guaranteed by the governments of France, Spain, or Holland, and even then to the amount of only $7,000,000 or $8,000,000. If General Hamilton had at any time a prospect of success, it was not because the moneyed men of Europe regarded as adequate such security as Texas could, offer, but because the French Government was disposed to add thereto its guarantee, in prosecution of its design of establishing close commercial and political connection with the rising Republic.

The Texan Government effected, in a direct way, loans abroad amounting in all to less than five hundred thousand dollars, viz.: the Triplet loan of $20,070, negotiated at New Orleans January 11, 1836; the Erwin loan of $45,820, negotiated in the same city and in the same year, January 16; some money lent by Samuel Swartwout, and others, amounting in all to $7,970 43; and the loan obtained from the United States Bank, the par value of which is set down by the comptroller at $400,000. Instead of wondering that the amount was so small, we should wonder that it was so large. That the United States Bank lent so much, was not owing to its riches, but to its poverty. It was at that time living by expedients, and one of the chief of these was getting possession of State and corporation stocks, and pledging them in Europe. The loan to Texas was intended to aid General Hamilton's operation in Europe, by showing that the rising Republic had some credit in America, with an ultimate view of establishing, out of the five or seven million dollars to be obtained from France, a national bank in Texas, which, under Mr. Jaudon's management, should act as a tender to the Pennsylvania Bank of the United States. The scheme was well contrived; but the fates determined it should not succeed. And yet Texas reaped the benefit of it in a loan of four hundred thousand dollars, which she could not otherwise have obtained.

Another illusion under which the Texans labored was as to the efficiency of their public lands as a means of supporting public credit and paying public debts. In a political point of view, wild lands are of great importance. If England and France had at their doors as extensive territories as have the United States, England and France would be prosperous and happy in spite of their monarchical institutions, their nobility systems, their church establishments, their large armies, their expensive navies, their heavy public debts, and all the accumulated corruptions of ages. In a politico-economic point of view, also, is land of great importance. It is an essential element of all wealth. Even if a man's business is polishing diamonds, he must have land, at least enough to stand upon. But in a commercial point of view, land is of little or no value, unless labor has been bestowed upon it or near it. The experience of the United States had shown that, even with the influx of emigrants from Europe, from two to three million acres per year of the public lands were all that was required on an average for purposes of cultivation. The amount of sales never exceeded this except when, in periods of bank inflation, speculation was directed to the public domain.

The Texan Government bestowed its lands with so much profusion on soldiers and settlers as to supply all demands, not only for cultivation but for speculation, for many years to come. It was, therefore, unreasonable in the Texan Government to regard its public lands as immediate means of great revenue, or as likely to afford much aid in supporting public credit. Yet, such was the infatuation on this subject, that we find even Samuel Houston, two years after the war commenced, speaking of the opening of the land-offices as 'almost certain to produce "boundless revenue to the Republic."

From this source, as well as from foreign loans, the Texans, after all, derived more aid than they had any right to expect. The sales of land were small, and the fees paid into the land-offices were small. But the Triplet and the Erwin loans were both repaid with lands; and the much-abused agencies at Mobile and New Orleans, if they did nothing else, helped to sustain the credit of Texan paper by redeeming treasury notes with land-script.

One characteristic of the revolutionary legislation of Texas was frequent changes in its revenue system. One scheme failing, another was tried. But even before opportunity was afforded to try some of the schemes, others were substituted. In some instances, a customs act had hardly time to reach the more distant sea-ports, before it would be made to give place to another. In the ten years Texas existed as an independent Republic, it had no less than seven distinct tariffs.

Almost as many changes were made in their plans of internal revenue; and the statesmen of Texas seem to have wondered that they all produced nothing, or next to nothing. But they ought not to have wondered. The most experienced financier would have found it difficult to collect a revenue of any amount from a community so small as the Texans, scattered over a large territory of one to every three or four square miles, and whose industry was liable to frequent interruptions from alarms of incursions by the Mexicans and the Indians. Even to assess taxes, in such a community, was an undertaking of no small difficulty. Much more difficult was it to collect them. Even in some cases where the taxes were assessed, it was found necessary to remit the payment of them, in whole counties, owing to what they had suffered from incursions of the enemy.

In most countries of Europe and in the United States, the collection of taxes goes on with the regularity of clock-work; but this is the result of long years of laborious preparation. When the Governments of Pennsylvania and of Maryland were compelled, owing to the breaking of the banks, to suspend the payment of interest on their public debts, or pay only in inconvertible paper, they found that new systems of internal revenue were necessary. But several years elapsed before they could bring their new systems into successful operation, and thus re-establish their credit.

Another marked feature in Texas revolutionary legislation was frequent changes of the public tender. "Your father hath deceived me, and hath changed my wages ten times," said Jacob to the sons of Laban. An equally strong complaint might have been made by those who had dealings with the Texan Government. These changes were so numerous that we cannot introduce them into the text, and must refer the reader to the synopsis of them in Appendix M.

All these changes of tender, changes in revenue laws, and all the other particulars that have been pointed out in the fiscal system of Texas, were, it may be said, necessary, as growing out of the state of the times, the people, and the country. In one sense of the word, whatever occurs is necessary, that is, it is the necessary effect of some pre-existing cause. Whenever there is vice or ignorance, there will be folly. The last is the necessary consequence of the two first. We pretend not to say that other men would have done better than did those who had the control of affairs in Texas. Nine men in ten would perhaps have done quite as bad, and some worse. But what we affirm is that, under a sound financial system (supposing it possible to have adopted it), Texas might have come out of the contest with only one-twelfth part of the debt she is now under a moral obligation to discharge.

If such a system had been adopted, there would have been economy in everything. No debts would then have been incurred
except for services and supplies indispensably necessary; for then,
only in cases where they were indispensably necessary, would the
people of Texas have furnished the required supplies and services.
There would not then have been one officer for every ordinary seaman in the Texan navy, and one officer for· every soldier in the
Texan army. The wild-goose expedition to Santa Fé would never
have been undertaken, and that to Meir would have perished in
the brains of its projector. A conciliatory policy towards the
Indians would have been adopted, and they would have been made
friends instead of enemies. Let the people be made to feel immediately but a part of the burden which public expenditure imposes,
and that expenditure will be brought within moderate limits. But
let the weight of this burden be postponed, or let its nature be con-
cealed from them by the issue of paper intended to pass as money,
and there will be no limit to the folly and extravagance of their
rulers, except such as is imposed by the depreciation of the paper.

Issues of paper intended to pass as money, and to which currency is given by making them receivable for public dues, afford
so easy a way of relieving immediate embarrassments, that ma-
nagers of fiscal concerns are under frequent temptations to resort
to them. But such temporary relief must, unless circumstances
are peculiar, increase subsequent embarrassments.

When a government issues small notes intended to pass as
money, and makes them receivable for public dues, it takes the last
step downwards in public credit. It has then no efficient revenue.
All it then does by means of its collectors of customs, and its collectors of taxes, is to redeem part of its floating debt ; and this
very act of redemption renders necessary the creation of a new
floating debt of equal amount with that redeemed.

Such a government can no longer negotiate a stock loan with
advantage, for it has no longer a revenue in specie wherewith to
pay the interest.

Nations who wish to borrow may learn wisdom from the British
Government. It has run in debt to the amount of four thousand
million dollars. It borrows on exchequer bills, or treasury notes,
as well as stocks ; but it always takes care that its exchequer bills
shall be for considerable amounts, and that they shall bear such a

rate of interest as will leave no inducement to the merchants to pay them in for duties. It always has a revenue in something distinct from its own paper, and thus has the means of supporting its credit.

The only safe mode for the United States Government to borrow is by means of stock loans of gold and silver, and treasury notes of such denominations (never less than fifty dollars) as will prevent their becoming a common circulating medium, and bearing such a rate of interest as will make them eligible investments. If these treasury notes are, in the aggregate, of any large amount, provision should be made to exchange them for stocks of long date, rather than attempt to redeem them by receiving them in payment of customs and other dues.

For want of strict attention to these principles, the United States Government was, in the war with Mexico, though that lasted but a short time, and though it pressed but lightly on the real resources of the country, brought into temporary though not serious embarrassment. Owing to a rise in the rate of commercial interest, the merchants found it to their advantage to pay in treasury notes, rather than gold or silver. The result was that, in some of the most important treasury offices, the amount of gold and silver was so reduced as but slightly to exceed the outstanding drafts against them. It was with difficulty that the daily expenditures were kept down to a level with the daily receipts. At one time there was even a talk of paying the salaries of the clerks in the departments with treasury notes. Fortunately, this state of things was but of short continuance. If it had lasted any time, it would have injuriously affected the price of United States securities in the market, and would have had an equally injurious effect on the negotiation of permanent loans, had any at that time been necessary.

The British Government seldom has afloat less than seventy-five million dollars in exchequer bills, and the amount frequently rises to one hundred and fifty millions ; but when it finds the rate of commercial interest rising, it raises the rate of interest on its exchequer bills. It thus prevents their being paid in for public dues, and thus escapes those embarrassments to which the United States Government has from time to time been subject.

CHAPTER XXIII.

PROCEEDINGS UNDER THE FIRST LEGISLATURE OF THE STATE OF TEXAS: 1845–46.

Improved condition of fiscal affairs—State constitution adopted—Government of the State *ad interim*—Immediate benefits of annexation—First meeting of the Legislature—Reports to the House and Senate in favor of ceding the public lands to the United States, as a means of paying the public debt—Scaling of the debt recommended—Its injustice—Instances in which the Governments of England and the United States have engaged to pay more than they received—Texas borrowed on good terms, all circumstances considered—Men who have bought Texan securities might have done better by other investments.

By the time annexation was effected, Texas may, in one sense, be said to have worked through her pecuniary difficulties. She had, indeed, a heavy public debt hanging over her; but, as she had for the three preceding years given over all attempts to pay either principal or interest, it caused her no immediate perplexity.

For the three years ending September 30, 1844, her expenditures were $511,083, equal to $170,361 a year. The amount was small; but, small as it was, it exceeded the aggregate of the receipts, in these three years, in the sum of $44,398 58.

In the fourteen months intervening between November 1, 1844, and January 1, 1846, her receipts amounted to $321,432 43, and then, for the first time in her history, did the revenue of Texas exceed her expenditure. The surplus was, indeed, not large, but any surplus was remarkable.

That she had such surplus was owing to her retaining the custom-house revenues till October 1, 1845, or for three months after her Convention had accepted the terms of annexation offered by the United States.

This Convention, as has been stated in a previous chapter, assented, on the 4th of July, 1845, to the term of annexation. They also adopted a constitution for the State of Texas, which was submitted to and approved by the people on the second Monday in October, 1845. But the new State Government did not fairly commence till February, 1846, when the first Legislature assembled.

There was thus, for several months, a kind of government *ad interim*, and this was favorable to Texas, as, though protected in that time by the United States forces, she still derived a revenue from her import duties. This advantage did not cease with the year, as the arrears of the customs yielded her a net revenue of fifty-one thousand two hundred and six dollars and thirteen cents, between the 19th of February, 1846, and the 31st of December, 1847, and some small sums in subsequent years. The precise time when the United States customs acts took effect in Texas is yet to be decided by the United States courts.

The benefits of annexation were felt immediately in increased immigration, and in the expenditures made by the United States Government for purposes of defence. The war with Mexico was, in a pecuniary point of view, of great advantage to Texas. Her citizens could not, indeed, supply any large amount of provisions to the army or the navy, but the transportation of troops and stores was to them great gain.

The first Legislature met at Austin February 16, 1846, and the subject of the public debt early engaged its attention. A report by a select committee appears to have been made March 1, though it was not read till April 1. A part of this we shall extract:—

"The committee to whom was referred the resolution of the House to inquire into the expediency of ceding the public lands to the United States, for a just equivalent, for the purpose of providing means for the discharge of the public debt, and to inquire into the propriety of classifying and defining the debt, and of organizing a board to ascertain and adjudicate upon the same, having considered each proposition, present the following report:—

"It is now more than ten years since Texas achieved and established her independence by a successful revolution. When she was driven into that revolution by the oppression of the Mexican Government, her population was extremely small, scattered over a widely extended territory, with little wealth, few sources of taxation, and, as a consequence, but ill able to procure the means to support a government, and sustain the military operations which the defence of the country demanded. The military service of the country diverting so large a proportion of the population from the industrial avocations of life, rendered it impossible for the government to draw any adequate revenues from its own population. In this state of things, many of the ardent friends of Texan independence, at home and abroad, stepped forward and advanced their money for the relief of the urgent wants of the country, at a time when doubt hung over the result of the contest.

"Texas came triumphantly out of the struggle, with less loss of blood and treasure than has ever attended a revolution of as much magnitude in the annals of history; but yet it has entailed upon her a considerable debt, which is strongly recommended to our sense of justice and honor for the earliest practicable payment. Your committee are confident the people of Texas feel keenly the weight of this obligation, and are anxious to meet it, although most revolutionary governments have been singularly disregardful of debts contracted under similar circumstances. Unfortunately, however, for Texas, owing to the peculiar condition of her past public affairs, her population has not increased with the rapidity which might have been anticipated from the salubrity of her climate and the fertility of her soil. Her resources and ability for raising revenue from direct taxation cannot, for many years to come, exceed the urgent and indispensable wants of her domestic administration. Nor can it be denied that annexation, however important and advantageous to this country in other respects, has, by destroying the revenue arising from the customs, taken from us a growing source of revenue, which might, in a short time, have afforded efficient means of providing for the public creditors. However strong, therefore, may be the desire of the country to provide for its creditors, it has no ability of doing so except through the means of the public lands. They can be made available for that purpose only by ceding them to the Government of the United States, in such a manner as to realize the money, or cash securities, or by making them the bases of land-script, to be located and surveyed by the public creditor at his own expense. For many reasons, the committee think the former course will prove the most advantageous both for the Government of the United States and the people of Texas."

The committee then state that Texas has not even the means of surveying these lands, the cost of which would be $500,000, and give a variety of reasons, political and pecuniary, to show that it would be to the advantage of the Federal Government to purchase them. But if the United States should not purchase them, they recommend that the public creditors

"Should be called upon to exchange their securities and evidences of debt for land-script, as the only means which the State would have to pay her public debt. And although such a measure would fall far short of the wish of Texas to protect her creditors, and would doubtless occasion much injustice and suffering in many instances, yet she would appeal to the civilized world, that she had performed all in her power to redeem her public engagements, and maintain her national faith."

* * * * * * * *

"Texas does not ask the United States to assume her public debt. She proposes, it is true, with the proceeds of such sale, honestly and faithfully to pay the debt, and pledges herself to that effect; but the two propositions are independent and distinct. Over the last, neither the agency nor control of the United States is invoked. Texas will determine what her debt is, and to whom it is due, and the proceeds of the land with which she pays it is the *property* of Texas, and not of the United States, and must pass to the treasury of the former, if no creditor should appear."

Thus far, no sentiment was uttered but such as must be approved by the reader. The debt was honorably admitted to be due, and every disposition evinced to pay it, so far as it was possible for Texas to accomplish this object with such means as she possessed, or could procure by means of a sale of her lands to the United States. But the residue of the report shows that the public mind in Texas had by this time become familiarized with the idea of repudiation, first brought forward by Mr. Secretary Chalmers, under the form of scaling the interest :—

"2. *The ascertainment and classification of the public debt.* The fact that the debt was contracted during a revolutionary struggle constitutes no reason, in the opinion of the committee, why we should not pay it in honesty and good faith. They, nevertheless, think that she should be bound to return to the public creditors only what, according to just average, they paid for her securities, with the rate of interest stipulated in the bond, or other evidence of debt; they have endeavored to place the scheme of classification on the broad basis of paying back with interest to every man every dollar advanced to her service or invested in the faith of her securities. They have made as near an approximation to truth and justice as so complicated a subject was susceptible of; but that there may occur some cases of individual hardship in carrying out any method of classification, they cannot doubt."

Here it appears that the committee proposed that Texas should pay, not what she had promised to pay, but what she had, according to their estimate, actually received. It was a pity this was not understood at first, for then she would have received nothing. No man would have given fifty cents, twenty, or even ten cents in the dollar for her paper if he had clearly understood that, after waiting an indefinite time, and with great uncertainty, he should ultimately receive no more than he gave. If Texas meant, when she issued her treasury notes and other obligations, to pay no more than one-half, one-fourth, or one-fifth of their face value, she ought to have said so. Then nobody would have lent to her.

What is called "interest" is made up of two distinct items, "rent or usage," and "insurance." Just in proportion as the risk of non-payment increases, does the rate of insurance rise. This shows itself, in the case of negotiable securities, in the ratio which the price offered bears to their face value. As Texas continued to issue her promises to pay, they fell in value, because every addition she made to her outstanding obligations diminished the chances of ultimate repayment. Hence her securities fell from par to fifty cents on the dollar, to thirty cents, to twenty cents, to sixteen cents.

With just as much reason might a merchant, having insured a ship at sea in a stormy time, and on a dangerous coast, afterwards refuse to pay the insurance when the ship is brought safely into port, as Texas now refuse to pay the insurance she engaged to give to those who, in an " exceedingly dark and gloomy period," risked their all in her securities.

Admit the principle which Texas has adopted, and it strikes a blow at the very foundation of public credit. No government could then borrow except under the most favorable circumstances, for it is only under such circumstances that governments receive as much as they promise to give.

The rate of commercial interest is sometimes one or two per cent. a month. Then a certificate of public stock for $100 is worth as an investment for immediate income no more than $25 or $50. If public stocks bring more in such times, it is because they are regarded as permanent investments which will yield a fixed income when the rate of commercial interest falls.

In addition to fluctuations in the value of public securities caused by fluctuations in the rate of commercial interest, there are others caused by changes in the prospective necessity of governments to borrow, and their prospective ability to pay what they owe. All these causes combined cause public securities to vary in price just as sugar and coffee vary. They are, in fact, merchandise subject to like laws of supply and demand with other merchandise. If, then, when, from one or more of those causes, these securities are low in the market, a government is under the necessity of issuing more, it must expect to receive for them less than it promises to give.

The histories of all civilized countries afford abundant illustrations of these truths.

According to Dr. Hamilton, the author of *An Inquiry into the Public Debt of Great Britain*, the British Government, between the beginning of 1793 and the close of 1812, issued certificates to the amount of 573,781,887 pounds sterling, for which it received only 384,616,705 pounds. For every bond of 1000 pounds, it received only about 670. In other words, it issued stock to the amount of about $2,865,000,000, and received in return the equivalent of only $1,945,000,000. The difference in the value it received and that it promised to give was $945,000,000—more than seventy-four times as much as the gross debt of Texas.

For stocks of the amount of 259,215,875 pounds sterling (included in the total above given), it received only 158,658,000 pounds, being at the rate of 611 pounds for every certificate for 1000 pounds.

In the year 1798, the same government borrowed 15,000,000 pounds sterling, for which it had to issue stocks to the amount of 30,000,000. In other words, it received but fifty cents in the dollar on the amount of its certificates.

A still stronger case than this occurred in the year 1797, when the British Government negotiated a loan for which it had to issue 226 pounds 10 shillings in stock for every 100 pounds it received; that is, it got but forty-four cents and a fraction for every dollar expressed on the face of its obligations.

In the year 1813, the same government negotiated a loan for nearly $200,000,000, for which it got apparently about fifty-six cents in the dollar ; but, as the whole amount was received in bank paper, then at a depreciation of about twenty-five per cent., " the actual par value which was realized" was less than forty-four cents in the dollar.

If the principles adopted by Texas are correct, the British Government would, especially when we take into consideration the fact that many of its loans were negotiated in depreciated bank currency, be justifiable in repudiating two-thirds of its debt.

In the year 1813, the United States Government borrowed about fifteen million dollars, for twelve millions of which stock was issued at the rate of one hundred and twenty-five dollars for every one hundred paid in. As much of this loan was received in depreciated paper, the Treasury Department did not realize more than seven hundred dollars, perhaps not more than six hundred dollars, for every one thousand dollar certificate.

In the last annual report which Mr. Walker made, as Secretary of the Treasury, is the following passage:—

" By the report of the Committee of Ways and Means, of the House of Representatives of Congress, of the 30th of April, 1830, it appears that of the loans of the war of 1812, for eighty millions of stocks and treasury notes, the government obtained but thirty-four millions, leaving a loss of forty-six millions on its transactions."

According to this statement, the American Government realized but forty-two cents and a half in the dollar on its bonds and treasury notes. On Texan principles, it would have been justifiable in repudiating more than one-half of its debts; but it acknowledged no such principles, and paid to the uttermost farthing what it owed.

Agreeably to the report of the auditorial board of Texas, that republic realized fifty-five cents, less a fraction, in the dollar, on the whole amount of its debts. It thus did much better than did either the British Government in the wars of the French Revolution, or the United States Government in the war of 1812–14.

The truth is that Texas did much better than she had any right to expect, and much better than she could possibly have done if her creditors had had the remotest suspicion that their claims were ultimately to be scaled down on the arbitrary principles she has adopted. When the interest on public securities is not punctually paid, they always decline in value. The British and the American Governments were always punctual in the payment of interests; but the Texan Government never paid a dollar of interest except in the way of other promises to pay.

All the causes we have mentioned as depressing the price of stocks operated with combined influence on Texan securities. The rate of commercial interest was high in Texas, and also in the United States. The prospective demand of the Texan Government for more money was great. Its prospective ability to pay was small. Under these circumstances, he who gave sixteen cents in the dollar for her securities gave more than they were worth, and this is proved by the fact that they fell soon afterwards to ten, five, and even two cents in the dollar.

Other proof may be given that he who received them from the government at sixteen cents in the dollar did not make a very profitable investment, even supposing the notes to be ultimately paid in full, but supposing that payment deferred for fifteen years. The commercial rate of interest in Texas was then very high, not less than twelve per cent. Commercial profits could not then have been less than twenty per cent. The gain which a merchant makes in one year is an addition to his capital in the next. He thus, if successful, increases his wealth in the ratio of compound interest. Now, one hundred dollars invested in trade, at this rate of profit, would, in fifteen years, amount to $1,719 48, while one hundred dollars invested in treasury notes, bearing ten per cent. interest, and supposing them bought at sixteen cents in the dollar, would, in fifteen years, amount to only $1,562 50. But at the time we are speaking of, the rate of interest in Texas was much nearer two or three per cent. a month than twelve per cent. per annum; and the profits of trade were correspondingly high. Many a man might, by investing his money in merchandise, have made as much in two or three years as by investing in treasury notes at sixteen cents in the dollar in fifteen years, even if these notes should be paid in full.

Many a man, by investing his money in lands in Texas, might have made more money than by investing them in treasury notes. Lands could then be bought in Texas at ten and fifteen cents which have since sold at five and ten dollars per acre. In this way a hundred dollars invested in lands might have been made to produce from $3,300 to $10,000.

Certain it is that many men in the United States have, out of very small capitals, made in the last fifteen years very large fortunes. But whether those who were so unfortunate as to make investments in Texan securities would have lost or gained by investments in other ways, is not the question. The question is, whether Texas has a right to violate her contracts simply because she did not receive two or three, or four or five times as much for her notes and bonds as anybody would then have given. We maintain that she has not. Her securities were sold in the open market. She got full value for them. She got for them far more than any cautious man ought to have been willing to give. And she is bound to pay the full amount she promised to pay, for it was through the most solemn promises to pay the full amount, and through them only, that she got what she actually received.

Instances of repudiation have occurred both in Europe and America; but never on the ground assumed by Texas. Former instances of repudiation have been, because the debts were contracted in violation of law or constitution; because gross frauds were perpetrated in the negotiation of loans; or because the government was not able to meet its obligations. But Texas makes none of these pleas. She repudiates simply because her commodities, her promises to pay, did not, when she offered them for sale in open market, bring from two to five times as much as they were worth.

On the 24th of March, a committee of the Senate made a report in favor of selling the public lands to the United States. It was similar in tenor to that read to the House :—

" They deem it is now the most important object to be consummated by the State of Texas, the adjustment and payment of the debt contracted by and under the Government of the Republic of Texas; a measure necessary for the redemption of plighted faith, from which no people should feel themselves relieved by change of government, and necessary in order that justice may be administered to those holding claims against the Republic of Texas ; many of whom have rendered timely and essential services at an important crisis."

All this is very good. But in what, in the opinion of the committee, " the administration of justice consisted," and what was necessary for " the redemption of plighted faith, from which no people should be released," will be seen in that which follows :—

" Nevertheless, your committee are clearly of opinion that there should be a legislative classification of all debts against the Republic of Texas ; and to each should be awarded such relief and payment as is due, according to the merits of each creditor ; for your committee cannot consent that the parties who have advanced cash and important services to Texas shall be placed on equal footing with those who hold the liabilities of the Republic of Texas, for which they have paid not more than twenty cents in the dollar, and for which Texas received perhaps a less amount, as it is notorious and universally admitted that a great portion of the liabilities now in circulation were issued and paid out at about sixteen cents in the dollar."

The committee reported " An act to Classify the Liabilities of the Republic of Texas," in which a distinction was made between original holders of claims and others. And another, entitled " An act for the Discharge of the Public Debt of the Republic of Texas," on the scaling principle supported by the House committee.

This was not the first time in the legislation of Texas that an attempt was made to draw a distinction between original holders of claims and those to whom they might be transferred. The reasons for such a distinction may, at first glance, seem plausible, but they are, in reality, contrary to all the sound principles of finance, and also of natural justice. The obligation to pay a debt is not in the least diminished by the evidence thereof changing owners. If a note or a bond issued by an individual, a bank, or a government, passes through five hundred hands, not one cent of the amount for which it has been given is thereby discharged. The obligation to pay the full amount is as complete when it is in the hands of the last holder as when it was in the hands of the first.

Negotiable securities owe much of their value to the facility with which they can be transferred. Few men would be willing to receive treasury notes, if it should be made a condition that they should be receivable for public dues, or payable in full to those only to whom they were originally issued. Still fewer would be willing to purchase stocks having many years to run, if it were made a condition that a deduction should be made from the annual interest, and ultimately from the principal, if the demand were made by any other than the original holder. But men are now willing to purchase both treasury notes and stocks, because they know that, when it is no longer convenient to hold them as investments, they can transfer their claim to others at its full value, whatever that value may be in the market.

If an individual, a bank, or a government, does, by refusal or delay to pay interest or principal as agreed on, make it necessary for the original or any other holder of a note or a bond to dispose of it to a disadvantage, he has a claim, in equity, for damages against the defaulting individual, bank, or government. On these principles, an immense number of suits might be brought against Texas, if it were possible to sue a sovereign State. But if all these damages should be paid in full, that would not in the least diminish the obligation to pay the original debt. Those who got the evidences at second or third hand paid for them what was then their full value.

To their transferable nature, the Texan securities owed much of the little value they at times possessed. And many an original claimant derived more advantage from parting with them, even at less than he gave for them, than he would have derived from holding them. A government security for one hundred dollars, bearing no interest (and such were the Texan "red backs"), and not paid till sixteen years after date, is, in a country where interest is at the rate of twelve per cent., worth, money in hand, but a fraction more than sixteen cents in a dollar.

But mere figures will not show all the disadvantages that the original claimants under the Texan Government would have sustained, if they could not have disposed of their evidences of government debt even, in some instances, for much less than they cost them.   The neglect to pay a single note when it is due may break up what might otherwise be a long train of profitable mercantile operations.   The inability to procure a few farming implements may cause hundreds of acres to lie desolate which otherwise might have been successfully cultivated.   Nay, many of the original holders of claims might have seen their families starving before them, if they could not have disposed of those claims to second and third parties.

The merchants of Texas received the evidences of public debt from the original holders, and disposed of them in the United States.   This enabled them to replenish their stock of goods, and thus grant supplies to the planters and farmers.   Through all the first years of their revolutionary struggle, the Texans were fed and clothed by means of transfers of the evidences of the public debt from the hands of the original holders.   Regarded in this point of view, as a merchant of Houston once remarked to us, no country ever derived more advantage from its public debt than did Texas.

But, we repeat it, whether this advantage was great or small is not properly the question.   The question is, whether Texas shall pay in full the debts she over and over solemnly promised to pay—debts which she never talked of scaling till her credit was sunk so low that she could borrow no more.   We contend that she is morally bound to pay to the uttermost farthing what she contracted to pay, no matter in whose hands the evidences of the debt are now found, and that, if she will not pay, she must share the disgrace that properly attaches to individuals, corporations, and governments that can pay their debts, and will not.

CHAPTER XXIV.

PROCEEDINGS UNDER THE SECOND LEGISLATURE: 1847–48.

The scaling policy sustained—The fact that the debt is due to persons abroad urged as one reason why it should not be paid in full—Act " to provide for ascertaining the debt of the late Republic of Texas"—Creditors ordered to bring in their claims to be scaled.

THE first Legislature of the State of Texas took the stand that a distinction should be made between original holders and assignees of the evidences of public debt, and that the gross amount should be scaled down one-half. The second Legislature, which assembled at Austin December 13, 1847, maintained the same stand.

On the 29th of December, the Governor, George T. Wood, sent in a message, in which he recommended a sale of public land to the United States, and the payment of the public debt by scaling, as had been urged by the committees of the previous legislature.

" As to our means of payment, our large and valuable public domain is the only ready resource we have.

" Our debt must be paid. The honor of the State must stand without blemish. We can never expect to attain a high and permanent prosperity until it is done; and the consummation of a purpose so noble calls for united and energetic action."

Scaling a debt, however, as recommended by Governor Wood, is not paying it. It is at best but *compromising* it. Necessity may induce creditors to accept terms by which they forego one-half of their claims; but if any State forces such a compromise on its creditors, " its honor cannot stand without blemish."

Texas, it may be admitted, has power, as a sovereign State, to determine, in the first instance, the amount of her debt, and to whom it is due; but she has no moral right to do wrong. As there is no Supreme Court before which her acts can be brought for adjudication, her creditors have no legal appeal from even her most unrighteous decision. In the exercise of her sovereignty, she can repudiate the whole of her debt as readily as one-half of it. Her political power in the premises is not disputed. But if she thus violates all the principles of natural justice and the laws of nations, she cannot expect her "honor to stand without blemish."

Her creditors will have a right to complain, although their oppressor may be a sovereign State. As one of her great men said, in an early period of her history, "Nations, as well as individuals, are amenable for their acts to the general opinion of mankind;" and Texas will sensibly feel this, if she persists in the violation of her plighted faith.

January 24th, 1848, a special committee made a report, in which they said:—

"It is, in their opinion, impossible to adopt any rule for the graduation of the liabilities of the late Republic, without doing a seeming injustice to a few individuals. * * * From these considerations, your committee have discarded the idea of even attempting to do all justice in a pecuniary way."

From this, it appears that the Texan authorities, from the very moment in which they began to apply their scaling principles, found it impossible to do even what they esteemed "justice to all," and when the report of the auditor and comptroller comes under review, it will be found that it is impossible on such principles to do justice to any.

"Your committee are fully of opinion that, of the audited evidences of indebtedness, not one-hundredth part are now in the hands of those to whom they were originally paid out by the government, but have been in circulation throughout the State ; and further, that it is probable that nine-tenths of its liabilities have found their way out of the State, and have been in circulation in other States, subject to the caprice of brokers and others, whose profession is to take advantage of the necessities and misfortunes of individuals, as well as nations, at various rates of discount. Your committee are therefore clearly of opinion that to graduate our liabilities, under these circumstances, will violate no principles of moral rectitude, but on the contrary is dictated by the soundest principles of justice, as well to the citizens of the country as to the creditor.

The reader will recollect that, as long as there was any necessity for Texas to borrow, the fact that great part of the debt was held in other States was regarded as an advantage ; but now, when the time comes for payment, it is conceived it will "violate no principle of moral rectitude" to cut down the debt one-half, inasmuch as "nine-tenths of the liabilities have found their way out of the State" !

The vulgar prejudice against stock and exchange brokers is, moreover, here embodied in a legislative report. It may be that some of them "take advantage of the necessities and misfortunes of individuals;" but if so, they in this only resemble some who are engaged in other branches of business. If there were no regular dealers in stocks, foreign bank-notes, and other negotiable securities, the fluctuations in the prices of these articles would be much greater than they are at present. The brokers in the United States did much more to prevent than to cause fluctuations in the price of "red backs" and other Texan vendibles.

"There is another difference between your committee and the comptroller, and that is in regard to interest on the promissory notes that were not intended to draw interest when they were issued. Your committee cannot consent to allow interest on these notes, as the holders or receivers had no right to, and consequently could not have expected interest on them. They were issued under the provisions of a law which expressly stated that they should not draw interest."

But they were not paid when they fell due, and, therefore, according to mercantile usage, interest on them commenced on the very day on which they were dishonored. They were, moreover, issued under a pledge that they should be received in payment of customs. In violation of its public faith, the Texan Government afterwards refused to receive them, and thus deprived these notes of much of the value they originally possessed. If Texas means to do justice to her creditors, she must allow interest on her "red backs."

In conformity with the principles expressed in the documents from which we have made quotations, an act was passed "to provide for ascertaining the debt of the late Republic of Texas." This divided the debt into three classes, including, in the first class, all claims which had been "audited or otherwise ascertained" at the time the law was passed; in the second class, "claims sufficiently authenticated to admit them to audit;" and, in the third class, claims which were known to exist, but which were not then "sufficiently authenticated to authorize their being audited under the laws of the late Republic." This law is of so much importance that we must give it at length.

"SECTION 1. *Be it enacted by the Legislature of the State of Texas,* That the auditor and comptroller of public accounts, as soon as practicable after the passage of this act, shall cause six months' notice to be given, by publication in some newspaper published weekly in the city of Austin, New Orleans, Washington City, and New York, requiring all persons having any claim or demand for money against the late Republic of Texas, to present the same to the auditor and comptroller of public accounts on or before the second Monday in November, 1849; and all claims that shall not be presented on or before that time shall be postponed.

" SECTION 2. *Be it further enacted*, That it shall be the duty of the auditor and comptroller jointly to receipt, under their seals of office, for all claims presented to them, setting forth the par value thereof, at the time the same accrued or were issued; the name of the person to whom the debt accrued, the date and amount thereof. The auditor and comptroller shall each keep a correct list, in books kept for that purpose, separately. First, the audited or ascertained claims, such as stock bonds, treasury notes, military script, or any other audited or ascertained claim. Second, àll claims with sufficient evidence and vouchers to authorize them to audit, under the late Republic of Texas. Thirdly, such claims as are not sufficiently authenticated by vouchers. It is hereby made the duty of the auditor and comptroller to report to the next session of the Legislature for its action.

"SECTION 3. *Be it further enacted*, That it shall be the duty of the comptroller and auditor jointly to report to the next biennial session of the Legislature, for final adjustment, the whole amount and character of the public debt ascertained, according to the provisions of this act, together with such suggestions concerning the same as they may deem just and proper; and they shall likewise report, semi-annually, from the first of May, 1848, to the Governor, the amount and character of claims presented and filed in their office; and it shall be the duty of the Governor to cause a synopsis of the report to be printed in some newspaper at the seat of government in the State.

"SECTION 4. *Be it further enacted*, That it shall be the duty of the auditor and comptroller of public accounts to classify all claims presented under the provisions of this act, reducing the same to the actual par value which may have been realized by the late Republic, and may report such further classification as they may deem best calculated to preserve the rights of the State, and to do equity to the holders of the claims: and the classification and rate of payment recommended by the auditor and comptroller shall be subject to the revision, amendment, and ratification of the next Legislature: and that this act take effect from and after its passage."

"Approved March 20, 1848."

Thus did Texas compel, or try to compel, her creditors to bring in their claims to be scaled down to one-half, one-fourth, or one-fifth of their original amount. Far different was the conduct of the United States Government when, in 1791, it passed a law to fund the revolutionary debt. So far was it from using compulsion, that it expressly enacted that such of its creditors as were not willing to accept the terms offered should be paid the same rate of interest as those that did accept.

An attempt has been made to justify this proceeding of Texas, under the plea that a sovereign State has "a right to define its debts." This cannot be either disputed or denied. But the debts of Texas were sufficiently "defined" in the laws under which they were incurred, and the acknowledgments issued to the creditors. Nothing can possibly be more "definite" than Texas's promise to pay dollars as expressed in her treasury notes, bonds, certificates of stock, and audited paper. In some cases, she "defined" the same debt as many as three times. She first passed the debts through regular audit, and granted drafts or certificates acknowledging the amount due to each creditor. Then she redeemed those drafts by giving in lieu of them treasury notes of the same amount. Then, in order to get these floating liabilities out of the hands of the holders, she funded them at par. Thus she, in three different forms, at three different times, acknowledged the amount due, which was, we think, "defining" them with sufficient exactness for all practical purposes. After this, to call in these evidences of debt, and scale them down to a small part of their original amount, and then sustain this proceeding under the pretext that Texas has "a right to define her debt" "by her municipal regulations" is to be very delicate in the use of language. The true name of the thing is "repudiation," and they who support the principle ought not to be ashamed of the word.

CHAPTER XXV.

PROCEEDINGS UNDER THE THIRD LEGISLATURE: 1849–50.

Governor Wood recommends that land be given to the public creditors—Reasons why Texas had no longer a deep interest in sustaining her credit—Hardships endured by civil officers, by soldiers, and others—Distinction between their cases and that of contract creditors—Auditor and comptroller make a report scaling down the claims of creditors to half their original amount—Time prolonged in which audited claims might be scaled without being "barred"—Audited claims made exchangeable for land-script at fifty cents an acre—Act declaring that all liabilities of the Republic shall cease to bear interest after July 1, 1850.

THE third Legislature met at Austin November 5, 1849, and on the next day Governor Wood sent them a message, some passages of which will be interesting to the reader :—

"The subject of our public debt is one of great importance, and in our situation so difficult as to forbid the hope that any action which may be taken upon the subject will be satisfactory to all parties, unless the United States should purchase a portion of our domain.

"Our only resource for the payment of the debt is our public lands.

"A large portion of our public domain lies remote from, and is inconveniently situated with reference to, the present settled and organized portion of our State, and of consequence is rendered of far less value and importance to the State than it is intrinsically worth. This territory would seem to be of great value and importance to the United States, viewed with reference to the purposes which it would serve that government in her settling her Indians, and in acquiring a complete jurisdiction over all her Indian relations, now rendered so difficult and complicated, by the fact that she has no jurisdiction over the soil. If, therefore, the United States Government should be disposed to purchase this territory for a fair consideration, I should conceive it to be the interest of the State so to dispose of it.

"The State has no disposition to evade the payment of her debt, and would sacrifice much rather than that history should record such a reproach against her. Nevertheless, it is not to be expected, nor is it our duty to sacrifice too much to this end. The only fund to which reasonable men ever looked for the payment of this debt was her public lands. To have expected twenty thousand tax-payers to discharge it from taxation on their own industry and wealth was an absurdity too gross to have been ever entertained.

"It is conceived that, if Texas makes proper provision by which the holders of her debt can convert it into land at fair rates, the State will not have failed in furnishing to the world the highest evidence of her disposition to pay it."

Let it be that " the only fund to which reasonable men [in Texas] ever looked for the payment of this debt was her public lands," such of her creditors as resided without the bounds of the Republic could not be supposed to be equally knowing. The Texan Government promised to pay them *money*, and they had a right to expect what was promised. Whether the money was procured by sale of lands, or by taxation, was to them matter of indifference. The calculations of the Texan Secretaries of the Treasury of the overflowing revenue that was to be, were well adapted to bolster up their hopes, and so were the expectations so confidently entertained that a loan would be negotiated in Europe. It was natural to expect that a part of this money would be applied to redeeming a portion of the floating debt, and paying the interest on the funded. Even supposing the whole five millions used in founding a national bank, as the said bank would have operated exclusively on national funds, and been closely connected with the national government, it could hardly have failed to have a favorable influence, for a time at least, on the price of the public securities of the Republic.

" The State," says Governor Wood, " has no disposition to evade the payment of her debt."

By this he meant paying just such an amount, and in just such form as the State might prescribe.

" And," he continued, " the State would sacrifice much rather than that history should record such a reproach against her. Nevertheless, it is not to be expected, nor is it our duty to sacrifice too much to this end."

The "sacrifice" contemplated, if sacrifice it could be called, was a very small one. If we are correctly informed, when the scaling system was projected, it was intended to pay the public creditors the reduced amount of their claims in lands at two dollars an acre, when at that very time land-script was selling in the streets of Austin at fifteen cents an acre. Had this scheme been carried out, the owner of eight per cent. bonds would, after finding his claim reduced to twenty cents in the dollar by the scaling process, have next found himself paid, not in money, but in a commodity worth not one-sixth the price at which he would have been compelled to receive it. The owner of a bond for one hundred dollars would then have been paid, not one hundred dollars in gold or silver, but land-script for fifty acres of the market value of seven dollars and fifty cents.

It may seem strange that a government which was always professing a desire honorably to fulfil its engagements should ever have entertained such a project; but for the state of feeling which then prevailed, various reasons may be given :—

1. As Texas was no longer an independent Republic, she no longer had a deep interest in sustaining her credit. If she had remained an independent Republic, the inability to negotiate a loan might, in some crises, have endangered her national existence. As a member of the American Union, ability to borrow was no longer necessary, though it might sometimes be convenient. The Federal Government was bound to protect her against foreign foes, and against attacks from the Indians. One of the Secretaries of the Treasury, under the Republic, had made a proposition to scale down, not the principal, but the interest. But it was not acted upon by the Congress. No measures of this kind were ever taken by the Government of the Republic. But in the very first Legislature of the State, the scaling principle was adopted, and it has been adhered to to this day.

2. At this time, the debtor interest was completely predominant in Texas. Nine-tenths of the public liabilities, as was declared in one of the legislative reports, were held beyond the bounds of the State. Few, comparatively speaking, had a personal interest in seeing these debts paid. Many had a personal interest in preventing their being paid, as then they would have been compelled to contribute their portion in the form of taxes. There was nobody to plead the cause of the public creditors, as it ought to have been pleaded, before either the Legislature or the people. He would have been a bold man who had dared to stand up in defence of their rights. If a candidate for public honors, he would, in an election, have been beaten ten to one by his competitor.

3. The longer a debt remains unpaid, the weaker becomes the sense of the moral obligation it imposes. A young widow will, in the first burst of grief for her departed lord, order a costly monument. If the stonecutter presents his bill in due season, he will be paid. If he delays presenting it, he will be paid, or not paid,

according to circumstances. A clerk in the Treasury Department
was once summoned before the Secretary for not having discharged
certain personal liabilities. "What did you say to the Secretary ?"
asked a fellow-clerk. "I told him," replied the other, "that I
had no notion of bothering myself about those *old* debts." "That
is right," continued his friend; "you stick to that. Why should
you trouble yourself about your *old* debts? It is quite enough that
you pay your *new* ones."

Independence of Mexico was fully achieved. Why should the
Texans concern themselves as to who paid for it? If an old debt is
a very heavy one, such as it seems impossible, or almost impossible,
to pay, the less does it afflict the debtor, be that debtor an individual or a government. This was the precise case of the Texans.
At no time had they had the ability to pay, in money, one-tenth
part of what they owed. For years they had given over all attempts to pay, even in the indirect way of receiving their public
securities for customs and direct taxes. To ask them to pay their
public debt, according to contract, was, in their judgment, very
much like asking a man to pay a debt which had long been "barred
by the statute of limitations."

4. The creditors, both within the bounds of Texas and without
it, were so disheartened by the repeated violations of faith they
had experienced, that they seem to have made no vigorous efforts
in defence of their rights. Many of them appear to have been
willing to accept of almost anything by way of satisfaction of their
claims, even land-script, at two dollars an acre, when the market
value of the same was only fifteen cents an acre.

5. The chief reason, however, why public opinion took the direction that the debt should be paid only in part was the notion that
all that morality, justice, and religion required was that the State
should give as much as she had received; and that the obligation
to pay a debt diminished if the evidence of it had passed from the
original claimant. These notions took very firm possession of the
public mind in Texas, and they are, to this day, the chief obstacles
her creditors have to contend with.

"I was," said one gentleman, "a custom-house officer. My
salary was five dollars a day. I was paid in treasury notes. On
one occasion, I parted with such notes, of the face value of fifteen
dollars, for three cents on the dollar. Do you think that I will

ever consent that the man in whose hands these notes may now be found shall be paid fifteen dollars in full, when I received but forty-five cents?"

The case of this gentleman, it must be admitted, is a hard one; and so is that of multitudes of others of the civil officers of Texas. But the State made an express stipulation with them that they should receive their pay in treasury notes. In paying them in this kind of paper, the State fulfilled its contract with them to the letter. The treasury note itself was not a contract to pay them especially, but any one into whose hands the notes might pass. If they disposed of this contract to another for a small consideration, they have no right to complain. It was their own fault, or, it may be, their misfortune; but, whether it was through fault or misfortune that they parted with it, that does not in the least affect the validity of the claim. The man who bought a treasury note at three cents on a dollar took on himself the risk of ultimate payment, a risk which the original holder was not willing to undergo. If, fifteen years afterwards, Texas has the ability to pay the note, she ought to pay it, no matter in whose hands it may be, for such is the contract.

Some of the speculators in *Morus Multicaulis* used to calculate their losses, not by the amount of money they had actually sunk, but by what they *might* have gained if they had sold their buds and roots when the price was highest. The original holders of Texan securities, who now oppose their payment, act on similar principles. But they do not carry their principles far enough. If they will take up the *New York Price-Current*, and calculate what they *might* have gained by buying certain stocks when they were at the lowest price, and selling them when they were at the highest, they will discover that they have lost millions.

It is a most unreasonable thing in a man to be uttering his lamentations because he sold his cotton in one year at six cents a pound, when, if he had kept it only a few months, he might have got ten cents; or to bewail his misfortune in having parted with his flour at five dollars a barrel, when a year or two afterwards it rose to ten. So it is most unreasonable in the original claimants against Texas to be regretting having parted with their evidences of debt; and most unjust in them now to prevent payment being made to those who bought those evidences when the debts were regarded as desperate.

When the Legislature at Austin was discussing the propriety of paying the public creditors, an old soldier made a speech outside of the capitol, which electrified his audience. We regret that we cannot give this speech *verbatim*. The substance of it was that coming, on one occasion, to Austin, he parted with all the treasury notes and other Texan securities he had received in pay of a long term of military duty, in exchange for a little coffee, a little sugar, and a calico gown for his wife—and that a "scant pattern." At that moment a cry was raised by a woman that her child had been carried off by the Indians. He had still remaining his "head-right," or claim as a settler to a league of land. On the impulse of the moment, he gave his "head-right" to a bystander in exchange for a Spanish pony. He pursued the Indians, and recovered the child. But he could no longer enumerate Texan securities among his possessions. He concluded by saying that nothing the Legislature could do by way of paying the public debt would afford any relief to the old soldiers, as they had long since disposed of the evidence of their claims.

Not only the old soldiers and the civil officers, but all the inhabitants of Texas have cause to complain of the losses they have suffered from the folly of their revolutionary leaders, in conducting the finances of the Republic on wrong principles, in removing the seat of the government to the foot of the Cordilleras, and in provoking conflicts with the Indians for the purpose of extending the area of land-speculations. But the Texan Government never made a contract that it would refund to such of its population as would follow it into the interior the additional price they would have to pay for sugar, coffee, and other supplies, or the cost of recovering such of their children as might be stolen by the Indians. Neither did it contract to make good to the original claimants the difference between the prices at which they received evidences of the public debt, and the prices at which they might part with them.

The case of the civil officers, old soldiers, and other inhabitants of Texas is one of great hardship. That of the holders of the notes, bonds, and other obligations of the Republic is one of positive injustice. The latter are statute creditors. Regular con-

tracts have been entered into with them, and these must be fulfilled to the letter: otherwise Texas will infringe that provision of
the United States Constitution which declares that

"No State shall pass any law impairing the obligation of contracts."

If Texas has no political power to pass laws impairing the obligation of private contracts, she has no moral right to pass laws
impairing the obligation of her own contracts.

If she persists in her present course, she will also violate the
important principle, contained in the 16th Article of the Declaration of Rights, which formed part of her constitution as an independent Republic:—

"No retrospective, or ex post facto law, or law impairing the obligation
of contracts, shall be made."

She will also violate the principles of that provision of her State
constitution which declares that

"No bill of attainder, ex post facto law, retroactive law, or any law
impairing the obligations of contracts, shall be made."

The contract debts of Texas stand against her in full, broad
daylight, supported by every principle of law, human and divine.
But political leaders in Texas had to address men situated like the
custom-house officer and the old soldier whose stories we have
given, and they had no difficulty in persuading them that paying
one-half, one-fourth, or one-fifth as much as the contract called
for was all that was required by justice, morality, and religion.   If
these old custom-house officers, old soldiers, and others had retained
their original claims, they would have seen the matter in a very different light.   And if the political leaders had been as deeply interested in Texan stocks as they were in Texan lands, their oratory
would have been of a different complexion.

If an impartial observer should suppose the case to have been
simply that of "the Land-Speculators versus the Stock-Specu-
lators," he would not err greatly.   And when informed that the
land-speculating interest was to the stock-speculating interest as
one hundred to one, in both numbers and influence, he will have
no difficulty in discovering why the scaling system was adopted.

In conformity with the requisitions of the scaling act, the auditor and comptroller made a report, December 27, 1849, from
which it appeared that the creditors had, under the threat of for-

feiture which had been held out to them, brought in their claims to the amount of about $7,000,000, and that these had been scaled down to about $3,000,000. The Governor, P. H. Bell, accompanied this report with a message (Jan. 1, 1850), in which he stated that there was "a very large amount of outstanding liabilities not presented for audit, and justice would seem to demand that the holders of these liabilities should not be excluded from the *benefits* intended to be conferred by the passage of the act of 20th March, 1848."

In conformity with this recommendation, an act was passed, February 8, 1850, extending the time for presenting claims to the first Monday in September, 1851, and declaring that all claims not presented at that time should be "barred."

On the 11th of February, 1850, an act was passed by which certificates of audited claims were made exchangeable for land-script at the rate of fifty cents an acre. This was offering the creditors much better terms than, we have been informed, it was intended to offer them, when the scaling system was first projected.

The same act contained a proviso

"That all liabilities of the late Republic of Texas, whether the same have or have not been presented to the auditor and comptroller under the provisions of the act" of March 20, 1848, "shall cease to draw interest from and after the first day of July, 1850."

This was an arbitrary measure. A government that is prepared to pay the principal of a treasury note or other obligation which has arrived at maturity has a right to say that interest thereon shall cease. But a government that has suffered its notes and bonds to be dishonored has no right to say interest on them shall cease till that day on which it is prepared to pay the principal in full.

CHAPTER XXVI.

PROCEEDINGS AT FIRST SESSION OF THE THIRTY-FIRST CONGRESS OF
THE UNITED STATES: 1849–50.

Few, if any, of the creditors embrace the offer of land in payment of their claims—
Reasons for this—Difficulties about land-titles—Change in the prospects of
Texas—Motion of Mr. Benton in the United States Senate—Motion of Mr. Clay
—Extract from Mr. Clay's speech—Motion of Mr. Pearce, of Maryland—Extracts
from Mr. Pearce's speech—Passage of the "Boundary Bill," or bill for drawing
the line between Texas and New Mexico, and for paying the creditors of Texas.

WE have noted the fact that the Legislature had, at its last session, passed an act authorizing the holders of audited claims to exchange them for land-script at fifty cents an acre. Nothing better can be hoped for from an insolvent debtor, when he cannot pay in money, than to pay in kind, as well as he can ; and it remains for the creditor to determine whether he will accept such offer, or wait for such better terms as the chapter of accidents may afford. Few, if any, of the creditors of Texas accepted this offer. The average value of all the lands in the State, subject to taxation, was, in the year 1850, according to the comptroller's report, sixty-six cents an acre. If the seated lands, with all the improvements on them, were worth only sixty-six cents an acre, fifty cents was a high price for lands in a state of nature. The creditor, after getting possession of the script, would have had to pay certain office-fees before he could get legal possession of the land. He might, indeed, retain his script ; but if he retained it too long, all the best tracts might be taken up.

To most of the creditors of Texas, this offer was not very tempting. The greater part of them resided at a great distance. From New York to Austin, by the post-route, is twenty-five hundred miles. Experience had shown that land-speculations, carried on by non-residents, are very seldom profitable. Everything must then be intrusted to agents, and the commission which can be allowed them is seldom such as to interest them deeply in the business.

After taxes on land have been paid regularly for years, the whole may be forfeited by a simple oversight of the owner or the agent, or it may be by some accident to the mail preventing the arrival of a remittance in due season.   In addition to this, as is well known, the land of non-residents is a fair object of plunder to all who live near it.

For United States land-script, there is a demand in the Northern cities, because there is a constant flood of emigrants from New England and the Middle States to the North-Western States. But though New England and the Middle States will furnish to Texas their full quotas of mechanical skill and mercantile capital, few farmers from New England or Pennsylvania will migrate to that distant region.   Besides this, the script was a poor investment for speculation, as Texas had, in satisfaction of soldiers' and settlers' claims, and in other ways, issued so many patents as to supply all the land wanted for cultivation for many years to come.

The public lands of the United States are regularly divided into sections of six hundred and forty acres, and these again into half and quarter sections and eighths.   There is no dispute here about metes and bounds, and the title which a patent confers is incontrovertible.   It is different in Texas, as is evident from the following passages in Governor Bell's message of November 3, 1851:—

"There is nothing which so much retards the growth and prosperity of a country as the unsettled condition of its land-titles.   This is an evil from which our State has greatly suffered, and though it has been partially removed by time and the adjudication of our courts, still it is a serious obstacle to her rapid advance in prosperity.   Whilst I do not pretend to be conversant with the intricate system of our land-laws, or to be able to devise any general plan for the quieting of land-titles, I will venture to suggest one enactment, at least, which, if made by the Legislature, would, in my opinion, be attended with the most beneficial results.

"Under the law as it now exists, locations may be made upon any lands claimed to be held by prior grants, and the parties holding by or under such prior grants may be forced into court to defend the validity of their titles.

"The only restriction known to me, upon this right of location, is that imposed by the act of February 5, 1850, which prevents them from being made upon lands previously titled or surveyed within the limits of the colonies of Austin, De Witt, and De Leon.   These locations are usually made, and suits instituted upon them for some supposed defects in the prior grant or title, and if the locator fails to defeat the same, he can lift his certificate, make new locations upon other lands, and test the validity of the title under which they are held.   This system of location may be carried to an indefinite extent, and the evils resulting from it are so obvious that I deem it unnecessary to mention them. The right of a person holding a genuine and valid certificate to locate the same upon any of the vacant and unappropriated domain belonging to the State, will not be denied by me; but this right of location, when extended to lands claimed to be owned by private individuals, should, in my judgment, be restricted, and guarded from abuse by legislative enactment.

"It is our duty as well as our policy to discourage litigation. This object will certainly be effected, to some extent, by restricting the facilities, now afforded to those who make locations upon titled lands, of contesting such titles. I respectfully suggest, therefore, for the consideration of the legislature, the propriety of passing a law which will prevent certificates, hereafter located upon lands which the records of the county show had been previously deeded or titled, from being removed or located elsewhere, in case such locations were not sustained by the judgment of a competent court; and I further suggest that the law should compel the locator, in such cases, within six or twelve months after making his locations, to bring suit upon the same against those claiming the lands under a previous grant, in order that the question of title may be settled in a reasonable time.

"It seems to me that those who seek to set aside prior titles for imagined defects in the same should run some risk as well as those whose titles they contest. It would check litigation by making locators cautious, and prevent much of that wild spirit of speculation which is at war with the true interests of the country."

Such a condition of things as this is very embarrassing to non-resident landholders. Those who are on the spot can better contend with such difficulties. They can manage their business without the intervention of agents. When immigrants arrive, they can deal with them directly. They have thus great advantages over non-residents. Yet few, if any, of the creditors residing within the State, embraced the offer of land-script in payment of their dues.

But a change was soon to take place in the circumstances of the Texan Government. It had long been desirous of making a sale of a portion of its domain to the United States. There was now a fair prospect of this object being accomplished.

On the 16th of January, 1850, Mr. Benton submitted to the United States Senate a bill, providing, among other things, that, if Texas would cede to the United States a certain portion of territory, and relinquish all claim on the United States "for liability of the debts of Texas," &c., the United States would pay to Texas the sum of fifteen million dollars in five per cent. stocks, redeemable fourteen years after date.

Mr. Benton supported this bill in a speech marked with his usual ability.

On the 29th of the same month, the subject was submitted to the Senate in a different form by Mr. Clay, as one of the " Compromise Measures;" a particular class of measures intended to satisfy both the North and the South, embracing the admission of California, the establishing of the boundary line between Texas and Mexico, the abolition of the slave trade in the District of Columbia, and the Fugitive Slave Act.

The fourth resolution was as follows :—

Resolved, That it be proposed to the State of Texas that the United States will provide for the payment of all that portion of the legitimate and *bona fide* public debt of that State, contracted prior to its annexation to the United States, and for which the duties on foreign imports were pledged by the said State to its creditors, not exceeding the sum of $—— in consideration of the said duties so pledged having been no longer applicable to that object after the said annexation, but having thenceforward become payable to the United States; and upon the condition, also, that the said State of Texas shall, by some solemn and authentic act of her Legislature, or of a convention, relinquish to the United States any claim which it has to any part of New Mexico."

In support of this resolution, Mr. Clay made the following remarks :—

"It proposes that the Government of the United States will provide for the payment of all that portion of the debt of Texas for which the duties received upon imports from foreign countries were pledged by Texas at a time when she had authority to make pledges. How much it will amount to I have endeavored to ascertain, but all the means requisite to the attainment of the sum have not been received, and it is not very essential at this time, because it is the principle, and not the amount, that is most worthy of consideration. Now, sir, the ground on which I base this liability on the part of the United States to pay a portion of the debt of Texas is not new to me. It is one which I have again and again announced to be an opinion entertained by me. I think it is founded upon principles of eternal truth and justice. Texas, being an independent power, recognized as such by all the great powers of the earth, invited loans to be made to her to enable her to prosecute the then existing war between her and Mexico. She told those whom she invited to make these loans that, 'if you make them, the duties on foreign imports shall be sacredly pledged for the reimbursement of the loans.' The loans were made. The money was received, and expended in the establishment of her liberty and her independence. After this, she annexed herself to the United States, who thenceforward acquired the right to the identical pledge which she had made to the public creditor to satisfy the loan of money which he had advanced to her. The United States became the owner of that pledge, and the recipient of all the duties payable in the ports of Texas.

"Now, sir, I do say that, in my humble judgment, if there be honor, or justice, or truth among men, we do owe to the creditors who thus advanced their money upon that pledge the reimbursement of the money, at all events to the extent that the pledged fund would have reimbursed it if it had never been appropriated by us to our use. We must recollect, sir, in relation to that pledge, and to the loan made in virtue and on the faith of it, there were three parties bound: the United States, Texas, and the creditor of Texas, who had advanced his money on the faith of a solemn pledge made by Texas.

" Texas and the United States might do what they thought proper; but in justice they could do nothing to deprive the creditor of a full reliance upon the pledge, upon the faith of which he had advanced his money. Sir, it is impossible now to ascertain how much would have been received from that source of revenue by the State of Texas if she had remained independent. It would be most unjust to go there now, and examine at Galveston and her other ports to ascertain how much she now receives by her foreign imports; because, by being incorporated into this Union, all her supplies, which formerly were received from foreign countries, and subject, many of them at least, to import duties, are now received by the coasting trade, instead of being received from other countries, as they would have been if she had remained independent. Considering the extent of her territory, and the rapid manner in which her population is increasing, and is likely to increase, it is probable that, in the course of a few years, there might have been such an amount received at the various ports of Texas, she remaining independent, as would have been adequate to the extinction of the debt to which I have referred.

" But, sir, it is not merely in the discharge of what I consider to be a valid and legitimate obligation resting upon the United States to discharge the specified duty; it is not upon that condition alone that this payment is proposed to be made; it is also upon the further condition that Texas shall relinquish to the United States any claim that she has to any portion of New Mexico. Now, sir, although I believe she has not a valid title to any portion of New Mexico, she has a claim; and for the sake of that general quiet and harmony—for the sake of that accommodation which ought to be as much the object of legislation as it is of individuals in their transactions in private life, we may do now what an individual in analogous circumstances might do, give something for the relinquishment of a claim, although it should not be well founded, for the sake of peace. It is, therefore, proposed—and this resolution does propose—that we shall pay the amount of the debt contracted by Texas prior to its annexation to the United States, in consideration of our reception of the duties applicable to the extinction of that debt; and that Texas shall, also, in consideration of a sum to be advanced, relinquish any claim which she has to any portion of New Mexico."

Mr. Clay omitted to mention that, in the articles of annexation (for so may the joint resolution be called), Texas gave a guarantee that the United States should not be responsible for her debts.

" In no event are said debts and liabilities to become a charge upon the Government of the United States."

It was, moreover, expressly stipulated that all the public lands in Texas should be applied to the payment of her debts, and to no other purpose, till the whole should be extinguished.

" Said State shall retain all the vacant and unappropriated lands lying within her limits, to be applied to the payment of the debts and other liabilities of said Republic of Texas; and the *residue* of said lands, *after discharging* said debts and liabilities, to be disposed of as said State may direct."

But Texas had, from inability, failed to make good her guarantee to the United States that in no event should said debts and liabilities become a charge upon them. Then commenced the responsibility of the United States, not to Texas, but the creditors of Texas. The import duties of Texas, which had been pledged to them, had been transferred to the United States. They petitioned Congress for redress, and it was plain that certain responsibilities, to guard against which express stipulation had been made in the articles of annexation, must come against the United States, unless Texas had increased means to discharge them. These increased means could be obtained only by a sale of the public lands, and, except the United States, no purchaser was to be found.

It is unnecessary to trace this business through the various forms which it assumed in the House and the Senate. The bill for passing all the Compromise Measures together, broke down; and it was resolved to try to pass them separately.

On the 5th of August, nearly seven months after Mr. Benton had brought the subject before the Senate, Mr. Pearce, of Maryland, proposed what has since been known as the " Boundary Bill." It contained some of the provisions of Mr. Benton's bill, with others intended to make it acceptable to the parties concerned.

In his introductory speech, Mr. Pearce, after showing what amount of land would be ceded by Texas, if the bill were passed, and the advantages that would be derived therefrom, proceeded as follows:—

" But, sir, there is another consideration, and it is one to which I have been exceedingly unwilling to give my assent, but to which, nevertheless, I have been unable to refuse it. The Senate are aware that the State [the Republic] of Texas has incurred, since her independence, a considerable debt. They know, also, that she has issued bonds to her creditors, in some of which the revenues from her customs are specially pledged for the payment of principal and interest. Upon the annexation of Texas to the United States, her right to levy duties upon imports was surrendered to the Government of the United States; so that source of revenue became extinct, or fell into the possession of the United States. The revenue derivable from this source is not at present large, but it is likely to become very large and valuable in future. I understand, from authorities on which I can rely, that the trade of Texas at this time amounts to five millions of dollars a year, and that in the city of Houston alone seven hundred and fifty thousand dollars' worth of dutiable goods are consumed annually. We know that the population is increasing with considerable rapidity, and in the course of a few years will swell to such an amount as would enable the State, if still in the possession of the revenue derived from the duty on imports, to defray the interest on the bonds, and finally to extinguish them by a full payment. True, Texas reserved to herself her public lands; but it is also true that they are at present a very inadequate source of revenue, and likely to continue so for some time. When a State pledges her revenue, it is with an understanding that the current expenses of the government shall be deducted, because if not, the government, unsupported by fiscal means, could not exist; anarchy would ensue, and the responsibility and obligations to the creditors would become absolutely valueless. But, sir, those creditors to whom the revenues of Texas were pledged for the payment of their bonds must undoubtedly have relied upon that source of revenue; they must have looked, not to the present productiveness of these Texan sources of income, but to their future productiveness; and, although they had no legal right to compel Texas to appropriate the revenue derived from that source to the payment of the bonds, and are utterly powerless to compel the United States, yet the very fact that they are powerless, that they rest entirely upon moral force for the performance of these obligations, gives them a higher claim to the equity and consideration of the Congress of the United States. I will not liken it to the case of a mortgage, because I do not suppose the operations of the government can be likened to a mortgage, being things different in their natures; but, so far as there is any analogy at all, it is undoubtedly in favor of the case which I now present. The creditors of Texas had a moral claim, at all events, upon the duties on imports into Texas. These duties have been taken by the United States, under the terms of annexation; and, although there was a special stipulation in the joint resolution of annexation that these creditors should not claim of the United States Government the payment of these duties, yet it may well be doubted whether that agreement between the United States and Texas can release the United States from its moral obligations to the creditors, or whether, as these duties have been specifically pledged by Texas for the payment of these bonds, it is not the duty of the United States, at all events, to make some compensation to these creditors. Well, sir, this being the case, I think I am perfectly safe in saying that the Congress of the United States need never expect to get rid of the claims of these creditors of Texas until they are paid. Considering the vast extent of Texas, the large population which must soon fill her settlements, that her productive capacity will soon be quadrupled, and that her ability to consume will keep pace with increasing production, we must see that no inconsiderable tribute to our treasury will flow from the customs duties on Texan commerce. It is not a sufficient answer to say that without annexation Texas would have had no security, and therefore no increase of commerce, for we know that her independence would have been acknowledged by Mexico, on the condition of eternal separation from the United States; and that if this scheme, guaranteed by England and France, had gone into operation, she would soon have gathered strength and grown in prosperity.

Besides, sir, I remember that, when we were opposing annexation, one prominent objection was that we should come under obligations to pay part of
her debt.   One of her bonds was exhibited in the Senate, and we were told
to mark the pledge and heed the liability which would devolve on us.   All
these are considerations which have weighed with me in determining the
amount of ten millions allowed in the bill.

"I have been furnished with a statement from the office of the auditor
and comptroller of Texas, which gives the names of the holders of all Texan
bonds for which the revenue from import duties was specially pledged, and
the amounts of principal and interest respectively due to each, calculated
up to some time in 1848.   The aggregate amount is $4,045,027 14 ;
which, by this time, as the interest is at the rate of ten per cent. per
annum, must be about four millions and a half.   If, to this sum, which
equity strongly calls on us to allow, we add a liberal amount for the territory which Texas undoubtedly cedes, and allow also for the territory which
she claims, and which some think she is justly entitled to, though I with
others differ as to that, you will have reached the aggregate amount of the
ten millions which is proposed to be paid in the bill.   I am aware that this
will be considered extravagant, especially after the expensive war in which
we have been engaged, and more especially when we consider the fifteen
millions to be paid for the cession, as many think, and as I think, of part
of this very territory ; still, taking all these considerations together, I think
a fair case is made out, in which every Senator could justify himself to his
conscience for allowing the sum proposed."

Mr. Pearce then dilated on the advantages which would arise
in settling the boundary line between New Mexico and Texas in
restoring peace and harmony to the country, after which he proceeded as follows :—

"There is another subject to which I must ask the attention of the
Senate for a few moments, and that is, the proviso attached to the last
clause of the bill.   It has been proposed by some that the United States
should reserve to itself the right of distributing the money we may vote to
Texas among her creditors; but I have put no such provision as that into
the bill, and for several reasons.   In the first place, I do not wish the
United States to become a commissioner in bankruptcy for Texas ; and, in
the second, I do not wish to place Texas in the condition of appearing to
be obliged to be placed in the hands of a commissioner of bankruptcy.   It
seems to me that, while it would have been impolitic in us to undertake
that which we have not the means of doing properly, Texas can, with safety
to her creditors and honor to herself, make this distribution.   It would also
be an indignity to the State of Texas.   Sir, one of the highest affronts that
could be offered to an honest man would be to say, when he has ample
means to discharge his debts, that you suspect his honor, and will not trust
him with the money devoted to this purpose.   It is quite as offensive, undoubtedly, to a State, to suppose that she will be faithless and fraudulent
in a settlement with her creditors.   I am not willing to make such an imputation on Texas, to suspect in the least her honor, or the honor of her
Legislature.   I am willing to submit the matter to her decision, and to let
her settle with her creditors with the means which we have provided her.

But I admit, at the same time, that it is right to guard the treasury of the United States from the contingencies which may flow from this measure, if Texas should not adopt this course, or if Texas were to settle with her creditors, not in full, but upon a reduction of their claims for principal and interest due them, even with their assent. It is possible that, at some future time, these creditors, even after having consented to take seventy-five cents in the dollar, if that can be supposed, may come back on the Government of the United States, and demand the full amount. I propose to guard against that, and for that purpose I have introduced the last proviso in the bill. It provides that, of the ten millions of five per cent. stock to be issued after the State of Texas shall have assented to these terms, and signified her assent in proper form to the Government of the United States, we shall retain five millions until such a time as a full release shall be filed, in the treasury of the United States, by the creditors holding those bonds for which the duties on the customs are pledged. The arrangement rendered necessary by this proviso may easily be effected by these creditors and Texas. On the presentation of these claims (and I believe they all have been presented under the act of the Legislature of 1848, which called upon the creditors to exhibit their claims), the amount of which is furnished in the statement I referred to, not long ago, to the treasury of Texas, it is perfectly competent for Texas to give them orders for stock on the treasury of the United States, for the amount to which they may be entitled, by any arrangement which may be agreed upon between them. And these orders, being filed in the treasury, will be ample security to the United States, and protect us from the possible demands to which I have referred. The necessary details can be prescribed by the authority of the Treasury Department."

The remarks of Mr. Pearce, taken in connection with those of Mr. Clay, give a very clear view of the relations subsisting between the Government of the United States and the creditors of Texas.

In the House of Representatives, on the 10th of August, Mr. Moore, of Pennsylvania, made a speech, in which he said:—

" And here let me also say that, while I may, perhaps, be willing to vote for a reasonable sum to Texas in the settlement of this question, not one dollar of it would I vote as a remuneration for the territory which she thus claims ; but because I feel that, having annexed that State to this Union, and taken all her means of revenue, we are, in a measure, at least equitably, if not legally, responsible for the debts due from her at that time, and for the liquidation of which debts these revenues were pledged."

Such, judging from the published reports of the debates, was the general feeling in Congress. If a direct vote could have been taken on the claim set up by Texas to the eastern half of New Mexico, and that claim could have been presented divested of all other considerations, very few members would have sustained it. But, in the excited state of the public mind, a direct vote on this question was very judiciously avoided, by including in the bill a portion of territory to which Texas had an undoubted right. But, if Texas had remained without the Union, Congress never would have settled with her on these terms. By conquest and by purchase, the United States came into possession of all the rights in New Mexico which Mexico had previously enjoyed. In settling the boundaries of that province with a foreign power, Congress would never have given five million dollars, nor one million dollars, nor one million cents, for the relinquishment of such a claim as Texas asserted. But settling the business with Texas, she having come into the Union, was a family matter; and family considerations alone led to the adjustment finally agreed upon.

As little disposed would Congress have been to give five million dollars, or one million dollars, or even one dollar, for the land which was undoubtedly Texas's, but for the sake of enabling Texas to pay her debts, and thereby release the United States from all responsibilities to the old creditors of Texas.

August 9th, the bill was ordered to be engrossed for a third reading by a vote of 27 ayes to 24 noes, and was afterwards, on the same day, passed by a vote of 30 to 20.

It was then sent to the House, where it was, September 4, ordered to be engrossed for a third reading by a vote of 108 to 98, and passed on the same day by a vote of 108 to 97.

We thus find that, notwithstanding the many influences that were brought to bear in its favor, it was by no great majority that the bill passed the two Houses.

CHAPTER XXVII.

PROCEEDINGS OF THE LEGISLATURE OF TEXAS AT ITS SPECIAL SES-
SION, NOVEMBER, 1850, AND AT ITS REGULAR SESSION, NOVEMBER,
1851.

The conditions of the "Boundary Bill" formally accepted—Proud position of Texas
—Different constructions of some provisions of the "Boundary Bill"—Extracts
from Governor Bell's message, with remarks on the same—Bill reported "to require
the creditors to sign releases to the United States"—The money received applied
to other objects than to the payment of the debts for which the United States
were liable.

THE "Boundary Act" was signed by the President on the 7th of
September. A special session of the Legislature of Texas was
held at Austin, and, on the 25th of November, a law was passed
accepting the propositions made by the United States.

This law, after reciting the provisions of the act of Congress,
enacts and declares as follows :—

" Therefore, first : *Be it enacted by the Legislature of the State of Texas*,
That the State of Texas hereby agrees to and accepts said propositions ;
and it is hereby declared that the State shall be bound by the terms thereof, according to their true import and meaning.

" Second : That the Governor of this State be, and he is hereby re-
quested to cause a copy of this act, authenticated under the seal of the
State, to be furnished to the President of the United States, by mail, as
early as practicable ; and also a copy thereof, certified in like manner, to
be transmitted to each of the Senators and Representatives of Texas in Congress, and that this act take effect from and after its passage."

In communicating this intelligence to the Senate, President
Fillmore said :—

" From the common sources of public information, it would appear that
a very remarkable degree of unanimity prevailed, not only in the Legislature, but among the people of Texas, in respect to the agreement of the
State to that which had been proposed in Congress."

Texas now stood in a proud position. She had succeeded in the
object she had so long had in view ; a sale to Congress of land
which was of no use to her as a State. As General Houston after-

wards said, in an address to the people of Galveston, "it was the best sale ever made of land of a worthless quality, and a disputable title." Texas was now rich. She had the means of paying her creditors in full. Whether Texas, in the days of her riches, repudiated the scaling system she had adopted in the days of her poverty, will be seen as we proceed.

It was not long before the authorities of Texas and those of the United States disagreed as to the amount of debts which the reserved five millions in bonds were intended to cover. The acting Attorney-General of Texas maintained that the only debts of the Republic for which duties on imports had been "specially pledged," were those where, in the laws authorizing such debts, said duties were expressly mentioned by name, distinctively from all others. There had been no such pledge, he averred, except in regard to the interest which had accrued on "the consolidated fund" issued under the act of the Texan Congress, approved January 7, 1837. This amounted to a fraction over six hundred thousand dollars. And he contended that, as soon as the claimants had signed releases to this amount, the United States were bound to surrender to Texas the residue of the five millions. The Texan authorities, generally, concurred in these views.

On the other hand, the authorities of the United States maintained that the genus could not be pledged without pledging all the species it included, and that, therefore, whenever the Republic of Texas had made a special pledge of her revenues, she had made a special pledge of the duties on imports as a part of these revenues. Thus, instead of pledging her customs for debts of the amount of only six hundred thousand dollars, as asserted by her acting Attorney-General, Texas had pledged them for debts amounting to at least six millions, probably eight, perhaps even more, at the unscaled rates. To determine the exact amount, more particular information was requisite in regard to certain branches of the debt.

Very soon after the "Boundary Act" was passed, the Texan delegation in Congress addressed a letter to the Secretary of the Treasury, in which they supported the construction given to the law by the acting Attorney-General of their State, thus maintaining that only six hundred thousand dollars of the debts of Texas were covered by the pledge of the duties on imports. This was a very different view of the subject from that given by Mr. Pearce when he introduced the "Boundary Bill." He then said—

"I have been furnished with a statement from the office of the auditor and comptroller of Texas, which gives the names of the holders of all Texan bonds for which the revenue from import duties was specially pledged; and the amount of principal and interest respectively due to each, calculated up to some time in 1848. The aggregate amount is $4,045,027 14, which, by this time, as the interest is at the rate of ten per cent. per annum, must be about four millions and a half."

This statement does not appear to have been controverted by the Texan members either in the Senate or the House, and with this understanding of the amount of debt for which the customs were pledged, Congress ordered the five millions in bonds to be retained till the creditors should sign releases to the United States.

The views of the Federal authorities are clearly set forth in the report of the Secretary of the Treasury, Mr. Corwin, to the President. We give it at length in Appendix T, as it will not admit of abridgment.

The views of the authorities of Texas will be seen in the following extracts from a message which Governor Bell sent to the Legislature of that State, November 10, 1851.

"The Republic of Texas having executed her bonds and other evidences of debt in an exceedingly dark and gloomy period of her history, it became necessary to issue them for nominal amounts, bearing no sort of proportion to the amount actually received; and to pledge her resources, arising mainly, at that time, from her revenues, for their redemption."

In this respect, the history of Texas is like that of other governments. Alexander Hamilton, in his report as Secretary of the Treasury, with his plan for supporting public credit, says: "When the credit of a country is in any degree questionable, it never fails to give an extravagant premium, in one shape or another, upon all the loans it has occasion to make." Every person who knows anything about debt and credit knows it necessarily must be so. But this is the first time, we believe, in the world's history, when the *necessity* a government is under, "in an exceedingly dark and gloomy period," of making large promises, is used as a *reason* for not fulfilling those promises in time of prosperity.

But, the Governor continues:—

"These securities, generally speaking, were concentrated at very low rates, in the hands of moneyed speculators, who had contributed nothing to the achievement of her independence, or to the relief of her actual necessities in the administration of the government at the time they were issued."

Admit all this to be so, and it does not in the least diminish the obligation of the government of Texas to pay its debts. The evidences of debt it issued owed great part of their value to their transferability. The original claimants transferred the whole of their rights to others. If they got but little for them, that was their misfortune. And if they were then worth but little, the fault was in the mismanagement and extravagance of the government of Texas. It is well, indeed, for a government to reduce the market value of its own securities by its own folly, and then give this as a reason why they should not be redeemed according to contract.

" This consideration, well understood and appreciated, induced an inquiry in respect to the mode of redeeming these securities; as no one could entertain the opinion, for a moment, that the government was under any obligation, either in justice or in morality, to redeem them by paying the amount expressed on their face; and that inquiry resulted in the passage of the act of the State Legislature of March 20th, 1848, " to provide for ascertaining the debt of the late Republic of Texas," which act required the auditor and comptroller of the State to reduce all claims presented for liquidation to the actual par value which was realized by the Republic at the time of their issue. The evident meaning and contemplation of that act was, that the holders of the claims should be paid in accordance with the amount thus ascertained by the auditorial board, subject to the revision of the Legislature; and the amounts so ascertained were considered as all that was actually due from the State to her several creditors. That the Legislature had the right to pass this law, there can be no question, and that the individuals holding the bonds or other evidences of debt against the late Republic, were bound by it, there can be as little."

.No one who knows Governor Bell will doubt his disposition to do what he believes to be right; and his entertaining such notions is only evidence of the extent to which, in some circumstances, an honest man's judgment may be perverted. There was a case of debtor and creditor. The creditor was absent, and his cause was feebly pleaded, if pleaded at all. The debtor was the sole judge, pleaded his own cause fully, and, as might have been expected, gave judgment in his own favor.

This was the precise case of Texas and her creditors. And from the one-sided view her citizens took from the beginning, and from their entertaining it uninterruptedly for several years in succession, they at length came to the conclusion that their decision was incontrovertible. A State may heap pledge upon pledge—pledge its public lands, its direct taxes, its license taxes, its customs, and, lastly, its public faith, and thus everything it possesses, or may hereafter possess. But if it makes these pledges "in an exceedingly dark and gloomy period of its history, no one can entertain the opinion for a moment" that it is bound by them in periods of prosperity. Such a government is under "no obligation, either in justice or morality, to redeem its securities by paying the amount expressed on their face." It may enter into contracts each as binding as if the great seal of the Republic had been attached to it, and it may cut down those contracts to one-half, one-third, or even the fifth of the original amount. As the debtor party is a sovereign State, there can be no question that it has a right to do this; and there is as little question that the creditor party, consisting of mere individuals, are bound by it!

Governor Bell seemed, however, to have his doubts whether this view of the case would be as satisfactory to the authorities of the United States as it was to himself and the great body of his constituents.

"It occurred to me, therefore, after a careful examination of the proviso, that difficulties and embarrassments would be produced in the settlement of our outstanding liabilities, unless the Secretary of the Treasury should give such a construction of the law on the subject as would enable the State of Texas to define who were the creditors therein referred to, and also to ascertain the amount of the liabilities of the State, which this reserved five millions of dollars was intended to cover. By the phraseology of the act, the decision of the question as to who were the creditors of the State, holding claims on which duties for imports 'were specially pledged;' and the amount of these claims, was referred directly to the Secretary of the Treasury of the United States; and as he could have no means of ascertaining these facts, except such as were derived from the State, through her proper officers, I deemed it my duty to dispatch an officer to the city of Washington, charged with instructions to ascertain what course he intended to pursue in reference to this matter."

Governor Bell was unquestionably right in supposing that difficulties and embarrassments would ensue, if Texas persisted in her scaling system. The possibility of this was mentioned by Mr. Pearce as one of the reasons for retaining bonds to the amount of five millions in the United States Treasury. His language was:—

"I am not willing to make any such imputation on Texas, to suspect in the least her honor, or the honor of her Legislature. I am willing to submit the matter to her decision, and let her settle with her creditors with the means which we have provided for. But I admit, at the same time, that it is right to guard the Treasury of the United States from the contingencies which may flow from this measure, if Texas should not adopt this course, or if Texas were to settle with her creditors not in full, but upon a reduction of their claims for principal and interest due to them, even with their assent. It is possible that, at some future time, these creditors, even after having consented to take seventy-five cents in the dollar, if that can be supposed, may come back on the Government of the United States and demand the full amount. I propose to guard against that, and FOR THAT PURPOSE I have introduced the last proviso in the bill."

Some of the Texans have expressed great indignation because the United States authorities will not give up the five millions; thereby, as they conceive, keeping them out of their rights. They may here see the reason of it. Scaling debts is not paying them. Unless Texas makes full satisfaction to a certain class of her creditors, they, according to the laws of nations and the principles of equity, become creditors of the United States. The United States are not willing to pay the same debts twice, and therefore holds on to the bonds, to the amount of five millions, till, all the releases shall be signed.

A little further on, the Governor makes the following remarks:—

" By adverting to the letter of the Secretary of the Treasury, under date of February 12, 1851, it will be perceived that he has decided not to issue to the State, *under any circumstances*, stock for any portion of the retained five millions of dollars, until *all* the creditors holding obligations, for the payment of which duties on imports were specially pledged, shall have relinquished to the United States their claims, notwithstanding it may be ascertained prior to such relinquishment that a very inconsiderable part of that five millions will be required to cover those claims; and that he has reserved to himself the right of deciding, from data to be furnished by the State, the amount of the claims now outstanding, for which duties on imports were specially pledged, and also the individuals entitled to receive these amounts."

The Secretary of the Treasury takes a very different view of the case. His inquiries have led him to believe that the customs of Texas were pledged for all the debts contained in Schedules A, B, D, and part of E, viz. :—

				Original claims.	Reduced amount.
"Schedule A,	.	.	.	$1,651,590 02	$1,164,482
" B,	.	.	.	2,582,902 70	1,651,200
" D,	.	.	.	1,472,918 90	294,581
Part of E,	.	.	.	509,000 00	289,000
				$6,216,411 62	$3,399,263
And it may be—					
Residue of E,	.	.	.	2,077,546 00	517,386
And part of F,	.	.	.	2,181,945 00	2,177,181"

There seems, therefore, little probability that only a " very inconsiderable part of that five millions will be wanted to cover those claims."

" From the opinions of the acting Attorney-General of the State, under date of September 8, 1850, it would seem that the payment of a very small portion of the public debt now outstanding was secured by ' a special pledge' of import duties, probably not exceeding six hundred thousand dollars ; and yet, according to the decision of the Secretary of the Treasury, the whole five millions must be retained in the treasury of the United States until every individual creditor owning any part of that six hundred thousand dollars, however small, shall have filed his relinquishment to the United States in the Treasury Department at Washington."

The acting Attorney-General of Texas was counsel for a party that had an interest in causing as little as possible to be paid to its creditors, that thereby as much as possible might be paid to itself, and he endeavored to do the best he could for his client. Hence his ingenious interpretation that, when a State made a special pledge of the whole of its revenues, that was not a special pledge of all its parts. But, admitting his construction to be correct, as but few of the claimants of the single class he supposes are alone entitled to the benefit of this provision of the act have signed the releases, the Secretary of the Treasury has no authority to surrender the bonds.

" A decision which would lead to such consequences cannot be in accordance with the spirit and intention of the compact between the Federal Government and Texas, although it may be within the strict letter of the law; and it has occurred to me that some further action by the General Congress is necessary to place this subject in its proper light; and it will be proper for the State Legislature to indicate, by resolution or otherwise, as it may deem best, what that action may be."

This provision of the law is too clear to admit of dispute, and the spirit of it is in exact accordance with the letter. It was voted for by all the delegates of Texas in Congress. It was fully and freely assented to by the Legislature of Texas in its act of November 25, 1850. It forms part of the compact between the United States and Texas, as set forth in the " Boundary Bill," and it ought not to be changed without a sufficient reason.

" If the decision of the Secretary of the Treasury remains unchanged (and we have no reason to expect a change in it, without an alteration of the law), the State may be kept for an indefinite, probably an interminable, period out of nearly one-half of the pecuniary consideration for which she relinquished a large portion of her territory; and this result may be produced by some obstinate and perverse creditor who, holding an amount not sufficient in importance to embarrass his own operations, may, by this means, seek to embarrass the interests of all others, by withholding a relinquishment of his claim to the United States."

Nothing like this has occurred, nor is it likely to occur. If it should, Congress will, no doubt, interfere.

"This difficulty may, perhaps, be obviated in the following manner: If the General Congress will so modify the act of September 9, 1850, as to authorize the Secretary of the Treasury to issue stock to the State of Texas for the whole amount of the retained five millions, upon the State, through her proper officers, filing at the Treasury Department a release and full exoneration of the Federal Government from all liability for any portion of the public debt of Texas, growing out of the transfer, by the act of annexation, of the resources arising from duties on imports, all difficulty would at once be removed, and the public debt could, without further delay, be placed in a train of proper adjustment, through the agency of our own officers, by whom it must be ultimately settled."

The liability of the United States is not to Texas, but to the creditors of Texas. Any release signed by the authorities of Texas would amount to nothing. Besides this, Texas, in the articles of annexation, entered into an engagement that "in no event should" these very debts "become a charge against the United States." As she has failed to fulfil this engagement, it is hardly to be expected that the United States will enter into another with her in relation to the same subject.

"To such a modification of the law, the Executive cannot perceive that any well-founded objection could be urged. The obligation to pay these debts rests entirely upon the State; and although the creditors, at the time they were incurred, may have had a view to the supposed and probable resources of the Republic for their payment, still they did not anticipate that those resources were to be applied by any other than the government with whom the contracts were made, and with whom necessarily remained the right to modify or change them, as it might deem best. Had the government, after these contracts were made, deemed that the interests of the citizens, or prosperity of the country, required her to reduce her duties on imports to a mere nominal amount, or to have taken them off altogether, and thrown her ports open to the free commerce of the world, no one would have questioned for a moment her right to have done so; and her creditors would have had no just cause of complaint of such an act, because they made their contract with the full knowledge that such a right existed, and would, to some extent at least, be exercised. Indeed, it was exercised every year, in the various modifications of the tariff laws of the late Republic; and, in 1842, upon the adoption of what was known as the Exchequer System, they underwent an almost radical change (a change which reduced the duties laid upon imports from a very large to a comparatively small amount); and yet no one then asserted that this change in the amount of duties to be collected was a violation of the previous contract entered into with these creditors."

A sovereign State may do a great many bad things; and Texas is not the only State that affords examples of this truth. Should a State, however, after borrowing money on the pledge of a particular branch of revenue, afterwards abolish that revenue, it would be bound, by regard to public honor and public faith, to make good the deficit from some other source. Mere variations may be made in the amount of taxes levied, and the manner of levying them, without any breach of faith. Such variations occur in all governments, and if they were more frequent in Texas than elsewhere, it was owing to the unsettled condition of her affairs during the whole period of her revolutionary history. The change made by the Exchequer System made only a nominal reduction in the revenue from imports. The specie value exceeded that of the revenue in the years in which treasury notes were received.

"The transfer by Texas of a portion of her sovereignty to the United States, and by which her right to collect duties on imports was given up, in its consequences was nothing more than would have resulted from a repeal of her own laws imposing such duties; and the Federal Government, by receiving that transfer, incurred no other obligation, in respect to the debts of Texas, than an equitable one to give the State such an equivalent for the loss of her revenues arising from import duties as would enable her to carry out her contracts with her creditors as effectually as she might have done had her revenues from imports not been surrendered; but that government incurred no other obligation whatever to the creditor individually; and the assumption of such an obligation was a gratuitous act, by which the State of Texas ought not, in any sense, to be bound. The debt is one which Texas owes, and which Texas has to pay; and no power can rightfully interpose between her and her creditors, and dictate the manner of its settlement."

The United States do not interpose between Texas and her creditors. Each and every one of them is at liberty to accept the composition Texas offers. But, then, in addition to the release he signs to Texas, he must sign a release to the United States, if the revenue from imports was pledged for the payment of his claims, or the United States will not give up the bonds. From the other creditors the United States require no such release.

The United States do not interfere between Texas and those to whom Texas is indebted. And it is very unreasonable in Texas to expect the United States to aid and abet her in the design she has of forcing a compromise on her creditors. In that case, the disgrace of a shameful act of repudiation, which now attaches to Texas exclusively, would be shared by the whole Union.

Texas had no " equitable claim for an equivalent for the loss of her revenues arising from import duties." When she was admitted into the Union, she was admitted to a participation in all the benefits which its original members enjoyed, and surrendered no more than others surrendered. Nay, she was admitted to more than equal benefits, for she was suffered to retain her wild lands, while the United States had to take charge of the wild Indians upon them. The expenditures of the United States in Texas, and for the benefit of Texas, have, in the seven years since annexation, exceeded the gross amount of the debt of the late Republic.

Different is the relation of the United States to the creditors of Texas. It is true, " the debt is one which Texas owes," and which Texas ought to pay. But Texas once could not, and now will not pay ; and here, according to the laws of nations and the principles of equity, commences the obligation of the United States, as Texas transferred, and the United States received, a branch of revenue, which was pledged to its full value to the old creditors of Texas.

" I therefore recommend to the honorable Legislature that our Senators in Congress be instructed, and our representatives requested, to use all proper exertions to procure such a modification of the fifth article of the second section of the act of September 9, 1850, as will authorize and require the Secretary of the Treasury to issue to the State all the stock contemplated by the fourth article of the said act, upon *her* filing such releases to the United States as may be deemed necessary to exonerate the Federal Government from any liability for any portion or all the debt of Texas."

Strange things happen in the political world, but it would be very strange if such an act should be passed, as it would make the United States liable for debts to the amount of millions, for which they have already appropriated millions, *nominally* for the purchase of worthless lands, but *really* for the payment of these very debts.

" I recommend this course because it is the best which my mind suggests to relieve this subject from all difficulty ; but, as it is possible that Congress may not concur in the propriety of making this modification, we should, in such a contingency, prepare ourselves in the best way we can to meet it. I trust I have shown the necessity of placing this matter upon a different footing from that on which it now stands, if we expect to close it within any reasonable period, or in any manner which would be at all satisfactory to the State. Indeed, the difficulties which must be overcome in its adjustment, so long as it remains in its present condition, are so obvious that it requires no argument to prove that immediate steps should be taken to obviate them. I therefore further recommend to the honorable Legislature that a law be passed, at its present session, limiting the time within which the creditors of the State, holding the class of claims referred to, shall file their releases to the United States ; declaring that, in default of their doing so within the prescribed time, the claims shall forever be barred."

Texas had already passed laws to compel her creditors to bring in their accounts to have them scaled down to one-half, one-fourth, or one-fifth of what was due to them, under the penalty of forfeiting the whole. Here is a suggestion that these same creditors, already scaled by force, shall by more force be compelled to sign releases to the United States, or have their claims barred forever !

The Governor did not stand alone in these views, for, even before he sent in his message, a bill was introduced into the Senate of Texas " to require the creditors to sign releases to the United States."

"It has further occurred to me, as the President has decided, that the revenues from imports were specially pledged (in contemplation of the 'Boundary Act') for an amount of our public debt, almost equal (if it has all been filed) to the reserved stock, that it might be advisable to appropriate the stock so withheld to the payment of that portion of the debt for which imports were pledged, and which would, consequently, come under this decision of the President; said stock to be issued to the creditors holding these pledges as soon as the United States will so amend the act of the General Congress as to give Texas control of the same."

There is no necessity for any new act. The moment the creditors, either voluntarily or by compulsion, sign the releases to the United States, Texas will get control of the bonds.

" I also recommend that a sufficient amount of the five millions of stock within the present control of the State be appropriated to the payment of that class of debts not covered by a pledge of import duties, under the decision of the President. This character of the indebtedness amounts to $985,422, and has been denominated the second class. It is due mainly to our own citizens for personal services rendered."

In this respect, it differs not from the evidences of the debts held by citizens of other States. They were all incurred, either directly or indirectly, for such services and supplies. But drawing a line of distinction between creditors residing within and without the bounds of the State appears to be a fixed principle of Texan policy.

" From the report of the comptroller, it is evident that the whole ten millions of dollars will not be required to discharge the outstanding liabilities of the State, according to the scale which has been adopted for ascertaining the actual amount of those liabilities, and from which I can see no just reason to depart; and it will, therefore, become a subject of interesting inquiry to you, as to the best mode of disposing of the surplus."

The Governor then recommends that the surplus be applied to fostering general education and internal improvements.

Again, we say, Governor Bell must not be held personally responsible for the false doctrines embodied in his message. In uttering them, he was the mouth-piece of the community he represented, or rather of the active politicians with whom he was most closely connected. He entertained these sentiments in common with them. But who can breathe an infected atmosphere and escape unharmed?

He was wrong throughout, because he viewed everything from a wrong stand-point. The evident expectation of Congress was that the five millions passed over unconditionally to Texas would be applied by her to the payment of these debts, for which, in a certain sense, the United States are regarded as responsible. How else could the releases be obtained, the filing of which, in the Treasury Department of the United States, was an indispensable prerequisite to the payment of the second five millions, according to the terms of the compact? No one could suppose that the creditors of Texas, holding securities for which the revenues of the Republic had been pledged, and which they, from the day of annexation, had contended had been virtually assumed by the United States, would file their releases unless they were paid. It is, therefore, obvious that the unconditional issue of the first five millions was intended to enable Texas to satisfy this class of creditors and obtain their releases, so that she could receive the second five millions, according to the terms of the act to which she had given her full and free assent.

Instead, however, of applying these five millions as they ought to have been applied, Texas applied part of the money to the payment of debts for which the United States are in no way liable, and another part to the payment of her State expenses! It was apparently only because some of the members of the Legislature favored railroads, and some the clearing out of rivers, that all that remained of the five millions was not appropriated to works of internal improvement.

By this strange proceeding, Texas has rendered it difficult, if not impossible, to comply with her own part of the compact, and thus greatly increased the perplexities of the question.

CHAPTER XXVIII.

PROCEEDINGS OF THE FOURTH LEGISLATURE, CONTINUED.

Report of the auditor and comptroller scaling down the public debt—Extracts from and remarks on the same—Treasury notes—Ten per cent. consolidated fund of 1837—Eight and ten per cent. funded debt of 1846—Treasury bonds—Loan from Bank of the United States—Debt due for steamship Zavalla—Debts to Dawson, Schott, and Whitney—Difficulties in applying the scaling principle—The cases of assignees in some instances of greater hardship than those of original claimants—Injustice of stopping interest after July, 1850—Act confirming the award of the auditor and comptroller—Governor Bell vetoes the act, but it passes by a large majority.

Two days after the Governor had sent in his message, the auditor and comptroller made a report, which, as it was the basis of the subsequent action of the Legislature, we have inserted at length in Appendix U. Inasmuch as the classification of the debts therein contained was finally adopted, a particular examination of this report becomes necessary.

After giving a table containing the original amounts of the debts, and the rates at which they had been scaled, the auditor and comptroller make some remarks on each class.

Speaking of the treasury notes, they say that for the first issue (the printed notes) the government had received par, and they had accordingly rated them at par. They then add:—

"To the engraved interest notes we have assigned an average value of fifty cents on the dollar. These notes were issued under the provisions of the same act that the printed bills were, and took their place; about the time of the first issue of these notes (the spring of 1838), this species of the government paper commenced depreciating in value, so that, when the act of 19th of January, 1839, prohibiting their further issue, went into operation, they were worth but about forty cents on the dollar."

Here we find that about the time this issue commenced, treasury notes *began* to depreciate. Hence the State got, for the first batch of this issue, par, or nearly par; for the next batch ninety cents in the dollar; for the next eighty, and so on till they fell to forty. The Republic received for these notes as many different values as there are between forty cents and ninety, or forty cents and a hundred. Yet the man who gave ninety cents in value for the notes is to receive no more than he who gave forty. Veritably, this is not equitable adjustment, even on Texan principles of equity. The State has professed a willingness to give back as much as she received. According to her own confession, she received in value for some of the engraved interest notes ninety cents in the dollar, and now she proposes to pay the holders of them only fifty cents.

" To the treasury notes not bearing interest, generally known as 'red backs,' we have assigned an average value of twenty-five cents on the dollar. These notes superseded the engraved interest notes above referred to, and the first issue of them was made during the spring of 1839, when they were worth about thirty-seven and a half cents in the dollar. They continued depreciating; so that, in 1841, the government was compelled to pay them out at from twelve to fifteen cents on the dollar. The value which we have given them is conceived to be equitable, as an average, both to the government and the holder."

Here is averaging again. John Smith gave the government the equivalent of thirty-seven cents and a half in the dollar, his brother Thomas gave twenty-five cents, and his cousin Samuel gave only twelve cents and a half. John gave three times as much as Samuel, and Samuel gave only half as much as Thomas. But thirty-three and one-third per cent. is deducted from John, while fifty per cent. is added to Samuel, in order that both may be placed on an equality with Thomas. As the amount of these "red backs" was nearly two millions, it is plain that individuals must here be wronged in the amount of thousands of dollars, even on Texan principles of dispensing justice.

But this is not all.

" It is impossible to ascertain, from the date of the issue of these bills, as shown on the face, what they were worth when last paid out. For instance, a bill issued in 1839, at say thirty-seven cents and a half in the dollar, and after having been returned to the treasury in the collection of revenue, may have been reissued, the year following, at twenty-five cents in the dollar, and so on; and, in 1841, when it may have been last paid out, at one-eighth of its ostensible value."

This is an admission, by the auditor and comptroller, that they could not carry out the principle they had adopted. Even the doctrine of averages failed them. The truth is that the Legislature imposed a task on them which neither they nor any other men could perform. Neither auditors, nor comptrollers, nor courts of law, nor courts of chancery can effect an equitable adjustment of debts contracted in a fluctuating currency, and the evidences of which pass from hand to hand by simple transfer. Unless, in such cases, evidence of what a State has promised to pay is regarded as evidence of what a State ought to pay, everything is thrown into uncertainty.

The like difficulties, it will be found, attended the scaling of the " consolidated funded debt of 7th June, 1837."

" The stock known by this title was issued under the provisions of an act of Congress, approved June 7, 1837, and, *could it be analyzed*, would be subject to *the greatest variety of equivalent rates*. We found it impossible to refer, in éach instance, to the original record, to ascertain at what rate each claim had been audited for which stock was issued. Even had, or could we have done so, we would have failed to a great extent in acquiring this information, for the reason that the government, for a long time, would not acknowledge any discount on her paper; and the result was that accounts were made out, augmented in amount, so as to make good the deficit in the value of the currency. Hence, the only practicable mode which suggested itself was *to make an average*, which we accordingly did, and assigned to it a value of seventy cents in the dollar. It is believed that this average is *about* what the government received *in the main*, and will, with a few exceptions (which will hereafter be alluded to), fully remunerate the present holders, as it is now generally in the hands of third parties, who, in most instances, acquired it at much less value from the original investor than that now assigned it."

In this place, it is acknowledged that it was impossible to ascertain either what value the original claimants had parted with, or what the government had received. The rates were various, and may have been from twenty-five cents up to ninety. But one average is struck for all. It is the case of the treasury notes over again.

A new principle of " equitable adjustment" is now, however, introduced. Before, it was what the government had received; now, it is what the " present holders" have paid. Admit this as a rule of settlement in regard to public securities generally, and what will be the consequence? Public stocks are not unfrequently above par. Then, if what a holder of public securities has *given* for them is to determine what a State is *to pay* for them when the time comes for redeeming them, the State must, in addition to the original amount of principal, pay five to twenty per cent. premium.

We pass on to the "eight and ten per cent. funded debt of the 5th February, 1840."

"We have assigned to this class of securities an average value of thirty cents on the dollar. This stock was issued under the authority of an act of Congress, approved February 5th, 1840, and was created for the purpose of withdrawing and lessening the amount of revenue currency then in circulation, with a view of enhancing the value of the residue. The inducement held out to the creditors to surrender a revenue currency, and to take one which could not be used in that way, was the promise of the government to pay the stipulated interest semi-annually in specie; which, it is well known, she was unable to do. The value attached to this stock may act onerously on some holders, but it will fully remunerate a large majority. *It would be much more difficult in this fund than in any other to ascertain the exact value the government received for the investments in it*, as it is composed of interest notes, 'red backs,' and audited paper."

Here let us stop, and drop a tear of pity on the hard fate of the original holders of this stock. We have no sympathy to spare just now for the innocent purchasers at second hand. They must weep for themselves.

But behold the hard fate of the original claimants. They had Texan securities with which they might, according to law, have paid their taxes. They parted with these in exchange for others not so available, because the Republic wished "to lessen the amount of revenue currency." "The inducement held out to them to surrender this revenue currency, and take one which could not be used in that way, was the promise of the government to pay the stipulated interest semi-annually in specie."

Does the government fulfil its promise? No, not for one single half year.

What then does it do? Why, after a lapse of some eight or ten years, it passes a law declaring that these public creditors shall be paid only thirty per cent. of their claims! By the funding law of 1840, these claims are fully and freely admitted to the amount of $778,280; by the scaling law of 1848, they are reduced to $233,484!

How much better it would have been for many of these claimants if they had held on to their original evidences of the public debt, and not been seduced into a surrender of them by the *promise* of the government to pay the stipulated interest semi-annually in gold and silver. Among the amounts thus surrendered were treasury notes of the first and second issue, and audited drafts and audited paper of equal value. If they had held on to the first issues till the scaling system was adopted, they would have obtained par for them. If they had held on to the second issues, they would have received fifty cents. But, having been induced by the fair promises of the government to surrender them, they now get but thirty cents!

The "eight per cent. treasury bonds" must next engage our attention.

"Twenty cents in the dollar is the average equivalent value assigned this class of the government paper. These bonds were issued to supersede, to some extent, and take the place of treasury notes. There is less danger of individual hardship growing out of the assignment of an average equivalent value to these bonds than that of any other of the government securities; they were seldom ever issued at more than twenty-five cents in the dollar, and rarely less than fifteen cents in the dollar. The value assigned them is deemed equitable."

Equitable, indeed! Twenty per cent. is deducted from one class of claimants, and thirty per cent. given to another. The man who invested the value of one hundred specie dollars in treasury bonds, when their market price was twenty-five cents in the dollar, is now to receive but eighty dollars; while he who invested the same amount in the same bonds when they were at fifteen cents, is to receive one hundred and thirty-three dollars. And in this way $766,800 of public debt is "equitably adjusted" down to $153,360!

"There is less danger," say the auditor and comptroller, "of individual hardship growing out of an average equivalent value to these bonds than that of any other of the government securities." Perhaps so. But hardship is one thing, injustice is another. It may be a hard thing to compel a poor man to pay his debts; but it is not unjust. There may be no hardship in depriving a rich man of half his dues; but it would be very unjust. It is the duty of legislative bodies to make just laws, and of auditorial boards to make equal awards to rich and poor—when the Legislature will let them.

But we do not think the case of the holders of these treasury bonds quite as free from hardship as has been represented. The government issued these bonds, and they gave services and supplies in exchange for them. The government promised that these bonds should be receivable for all public dues, and in about two

years it revoked its promise. The government made a special
pledge of the revenue arising from the license-tax and the tax on
personal property for the payment of interest on these bonds,
and afterwards applied the revenue to other purposes. The
government, to induce people to part with their substance in exchange for these bonds, promised to pay them, semi-annually,
eight per cent. interest in gold and silver. It has never in one
half year fulfilled its promise. Finally, after keeping these claimants out of their just dues for twelve years, the government re-
solves to pay them only one-fifth as much as it had contracted to
pay. If this had been understood when the issue of the bonds
commenced, their value in the market would have been reduced
four-fifths, so that, instead of twenty-five cents, only five cents in
the dollar would have been given for them, and instead of five
cents, only one. Such would then have been the value of a Texas
promissory dollar, as Texas now interprets her promises.

"Audited paper," continues the auditor and comptroller, "when
issued at par, has been allowed accordingly; when less than par,
a corresponding deduction has been made; the records and vouchers showing the rate at which it was audited."

This proceeding was on correct principles. There were two
currencies in Texas, and as bills were sometimes made out in the
one, and sometimes in the other, it was necessary to make an equation of them. Here are four men, each of whom furnishes one
hundred beeves to the army. The first makes out his bill in specie,
and charges five dollars a head. The remaining three make their
charges in paper currency, designing in each instance to charge
the equivalent of specie; but, as the paper currency is subject to
successive depreciation, their charges are respectively $750,
$1000, and $1500. Without an equation of currencies, justice
could not be done to the State and to them also.

The auditor and comptroller then proceed to speak of some
special debts of the Republic.

"In the first class are included the bonds issued to the Bank of the
United States for a loan of $400,000, obtained from that institution in the
year 1839; also, the claim of James Holford and associates for the purchase
of the steamer 'Zavalla.' A value corresponding to what the government
actually received has been assigned to each."

The value the government actually received! But what was

the value it engaged to give? Waiving the case of the United States Bank, we may remark that it is not at all likely that the owners of the steamboat "Zavalla" would have parted with value in hand, certain and immediate, without the expectation, or at least the promise made to them, of receiving greater value in time, especially in a case in which the prospect of payment was so very remote and dependent on so many contingencies. The debtor is not the sole judge of the value he receives. The creditor, also, must be allowed some say in such matters. The steamboat "Zavalla" was worth to the Republic of Texas all she engaged to pay for it. Else, why did she engage to pay that for it? What Texas promised to pay the former owners of the "Zavalla" is what she owes them.

Next come the debts of Messrs. Dawson, Schott, and Whitney.

"Since our last report, Messrs. James Schott and E. D. Whitney have filed their claims, composed of one of the bonds issued to Frederick Dawson, of Baltimore, in payment for the navy. These gentlemen, although not known in the contract, are acknowledged by Mr. Dawson to have been equally interested in that transaction; and the readiness manifested in aiding the cause of Texas, by undertaking and carrying out a contract requiring a large pecuniary outlay, at a time when the public credit was at an exceedingly low stage, procured for the contractors the commendation of the late Republic."

All this is very well. But resolutions of thanks will not pay for vessels of war. These commendations were, no doubt, very delectable to Messrs. Schott, Whitney, and Dawson; but, as these gentlemen are not pure spiritualities, they cannot live on commendations. What of a more substantial nature does Texas propose to allow them? Listen.

"In assigning to this claim fifty cents on the dollar, as the value received by the government, we have been governed by the law making the appropriation, and the contract entered into by the agent of the government and Mr. Dawson. This contract, subsequently recognized by legislative enactment (a copy of which accompanies), stipulates the price of the vessel at $280,000, to secure the payment for which, two bonds of the Republic, for $280,000 each, were deposited with the President of the Girard Bank at Philadelphia, with the understanding that they could be redeemed at the end of twelve months by the payment of the $280,000, and ten per cent. interest on the two bonds; otherwise, the said bonds to become the property of Mr. Dawson. The government was unable to make the payment at the time specified; and the president of the bank, according to instructions, delivered the bonds, amounting to $560,000, to Mr. Dawson."

Here is a contract as solemn as contract could be, ratified by legislative enactment. "The government was unable to meet the payment at the time specified," and then, after thirteen years' delay, the contract is further violated by reducing the claim to fifty cents on the dollar!

But this, say the Texans, is all the value our government received. That, we reply, is not so certain. Value is not something fixed, absolute, and immutable. It is always relative, and varies with circumstances. Ships of war were of great value to Texas then: they would be of no value to her now. The commissioners of Texas were, for a long time, hawking about Texas bonds, their only marketable commodity. It was offered for sale in open market; Messrs. Dawson, Schott, and Whitney gave for this merchandise full value. They gave more than anybody else was willing to give—more than they themselves would have been willing to give if they could have foreseen the length of time they were to be kept out of their just dues.

If these gentlemen should now be paid in full, it would be no compensation for the injury done them. He is not a very successful merchant who cannot double his capital in twelve or thirteen years. Dawson, Schott, and Whitney, but for their connections with Texas, might have trebled their fortunes; perhaps quadrupled them, perhaps not. But, whether loss or gain would have attended their exertions, one thing is certain, that, according to contract, Texas owes Dawson, Schott, and Whitney $560,000, and interest.

Two of these claimants, Messrs. Schott and Whitney, in a letter to the Governor of Texas, dated October 9, 1851, make the following statement:—

"By the contract concluded on the part of the Republic of Texas, by Mr. Samuel M. Williams, with Mr. Dawson, then acting also for us, two prices were fixed for the construction and equipment of the vessels required for the service of the government—one a cash price of three hundred and thirty-six thousand dollars, and the other a credit price of five hundred and sixty thousand dollars.

"The difference between these two prices was occasioned, not only by the uncertainty of the continued political existence of the Republic, but also by the consideration of the great embarrassment which the advance of so large a sum of money might occasion to the business of the contractors. The Republic *selected* the latter price, and we received, in payment for our part of the work, the bond for two hundred and eighty thousand dollars above mentioned.   *   *   *   *   The choice which the Republic made of the credit price, and her failure to pay at the maturity of the bonds, compelled us to sacrifice all our available means at a ruinous discount—exhausted our private fortunes—and entirely destroyed the very profitable business then in our hands. There can be no 'instance of hardship,' it seems to us, greater than to be compelled to lose, for the benefit of others, mercantile credit and position; and to support through life a weight of indebtedness incurred from a generous confidence in the honor and success of a rising State. Such is our position; and if the Legislature of Texas should restrict the payment of our claim to what was once fixed as the cash price, the amount, at this late day, will be insufficient to satisfy the debts which we still owe on her account."

Such have been the calamities of two of the creditors of Texas; and hundreds of others have been made to suffer in the same way, though not many in as large an amount. It is a mistake to suppose that the great body of the present holders of Texan securities got them at very low rates. The writer of a letter, now before us, states—

"The interests of creditors have been somewhat prejudiced by the prevailing error that the present holders of the eight or nine millions of claims hold them at a low cost. Those conversant with the position of this debt know that it is held by the present holders at a cost of fully seven millions of dollars. It is true that Texan securities have seen a very low mark; but a large portion of the claims are held by those to whom they were originally issued, while the vast majority of those that were sold and resold are now lodged in hands of purchasers whose confidence in a sacred promise and pledge had led them to bid correspondingly high."

The remarks made in relation to the case of Dawson, Schott, and Whitney apply to the case of Mr. Holford, for, as the auditor and comptroller correctly say, " The terms of contract between the government and James Holford and associates, for the purchase of the steamer ' Zavalla,' are similar to those entered into with Mr. Dawson." Setting aside such positive contracts as these is an action far more becoming a despotism than a republic.

The next paragraph shows that the auditor and comptroller met with other embarrassments in applying the principles which the Legislature had laid down for their guidance.

"In the average value assigned to the consolidated fund of June 7, 1837, there came to our knowledge a few cases of hardship where the government had received full consideration for the original obligation which had been converted into this fund, and yet owned by the original investor. Had we departed from the rate we had assigned to this or any other character of liability, in any one instance, no matter how justifiable, others not possessing the same merit would have claimed it, and the consequence would have been that but few claimants would have been satisfied with any other classification than that of par. For this reason, we determined, in all instances, to adhere to the rate affixed to each class, and report such cases of hardship as might arise to the Legislature, in order that such relief may be awarded in the premises as appears to be just. We, therefore, accompany this report with a statement marked ' C,' of such cases, and hope the same will receive your favorable consideration."

In this place is again brought forward the favorite Texan notion that more justice is due to the original holder of a public obligation than to him to whom it may have been transferred. Nothing can be more erroneous. If a bank-note passes through five thousand hands, the obligation of the bank to pay the full amount to the last holder is just as strong as it was to pay it to the first. The like is true in regard to treasury notes, certificates of stocks, and other evidences of public debt. And there may, sometimes, be greater hardship in refusing payment to the last holder than to the first. If a man dies, and his treasury notes and other securities pass to his wife and children, they are no longer in first hands. Waiving cases of this kind, there are others equally worthy of consideration. The receipt of public securities from their original holders is not always matter of choice. Their creditors may be compelled to take them in payment of debts long due, because they can get nothing else. It is very hard, then, in the State to mulct these second and third hand holders of one-half of their dues, because they were under the necessity of receiving from their debtors government paper instead of money, when that very necessity was created by the State in putting off its own creditors with paper instead of money.

The creditors of a State living within the bounds of the State, though they may be directly injured by the receipt of government paper, may receive some compensation in the improved state of public affairs consequent on a successful revolution. This is the case of the creditors of Texas resident in Texas. Their political, civil, and religious rights are now secure. Their lands have increased in value, in some instances many fold. In this way, they may have been amply compensated for all their losses through "red backs," and the various other paper devices to which their government resorted in order to get from them their property and their services. Very different, however, is the case of those creditors who reside in other States. Their lands have not been increased in value by the annexation of Texas to the Union; and their political, civil, and religious rights are no more secure than they were before the Texan revolution commenced.

If the public securities of Texas had not passed into the hands of the residents of Louisiana, Arkansas, Georgia, and other States, that revolution could never have been brought to a successful issue. As it was, the original claimants passed them over to the Texan merchants; these sent them to the United States, and exchanged them for merchandise. In this way, Texas obtained her supplies of arms, clothing, and provisions. It was this, and this alone, that saved the Republic. But, now that the Republic is saved, this is to be made a reason for depriving those who were the indirect instruments of its salvation of from one-fourth to four-fifths of their dues.

Who in Texas was able to hold on to such an immense amount of securities as the Republic issued? Who would have received them at all if it had been a condition that he must hold them till the Republic might be able to redeem them, perhaps in five years, perhaps in ten, perhaps never? What soldier would have received the treasury notes in pay for services, or what farmer would have received them in pay for provisions, if he had not known that he could pass them off to the merchant? And what merchant in Texas would have been willing to receive them if he had not supposed the whole claim thus conveyed to him might be transferred by him without diminution to whomsoever he chose? Whatever value Texan securities may have had, whether little or great, they owed that value quite as much to the action of those who got them at second or third hand as to the action of the original claimants. And unless Texas redeems those securities in full, no matter in whose hands they may now be found, she will not give back the value she has received.

We pass next to the subject of interest :—

"On the liabilities stipulated to bear interest, we have calculated it from the date of the last payment to the 1st of July, 1850, in accordance with an act approved February 11, 1850, except the interest treasury notes, on which we have allowed interest to the 1st of January, 1841, as all holders of this character of notes were required to fund them by that time, and the appropriation for the further payment of interest on said notes was cancelled."

Yes, but cancelling an appropriation is not paying a debt. The Legislature could not in justice *require*, all it could do was to *invite*, the holders of treasury notes to fund them on a certain day. If any of them chose not to accept the invitation, that did not, in the least, lessen the obligation of the Republic to pay what it had promised. Interest on a debt is due till the principal is paid. No government that issues obligations bearing interest has any right to cease paying interest till it offers to its creditors the full amount of said obligations.

Equally arbitrary and inequitable is that provision of the law of February 11, 1850, which declares that "*all* liabilities of the late Republic of Texas shall cease to bear interest from and after the 1st day of July, 1850." Just as much right would the Legislature have had to say that they should not bear interest after the 1st day of July, 1840. A retrospective act of this character would have been quite as just as a prospective one. Not till two years afterwards, or February, 1852, did Texas even commence paying her debts at the scaled rates; and till she pays all her debts in full, interest will, on principles of equity, be continually accruing thereon.

It is unnecessary to give any further analysis of the report of the auditor and comptroller. They are estimable men and able officers; but the Legislature devolved on them a task which neither they nor any one else could perform.

It might be supposed that such a report as this would induce the Legislature to pause in its career ; but it did not. The report itself (though that was not the object of its authors) contained the most indubitable evidence that it was impossible to carry out the principles that had been adopted: namely, that of giving to each claimant the value the government had, according to its own estimate, received for the claim he held. But the Legislature did not see this; or if it did, it did not care for it. It passed the law following :—

" An act confirming the action of the auditor and comptroller, under the provisions of an act of the Legislature to provide for ascertaining the debt of the late Republic of Texas, approved March 20, 1848, and the act supplementary thereto, approved February 8, 1850.

" SECTION 1. *Be it enacted by the Legislature of the State of Texas*, That the rate of payment and classification assigned to each class of debt of the late Republic, by the auditor and comptroller, under the provisions of an act entitled ' An act for Ascertaining the Debt of the late Republic of Texas,' approved March 20, 1848, and the act supplementary thereto, approved February 8, 1850, as reported by said officers in their report to the Legislature of date the 12th of November, 1851, is hereby recognized and adopted by the State of Texas ; and the value assigned to each class of liabilities by said officers in their report aforesaid is what the State of Texas recognizes as due to the respective claimants."

The bill was sent to the Governor the 23d of January, and on the 29th he returned it with a message, in which he said—

"I have, both in my official capacity, and as a private citizen, expressed my approbation of, and concurrence in the general basis upon which the auditor and comptroller have classified the public debt of Texas, and the value assigned to them; but there is no general rule without its exception; and with those officers, I do think that there are cases of individual hardship to which an application of the general basis, upon which they felt themselves constrained to act, does not render justice."

The Governor then mentions the cases referred to in statement "C" of the auditor's report, and, conceiving that they are not properly provided for in the bill, refuses to sign it. Towards the close of his message, he says—

"It is my anxious wish to see the State of Texas, at this time attracting universal attention, assume a position in reference to her debt which will not only command the admiration of her sister States and of foreign powers, but save her also from any just charge of repudiation. So far as it lies in my power, I desire every creditor of Texas to have what in justice and equity is due to him. Such, too, I believe, is the sentiment of the people at large, and of the Legislature."

The bill was passed in opposition to Gov. Bell's veto: in the Senate by a vote of 29 to 5; in the House by a vote of 47 to 12.

CHAPTER XXIX.

PROCEEDINGS OF FOURTH LEGISLATURE, CONTINUED: 1851-'52.

Act passed for the liquidation of the public debt—Debt payable and debt suspended—Effects of this act in dividing the creditors into two parties, and throwing the odium of non-payment on the United States—The money received from the United States applied to pay the current expenses of the State Government.

THE Legislature did not confine itself to an act giving a legal sanction to the awards of the auditor and comptroller. It made provision for an agent to proceed to the city of Washington to receive the bonds to the amount of five millions, about which there was no controversy, and the interest that had accrued on the same. And on the 31st of Jan., 1852, it passed a law entitled "An act providing for the Liquidation and Payment of the Debt of the late Republic of Texas."

In Appendix S, this law will be found at length; but it is so intricate in its provisions, that many will find it difficult to understand. We shall therefore state that the effect of it was to divide the whole of the acknowledged audited debt of Texas into two classes, debt payable, and debt suspended.

The debt which was made payable immediately after the passage of the act embraced the following items:—

	Original amount.	Scaling rate.	Scaled amount.
Ten per cent. funded debt created by act of Feb. 5, 1840	$754,000 00	30 cts.	$226,200 00
Eight per cent. funded debt created by act of February 5, 1840	24,280 00	30	7,284 00
Audited paper issued under various enactments	74,441 26	various	69,451 12
Miscellaneous liabilities . .	26,129 87	1 00	26,129 87
Amount filed and receipted for as second class debts . .	748,899 89	various	679,222 50
Ditto, third class, since recognized as second class . .	16,467 95	1 00	16,467 95
Amount audited by special acts	34,023 55	1 00	34,023 55
	$1,678,242 52		1,058,778 99

For the payment of these debts, and the interest thereon, bonds to the amount of two million dollars were appropriated.

The reader will observe that, with the exception of the eight and ten per cent. funded stocks, the evidences of these debts were in such a form as to be likely not to find a general market beyond the limits of the State. Thus, the debt made payable was the " domestic debt" of Texas. He will also observe that this domestic debt was subject to a very small scaling, when compared with the "foreign debt," i. e., the debt the evidences of which are held principally by the citizens of other parts of the Union.

Having still on hand bonds to the amount of three million dollars, the Legislature might have gone further in its payments; but it was not disposed so to do. It made the payment of the whole of its treasury notes, and of the residue of its stock and funded debt, dependent on the future action of the United States. These debts were not to be paid till the bonds reserved in the treasury of the United States should be paid over to Texas, or such portions thereof as might equal in amount the claims for which the creditors might sign the required releases.

We have seen that a bill had been brought before the Legislature to *compel* the creditor to sign releases to the United States. But this was abandoned as too bold a measure, and what was, no doubt, regarded by its authors as a master-stroke of policy, adopted in its stead. This would throw the *odium* of non-payment on the United States, and cause the creditors of Texas to make common cause with her in getting the bonds out of the federal treasury. The five millions already received, with the interest accrued thereon, would, indeed, pay the whole of the "filed" debt, as scaled by the auditor and comptroller; but two millions would satisfy the domestic creditors. The remaining three millions might be applied to purposes of internal improvement; and the "foreign" creditors wait till the United States could be forced or persuaded to modify the obnoxious provision which denied to Texas the absolute and unconditional control of the remaining bonds.

The scheme was cunningly contrived, and not the less so in being embodied in an act so involute and convolute that probably many who voted for it did not see its true bearing.

The effect intended has, in part at least, been produced. Some of the people of Texas are loud in their complaints " about the injustice of the United States in withholding from the State the bonds which are her own property, thereby preventing Texas from paying her creditors;" when the truth is that already more than enough bonds have been passed over to Texas to pay all her debts, both domestic and foreign, according to her " plan of settlement." The whole amount which Texas has to pay, according to the award of her auditor and comptroller, is, interest included, only $4,807,764 37. Supposing the bonds to bring on an average only four per cent. premium, they are worth $5,200,000. To this add interest for one year $250,000, and the total is $5,450,000, being nearly $650,000 more than Texas is willing to pay.

In the other object they had in view, the framers of this bill have also partially succeeded. A portion of the creditors finding that Texas, though she had ample means in hand, would not pay them even the scaled amount of these debts, have united their efforts with those of the Texas politicians to induce the United

States to give up the reserved bonds, or so many of them at least as will cover the amount of their scaled claims.

A statement follows of the various items of debt, the payment of which has been suspended by the complicate action of Texas:—

	Original amount.	Scaling rate.	Scaled amount.
Ten per cent. consolidated fund, created by act of 7th June, 1837	$632,526 80	70 cts.	$442,768 76
Ten per cent. consolidated fund, created by act of 7th June, 1837, issued under an act for the relief of Swartwout and others	7,970 43	1 00	7,970 43
Eight per cent. treasury bonds, created by act of 5th February, 1840	766,800 00	20	153,360 00
Ten per cent. treasury notes issued under act of 9th June, first issue	41,630 00	1 00	41,630 00
Ten per cent. treasury notes issued under act of 9th June, second issue	331,371 00	50	165,685 50
Treasury notes, without interest, issued under act of 19th Jan. 1839, third issue . .	1,828,192 00	25	457,048 00
Ten per cent. bonds issued by commissioners to negotiate a loan for $5,000,000, viz.:— For loan obtained from Bank of United States . . .	457,380 00		400,000 00
For purchase of steamer "Zavalla"	195,907 00	50	90,014 84
For purchase of naval vessels under contract with F. Dawson, now owned by James Schott and E. D. Whitney	280,000 00	50	140,000 00
Total of debt suspended . .	$4,541,777 23		$1,898,477 53

In addition to this act, the Legislature passed two others, one appropriating $123,220 33 for the payment of other portions of the second class debt, and another appropriating some forty or fifty thousand dollars to cover third class debts, which had not been formally decided on when the auditor and comptroller made their reports.

It also passed a law authorizing a sale to the amount of a million of the bonds, and another appropriating so much of the money received from the United States as might be necessary to the payment of the current expenses of the State Government for two years to come.

Just before the Legislature adjourned, Mr. Shaw, the comptroller, who had been sent to Washington City as agent of the Texan Government, arrived at Austin with the bonds to the amount of five millions, and the interest that had accrued thereon, to the amount of $250,000, in gold. The members received their pay out of this gold, and went rejoicing to their homes.

The treasurer then commenced making payments in gold ; but as his coffer soon gave signs of exhaustion, he began (with the sanction of the other high officers of State) to pay the public creditors in United States bonds at three per cent. premium.

A sale of bonds to the amount of upwards of $800,000 was afterwards effected at a premium as high, in some cases, as five per cent., and thus Texas realized an additional profit.

CHAPTER XXX.

PROCEEDINGS OF THE THIRTY-SECOND CONGRESS OF THE UNITED STATES: FIRST SESSION, 1851–52.

Diversified action of the creditors—Report to United States Senate by Mr. Pearce, of Maryland—Motion by Mr. Mason, of Virginia—Remarks of Messrs. Houston, Pearce, Butler, Pratt, and others—Present condition of the creditors of Texas—Distinction between debts of the Republic and debts of the State.

THE action of the Legislature of Texas had, as has already been observed, the effect of dividing the creditors into two parties. Part of them applied to the Congress of the United States for payment of the amounts due to them. Another part petitioned the same Congress to surrender the bonds to Texas in proportion as releases to the United States should be filed at the Treasury Department.

The Finance Committee of the Senate, to whom these petitions were referred, after duly considering the same, made report, through Mr. Pearce, of Maryland, on the 17th of August, 1852.

In this report, the committee, after showing in what manner and to what extent the United States had become responsible to the creditors of Texas, recommend the passage of a bill for issue of stock of the United States to the amount of eight millions and a third, bearing an interest of three per cent. per annum—the said stock to be paid to the creditors on their giving receipts in full and assignments of their evidences of debt, which may be held by the United States as a set-off to the claims of Texas to the five millions reserved under the act of September, 1850. This report is so important that we have inserted it at length in Appendix V.

When the report was laid before the Senate, no remarks were made except by Mr. Hunter, of Virginia, one of the members of the committee. He said he was in a minority as respected the bill, but that pressing duties at that juncture would not permit him to draw up a counter report.

Nine days afterwards, or on the 26th of August, when the general Appropriation Bill was under discussion, Mr. Mason, of Virginia, proposed an amendment to it, the purport of which was that the Secretary of the Treasury should release to Texas the reserved bonds in proportion as the creditors of Texas should file releases to the United States.

Mr. Mason, in supporting this amendment, said :—

" I am told, and I have no doubt correctly, that the State of Texas, before the passage of the act, passed a law determining in what proportion she would pay that debt; in other words, that it should be scaled at prescribed rates. I have not felt myself at liberty to enter into the consideration of the subject how Texas proposes to pay the debt. Whatever my opinions may be, they are not to be expressed here. She is to determine for herself, upon her own ideas of propriety, what to do with her creditors. I have nothing to do with that subject. My object alone is to say that I do not believe the interests of the United States, which I am here to represent, will be affected by authorizing the stock to be issued as fast as the releases come in; and that is the whole object of the amendment."

Messrs. Gwin of California, Clemens of Alabama, and Bright of Indiana, opposed the discussion of the amendment on the ground of want of time. Mr. Clemens said :—

" My State is one of the creditors of Texas. We are willing to trust Texas. We believe that Texas will pay us : at all events we are willing to trust her."

Mr. Houston, of Texas, supported the motion of Mr. Mason,

and expressed his regret that the subject had not sooner been submitted to the Senate. He added :—

" If the Senate were to act upon it, and to adopt the measure now proposed, I believe it would not only benefit the creditors of Texas, but it would attain all the ends of justice that they can ever expect, or that Texas can ever accord to them, which will, I think, be complete. Whether they will act upon it or not, Texas will take care of herself, and her creditors, too, if she can."

The debate was continued by Mr. Pearce of Maryland. He said:—

" Mr. President, if the State of Texas and her creditors were the only parties concerned, I should not be inclined to offer the least opposition to the amendment of the Senator from Virginia. But the Senate must all know that the United States are concerned, directly concerned; that it was the supposed liability of the United States which induced us to make that provision in the bill of 1850, by which five of the ten millions of stock, which the bill proposed to grant to Texas, were reserved and retained in the Treasury, until releases should be filed by the creditors of Texas, of a certain class. That class of creditors, as the Senate will remember, were those who held bonds for which the revenues of Texas, arising from imports, had been pledged. It had been alleged here that the United States were liable for the bonds for which these revenues were so pledged. Even during the discussion of the annexation of Texas, I well recollect that the honorable Senator from Massachusetts (Mr. Davis), in the course of a speech which he made on that occasion, produced one of the revenue bonds of Texas, held it up, showed it to the Senate of the United States, and urged it as an argument against annexation that we should be inevitably obliged, at some future day, to pay that class of debts, at all events. That was one of the considerations which induced the Congress of the United States to agree to give to Texas, by the bill of 1850, the large sum of $10,000,000. It was held that the United States were liable—at all events, such was the opinion of a great many persons, and probably of a majority of Congress—because, if the United States, upon the annexation of Texas, took possession of the funds which were pledged by that Republic to one class of her creditors, they must take those funds *cum onere;* they could not be diverted from the purpose to which they had been pledged by the Government of Texas; and when they were received into the treasury of the United States, the United States having so diverted them became liable, at least in some degree, to the parties to whom those bonds were pledged.

" Well, sir, that being the case, the United States, having that view, reserved the five millions, and declared that they should not be paid over to Texas until the creditors filed their releases. It is manifest, when we come to consider this proposition, that we are considering that which does not concern Texas and her creditors alone, but which concerns the Treasury of the United States. Texas has passed a law proposing the liquidation of her debt, and has classed her creditors variously.

" I have not yet ascertained the exact amount of those claims for which her revenues from customs were specially pledged by that name, or generally as revenues, or as being made receivable in payment of public dues. The Secretary of the Treasury, in the opinion which he has filed on this case, has stated that he supposes that the class of claims which came under that description are not to be confined to those claims for which the revenues from customs were pledged on the face of the bonds, but that other classes, also, are equally pledged, though in a different form. For example, some of these obligations of Texas are made receivable for all public dues. If they are receivable for all public dues, they are receivable in payment of *duties on imports;* and if so, duties on imports may be considered as pledged for their payment. Texas, by the act of their Congress, though it does not appear on the face of many of her obligations, pledged all her revenues for the payment of those obligations prior to January, 1840. Of course, a pledge of revenue from all sources included a pledge of revenue from customs just as effectually as if that source of revenue was specially named; since otherwise a general pledge of the revenues would be a pledge of no particular item of revenue at all. These are classes of which we were not aware at the time we passed the act of 1850. These classes amount to a much larger sum than the five millions reserved, and hence it is that the United States become interested; for these different classes of claimants amounting to more than five millions, it follows that, if we allow these claims to be admitted by payment to one portion of the creditors, still we would remain liable to another portion, and so we should not escape that which it was our purpose to avoid when we made the reservation.

" Texas has scaled her debts; that is, she proposes to liquidate them by paying some creditors the par value, as we call it, or the ostensible value, as they call it at the treasury of Texas; others she proposes to pay at the rate of seventy cents on the dollar; another class at fifty cents; and another, I think, at twenty cents on the dollar. With regard to some of these claims, Texas alleges that she received only so much as she is now willing to pay; that those who took her obligations bought them under par, or advanced less than their nominal amount. Then again, in regard to some classes, it is impossible to ascertain what the different creditors have advanced on those bonds, some having given more, and others less. These Texas has averaged. This proceeding is not satisfactory to those who have been scaled at the low rate; and they, naturally enough, are disposed to hold, not Texas only, but the United States liable for the whole amount of what is due upon the face of the bonds. They say, and it is very difficult to deny it, that, at the period when they took those obligations, the affairs of Texas were in a very critical, if not almost desperate state; that the reduced rates at which they paid for their bonds was but fair, when you consider the risk they run; and they say that they are entitled to all, now that Texas has got out of her difficulties, and especially as the United States have in some measure acknowledged their liability for them. And then, as it has not been the practice of the Government of the United States to scale her debts, to refuse to pay her liabilities in full, it is difficult for us to say that we will sanction any proceeding by which payment for one portion of these debts, at one rate, should be paid at the treasury at a rate which will leave a remainder of the five millions insufficient to pay the other creditors at the same rate.

" I wish to say that I trust these remarks will not be considered offensive to Texas. It is impossible to avoid speaking of the effect of the scaling act; but neither in the report of the Committee on Finance, ncr in any remarks which I may make, is there any desire to cast any reproach upon that State. On the contrary, I have endeavored to avoid any expression which might justly cause irritation.

"I suppose that, if you adopt this proposition of the Senator from Virginia, 'the consequences would be, that something like $1,800,000 would be paid out of the treasury of the United States in favor of the claimants, scaled at the high rate, and they most probably would be satisfied; but those scaled at the low rates would be utterly dissatisfied; and they would hereafter be calling on the treasury, and calling until, at last, I have no doubt, we should yield to their demands, and exhaust, not only the whole amount of the $5,000,000 left, after the $1,800,000 were paid, but even $6,000,000 or $7,000,000, to which, with the accumulated interest, in the course of a few years, the remainder of the debt would amount. If we adopt this amendment, the amount remaining of the $5,000,000 will not more than one-half satisfy these demands.

"Now, will the United States, under these circumstances, give their sanction to a proposition, by which one class of creditors, having quite an equal claim upon them as the other class, shall be paid at the treasury out of this reserved fund, at the larger rate at which their claims were scaled, and leave the others to receive the reduced rate at which they were scaled, or wait an indefinite series of years, besieging us all the time for the full rate which they say they have the right to demand, and which, according to our usage, we have not a right to deny? If we are not prepared to say that we will discriminate between the classes who have equal claims against the United States, we must reject this amendment.

"The Committee on Finance have, through me, submitted a proposition which, we believe, will be satisfactory to all the creditors of Texas. That proposition is to appropriate $8,333,000 in bonds, bearing an interest of 3 per cent., to be divided equally among all the claimants, according to their claims. I do not propose now to vindicate that bill, but I shall be prepared to do so whenever it comes up properly. We hope that it will prove satisfactory to Texas, as we are sure it will be to the creditors. But while that is pending, it seems to me that we can scarcely, without entering into its consideration, undertake to dispose favorably of this proposition of the Senator from Virginia. I will not pursue the debate further. I have stated these considerations in order to show the difficulties in the way of the adoption of the proposition of the Senator from Virginia."

Mr. Hunter, of Virginia, preferred the amendment offered by Mr. Mason to the report of the Finance Committee, but he did not wish the general appropriation bill encumbered by any provision relating to the debt of Texas.

Mr. Houston said:—

"Without the reservation having been made in the law of 1850, I never should have supposed, for one moment, that the United States were liable for any portion of the debt of Texas. Nor do I believe that by any but an open declaration of theirs can they even assume the responsibility of her debts. * * * Texas has not repudiated any of her liabilities. She has arranged that by her municipal regulations. She had a right to do that.

* * * She is competent to regulate her own matters, and she will reserve that power, let the United States take what action they please."

Mr. Bayard, of Delaware, said he should vote against the amendment, because there was no time to discuss the principles involved in it, and the relative importance of the two propositions—this and the one reported by the Finance Committee.

The debate was continued by Mr. Butler, of South Carolina, and Mr. Pratt, of Maryland, whose words we must give *verbatim*.

"Mr. BUTLER.—Mr. President, I have not now time to say what I would wish to say upon this subject, but I will say one thing pretty decidedly—that I think Texas ought to be the administrator of her own affairs; and when the United States undertook to supervise and correct her, and assume for Texas a responsibility which she is not disposed to assume for herself, it is the climax of Federal assumption.

"Sir, some gentlemen say there is not time to consider this subject; others say if there were time it ought not to be considered one way or the other; but I choose to say that there is time enough to consider this in any point of view in which I believe the subject ought to be considered; and that is, to allow those who may be willing to receive their money according to the scale of Texas, to come in, file their releases, and receive their money. What objection is there to that? That is the object of the amendment of my honorable friend from Virginia.

"There is now an injunction upon that; and upon what ground? That by delaying this subject, and managing, perhaps, upon a very high consideration of political morality—no speculation, of course; I suppose speculation has nothing to do with this subject—the Federal Government is to rebuke Texas by saying to her: 'You have not scaled your debt correctly, and we will assume to honor a draft which you do not choose to pay, on the ground that you have disgraced yourselves.' That is the amount of it. We have said to Texas: 'Say what you owe, and we will pay it; and to save ourselves from any further liability hereafter, we will give you $5,000,000 positively, and $5,000,000 on certain conditions, that your creditors file releases.' Well, all do not come in. Here are women and children absolutely perishing because they have not liberty to come in and take their money; and then, from a high morality—political morality, of course—the United States tell Texas: 'You have disgraced yourselves by the manner in which you have scaled your debts; we will save you from disgrace by assuming the debt; we will accept the draft which you have dishonored.' I do not stand here to be the guardian of the honor of Texas —not at all. But one thing is very certain; and I leave the proposition to the public to say whether there is more political morality or speculation in it."

"Mr. PRATT.—Mr. President, if I admitted the obligation supposed to exist by the Senator from South Carolina (Mr. Butler), I should, of course, agree with him in opinion; but I do not think the obligations of Texas have anything to do with the question presented by this amendment. The sole question for us to consider is whether the Government of the United States is bound for all these debts.

"The Senator makes light of the proposition. I know him to be a good lawyer, and I venture to say now that he cannot answer the argument which so humble an individual as myself may make on the subject.

"Mr. President, I do not propose to say anything as to the honor of Texas. The question here is whether the United States are liable for these debts or not. If the United States be answerable for them, then it is the honor of the United States, not the honor of Texas, that we are to consider. Now, I assume, as a legal proposition which my honorable friend from South Carolina cannot deny, that, whenever any one State becomes, by compact, amalgamated with another, the State into which the sovereignty is merged is liable for all the obligations of the government thus united with it.

"My constituents are deeply interested in this question. I do not intend to say aught against Texas. I am speaking of the obligation of the United States to pay my constituents the debt which I believe is now due from this government to them.

"Texas was a sovereign State; the United States cannot deny that proposition; it must be conceded by us, at least, that Texas was a sovereign State. She has yielded that sovereignty to the United States. What, permit me to ask, was pledged for the payment of her debts? I differ here somewhat from my honorable colleague. I say that the national faith of Texas, her faith as an independent nation, was pledged. She has ceased to exist as a nation. The United States now possess that former sovereignty which was originally pledged by Texas for the payment of these debts. Now, I say that it is a proposition of national law, running down from the first elementary works to the latest writer on the subject, that, where that case exists, where the sovereignty of one State has been merged in that of another, the State into which it is merged is liable for all the obligations of the other. I hold before me Rutherford's *Institutes*, who, speaking of the effect of the union, by compact, of two States into one, says:—

"'Since both States thus continue in this united body, and neither of them ceases to exist, the rights and the obligations of both will remain, and will become the rights and obligations of the united body—that is, whatever rights belonged to each State separately before they were united will afterwards be the rights of the collective State; and the same obligations that each State was under separately before, the collective State will be under afterwards.'

"You will find in all the elementary works this proposition broadly laid down, and it is, I submit, a proposition right in itself. Texas was entitled to enter into these obligations. She was a nation, existing in the eyes of the civilized world as a nation, when she entered into these obligations."

"Mr. BAYARD.—Allow me to ask the honorable Senator from Maryland whether he argues that the entire nationality of Texas was all amalgamated into the United States? Did her entire sovereignty pass to the United States? I say the entire nationality of the nation amalgamated with another must be destroyed before the nation into which it is amalgamated is liable for the debts of the other."

"Mr. PRATT.—The Senator says that the entire nationality must be destroyed. Now, I say the entire nationality of Texas was destroyed. I do not mean to say that she is not a State equal to any in this Union. I am proud to consider her as a sister State, equal to any other State in the Union.

But I say that Texas has surrendered the entire nationality which was pledged for the payment of these debts.

"The proposition of my honorable colleague is that the United States are bound for that class of debts for which she had pledged her revenue from imposts, and which were of course expressly ceded to this Union by her becoming a member of it. No one can doubt that proposition. My honorable friend from South Carolina says there is nothing in it; but he adduced no argument to show it."

"Mr. BUTLER.—I had not time to do so."

"Mr. PRATT.—Nor could you, if you had time; nor can any man living refute the proposition, *that, so far as the obligations of Texas were secured by her revenues* from imposts *which have been surrendered to this Union*, our government, having taken those revenues, took them *cum onere*, and are bound for the debts for which Texas pledged them. But I go further, and I say that, in reference to all the debts of Texas for which the national faith was pledged, we, having assumed the nationality which was pledged for their payment, assumed the debt.

"My honorable friend from Delaware has asked me whether Texas surrendered her nationality—her entire revenue, and ability to pay, which, as a nation, she possessed antecedently to her annexation to this Union. Well, I say that she has ceased to exist as a nation."

"Mr. BAYARD.—She possesses a *quasi* sovereignty."

"Mr. PRATT.—We have peculiar institutions. The sovereignty which she possesses is a *quasi* sovereignty : but the sovereignty which she had pledged for the payment of these debts was an absolute sovereignty, and has been surrendered. She entered into these debts as a nation. As a nation she has ceased to exist; and she is now a member of this Union, possessing, as my friend says, a *quasi* sovereignty; but not possessing *the* sovereignty which was pledged for the payment of those debts. It is sufficient, however, for the purpose of this argument, to show, what cannot be successfully denied by any one, that the class of debts embraced by the amendment were secured by an express pledge of revenues of Texas which *have been* surrendered to the United States. In regard, therefore, to the class of debts affected by the amendment under consideration, Texas has surrendered to the United States the revenues which she had pledged for their payment; and in regard *to them*, the Senators from South Carolina and Delaware must admit that Texas has ceased to be sovereign; and by the admission necessarily inferred from their argument, we (the United States) are answerable for them, the thing, the revenue, pledged by Texas for their payment, now belonging to the United States, and she receiving the money arising from it. This proposition, therefore, with due submission to the judgment of others, I say, cannot be successfully denied with reference to that class of debts intended to be embraced by this amendment, because, by assuming the means which Texas pledged for their payment, the United States *with them* necessarily assumed the payment of the debt for which those means were pledged."

The Senate adjourned without taking a vote on the question; and for the present the condition of the creditors of Texas is as follows:—

With claims on two governments, which claims are, to a certain extent, recognized by both, they are paid by neither.

Texas, although she has abundant means, will not pay them so much as one cent of even the scaled amount, because she wishes them to unite with her in *forcing* the United States to give up the reserved bonds.

The United States will not pay them, because this would be in reality exacting the amount from her twice. If she should make an unconditional surrender of the bonds, or any surrender of them whatever, except on the terms stipulated in the act of September, 1850, she would make herself liable to the creditors for the difference between the scaled and the original amount of their claims.

One class of creditors join with Texas to wrest the reserved bonds from the United States Government; but they show by their language and their conduct that, if the United States should pay the others in full, they would expect to be paid in full also. What they aim at, is, to be paid the scaled amount by Texas now, and the residue by the United States some time hereafter.

What the result will be, we pretend not to augur. If the question could be kept clear of all others, there would be little difficulty in effecting an adjustment. But this can hardly be hoped. Our leaders of all parties are always on the look-out for something out of which to make political capital. It was of very little importance to the great body of the people of the United States where the line was drawn between Texas and New Mexico. But the controversy on this question (if the speech-makers are to be believed) brought into danger the very existence of the Union. The truth is that various aspirants for public honors wanted something to quarrel about, and if they could have found no better subject of dispute, they would have quarrelled about a stick or a straw. Not a few of them seem ready at any time " to bring the Union into danger," so far at least as can be done by their speeches, in order that they may afterwards have the honor of saving it by other speeches.

Judging by past experience, there is little hope that this case will be decided solely on its merits. Perhaps the doctrine of " State Rights" will be invoked to bring it within the limits of the political arena. If so, we protest against any such abuse of what is, when properly understood, a most excellent doctrine. A State has an undoubted power to contract debts, and pay them in whole or in part, or not at all, just as she pleases; and the United States have no power to interfere. So a State may, by what General Houston is pleased to denominate "her municipal regulations," call in her evidences of public debt, and scale them down to one-half of their original amount. She may call them in, in this way, again and again, till finally she scales them down to zero. "She has a right to do that." "She is quite competent to regulate her own matters," and in this way "to take care of herself, and her creditors too;" and the United States have neither the ability nor the disposition to interfere with this "arrangement."*

* Far be it from us to doubt or deny the sovereign right of a sovereign State to cheat its creditors. This is an attribute of sovereignty which the States have never surrendered. On this point we are of perfect accord with Mr. Mason and Mr. Hunter of Virginia, Mr. Butler of South Carolina, and General Houston of Texas. But does the case of Texas fall strictly within the limits of the principles laid down in our text? The constitutional right of a State to repudiate its debts, either in whole or in part, we freely admit. But the debts in question are not the debts of the *State* of Texas, but the debts of the *Republic* of Texas. Some of the citizens of Texas show that they have a very clear notion of the distinction, when they say their State "is administering on the effects of a *dead* Republic."

The State has, indeed, assumed the debts of the Republic, for in her constitution it is expressly said that "the ordinance passed by the Convention on the fourth of July, assenting to the overtures for the annexation of Texas, shall be attached to the constitution, and form part of the same." And in this ordinance (see Appendix R) these debts are recognized, and a guarantee given that they should not come against the United States.

Does such an assumption of the debts of the Republic by the State give the latter the right "to arrange them" "by municipal regulations" as she might her own proper debts? The debts were incurred by the Republic, and "defined" by the Republic. As so "defined," they were assumed by the State, and now for the State to attempt to "re-define" them seems to detract somewhat from the sovereignty of the Republic.

It is evident that the Congress under which annexation was effected was aware of the distinction between the debts of the Republic and the debts of the State of Texas. They knew that, according to the laws of nations, all those debts for which the transferred revenues had been pledged would, without some express stipulation to the contrary, become a claim against the United States. They, therefore, made it an indispensable condition that the *State* of Texas should assume the debts of the *Republic* of Texas.

The question is a very different one from that which would be presented, if the debts had been incurred by a State within the Union. And, perhaps, even as matters now stand, the question is more curious than useful. The United States Government took the initiative in annexation, and by the very terms it proposed,

The United States leave Texas at liberty to make the best compromise she can with her creditors. But the case of the United States and the creditors of Texas is different from the case of the United States and Texas, though the two cases are necessarily connected. If Texas will not, or cannot pay the holders of the evidences of her circulating debt, the United States are bound to pay them. And, under these circumstances, the United States will not surrender the bonds till the creditors shall sign the required releases. It was to guard against such a contingency as has occurred that the last proviso was introduced into the "Boundary Act;" and, as Texas freely assented to this proviso, she has no right now to object, even if it does present an obstacle to her plan of coercing her creditors into a compromise.

CHAPTER XXXI.

TEXAN PLEDGES OF FAITH AND TEXAN BREACHES OF FAITH.

Solemn league and covenant of the Provisional Government—Audited drafts—Five million loan act and supplement—Act of June 7, 1837, for consolidating public debt—Treasury notes—Act of 1837 authorizing receipt of audited drafts for direct taxes—Act of 1838 for payment of interest on the funded debt—Treasury bonds act—Funding act of 1840—Act to repeal the act providing for the redemption of promissory notes—Act for the issue of exchequer bills—Resolution of annexation—Scaling act of 1848—Act barring all claims not presented before September, 1850—Act stopping interest after July 1, 1850.

It will be proper to give a summary view of Texan pledges of faith and Texan breaches of faith, if it be only to show what governments will promise, and what, in some instances, they will not perform.

In the preamble to the plan of a Provisional Government, adopted in November, 1835, the people of Texas do solemnly declare :—

---

admitted, by implication, that it would be responsible for the debts, if they were not paid by Texas. In the "Boundary Act," it fully and positively admits its responsibility for all the debts for which the transferred revenues had been pledged.

" 6. That Texas is responsible for the expenses of her armies now in the field.

" 7. That the public faith of Texas is pledged for the payment of any debts contracted by her agents.

" These DECLARATIONS we solemnly avow to the world, and call GOD to witness their truth and sincerity ; and invoke defeat and disgrace upon our heads should we prove guilty of duplicity."

This is a solemn league and covenant, as solemn as words could make it. It has never been fulfilled. The expenses of the army then in the field were paid with audited drafts, many of which were afterwards commuted for treasury notes, while many of those treasury notes were subsequently exchanged for certificates of stocks. These debts have been so mixed up with the other debts of the Republic, that it is impossible to separate them. The only way in which the Texans can fulfil this solemn league and covenant is by paying to every man what they have promised to pay.

December 20, 1836, an act was passed imposing duties on imports. By the fourth section of this act, it was declared—

" That it shall be the duty of the several collectors to receive the orders of the auditor upon the treasury of the Republic when offered by importers in payment of duties at the time of importation."

This was followed by an act, June 12, 1837, " to raise a revenue by direct taxation," one provision of which was :—

" That properly audited drafts on the treasury of the Republic shall be received in payment of taxes imposed in this bill, except on billiard tables, retailers of liquors, and nine-pin alleys, or games of that kind."

By these two acts, Texas gave to her audited drafts a greater value than they would otherwise have possessed, and caused them to pass into hands that otherwise would not have received them. She thus entered into a contract with the holders of these drafts to take them in payment of debts due to herself. By another act, passed December 14, 1837, she violently set aside this contract, declaring that such drafts should no longer be so received. She made the holders thereof no compensation for the wrong done them ; and as these debts have become so mixed up with other debts subsequently incurred that they cannot be separated from them, the only way for her to do justice to those who were thus wronged is for her to discharge all her outstanding obligations according to the letter of the contract.

June 7, 1837, was passed "an act to authorize the consolidation and funding of the public debt."

The preamble was in the words following:—

"Whereas, it is deemed expedient to consolidate the public debt, by the creation of a stock fund commensurate therewith, by issuing certificates of stock in suitable and convenient shares: it is also deemed expedient, *in order that the public credit be sustained, and the public creditors be relieved by the payment of fair interest on the government liabilities,* that the same be thus consolidated and placed in a tangible form, *so that the interest may be annually paid, and the debt secured to the public creditors until its final redemption, &c.* Therefore," &c.

This was a new pledge of faith to the public creditors, holding out to them inducements to exchange the evidences of the public debt they then held for others in a form more convenient to the government. The first section provided that these certificates of stock should bear an interest of ten per cent., payable semi-annually, and another section was in the words following:—

"*Be it further enacted,* That the public faith is hereby pledged for the redemption of said stock agreeably to the foregoing provisions ; and so much of the public revenue, arising from imports and direct taxation, as may be necessary to meet the annual interest of the funded debt, is hereby appropriated and set apart for that special purpose."

These pledges have been violated:—

1. In not applying the revenues from imports and direct taxation to the payment of the interest on this funded debt; but in appropriating them to the current expenses of the government.

2. In arbitrarily declaring that interest on this funded debt should cease on the 1st of July, 1850, on which day not one dollar of the principal had been paid.

3. In scaling down this debt to seventy cents in the dollar, which is an express violation of the letter of the contract.

June 9, 1837, was passed "an act authorizing the issuing of the promissory notes of the government," some of the provisions of which were as follows:—

"That the said notes shall be payable twelve months after date, and shall draw an interest of ten per cent. per annum from date.

"That the said notes, at any time before or after maturity, shall be considered as cash, and shall be received as cash for all dues owing or coming to the government.

"That one-fourth of the proceeds arising from the sales of the lands contemplated to be sold by an act of this Congress shall be paid into the treasury, to be paid out only for the redemption of the promissory notes of the government.

"That the President is authorized to sell five hundred thousand acres of land-script, the proceeds of which shall be paid into the treasury, to be paid out only for the redemption of these promissory notes of the government."

These pledges have been violated :—

1. In not paying the notes with the interest thereon in twelve months after date.

2. In arbitrarily declaring that the said notes should not, after Feb. 1, 1842, be receivable in all payments to government, and that at a time when their being so receivable gave them the little value they then had left.

3. In not setting apart one-fourth of the proceeds of the sale of the lands for the redemption of these notes, but in appropriating them to the current expenses of the Republic.

4. In appropriating the proceeds of the land-script above mentioned to the current expenses of the government, instead of applying them to the redemption of these notes.

5. In arbitrarily declaring that such of these notes as remained unfunded should, after January 1, 1841, cease to bear interest.

6. In scaling down these notes to fifty cents in the dollar.

May 16, 1838, was passed an " act to authorize the President to negotiate a loan on the bonds of the government, not exceeding five million dollars," one section of which was as follows :—

"Section 7. *Be it further enacted*, That, for the punctual payment of the interest and final redemption of said bonds, the public faith is hereby solemnly pledged."

Such a pledge covers everything a government possesses, or may hereafter acquire.

Comprehensive, however, as was this pledge, it was found impossible to borrow money under it, and a supplementary act was passed January 22, 1839, some of the provisions of which we shall introduce at length.

"Section 4. *Be it further enacted*, That in case the said loan of five million dollars, or any part thereof, should be negotiated by virtue of the aforesaid act of May 16, 1838, in addition to the general pledge of the faith and credit of the Republic, contained in said act, for the payment of the interest and redemption of the principal of said loan, so much of the revenues of the Republic as may be necessary shall be set apart and semi-annually remitted to the Bank of the United States, in Philadelphia, to meet the semi-annual interest on any bond or bonds issued under said loan. And as soon as the government shall deem it expedient to sell the said lands, of the proceeds thereof three hundred thousand dollars shall be annually appropriated and set apart, and invested in public securities or corporate stock, to form a sinking fund for the ultimate redemption of the aforesaid loan of five millions of dollars, which said appropriation shall be continued annually to be made, until, with the interest accruing and accumulating on the same, a sum shall be raised equal to the five million dollars, or any part thereof which may have been negotiated."

These pledges were further strengthened by an act passed January 14, 1840, entitled

" An act to provide for the more certain operations of the Sinking Fund created by an act of Congress of the Republic of Texas, passed January 22, 1839, to extinguish the five million loan authorized to be raised under two several acts of Congress of November 18, 1834, and 16th of May, 1838 ; and such further loans as the Republic may cause to be negotiated, and for other purposes."

The third section contains the following provisions :—

"SECTION 3. *Be it further enacted*, That in case, from consideration of public convenience or policy, it shall be deemed inexpedient to bring the public lands into the market on or before the 1st of January, 1842, or that, when so brought forward, it should be deemed inexpedient to sell them, it is hereby declared to be then and after that period the duty of the Secretary of the Treasury to provide from other sources of revenue, and to pay over to the aforesaid Commissioners of the Sinking Fund, the full sum of three hundred thousand dollars in the instalments before mentioned, or such sum as, with the amount realized from sales of public lands, shall make up, at the period stated, the sum of three hundred thousand dollars, to be remitted to the agents aforesaid, or wherever the said loan may be effected."

Another section of this act is in the words following :—

"SECTION 15. *Be it further enacted*, That for the redemption of all loans negotiated by the authority of the Republic of Texas, independently of the reservation of the Sinking Fund, the proceeds of the public lands generally, its revenues and public faith, are solemnly pledged."

Under the pledges of faith, general and special, contained in these acts, bonds were negotiated to the amount of $1,213,287 : namely, $560,000 with F. Dawson and others, $457,380 with the U. S. Bank of Pennsylvania, and $195,907 with J. Holford and others.

These pledges of faith, general and special, have been violated in the following particulars :—

1. So much of the revenues of the Republic as was necessary to meet the semi-annual interest on the bonds was *not* set apart and semi-annually remitted to the United States Bank in Philadelphia. The revenues were, on the contrary, used to defray the general expenses of government.

2. The government did not deem it expedient to bring the public lands into the market on or before June 1st, 1842, and yet the Secretary of the Treasury did not, from other resources, pay over to the Commissioners of the Sinking Fund the full sum of $300,000 annually.

3. In a subsequent year, the government did deem it expedient to sell a portion of the public lands, and made a most excellent sale to the amount of $10,000,000; and yet it did not appropriate and set apart annually $300,000 of the proceeds thereof for the redemption of these bonds, principal and interest.

4. These pledges have been further violated in scaling down the debt to fifty cents on the dollar, in direct violation of the letter of the contract.

5. They have also been violated in arbitrarily declaring that interest on this debt should cease on the 1st of July, 1850, when not one dollar of it had been paid.

February 5th, 1840, was passed " an act for creating funds for the support of government for the year 1840."

SEC. 1. Bonds to be issued of the denomination of $100, $500, and $1000, " bearing an interest of eight per centum per annum, payable in gold and silver."

" SEC. 3. *Be it further enacted*, That the bonds before referred to shall be at all times receivable by any collector of revenue, or at the Treasury Department, in payment of any debt to the government, or any duties by impost or direct taxation, for the amount value of such funds, and the interest which may have accrued thereon."

" SEC. 4. *Be it further enacted*, That for the payment of the interest on the bonds before referred to, the revenue accruing from license-tax, and the tax on personal property, is hereby set apart for that purpose."

The pledges of faith herein given have been violated :—

1. In not paying the interest on these bonds in gold and silver ; no, not so much as for one half year.

2. In appropriating to other purposes the proceeds of the license-tax and the tax on personal property, instead of applying them exclusively to the payment of interest on these bonds.

3. In declaring that these bonds should not be receivable for duties or taxes after February 1, 1842, by which they were deprived of the little value that then remained to them.

4. In arbitrarily determining that not one cent of interest should be paid after July 1st, 1850, though not one dollar of the principal of these bonds had then been discharged.

5. In scaling down these bonds to twenty cents in the dollar.

February 5th, 1840, was passed "an act to provide for the redemption of the promissory notes of the government now in circulation, and for funding other liabilities of the government."

SEC. 1 required blanks to be provided for sums of $100, $500, and $1000, transferable by simple indorsement.

" SEC. 2. *Be it further enacted*, That all sums of the promissory notes of this government in circulation, which shall be presented to the stock commissioner prior to the first day of July next ensuing (if in sums to suit the denominations of the certificates), shall be admitted for funding, and certificates of stock, as before provided, shall be issued to the holder or holders of such promissory notes for the amounts so presented ; which certificates so issued shall bear on them an annual rate of interest of ten per cent., payable semi-annually in gold or silver at the Treasury Department.

" SEC. 3. *Be it further enacted*, That all other liabilities of the government, which may have been properly and regularly audited, shall be admitted for funding, and certificates for the same shall be issued by the stock commissioner, bearing the same rate of interest of ten per cent., and payable semi-annually in gold or silver.

"SEC. 4. *Be it further enacted*, That from and after the first day of July next ensuing, the promissory notes of the government, which may be presented for funding, shall only be entitled to receive from the stock commissioners certificates of stock bearing a rate of interest of eight per cent. per annum, interest payable semi-annually in gold and silver."

There was something arbitrary in requiring men who had notes bearing an interest of ten per cent. to bring them in prior to the 1st of July, 1840, under penalty of having the interest on the certificates, for which they were to be exchanged, reduced to eight per cent. But, waiving this, the pledges of faith contained in this act have been violated in the following particulars :—

1. In not paying the interest, semi-annually, in gold and silver, as promised, not even for one half year.

2. In arbitrarily declaring that interest on these certificates should cease on the 1st of July, 1850.

3. In scaling down the face of these certificates to 30 cents in the dollar.

Feb. 5, 1841, was passed "an act to repeal an act to provide for the redemption of the promissory notes."

"That from and after the passage of this act, so much of the above act as relates to the bonding or funding of the promissory notes or liabilities of the government be, and the same is hereby repealed."

This left the holders of "red backs" and of unfunded audited paper, without even the promise of interest, though they were, in justice, as much entitled to such promise as the other creditors of government.

Jan. 19, 1842, was passed "an act to authorize the President to issue exchequer bills, and to declare what shall be receivable in payment of taxes and duties on imports."

"SEC. 1. *Be it enacted by the Senate and House of Representatives of the Republic of Texas in Congress assembled*, That, from and after the first day of February next, it shall not be lawful for any collector of customs of this Republic to receive in payment of imposts or duties upon goods, wares, and merchandise imported into this Republic, after the day above specified, anything but gold or silver, or the exchequer bills hereinafter authorized to be issued.

"SEC. 2. *Be it further enacted*, That it shall not be lawful for the sheriff and collectors of direct taxes, to be assessed for the year 1842, and all subsequent years, to receive anything in payment of such taxes except gold or silver, or the exchequer bills authorized to be issued by the provisions of this act.

*   *   *   *   *   *   *   *

"SEC. 9. *Be it further enacted*, That all land-dues (except the land-tax) and all payments for patents be made receivable, as heretofore, in the liabilities of the government.

"SEC. 10. *Be it further enacted*, That all laws heretofore passed, authorizing the issue and reissue of promissory notes, and their reception in payment of duties or taxes hereafter to be assessed, be, and the same are hereby repealed."

Necessity led to the passage of this act; but that did not make it the less a violation of public faith. The promissory notes had been issued with a proviso that they were to be received in payment of all dues to government. This provision, on principles of equity, should have remained in force till all the notes were redeemed. Depriving them of the quality which gave them their chief value was a manifest injustice to the public creditors.

It was not long before the holders of exchequer bills received much the same treatment that holders of treasury notes had experienced. July 29, 1842, an act was passed "to regulate the collection of import duties," two of the sections of which we shall give in full:—

"SECTION 1. *Be it enacted*, That the collectors of revenue are hereby required, from and after the passage of this act, to receive the exchequer bills, in the collection of impost and tonnage duties, only at the current rates at which such bills are selling in the market.

"SECTION 4. *Be it further enacted*, That all sheriffs, clerks, and postmasters throughout the Republic are hereby authorized and required to collect the direct and license-taxes and postages in accordance with the provisions of this act."

This was a violation of the act passed only six months before, which, if it meant anything, meant that exchequer bills should be received at their face value for public dues.

March 20, 1848, an act was passed "to provide for ascertaining the debt of the late Republic of Texas." And February 9, 1852, was passed "an act confirming the action of the auditor and comptroller under the provisions of an act of the Legislature to provide for ascertaining the debt of the late Republic of Texas, approved March 20, 1848, and the act supplementary thereto, approved February 8, 1850."

From beginning to end, these acts were violations of the public faith, as they provide for the scaling of the debts, contrary to the very face and tenor of the evidences of these debts. Every treasury note, every bond, every certificate of stock, every audited draft she issued was a pledge of the public faith of Texas. Just so many pledges of faith as she gave, just so many did she violate when she scaled them down below the contract amount.

February 8, 1850, an act was passed extending the provisions of the act of March 20, 1848, to the first Monday in September, 1850, and declaring that "all claims not presented by that time shall be barred."

Texas has no right to bar the claims of such of her creditors as may not choose to submit to her scaling system. On principles of equity, these claims will remain in full force against her, though a dozen legislatures should each in succession determine that they should be barred.

February 11, 1850, was passed "an act to provide for the liquidation of the public debt of the late Republic of Texas." The sixth section enacts

"That all liabilities of the late Republic of Texas, whether the same have or have not been presented to the auditor and comptroller under the provisions of the 'act to provide for ascertaining the debts of the late Republic of Texas, approved March 20, 1848,' shall cease to draw interest from and after the first day of July, 1850."

If, of a debt matured, full payment is not made when demanded, interest is, on principles of equity, due on that debt till it shall be paid in full. The debtor has no right to say to the creditor, "I will not pay you, neither will I pay interest longer than to me seems fit."

Therefore, notwithstanding this enactment, the debt of Texas goes on accumulating at the rate of ten per cent. per annum, and will go on thus accumulating till either she or Congress shall pay in full the debts for which the revenues were pledged.

We pass next to the pledges of faith Texas has given in relation to these debts in her compacts with the United States.

In the resolution of annexation, to which Texas gave her most cordial assent, it was expressly provided that said State

" Shall also retain all the vacant and unappropriated lands lying within its limits, *to be applied to the payment of the debts and liabilities of Texas;* and the RESIDUE of said lands, after discharging said debts and liabilities, to be disposed of as said State may direct, but in NO EVENT are said liabilities to become a charge against the United States Government."

Here were two distinct pledges; first, that the public lands of Texas should be applied *exclusively* to the payment of the debts of Texas, till the whole should be discharged; secondly, that in no event should these debts become a charge against the United States.

Both these pledges have been violated.

Texas has appropriated her public lands for the promotion of internal improvements and other objects just as freely as she could have done had no such pledge been made. Every inch of her public domain is mortgaged to her public creditors, and she has no right to give or grant one acre, except for the purpose of redeeming this and other mortgages.

The second pledge has also been violated. Texas has suffered her debts and liabilities to come against the Government of the United States, and that, even after the United States had appropriated ten million dollars for the express purpose of paying these very debts.

The compact entered into between the United States and Texas, in the "Boundary Act," has also been violated.

It is evident, from the terms of that act, that its intent was that the five millions paid over unconditionally should be applied to the redemption of those debts for which the United States were considered liable. But Texas applies part of the money to the redemption of her "domestic debt," for which the United States were in no way responsible; another part to the payment of the expenses of her State Government; and not one dollar to the redemption of the debt for which the revenues had been pledged !

Admit, by way of argument, that Texas, as a sovereign State, has a sovereign right to violate her contracts with her private creditors, she has no right thus to violate her compacts with the United States.

CHAPTER XXXII.

GENERAL VIEW OF CURRENCY IN TEXAS.

"Hammered dollars" the chief currency of Texas previous to the revolution—Influx of bank-notes from the United States in 1835–37—"Shin-plasters"—Treasury notes, first, second, and third issues—Evil consequences thereof—Exchequer bills—Gross amount of circulating paper—Bank of Agriculture and Commerce—Texas Railroad, Navigation, and Banking Company—Other bank projects—Laws of the Republic and the State, and constitutional provisions to prevent the issue of circulating paper—"Mills's money"—A little paper-money panic in Texas—Good effects of the hard-money laws of Texas—Efforts to change the constitution so as to allow of paper-money banking.

THAT the reader may have a clear view of the changes in currency that have taken place in Texas, it will be necessary to bring together various facts scattered through different chapters, together with others which could not before be conveniently introduced.

While Texas was a part of Mexico, the currency consisted of gold and silver, with a sprinkling of the notes of various banks of the United States. As the civilized population was small, amounting, in 1834, according to Mexican official statements, to no more than twenty-one thousand, no large amount of currency of any kind could have been required for the transactions of business. Accordingly, we find Almonte declaring: "Money is very scarce in Texas ; not one sale in ten is made for cash. Purchases are made on credit, or by barter, which gives the country, in its trading relations, the appearance of a fair."

An old Texan, however, assures us that it was only as compared with Mexico that money was scarce. As compared with most newly-settled countries, money was plenty in Texas. A great part of the currency consisted of "hammered dollars," that is, of old Spanish dollars, from which the royal effigy had been effaced by the Mexicans, as a testimony of their indignation towards their ancient rulers. This "hammered money" was the common currency, but time-contracts were made in "eagle-money," by which were meant new Mexican dollars, which were valued at one hundred cents, while the "hammered dollars," though containing full as much silver, were valued at only ninety cents.

At Brownsville, and other towns on the Rio Grande, there is much of this "hammered money" still in use. But there a different reason was given for the stamp's being defaced. It was done, we were told, by the Mexicans, " in order to keep the money in the country." If so, they act on much the same principle as some of our own people who are now endeavoring to deteriorate the silver coinage. Their object is to keep our silver money in the country by diminishing the quantity of pure metal in our half-dollars, quarter-dollars, dimes, and half-dimes. The Mexicans, with the same object in view, did not diminish the intrinsic value of their coin, but sought to prevent its exportation by effacing the stamp, which was the certificate of its value. Of the two plans we prefer the Mexican.

After the revolution broke out, "hammered money" was not for a long time the chief currency of the Republic. In 1835, bank-notes began to come in freely from the United States, more freely in 1836, and still more freely in 1837. Then the banks suspended specie payments. The paper of most of the banks of Mississippi, which formed much of the currency of Texas, depreciated greatly, and that of some of them became worthless. Many of the people of Texas suffered severely thereby, but their aggregate losses did not equal their aggregate gains, as many of these notes had been obtained on loans, and many of these loans were never repaid.

To these notes of suspended banks, were added " shin-plasters," or notes for fractional parts of the dollar, put into circulation by individuals and municipalities. The issue of these began in 1837, and continued till 1840, when an end was put to them by the bankruptcy of the issuers.

For two years after the revolutionary outbreak, or from the fall of 1835 to the fall of 1837, bank-notes and " shin-plasters" formed almost the exclusive medium of Texas. The government had issued a large quantity of drafts on its empty treasury, and these were a tender for public dues; but, as they were for odd numbers of dollars and cents, they never became a common currency.

The first issues of treasury notes were in November, 1837, though some of the notes are said to bear date in September. As these were for round sums and for small amounts, they were much better fitted to serve the purposes of a circulating medium than were the audited drafts. As the notes of the banks of the United States were of almost as many different values as the banks that issued them, the want was sensibly felt of some one medium that should have one value. As the treasury notes bore on the face an interest of ten per cent., this was an inducement to hoard them, on the part of such Texans as could afford it; and this, also, gave them a market in the United States.

Through these causes combined, as explained at length in a preceding chapter, these notes were kept at par with specie, or nearly at par, for several months, and till the issues exceeded half a million. They then, in the spring of 1838, began to depreciate, and as each additional emission increased the depreciation, they were, in January, 1839, worth no more than forty cents in the dollar.

To these treasury notes bearing interest, the first issues of which were known as the "printed," and the second as the "engraved," succeeded, in the spring of 1838, treasury notes bearing no interest, and which were familiarly known as "red backs," on account of a red impression on the back. When first issued, in the spring of 1839, they were worth thirty-seven and a-half cents in the dollar, but in 1841 they were worth no more than twelve to fifteen cents. In the winter of 1841–42, they fell to ten cents, to five cents, to four, to three, to two cents in the dollar. Finally, they became worth nothing in many parts of Texas.

Thus, in little more than three years, the treasury note system ran its course. As soon as it was fairly established, it supplied Texas with its only general circulating medium. Just on the same principle that bank-notes in the United States displace gold and silver, did treasury notes in Texas displace bank-notes. For, where there are two currencies of like denominations, that of the least value will always drive the other out of circulation.

The evils this system did were immense, and such as for which,

even if it were so disposed, the government could afford no compensation to the sufferers. A receives a treasury note at par. He
keeps it, for a time, and then passes it to B at ninety cents in
the dollar. At the end of a week, a month, or a day, B passes it
to C at eighty cents. So it passes to D, E, F, G, H, I, till, finally,
it reaches J at ten cents. J passes it to K at nine cents, who passes
it to L at eight cents, and thus it passes on to M, N, O, P, Q, R,
S, till it reaches T at one cent. In this way have the poor Texans
been "scaled" by their government, and this may be one reason
that they wish to scale others in their turn.

It would be curious to calculate the amount of evil that may
be done, and the number of persons that may be made to suffer,
through a government note for one dollar. It is true that a fluctuating bank currency may produce the like evils, but that we have
not immediately under consideration. One thing is certain, that,
as neither bank nor government can afterwards ·atone for such
wrongs, neither bank nor government ought to be suffered to inflict
them.

Great, however, as were these evils, they were small compared
with those produced by continental money, for that was made a
legal tender, and supported by penal enactments. In Texas, on
the contrary, every man was at liberty to refuse or receive treasury notes at his option. As the most general circulating medium,
they regulated prices ; but, as it was known that they were continually varying in value, if a man gave a note payable at a distant
day, it was understood that he was to pay it in silver, or in so
many treasury notes as might then be the equivalent of the silver
money therein expressed.

To the treasury notes succeeded the exchequer bills, which were
but treasury notes in a new form. These were so few in number,
and so variant in value, that they never became a common circulating medium. They were merchandise, and a tender to government for public dues.

By this time, there was little circulating medium of any kind in
Texas; but this was no great calamity, as the people had but little
left to circulate. They no doubt, however, like others in similar
circumstances, attributed to want of circulating *medium* the evils
they suffered from want of circulating *capital*.

As the issues of audited drafts amounted to $7,834,207 57,

those of treasury notes to \$4,717,939, and those of treasury bonds to \$766,800, or, in all, to \$13,318,146 57, if paper issues could make a people rich, the Texans would have been the most wealthy people in the universe.

What they suffered from this policy is sufficiently attested by a provision inserted in their State Constitution, adopted August 27, 1845, which declares that

"In no case shall the Legislature have power to issue ' treasury warrants,' ' treasury notes,' or paper of any description intended to circulate as money."

It is never without deep experience of the evils of paper issues that a people impose such restrictions on their rulers.

It is now time to turn our attention to the policy of Texas concerning banks.

It has already been mentioned that the Congress of the Republic made full recognition of the Coahuilan decree for the establishment of the Agricultural and Commercial Bank, and also that it passed an act to incorporate the Texas Railroad, Navigation, and Banking Company, with a capital of five millions, to be increased to ten millions, and with a charter for forty-nine years. Other schemes, equally magnificent, were, as has been duly recorded in other parts of our history, favorably received by the Texan Congress. But, about this time, the banking system of the United States descended with a mighty crush; and this produced a change in the minds of the Texan lawgivers. On the 14th of December, 1837, they passed an act by which it was made unlawful for any person or persons to either issue or put in circulation any printed or lithographed promissory note, under a penalty of not less than five nor more than fifty dollars for each offence. A like penalty was imposed on any person who should so much as present in payment for debt, or for the purchase of property, any such notes; and it was made the special duty of all grand-juries to inquire into and present all persons offending against the provisions of this act.

Perhaps this law was intended in part to secure an exclusive field for the circulation of treasury notes, by forbidding the issue of small notes by individuals and municipalities.

After the explosion of the treasury note 'system, an act was passed February 3, 1841, to authorize McKinney and Williams to issue their notes to the amount of thirty thousand dollars for circulation as money; but a declaration was added:—

"That banking privileges, as a general rule, being inexpedient, the privileges hereby granted to McKinney, Williams, & Co. are conceded to them in consideration of their having made large advances to this government at an early period of its existence."

The next law that we can find having a bearing on the subject, is entitled "An act to Suppress Private Banking," passed February 5, 1840. In this, it is provided

"That all laws granting to any individual, individuals, or corporations the authority to issue either bills or promissory notes, to pass or circulate as money, are hereby repealed."

For each offence against the act, the penalty was a fine of five hundred dollars, and imprisonment for not less than three nor more than twelve months; and it was made the special duty of the judges of the District Court to give the act in charge to the grand-juries of the several counties, at the beginning of each term of said courts.

This act took from McKinney, Williams, & Co. the privilege conferred by the law of February, 1841 (a privilege, by the way, of which they could not avail themselves), but it did not repeal the charters of the Commercial and Agricultural Bank, or of the Texas Railroad, Navigation, and Banking Company. It simply deprived them of the power to issue paper to circulate as money, but left them with full power (if so be they had any legal existence) to discharge the functions of banks of deposit, transfer, discount, and exchange.

These are the only acts relating to banking that appear to have been passed by Texas as an independent empire; and the result was that Texas, as a Republic, had no banks in operation.

To prevent their suffering in future such evils as the citizens of other parts of our Union have been subjected to, the people of Texas embodied the following provisions in their State Constitution:—

"ART. VIII. SECTION 28. No corporate body shall hereafter be created, renewed, or extended, with banking or discounting privileges.

"SECTION 32. The Legislature shall prohibit by law individuals from issuing bills, checks, or promissory notes, or other paper, to circulate as money."

These provisions are sufficiently stringent; some of them, perhaps, almost too much so. It is only as paper-money factories that banks do harm. We can see no objection to banks of deposit, discount, transfer, and exchange, provided they operate with hard-money only, or with paper which shall be, dollar for dollar, the representative of specie actually in their vaults. But the Legislature of Texas is by the constitution prevented from establishing even hard-money banks.

In accordance with these constitutional provisions, an act was passed on the 7th of April, 1846, declaring that

" No person or persons within this State shall issue any bill, promissory note, check, or other paper, to circulate as money.

" Every person who may violate this act shall be subject to indictment therefor, by a grand-jury, as for a misdemeanor, at any time within twelve months after so offending ; and shall be subjected to a fine of not less than ten dollars, nor more than fifty dollars, for each and every bill, promissory note, check, or other paper, issued by them in violation of the first section of this act."

Another act was passed, nearly two years afterwards, or on the 20th of March, 1848, the first section of which provides

" That any corporation, company, or association of individuals who shall use or exercise banking or discounting privileges in this State, or who shall issue any bill, check, promissory note, or other paper in this State, to circulate as money, without authority of law, shall be deemed guilty of a misdemeanor, and shall be liable to a fine of not less than two thousand dollars, nor more than five thousand dollars, which may be recovered by a suit in the District Court, in the name of the State."

The second section makes it the duty of the attorney-general to institute suit against offenders, makes simple service of citation sufficient service, and provides that, in any judgment that may be obtained, execution may be levied upon the estate of the corporation, company, or association of individuals, and in default of such estate, on the estate of the officers of such corporation, company, or association.

The third section enacts " that in any suit instituted under the provisions of this act, either party may appeal to the Supreme Court of the State, and no bond or security shall be required of the State on any such appeal."

The fourth section provides that each and every month that any corporation, &c. shall exercise banking or discounting privileges, shall be deemed a separate offence ; and each and every bill, &c., issued to circulate as money, shall be deemed a separate offence.

As the laws of the Republic, of December 14, 1837, and February 5, 1844, remain unrepealed, they would seem quite sufficient, with the provisions of the constitution, and the acts of the State of April 7, 1846, and March 20, 1848, to put an end to paper-money evils in Texas. But the reader may be disposed to ask if these various provisions produce the effect intended, for he is well aware that laws often prove nugatory, sometimes through the faults of the officers whose duty it is to execute them; sometimes through the state of public opinion being such as to prevent their proper enforcement; sometimes through defects in the mere wording of the law; and sometimes through a neglect to provide the necessary auxiliary means to carry the law into operation.

We answer that the effect intended has been produced, though not to the whole extent that the framers of the constitution desired.

Through some mysterious means, the Commercial and Agricultural Bank has been brought into operation, for it does not appear that it has ever been certified to the Executive "that one hundred thousand dollars had entered its vaults," and this was an indispensable condition of its charter. A writer, in the sixth volume of De Bow's *Commercial Review*, states that

"Messrs. J. Lake & Co., by means of the credits which they got through the Ohio State Bank law, started three other Ohio banks (in addition to the Bank of Wooster), besides buying the Mineral Bank of Maryland and a bank in Texas. 'The foundation of the whole is $171,900 of stock owned by Lake in the Wooster Bank. It is possible that not a cent of money was paid at all, but stock notes given.'"

As the Commercial and Agricultural Bank is the only bank in Texas, the fair inference is that this is the bank affirmed to have been bought by J. Lake & Co. But this is inference. Wherever it obtained the means, certain it is that the Commercial and Agricultural Bank commenced operations at Galveston some six years ago, and continues them to this day. It has also established a branch at Brownsville, with the view of circulating its paper in the adjoining State of Tamaulipas. But the Mexicans will have none of it. They prefer their own defaced silver coin to any "promises to pay," however prettily they may be adorned by the art of the engraver.

The Attorney-General of Texas has been, for some time, contesting with the bank the legality of its existence; but, as he was the private counsel of the bank before he was elevated to his present dignity, the opinion of some people is that the State will not gain much in the contest. Texas found no difficulty in abolishing the privileges which the Mexican laws conferred on the *empresarios*, or contractors for settling the public lands. But when it comes to a question about privileges conferred on a bank, the case is very different. The bank then proves too powerful for the State, with all its hard-money laws, and its hard-money constitution.

The laws of Texas are, as we have seen, very strict in regard to paper currency; but a certain English judge once said that he never saw an act of Parliament through which he could not drive a coach and four horses, and our paper-money men in America can, when necessary, drive a whole ox team, horns, hoofs, and all, through acts of Assembly. If the reader will scan the laws of Texas in regard to paper currency, he will find that, though they rigidly prohibit the issue of bank-notes, they do not prohibit their *reissue*, much less the simple passing of notes issued by banks in another State. Neither do they prohibit any citizen of Texas from indorsing such issues, although such indorsement may give them a currency in Texas they would not otherwise obtain. Penal acts are to be strictly construed. Constructive offences are not to be admitted in a Republic; otherwise, no one citizen knows how soon he may be arraigned as a criminal.

Taking advantage of these most excellent principles, the house of R. & D. G. Mills, of Galveston, have for years been in the habit of indorsing the notes of the Northern Bank of Mississippi at Holly Springs, and thus giving them a currency in Texas, as the *Texas State Gazette* expresses, "not for the purpose of making money, but to facilitate the operations of their own business, by affording a convenient medium of circulation." The Bank of Holly Springs is of very doubtful reputation, the notes of which would never of themselves have obtained currency in Texas. But being indorsed by what was long regarded as the richest commercial firm in the State, they passed freely, to the amount, as the *Houston Telegraph* supposes, of three hundred thousand dollars, though the *Austin State Gazette* asserts "it is scarcely possible that there ever was, at any one time, more than forty thousand dollars in circulation."

All this did very well for years in succession. "Mills's money," as it was called, was regarded as being as good as gold and silver, or even better, inasmuch as it could more readily be carried from place to place.   The rest of the story we will let the editor of the *Texas State Gazette* tell in his own words, as we find it in his paper of February 7, 1852, premising the fact that Austin, the home of the editor, is, by the post-route, two hundred and fifty miles inland from Galveston, the home of the Messrs. Mills.

"The news of the suspension of the house of R. & D. G. Mills was received in town a few days since, and of course created no little excitement, as the bills of the Northern Bank of Mississippi, bearing their indorsement, had for some time circulated among us with all the facility of gold.   The sudden and unexpected announcement of this fact of course created a great revulsion, and for a time all confidence was destroyed in this money; subsequent advices, however, and the opinion of men acquainted with the members of this house, and not altogether unadvised of their true condition, have produced a considerable modification of the panic and a restoration of confidence."

From this it will be seen that the people of Texas have, in spite of their hard-money laws and hard-money constitution, had a very pretty little paper-money panic.   And they will have more, unless those whose duty it is to administer the laws shall discover that putting foreign bank-notes in circulation, by indorsing them, is a mere evasion of the act of Assembly which forbids the emission of paper for circulation.   By the method they pursued, Messrs. R. & D. G. Mills made their house at Galveston a branch of the Bank of Holly Springs.   If this practice is tolerated, other "wild-cat banks" will have their branches in Texas.   The Bank of Holly Springs and its agents will not be suffered to monopolize so very profitable a business.

It is to be observed that the Messrs. Mills are, as are also Messrs. McKinney and Williams, of the Commercial and Agricultural Bank, very amiable men in the private walks of life, and highly meritorious citizens, who rendered great aid to Texas in her hours of adversity.   But they would add greatly to the esteem in which they are justly held by their fellow-citizens if they would set a proper example of obedience to those provisions of the law and the constitution which are designed to insure to Texas the benefits of a sound circulating medium.

Notwithstanding the subterfuges by which they are violated or evaded, the hard-money laws of Texas have done much good.   The

Commercial Bank has, as is said by some, not more than fourteen thousand paper dollars in circulation, and if the editor of the *State Gazette* is correct, the circulation of the Holly Springs branch notes hardly amounts to twenty-five thousand dollars. These sums are necessarily conjectural: but it is agreed on all hands that at least nine-tenths, perhaps nineteen-twentieths, of the circulating medium of Texas consists of gold and silver. The notes of the banks of other States are brought into Texas by immigrants and travellers, but they are soon sent out again in pay for commodities. They form no permanent part of the circulating medium of the State; and so little inconvenience do they occasion that, within the bounds of the commonwealth, there is not one broker, exchange merchant, or other person, whose business is to buy and sell bank-notes.

To this exemption from the curse of paper-money, Texas is in part indebted to her situation. If she had, by her side, a petty State, like Rhode Island, with a hundred petty banks, each issuing petty one and two dollar notes, her hard-money laws and hard-money constitution would avail but little. The public good would then prove no match for private cupidity. But Arkansas, one of the States adjoining Texas, has no banks, and Louisiana, the other adjoining State, permits her banks to issue no notes of a less denomination than five dollars.

The result of this hard-money policy is that business in Texas rests on a more stable foundation than it does in many other parts of the Union. That it is absolutely free from vicissitude is what we do not assert. That would be impossible in a State containing some two hundred thousand inhabitants, connected by strong political and commercial ties with other States containing upwards of twenty millions, most of whom are subject to paper-money vacillation, as certain, though not as regular as the return of the seasons. The main export of Texas is, moreover, cotton, and the chief market for that is England, another paper-money country, subject to money revulsions, not as frequent, but sometimes as violent as our own. In addition to this, it should be taken into consideration that, in all new settlements, some time must elapse before the different relations of supply and demand can attain the regularity which they have in old communities.

All these difficulties Texas has to contend with. But, unbolstered by bank credits, and governed by that best of all regulators, gold and silver, her merchants limit their purchases of goods abroad by the actual demands of the planters at home, measuring that demand by the surplus crops the planters have to dispose of. Exchanges are regular. The maximum. rates never exceed the cost of transporting specie, and often fall below it. A gentleman of Austin told us that he had, in the course of years, negotiated bills on New York to the amount of two hundred thousand dollars, and had seldom given or received either premium or discount. At Galveston, from what we could learn, exchanges on New York have not for years been at any time at more than one and a half premium. Sometimes exchanges set against the North and in favor of Texas.

Prices are not low. At Austin, in March, 1852, butter was from thirty-five to forty cents a pound ; flour was ten dollars and a half a barrel; beef five cents a pound; chickens twenty-five cents a piece ; eggs twenty-five cents a dozen. These facts show that hard-money and high prices are not incompatible, though it is proper to observe that the prices in that particular neighborhood at that time were owing in part to demands from immigrants, and in part to a detachment of United States forces having been quartered in the town. Throughout Texas, however, prices are quite as high as they are (other things considered) in the most paper-money loving parts of the Union.

The rate of interest is high, because the profits of trade are great. Money is scarce, as money ought to be, for without scarcity it would lose its value. But gold and silver money is in Texas quite as plentiful, in proportion to other circulating wealth, as paper-money is in New York or Massachusetts.

How long this state of things will last, we know not. The editor of the *Texas State Gazette*, the government paper, states that it was want of time only that prevented the Legislature, at its recent session, from taking the initiatory steps to such a change in the constitution as will make it possible to establish paper-money banks. The editor himself is in favor of the change. The Democratic party, he observes, is not opposed to banks; it is only opposed to a bank of the United States. It is an error, moreover, he asserts, to suppose that banks are intended for the benefit of the rich ; they are, in reality, intended for the benefit of the poor.

Arguments like these will hardly fail to have their effect in a country where many must be desirous of an inflation of the currency, even if it should last only long enough to enable them to get high prices for the square leagues of land for which they cannot now find purchasers. The Legislature being already gained, all the editor has to do is to unite with himself one-half of the other able editors in the State, and the work is accomplished. It may be very true that three-fourths of the people of Texas may be, in their hearts, opposed to a renewal of the paper-money policy; but Americans are always in haste to be rich, and the Texans are (whatever some people may think to the contrary) full-blooded Americans. Many will favor the projected change, not because convinced that it will benefit the community, but because they will hope thereby to benefit themselves.

Even supposing the paper-money men to remain a minority, a well-organized minority, closely bound together by selfish interests, is almost always too strong for a majority that has only the public good in view.

At first sight, indeed, there would seem to be some difficulty in effecting the desired amendment to the constitution. First, it must receive the approbation of two-thirds of each House; secondly, it must be published in the public prints for at least three months before the next general election of representatives; thirdly, it must receive a majority of the votes of all the citizens voting for representatives; fourthly, it must have the sanction of two-thirds of each House of the next Legislature; and fifthly, the amendment must be read on three several days in each House.

These are obstacles indeed. But greater obstacles than these can be overcome, when the object is individual enrichment through legislative enactment.

CHAPTER XXXIII.

COMPARISON OF THE ACTION OF TEXAS, THE OTHER STATES, AND THE UNITED STATES, IN RELATION TO PUBLIC DEBTS.

Laws of Texas concerning interest on private debts—Their good effect—Erroneous views of the Texans concerning their public debts—Arguments drawn from the action of the United States in relation to continental currency shown to be unfounded—Contrast of the conduct of Texas and that of the other States in relation to public debts.

THE chief arguments adduced by the Texans in favor of their scaling system are the examples set by other governments in times of difficulty, and that the value a government receives in time of trouble is all that it is honestly bound to pay in times of prosperity—in other words, that no insurance is due on public debts. They do not carry the doctrine so far as to say that no insurance is due on private debts. From the remains of that superstition of the Middle Ages, which teaches that the receiving of interest is a sin, they are freer than the people of most other countries. They regard it as almost as absurd for the Legislature to attempt to regulate the rent (*i. e.* interest) of money as to regulate the rent of houses and lands (*i. e.* the interest of money invested in houses and lands). Their statutes make a distinction between "legal and conventional interest." "On all written contracts, when no specific premium or rate of interest is expressed, interest shall be allowed at the rate of eight per cent. per annum." But "the parties to any written contract may agree to and stipulate for any premium or rate of interest, not exceeding twelve per cent. per annum on the amount or value of the contract; and the same may be taken, 'recovered,' and allowed."

Thus, under specific contracts, the lender can, by law, recover twelve per cent. interest. He is free to take more, if he can get it. But the law will not aid him in collecting it. It is then a debt of honor between the parties; and due means are taken that the creditor shall not convert this debt of honor into a debt recoverable by law. To insure this, it is provided

"That all contracts or instruments of writing whatever, which may, in any way, directly or indirectly, violate the foregoing provisions of this act, by stipulating for allowing or receiving a greater premium or rate of interest than twelve per cent. per annum, for the loan, payment, or delivery of any money, goods, wares, merchandise, bonds, notes of hand, or any commodity, shall be void and of no effect for the whole premium or rate of interest *only;* but the *principal* sum of money, or the value of the goods, wares, merchandise, bonds, notes of hand, or commodity, may be received and recovered."

This law has been pretty well tested, for it was passed in 1840, and remains to the present day unmodified, affording an example of stability that is quite remarkable in Texan legislation.

Perhaps a better láw could not be devised. The business of borrowing and lending is left free, as it ought to be. But it is free all round. The borrower is free to pay a sum exceeding twelve per cent., if he chooses; and the lender is free to receive whatever the borrower is willing to give. At the same time, the courts of justice are left free not to interfere with the parties.

But cases of *extortion* may occur. Then the debtor has his remedy; and the would-be extortioner is punished by being deprived of the *whole of the interest* he has bargained for. If the law went further than this—if it deprived the money-lender of principal also, it would hold out inducements to dishonest borrowers to defraud their creditors.

The money-lender has an interest in not charging more than twelve per cent., for if he charges fifteen, fourteen, thirteen, or even twelve and a half, he may forfeit the whole of the interest, and not recover the principal without a lawsuit. At the same time, if commercial interest rises above this rate, he has an interest in lending, because the borrower has an interest in paying. If he does not pay according to agreement, his credit is (except in attempts at extortion) forever gone in the money-market of Texas.

Borrowers and lenders ought to be at liberty to make such contracts as they choose, and it is proper for the law to enforce these contracts when neither party takes undue advantage of the other. But there is no good reason why all the judges, all the jurors, all the sheriffs, all the constables, and all the prisons of a country should be put in requisition to enforce extortionate contracts. On the contrary, those who attempt to enforce such contracts ought to be punished; and for this the laws of Texas sufficiently provide in compelling the would-be extortioner to forfeit the whole of the interest he may have bargained to receive.

The law works well. Texas is a country of unlimited natural resources, but of very limited capital. The demand for capital is consequently great, and the rent of loanable capital is very high. This is shown not only in the rent or interest demanded for money loaned, but in the rent demanded for improved lands. In the neighborhood of Austin, two hundred and fifty miles in the interior, improved lands rent for ten dollars an acre per annum, while lands nearly as good and but a few miles distant can be bought, in fee simple, at one or two dollars an acre. The immigrants from the old States, bringing their working hands with them, find it more advantageous to pay this high rent for lands on which their labor will be immediately productive, than to purchase provisions till they can bring their own lands into cultivation. As the number of acres of improved land offered for rent is relatively small, and the number of persons who wish to rent is relatively great, the high price above stated is given and received.

So in the case of loanable capital in the form of money. The demand for it is great. The supply is limited, and the rate of commercial interest is consequently high. At Galveston, it is seldom below twelve per cent., and sometimes rises to twenty. It has been known to be sixty, but then only for a few days. In New York and Boston, commercial rates rise sometimes in the same ratio above legal rates, for laws cannot give fixidity to that the very essence of which is variability.

In such a country as Texas, any restrictions on the free circulation of loanable capital would be very injurious; and so well are the laws of Texas adapted to the circumstances of the country, that we could hear of but one case in which a debtor refused to pay interest on the ground of having been charged more than the law allowed, and then the jury brought in a verdict in favor of the lender.

One consequence of this freedom of borrowing and lending is an increase in the amount of capital loaned. Many persons lend at commercial rates who would not lend at all, if the laws (as in some of the old States) made it a crime to lend above a specified rate.

In Texas, moreover, loanable capital is not collected into banks, and there placed under the control of irresponsible boards of directors. Every man lends his own capital without the intervention of banks or brokers. No " go-between" is necessary to evade unjust and oppressive laws, for there are no unjust and oppressive laws to evade.

One consequence is an escape from much of that litigation which is so common in the old States. The money which debtors in New York and Pennsylvania pay to their lawyers, they pay in Texas to their creditors. The lawyers in Texas have much cause of complaint as to this freedom of borrowing and lending, as it deprives them of much of their business. But they are the only men who have cause to complain.

We do not pretend to say that credit in Texas is unattended with evils. Wherever there is credit, there must be debt. Where profits of trade are high, men are naturally disposed to stretch their credit to the utmost in order that they may get the capital of others into possession. They thus involve themselves in debts, from which in some cases it is difficult, in others impossible, to extricate themselves. This occurs in Texas as elsewhere. In addition to this, Texas, as part of a paper-money confederation, suffers from every contraction and expansion of the banks of New York and Philadelphia ; but having no banks of her own, or none of much account, and being exempted by her location from the operations of the banks of the other States, except in a secondary degree, she suffers much less than other parts of the Union.

Some readers may regard this as an episode. If it is, we cannot help it. It is connected with the main chain of our history. The laws have much to do in forming public opinion. The laws of Texas cause a distinction to be made in the public mind between legal and conventional rates of interest. The former may be recovered by law ; the latter cannot when they exceed a certain rate, but ought to be paid, except when the amount is extortionate.

The Texans regard their public debt as falling within the last category. The full amount may be due according to the letter of the contract, but it is not due in equity ; it is not due in honor, for the government never received (as they maintain) adequate consideration for it.

We differ from them in judgment. If a private individual wishes to borrow, there are relatively few to whom he can make known his wants. The whole world knew of the necessities of Texas, and by issuing her securities in as small amounts as five, three, two, and even one dollar, she took every means in her power to enlist every man, woman, and child who had a dollar to lend among her creditors. She sent agents to the United States, agents to England, and agents to France, and all for no other purpose in the world than to get people's dollars from them. In order to induce folks to part with their money, she pledged everything she had in the world —her lands, her customs, her direct taxes, her license-taxes, and above all her "public faith," which is her public honor. To suit the various tastes and fancies of men and women, who had money to lend, she issued her securities in every variety of form, treasury notes and exchequer bills, printed notes and engraved notes, notes with interest and notes without, "red backs," and star notes, and change notes, eight per cent. treasury bonds and eight per cent. funded, and ten per cent. consolidated debts.

Texas borrowed in the open market of the world, and if she got but little for some of her securities, it was because they were worth but little. That they brought even the little they did was because Texas promised much. If her meaning was, "Though I promise to pay one hundred cents, I intend to pay only fifty cents, or twenty cents, as suits my convenience," she ought to have said so. Then she could not have borrowed at all.

If hard pushed by arguments of this kind, the friends of the scaling system in Texas attempt to defend themselves by saying that the United States scaled their debts in the case of the continental issues. Those who are in want of precedents for injustice will never be at a loss to find them. It would have been better if the Texans had so used the experience of the United States in the case of continental money as to avoid striking on the same rock. Speaking of this same continental money, an eye-witness of its effects says:—

"We have suffered more from this cause than from every other cause of calamity. It has killed more men, pervaded and corrupted the choicest interests of our country more, and done more injustice than even the arms and artifices of our enemies.　＊　　＊　　＊　　＊

" It has polluted the equity of our laws, turned them into engines of oppression and wrong; corrupted the justice of our public administration; destroyed the fortunes of thousands of those who had most confidence in it; enervated the trade, husbandry, and manufactures of our country, and gone far to destroy the morality of our people."*

The Revolutionary Congress did scale this continental money; and by the very act of scaling greatly aggravated the evils above described. Deeply did it deplore the necessity for the act. Speaking of it in after years, Mr. Gerry said:—

" Congress were reduced to the necessity of scaling the old debt, to sink it, and of beginning anew, or of giving up the cause. Sad alternative! to violate the public faith, or be enslaved."

The first Congress, under the present Constitution of the United States, took measures for funding the revolutionary debt. The foreign debt was paid at par, the domestic certificate debt was funded at par, and the continental bills were funded at one hundred for one. While they were yet a common circulating medium (ten years before), they had depreciated to a thousand for one. " Their circulation was never more brisk than when they were five hundred for one." As they were in everybody's hands when they became worthless, it was argued that the sinking of them in this way by depreciation was equivalent to sinking them by general taxation; and that to impose a general tax for the sake of redeeming them in the hands of those with whom they chanced to be found ten years afterwards, was very like taxing the community a second time for the sake of that for which it had been very heavily taxed already.

Whatever may be thought of this argument, a better may be found in the fact that it was utterly impossible to redeem the continental bills at par, or pay the interest on them if funded. The issues amounted to $357,000,000, without including the counterfeits thrown into circulation by the British. Even supposing it possible to distinguish the clumsily executed originals from the counterfeits, the attempt to pay the interest on them would have crushed the government.

The United States assumed all the rest of the revolutionary

---

* See Essays by Pelatiah Webster, a merchant of Philadelphia, published at different intervals from 1776 to 1780, in pamphlet form, and collected into a volume in 1790.

debt at par, and thereby assumed as much as they could bear. Even to enable them to bear so much as they assumed, it was found necessary to defer for ten years the payment of interest on one-third of the debt.

The cases of the United States and Texas are so different that the action of the first in funding the continental bills at one hundred for one, cannot be adduced as an excuse, much less as a justification of the latter for the course she is pursuing.

The continental bills were sunk by a depreciation equivalent to a tax to that amount on the people who were benefited by the Revolution. Not one of them was exported. This cannot be said of the promissory notes of Texas. And if Texas insists on scaling them, she will throw great part of the costs of her revolution on people deriving no benefit from it. This is a point of great importance. Some of the Texans seem to think that the notes being held by non-residents is reason enough in itself why they should be scaled down to the lowest rate possible. To us it is an additional reason why they should be paid in full. If the notes were held by residents of Texas, it might be supposed that they received some compensation in the increased value of their lands and the general prosperity consequent on the successful issue of the struggle. But no such compensation can be afforded to non-residents. They suffer all the injustice, without any abatement.

The other point of distinction is that the United States had not the power to redeem their continental bills, while Texas has full ability to pay her promissory notes.

None but those who have turned their attention specially to the subject know the state of poverty and destitution in which the old thirteen States were left by the revolutionary war—a state from which they hardly began to emerge till the present Constitution was brought into operation, and till the wars of the French Revolution created a new demand for our products, and gave employment to our shipping. In the very debate which was had on the funding of the public debt (1791), Mr. Boudinot said there was one township in New Jersey in which three hundred executions were out for non-payment of taxes. And the Secretary of the Treasury, in his report, "with his plan for supporting public credit," made the following statement in regard to the value of land :—

"The present depreciated state of that species of property is a serious calamity. The value of cultivated lands, in most of the States, has fallen, since the Revolution, from twenty-five to thirty per cent. In those further south, the decrease is still more considerable. Indeed, if the representations continually received from that quarter may be credited, lands there will command no price which may not be deemed an almost total sacrifice."

How different the condition of Texas, with her lands rising in value, and prosperity in all her quarters!

If any foreign government had bestowed on the United States, either in payment for wild lands or for any other cause, a sum of money equal to their debts, they would have redeemed every dollar of the continental bills. But the United States have bestowed on Texas, in payment for wild lands, a sum exceeding the whole amount of her circulating debt, and yet Texas will not pay.

As little of excuse or justification can Texas derive from the recent conduct of some of the States of our Union. Mississippi has repudiated the Union Bank bonds, because, as she avers, they were issued and negotiated in violation of law and of constitution. Texas cannot make this excuse. All her debts were incurred in strict conformity with both law and constitution.

Florida pleads minority: that she was a mere territory, and that the United States, as her guardian, ought to have prevented her running into debt. Texas cannot set up this plea, for she was an independent Republic, in the plenary enjoyment of all the attributes of sovereignty.

The only two of the remaining States that have repudiated any portion of their debts are Indiana and Michigan, and they have done it on the ground that gross frauds were practised in their negotiation. Texas cannot make this apology. All her debts were fairly and openly contracted.

Arkansas does not pay; but she has not repudiated. She acknowledges the amount due, and once every two years, through her Governor, expresses her deep regret that she cannot discharge her obligations. Texas can pay, and will not.

Illinois, Indiana, and Michigan, finding it impossible to pay in money certain of their admitted debts, freely surrendered to their creditors the railroads and other improvements on which the borrowed money had been expended. To this they added lands. They did the best their circumstances would permit. If Texas would do likewise, her creditors would have no cause of complaint.

Pennsylvania, Maryland, and perhaps some of the other States, suspended for a time the payment of interest, or paid only in inconvertible paper. But this was matter of stern necessity, caused by the suspension of specie payments on the part of the banks, with the derangement of commerce and the prostration of industry thereon consequent. But, as soon as the banks resumed specie payments, and as soon as Pennsylvania and Maryland could bring into successful operation the new revenue systems which the change of times made necessary, they resumed the payment of interest in full.

Texas stands alone. She repudiates on principles on which the other States have never acted. They all, except her, admit, in the language of Mr. Sedgwick, that, " whenever a voluntary engagement is made for a valuable consideration for property advanced, or services rendered, and the terms of the contract are understood, if no fraud or imposition is practised, the party engaging is bound to the performance, according to the literal meaning of the words in which it is expressed." None of the States except Texas attempts to set aside such contracts on the plea that they have not received as much as they have promised to give. None of the States but Texas maintains that insurance is not due on money borrowed in times of adversity. None of the States but Texas thinks of reopening accounts ten years after they have been fairly audited, and ten years after the negotiable certificates of the same have been in circulation. None of the States but Texas gives a preference to domestic over foreign creditors. None of the States but Texas attempts to draw a line of distinction between original holders and assignees of evidences of public debt. None of the States but Texas has, or might have, ten millions in her treasury, and fifty million dollars' worth of public lands. The public lands in the other States are, for the most part, the property of the Federal Government. In this respect, Texas has great advantages over the other States. Yet she will not pay what she owes.

CHAPTER XXXIV.

PRESENT CONDITION OF TEXAS.

Improved condition of Texas as set forth in the inaugural address of Governor Bell and Lieutenant-Governor Henderson—Contrast with its condition a few years previous as set forth by President Houston—This the result of annexation, and this " a sufficient consideration" for all the debts Texas has incurred—Complaints against Texas—Unreasonable demands of her public men—Land-speculations in Texas—Their effects on the public mind—Popular arguments of the Texans in favor of scaling—Led to scaling in part by the necessity of making equation of currencies—Audited claims not to be reopened—Popular arguments in favor of scaling briefly examined—Less made by investments in Texan securities than by other investments—Prices of leading stocks in New York market in 1842, 1845, and 1852—Prices of bank and other stocks in Philadelphia in 1842, 1845, and 1852—Bad effects on American reputation in Europe if Texas does not review her course—Indications of a change for the better in public sentiment in Texas—The interest of Texas will be promoted by her complying with her contracts.

Since annexation to the Union, the fiscal concerns of Texas have undergone a striking improvement. Her revenues have exceeded her expenses, and the interest on the bonds received from the United States has enabled her to release the State tax collected in each county for the benefit of such county.*

General prosperity prevails ; but on this point it will be best to let the Texans themselves speak.

In the address which Governor Bell made to the Legislature, December 22, 1851, at the commencement of his second term of office, he uses the following language :—

" I cannot conclude this address without expressing to you who are now present, and to my fellow-citizens generally, my heartfelt congratulations upon the prosperous condition of our young State. To me, the contrast between what Texas is, and what she was in 1836, is indeed most striking: it is difficult to realize the great and happy change that has taken place. *   *   *   * A dark cloud then hung lowering over this fair land. The 'Lone Star' shot fitful through the gloom—now beaming with the light of peace and hope—now almost quenched in blood, yet ever with a

* See Appendix N for revenue of State of Texas ; Appendix O for assessment of taxes ; Appendix P for agricultural statistics.

halo of glory encircling it. We have lived to see that lost pleiad restored to its proper place among its sisters, no longer obscured by doubt or difficulty, but shining far abroad to the nations of the earth a beacon, which every day grows brighter and more glorious."

This is magniloquent; but magniloquence is excusable in the Governor of a State, which, even in its reduced limits, is larger than the whole empire of Austria.

Similar is the language which James W. Henderson, the newly elected Lieutenant-Governor, used on the same occasion :—

"I may be permitted to offer to the Senators and Representatives of Texas, and to my fellow-citizens, my sincere congratulations upon the happy and prosperous condition of all the States of this now glorious Union.

  *   *   *   *   *   *   *   *

"Whilst these prospects are gratifying to us as citizens of the great Republic, we have, as citizens of Texas, equal cause to rejoice in the vast improvements which are everywhere presented throughout the broad limits of our own State. When we contrast our present condition, social, moral, and political, with that of a few years past, we are astonished at our rapid advancement; and look back with the deepest interest to the time when Texas, without organization and without means, yet impelled by a strong sense of the value and blessings of liberty, dissolved her political connection with Mexico, and established an independent republican government, under the most trying and discouraging circumstances that ever befel an oppressed and resisting people.

"Yes! at a time when Texas, without a dollar in her military chest, not a bayonet bristling in her ranks; with the hopes of her people depressed by the atrocities committed upon her citizens and soldiers: when the homes of her citizens were in flames, when her soldiers lay butchered upon the ill-fated plains of Goliad, and around the desolated walls of the Alamo—nay, at a time when the progress of desolation and hostility marked the track of the invader as visibly as if the besom of destruction had swept over the land—the hearts of the people failed not; and they met in convention to deliberate upon the affairs of Texas.

  *   *   *   *   *   *   *   *

"Since that day [the day of the battle of San Jacinto] the prosperity of Texas has been steadily advancing: her march has been onward, until we now behold her happy and prosperous, and rejoicing in the beautiful blessings of a kind and beneficent Providence."

Some of the politicians of Texas maintain that she ought not to pay her debts, because, as they say, "she received no consideration for them." We assert that she has received ample consideration for them in all the blessings attendant on liberty and independence so eloquently set forth in the discourses of Gov. Bell and Lieut.-Gov. Henderson. All the courage and all the wisdom of the men of Texas would have availed them nothing without the auxiliary aid of money. Without the supplies obtained from the United States, and for which her present certificate debts were exchanged, the struggle with Mexico could never have been brought to a successful issue.

One way of testing the value of what we part with is by considering the value we thereby acquire. To do this fairly in the present instance, let us suppose that all the land and all the other wealth of Texas had been the property of one man. Would not that man consider himself fortunate if, by an expenditure of ten or twelve millions, he could bring his property from under an anarchical and unenlightened despotism into the control of a free, stable, and enlightened government. Lands which, when Texas was part of Mexico, were worth but from one cent to fifty cents an acre, are, now that Texas is part of the United States, worth from one dollar to fifty dollars an acre. The case is not weakened by the fact that the advantages of this rise in value are shared by many men, instead of being monopolized by one.

Verily, Texas got her independence cheap. There are few people suffering under the yoke of oppression who would not be willing to pay many times as much to obtain their liberty. Even if the Texans should esteem religious and political freedom as not worthy to be taken into the account, they have gained more in their increase of wealth than they have promised to pay to those who aided them in their struggles.

The present condition of Texas will appear the more remarkable if we contrast it with her condition a short time before she was annexed to the Union, as depicted by President Houston in his message to the seventh Congress, December 1, 1842 :—

" The nation has been gradually declining. Instead of deriving facilities and advantages from the march of time, its decline since the year 1838 to the present period of depression has been more rapid than perhaps that of any other country on the globe possessing the same natural advantages."

The rapid improvement that has since taken place has been chiefly owing to annexation. This is admitted by Governor Bell, in the message from which we have already made quotations.

"It was not until Texas took her place as one of the States of the great American Union that she occupied the position which nature designed for her. From that period to the present, her onward march to power and improvement has been unexampled. Nations behold the position of our hopes. From every land immigrants are flocking in welcome crowds to partake of our prosperity. From the vine-clad hills of France and Germany, from Ireland's green shores, and England's smiling fields, and from our own sister States, they swell the flowing tide, until the solitary plains have been made to rejoice, and the wilderness to blossom as the rose. A land more fair and happy never sun viewed in its wide career; salubrious, mild, its hills are green, its woods and prospects are fair, prairies fertile, and, to crown the whole, it is our home—the land of liberty and all its sweets."

All this is true; but all who have had any transactions, in the way of dollars and cents, with the government of this fair land, have abundant cause of complaint, and the United States among the rest. The war with Mexico, which was brought on by the annexation of Texas, cost, as has been computed, $300,000,000. This expense was borne by the United States. Texas was enriched by the expenditures it caused within her borders; so much so that it is said a part of her population would be very glad if hostilities should be renewed. Part of the gross cost of the war must be charged to the account of California, Utah, and New Mexico. But, independently of this, the United States have expended in Texas, and for her benefit, more millions than her debts amount to. Nearly half the army of the United States is employed in Texas. Yet Texas, with all these liberal outlays in her borders, is not content unless she can wrest from the United States five millions in bonds, to which she has no claim till the conditions to which she assented in her act of November 25, 1850, are fully complied with.

The truth is that some of the politicians of Texas seem to think that the United States have been annexed to Texas, and not Texas to the United States. If any demand they make, no matter how unreasonable it may be, is not at once granted, they are loud in their outcries about the grievance to which their State is subjected. In view of this state of feeling that prevails among them, it is a pity that a direct vote was avoided in Congress on their unjust pretensions to one-half of New Mexico. We have already said that it was judicious to avoid that vote, seeing the condition into which public affairs had been brought by the insane doings of politicians of different parties. Yet an evil has attended what Texas has interpreted as an implied acquiescence in her claims. Grant one unreasonable demand to an unreasonable man or an unreasonable State, and you pave the way for other demands equally unreasonable. Let Texas have the reserved bonds, and there is no knowing what new claim she will set up.

If her politicians are frustrated in their present design, they will, it may be, commence a new agitation, and perhaps appeal to sectional feelings to give it additional force. They have, no doubt, still in them much of the remains of the "old Adam," which led to such violent party conflicts in the days of the Republic; exemplifications of which are to be found in the bitter controversies of Gov. Smith and his council, in the land-speculator's rebellion, and in the war about the land-office archives. The wrath which they formerly poured, in all its concentrated energy, on the heads of one another, they may now pour out on the people of other States. But if they do, its venom will be weakened by its diffusion.

Whatever their policy may be, their demand for the reserved bonds should be resisted—calmly resisted, but firmly resisted—till the conditions set forth in the act of Congress of September, 1850, and assented to by the Legislature of Texas in its act of November 25, 1850, are fully complied with.

That there is this strong disposition to get hold of the bonds, and at the same time pay the public creditors but half their dues, is owing to a wish to apply the money to internal improvements. "It was great folly in Texas," said one of her Senators, "to pay her debts at all." "What," said a gentleman from Louisiana, "folly to pay them at all?" The Louisianian being a creditor of the State, felt some alarm. "Yes," replied the Senator, "it was folly to pay them at all. Texas ought to have taken the money she got from the United States, have invested the same in railroads, and then given the public creditors shares in those railroads."

We have mentioned elsewhere that land-speculations afford the key to all movements in Texas. They had, if some authorities are to be believed, much to do in bringing on the revolution; they caused the wars with the Cherokee Indians; and they are now the chief obstacle to the creditors of the State being paid their just demands. The money is wanted to make railroads, in order to promote sales of land in larger quantities, and for higher prices than would otherwise be possible.

Certainly no other country affords such beautiful opportunities as Texas for land-speculations, and her inhabitants have taken full advantage of them. From the best accounts that can be collected, the whole number of acres in cultivation in 1848 was only 512,641, while the number of acres assessed and subject to taxation was 38,788,439.* According to a more recent statement, the whole amount of land owned by individuals is 63,783,054.† In a community in which each land-owner has one hundred times as much land as he has either ability or disposition to cultivate, there must naturally be a strong wish to dispose of the surplus to advantage. The necessary result is that the land-speculation interest is predominant. Compared with it, the creditor interest is feeble indeed, as nine-tenths of the public creditors reside in other States. We met with many persons in the State who were dissatisfied with the scaling system; but, as they are without organization, they are without influence. Some of the newspaper editors are of this number; but arguments in favor of paying the debts of the Republic are hardly agreeable to the majority of their readers, and a stump orator who should take the field in behalf of the public creditors would find little sympathy in his hearers.

"Rapacious bond-holders," and "greedy speculators," are among the mildest of the epithets bestowed on such of the creditors as seek payment according to the letter of the contract. Land-speculations are, in Texas, quite in accordance with the orthodox faith. It is only stock-speculations that are criminal.

When men have a deep interest in any scheme, it is not very difficult for them to persuade themselves of its entire justice. And hence it ought to occasion no surprise that the project to take the money belonging to the public creditors, and apply it to the promotion of land-speculations, has considerable popularity in Texas. We have already treated at some length of the arguments by which this project is supported; but more on this head is necessary. So many phases as error assumes, so many is it necessary to expose.

One reason why the arguments in favor of scaling have had so much effect on the Texan mind is that scaling, in a certain sense, and to a certain extent, in non-audited debts, was just and proper. This was the case in regard to a part of the second and third class debts. If any man made out his bill for services or supplies at

---

* See Appendix P.   † See Appendix K.

treasury note prices, it was just and proper for the auditor and comptroller to reduce them to their equivalents in specie. This scaling, if it may so be called, was a mere equation of currencies; and as payment was to be made in the better currency, no one could object to it. This kind of scaling was righteously applied to the non-audited, or second and third class debts, and it is well worthy of remark how little it reduced the original amount. The ostensible sum of the second class debt was $968,763 28, reduced by scaling to $896,217 80, being a deduction of only $7\frac{1}{2}$ cents in the dollar. The ostensible amount of the third class debts was reported by the auditor as $97,675 10, and the par value as the same. From this it appears that nearly all those whose accounts were unaudited when the scaling act was passed, had made out their accounts in specie; and it was right that the few who had made out their accounts in treasury note prices should have the amounts reduced to their equivalents in specie.

Thus far, then, the scaling was unobjectionable. But the auditor and comptroller had no right—the Legislature had no right—to direct them to go further. After an account has once been regularly audited, and a certificate thereof duly issued, it is too late to change it. A treasury note, or certificate of stock, or any other negotiable public security, is like a bank-note. It is evidence that the amount expressed on its face is due to the holder, and so acknowledged by the government. If the government, in auditing any claim, neglected to make a proper equation of currencies, the fault was the government's, and it ought to suffer the loss, if any. The loss ought not to be thrown on innocent third parties, who have no means of knowing what a government owes, except the government's own acknowledgments of what is due. Hence the whole of the first class debts, " consisting," in the language of the auditor and comptroller, " of *audited* and *ascertained* claims," ought to have been left untouched. After the evidences of them had been in circulation, none of them for less than eight years, and some of them for twelve years, they ought not to have been subject to a re-audit.

To admit any other principle than this would be to overthrow the very foundation of all negotiable securities. The amount expressed in the treasury notes and certificates of stock is what

Texas owes, and this amount she must pay, unless she means to violate her contracts.

Suppose the Republic of Texas, instead of constituting herself a bank of issue, had, after the manner of South Carolina, established a public bank, to issue notes and aid in fiscal operations. If Texas had done this, she would have done what she had a perfect right to do; for, as she was then without the Union, she was not bound by the provisions of the United States Constitution.

Suppose, then, that this Bank of Texas, founded exclusively on the credit and resources of the Republic, and carrying on operations for its exclusive benefit, had done just what the Republic did, that is, issued notes in such excess that they depreciated to fifty, forty, thirty, twenty, ten, and even fewer cents in the dollar. Suppose, finally, the Bank of Texas should, by some turn of fortune, become suddenly rich—become possessed of ten millions in United States bonds, besides much other wealth worth millions more; would not the Bank of Texas, under such circumstances, be expected to pay its notes in full?

If it did not, it would do worse than our incorporated banks in the United States have done. They all, like the Republic of Texas, issued notes in excess. They continued to issue them at various stages of depreciation. But all, such of them as have any credit or character to sustain, have paid their notes in full, without regard to the rate of depreciation at which they were issued.

The case is not altered by the fact that the Republic of Texas, instead of establishing a separate bank, constituted herself a bank of issue.

"It is pretty well," said one Texan, "for the State to pay as much as she does. Those who bought the paper of a revolutionary government had no right to expect any more." This argument is not satisfactory. A revolutionary government is as much bound as is an established government to fulfil its contracts. Nothing but inability will excuse either. And till it can be shown that other revolutionary governments have had as ample means as Texas, their defaults of payment will not afford her even the shadow of an apology.

Another Texan is willing to admit that, "if the loans had been in gold and silver, Texas would be bound to pay in full; but as they were obtained in another way, it is quite enough if she pays in part. He forgets that, if the loans had been in gold and silver, they would have been expended for the very articles of clothing, provisions, and munitions of war, that Texas obtained by the simple intervention of her paper. Texas is as much bound to pay for value in kind as for value in cash.

Through trading connections, a market was got for Texan securities that could not otherwise have been obtained. A man may be very unwilling to lend a government, especially a foreign government, one hundred dollars in gold and silver, and yet be ready to sell goods to that value, and receive pay in the obligations of such government. Much more ready may he be to receive payment of old debts in such obligations. In this way, Texas borrowed to a large amount from the people of the United States, and it was the only way in which she could borrow.

A third Texan says, the holders of her securities will, under the scaling system, get more than they expected when they bought them, and therefore they ought to be satisfied. No doubt many holders of Texan securities had, at times, very faint hopes of their ever being paid at all; and when they purchased such securities, it must have been at a price which they regarded as proportionate to the risk. But this is not a good reason that they should not be paid in full, when the State has ample ability. If the "degree of hope" of the creditors is to be the standard of adjustment, the State owes compensation not only to those whose hope has been so long deferred, but to those who have been doomed to absolute disappointment. When hope was raised high by the Texan official announcements that General Hamilton had negotiated a loan in Europe, some men invested their all in Texan securities, and thereby lost their all.

Besides this, it should be recollected that the receipt of these government liabilities was not always matter of choice. It was sometimes matter of necessity. The government had nothing else to give its creditors, and they consequently had nothing else to pay to those to whom they were indebted. Texan securities had a *forced* circulation, not through law, but through circumstances. As an example, we may mention the case of a lady of Washington City, who could get nothing else from a Texan minister to the United States but Texan securities in pay for his board. After waiting some ten years, the Texan authorities are trying, by their scaling, to deprive this widow of a great part of her just demands.

The prospect that "speculators" will be enriched, if the State pays her debts in full, seems, with some Texans, quite reason enough why she should pay only one-half. For, as already remarked, growing rich by speculations in lands is quite consonant with Texan principles of morality, because the Texans hold many lands; while growing rich by speculations in stocks is wicked, because Texans hold few stocks.

In our view, speculations in stocks are just as conformable with the principles of morality and religion, as are speculations in lands, or speculations in anything else. When men buy any commodity with the intention of reselling it, they do so with the hope of gain. At the same time, they know there is a risk of loss. This was the precise case with those who dealt in Texan securities, and we know not why they, among all dealers in commodities, especially when they ran so great a risk of loss, should alone be deprived of all chance of gain.

The Texan Government had for sale two kinds of merchandise —land and paper. Some took the one, and some the other. Both its land and its paper were then very low—the one worth, perhaps, ten cents an acre, the other ten cents in a dollar. Many who took the land at these low rates have done very well by it, it being now worth two, five, ten, and twenty dollars an acre. There is no murmuring at the good luck of those who took land, because it is now worth many times as much as it was ten years ago. Neither should there be any murmuring at the good luck of those who took paper, if it should now be worth more than it was when they received it.

As there is no law of nature fixing the value of the interest on debts, so there is no law of nature fixing the market value of the principal of debts. As flour is sometimes worth ten dollars a barrel, and sometimes only five, and as cotton is sometimes worth twelve cents a pound, and sometimes only six, so stocks are sold sometimes at a premium, and sometimes at a discount. Public securities are, as has elsewhere been observed, a merchandise subject to like laws of prices with other merchandise. But these general laws of prices have particular effects on each species of merchandise, according to its particular nature. Supposing the

money-market to be the same in other respects, government securities rise or fall in price according to the supposed ability and the
supposed inclination of government to pay. Texas Government
merchandise was low in the market, because the ability to pay at
all depended on remote and uncertain contingencies. Texas securities have since risen, because the ability of the government to
pay has been increased. But Texas securities have not risen to
par, because, though the government can pay, it will not.

But, supposing all the creditors of Texas to be paid in full, and
that they purchased their claims at second hand, and at very low
rates—have they, after all, done so very good a business? Might
they not have made more money by other investments? Twelve
per cent. interest may be recovered by law in Texas, and as money
is freely borrowed at that rate, we may rest assured that the profits of trade are rather above than below it. At compound interest, paid semi-annually, money, at twelve per cent., will double
itself in six years. The government admits that it obtained the
equivalent of fifty cents in silver from those who received its second
issues of treasury notes; and, though it promised interest, it ceased
to pay interest, even in paper, after the 1st of January, 1841. A
man who gave one thousand dollars in specie, or its equivalent,
for these notes, might, if he had kept that money in trade, have
made it two thousand dollars at the end of six, and four thousand
dollars at the end of twelve, years. But at the close of this period, he gets from the Texan Government—how much? One
thousand dollars, or exactly what he advanced twelve years ago!
The government did promise to pay him two thousand dollars;
but it pays only one thousand. It did promise to pay him interest;
but it does not.

If the matter be fairly investigated, it will be found that those
Texans who kept their money in trade, or who invested it in lands,
have done much better than those who invested it in government
securities. The value of money to the man who parts with it is
to be estimated by what he would have gained by it, if he had
kept it in his own hands.

In regard to those citizens of the United States who made investments in the securities of Texas, it will not be hard to show that
they could have done much better by employing their money at
home. In evidence of this, we give the following table. The quota-

tions for 1842 are from Hunt's Merchants' Magazine for January, 1843; those for 1845 from the same work for July, 1845; those for 1852 from the Journal of Commerce, and the Courier and Inquirer:—

Prices of State Stocks in the New York Market.

Stock.	Interest.	Redeemable.	Price, April, 1842.	May, 1845.	Nov. 1852.
New York State,	6	1860	82 a 84	108	120
" "	5½	1861	77 a 80	104	
" "	5	1855	75 a 77	106¾	114¼
Pennsylvania,	5		31 a 33	73½	96
Ohio,	6	1856–60	50 a 55	97¾	110
Kentucky,	6	1860	68 a 70	101¾	110
Alabama,	5	1865	35 a 40	72½	95
Indiana,	5	1861	15 a 17	34½	99
Illinois,	6	1870	15 a 16	39	83
Maryland,	6		40 a 45		109
Michigan,	6	1860	15 a 30		

New York stocks were, March 1, lower than they were April 15, 1842, five per cents. being then 68 a 72, and five and a half per cents. 71 a 73. Others of the stocks above quoted were at times lower than they were April 15, 1842. Illinois sixes have been sold at 13.

It is evident that, if a man had bought these stocks at the rates they were in 1842, and sold them at the rates at which they were in 1845 or 1852, he would have made immense sums of money. But if he had bought and sold at shorter intervals, his gains would have been proportionally much greater.

New York sixes, in April, 1842, averaged 83; in April, 1843, they averaged 1 04. Gain on investment in one year equal to twenty-five per cent.

Ohio sixes averaged, in April, 1842, 52½; in May, 1843, they averaged 86. Gain on investment in thirteen months equal to 65 per cent.

Kentucky sixes were, in April, 1842, at 69 on an average; in May, 1843, at 95. Gain in one year equal to 36 per cent.

Illinois sixes were, in December, 1842, 18 a 18¾ ; in May, 1843, they were 29½ a 30¼. Gain in the short period of six months equal to 61 per cent.

Indiana fives were, in December, 1842, 20 a 21¾. In May, 1843, 28 a 30. Gain in six months equal to 38 per cent.

Considering the quickness of the returns, any of these stocks were better speculative investments than the best securities Texas could offer.

Such fluctuations in stocks are great evils, but where paper-money is used, they are unavoidable.

Take next the prices of bank and other stocks at Philadelphia, on the 1st of January, 1842, and compare them with their prices in May, 1845, and November, 1852.*

Banks.	Jan. 1, 1842.	May 2, 1845.	Nov. 1852.
Pennsylvania, . .	150	258	480
North America, . .	160	380	620
Philadelphia, . .	46	110	140
Farmers' & Mechanics',	29	42½	71
Commercial, . .	35	53	65
Northern Liberties, .	25	42	60
Mechanics', . .	17	25	33
Southwark, . .	48	63	80
Kensington, . .	30	57	68
Penn Township, . .	30	29	32
Girard, . .	12	8⅝	13
Western, . .	26	46	70
Manufacturers' & Mechanics',	21	23½	30
Moyamensing, . .	32	41¼	75
New Orleans Gas, .	4	35	125
Lehigh Coal & Naviga-tion (shares), . .	10	14½	70
Lehigh loans, 6.per ct.,	40	45	95
Chesapeake & Delaware Canal (shares), .	5	29	135
Chesapeake & Delaware loans, 6 per ct., .	20	71	101¼
Camden & Amboy Rail-road shares, . .	75	110	147
Norristown Railroad, .	¼	7½	45

Some of these stocks have been sold at much lower rates than those mentioned in the first column. Philadelphia Bank shares, for example, have been sold at 25; Farmers' & Mechanics' at 19; Penn Township at 20; Mechanics' at 7; and Girard at 2.

On stock-jobbing principles, the securities of Texas have been among the poorest investments, considering the risk attendant

* The prices for 1842 are from the Journal of Banking; those for 1845 and 1852 are from the Philadelphia Commercial List and the books of a leading broker. The shares of the Bank of Pennsylvania and of the Bank of North America were originally $400 each. Each share has since been divided into four, of $100 each; but, to facilitate comparison, we have made our quotations as if the shares had not been divided.

on them, and the slowness of the returns. A man might have made more money by investing in almost anything else.

It may be that they who have been so unfortunate as to invest their earnings in Texan bonds and treasury notes would, if they had employed their money in other ways, have lost instead of gaining. But this does not, in the least, affect the validity of their claims. And if Texas does not pay them dollar for dollar what she has promised, Texas must bear the infamy (the term is not too strong)—Texas must bear THE INFAMY that properly attaches to men and States that can pay their debts and will not.

Nor will Texas bear this infamy alone. The whole family of States of which she is a member must share it with her. An American cannot now enter certain circles in Europe without being reproached with what Pennsylvania has done in relation to her debts. Yet Pennsylvania never repudiated one dollar of her obligations. The most she did was to defer payment of the interest, or pay in inconvertible paper, till she could bring a new revenue system into operation, and till her banks could resume specie payments. This was matter of stern necessity. But State credit is like female reputation. The greatest circumspection is necessary for its preservation.

But we are not without hopes that Texas will yet redeem her character. If the case of her creditors could be fairly presented before her people, we should have no fears of the result. But there is great difficulty in doing this, owing to the scattered state of the population and the few persons in Texas who have any interest in supporting the creditors' cause. The men of Texas are just as honest as the men of France, England, or Germany, or the men of New York, Massachusetts, or Virginia. Their minds have, unfortunately, got a wrong twist on the subject of their public debt; but all would soon be right if the truth could only be fairly laid before them.

Already are there indications of a change of sentiment. The *Texas State Gazette* declares that the number of those who believe the debt must ultimately be paid in full increases every year. Attention has been awakened by the cases of individuals to whom gross injustice has been done by the scaling system; and the further these inquiries are pushed, the greater will be found to be the number of cases of hardship. What but injustice can be done when debts are *averaged*? How perfectly absurd it would be in a State to strike an average of the debts due *to* her! Not less absurd is it for one to strike an average of the debt due *by* her.

It was a monstrous thing in Texas to reopen accounts which all those concerned supposed had been finally passed upon some eight or twelve years previous. The reaudit, if made at all, should have been as careful as the original audit. But this was impossible. Many of the original claimants were dead; others had lost their vouchers; others had no interest in seeing the audit fairly made, as they had long since parted with the treasury notes or the stock certificates they had received in satisfaction of their claims.

Under these circumstances, it was impossible to ascertain the exact value Texas had received in each case, even according to her own estimate of such value; and, as it was thus impossible to carry out the principles she has adopted, this of itself is sufficient reason for abandoning it.

Motives of interest and motives of duty point in this instance in the same direction. The celebrated Col. Chartres said he would give one hundred thousand pounds for a character—not for its own sake, but because he would get two hundred thousand pounds by it. Texas will do well in buying a character, even if it should cost her ten million dollars. She would gain by it one hundred millions. By this is of course meant a character for paying debts. A character for courage and conduct she has already.

If the land-speculating interest in Texas only knew where its true interest lies, it would be foremost in abandoning the scaling system. No State in the Union stands more in need of railroads, and in few States could they be made at less expense. If the whole five millions that would be acquired by repudiating half the public debt should be applied to internal improvements, it would go but a little way in constructing the works that are wanted. It will require many millions more to construct the railroads which are so desirable in Texas, and which she will have in a few years, if she now redeems her plighted faith. But if she persists in repudiating regularly audited debts, for which her truth and honor were solemnly pledged, the whole world (that is, the money-lending world) should unite in one combination against her. Texas will then, notwithstanding her great natural advantages, be far behind her sister States ; for no extensive system of railroads can be completed without resort to loans.

We trust, however, in this case, more to natural sentiments of justice than to hopes of gain.

It is true, indeed, that the United States are bound for the whole of the debt for which the revenues were pledged ; but Texas must evince a hearty concurrence with the United States in the payment of these debts, and interpose no further obstacles in relation to the reserved bonds. In justice to herself, Texas must go further. She must repeal all her scaling-acts, and pay the residue of her creditors in full, according to contract.

The case of one class of them is peculiarly hard. We allude to the holders of eight and ten per cent. funded debt of 1840. It is true that they are the only owners of circulating evidences of debt who have as yet been paid anything; but they have been scaled most awfully—down even to thirty cents in the dollar. If something be not done for their relief, their condition will be worse than that of any other contract creditors.

They have strong claims on Texas. From the supplement to the report of the auditor and comptroller, Dec. 27th, 1849, it appears that treasury notes to the amount of $777,080 were invested in the ten per cent. funded debt of 1840, and notes of the same kind to the amount of $22,800 in the eight per cent. funded debt of the same year. Thus the whole, or nearly the whole of their stock represents debts for which the revenues were originally pledged. It will be very hard if these creditors, having parted with these evidences, and taken others in exchange for them, in order to promote the convenience of the Republic, shall now be paid only thirty cents in the dollar. If they had retained their original evidences, they would have come within that class of creditors for whom, agreeably to the decision of the President and of the Secretary of the Treasury, the United States are, in the default of Texas, bound to provide.

Texas has still from three to four millions in her treasury. She cannot apply this amount, or so much of it as may be necessary, in a better way than by making up to the holders of the funded debt of 1840, and others who have been improperly scaled, the sum that is justly their due.

If the United States should pay all the debt, the creditors would indeed be satisfied, but the reputation of Texas would not be left without blemish. Her breaches of faith have been many. She must show to the world, by her present and her future conduct, that those breaches of faith were produced by necessity, and not by inclination, and that if she at any time favored the scaling system, it was through want of acquaintance with the true nature of stock securities. She will thus effectually wipe off the reproach of repudiation, and take her stand proudly in the foremost ranks of the States of the Union.

APPENDIX.

A.

FROM Jan. 1, 1836, to Dec. 31, 1836, one year,*	$502,179 23
" Jan. 1, 1837, to Dec. 31, 1837, one year,*	718,258 98
" Jan. 1, 1838, to Sept. 30, 1838, nine months,*	885,458 61
" Sept. 30, 1838, to Sept. 30, 1839, one year,*	1,370,810 15
" Sept. 30, 1839, to Sept. 30, 1840, one year,†	2,245,244 62
" Sept. 30, 1840, to Sept. 30, 1841, one year,‡	1,265,038 70
" Sept. 30, 1841, to Feb. 19, 1846, 4 yrs. & 4 mos.,§	694,791 81
Total to February 19, 1846,§ . .	$7,681,782 10

The total given by the auditor and comptroller does not include the drafts issued under the Exchequer System.

A small amount issued in 1835 appears to be included in the accounts of 1836.

For two years, these audited drafts were, with the exception of land-script, the only governmental paper tender; yet the amount redeemed in these years, by receiving them in payment of public dues, appears to have been only $8,687 97, besides $16,134 02, redeemed by drafts on agents in the United States.

As before the close of these two years, the amount of audited drafts afloat considerably exceeded one million dollars, and as they had in May, 1837, fallen so low as to be worth only fifteen cents in the dollar, this fact affords indubitable evidence that the Texans of those days had little dispo-

* First Auditor's Report, October 25, 1839.

† Comptroller's Report, October 1, 1840.

‡ Secretary of the Treasury's Report, October 20, 1841.

§ Supplement to Auditor and Comptroller's Report, December, 1849. The amount from September 30, 1841, to February 19, 1846, has been obtained by deducting from the total the amounts that were issued previous to September 30, 1841.

sition to pay taxes, or that those whose business it was to collect them were strangely negligent of their duty.

This table is the best we can give of the expenditures of the Texan Government in different years. By scanning it, the reader will find that in those years in which the exigencies of the government were the least, its expenditures were the greatest.

According to the supplement to the auditorial report of December, 1849, the final disposition of these drafts was as follows :—

Received in payment of public dues, . . .	$636,322 66
Invested in ten per cent. fund of 1837, . .	837,500 00
" " " of 1840, . .	45,600 00
Amount paid at the treasury, ...	5,985,131 21
Leaving unliquidated, ...	177,228 23

The reader must not suppose that the amounts paid at the treasury were paid in gold and silver. Giving treasury notes in exchange for audited drafts was called paying them.

In addition to the above, outstanding claims to the amount of $72,077 28 have been audited by virtue of a special act of the Legislature at its second session; and, by virtue of other special acts, other claims to the amount of some two hundred thousand dollars have been brought in, and duly audited.

B.

PROMISSORY NOTES.

First emission, printed notes, Nov. 4, 1837, to Jan. 15, 1838,*	$514,510
Second emission, engraved notes, Jan. 15, 1838, to Nov. 3, 1838,*	436,289
" " " Nov. 3, 1838, to Jan. 1, 1839,†	214,340
Third emission, "red backs," Jan. 1, 1839, to Sept. 30, 1839,†	1,569,010
" " " Sept. 1839, to Sept. 1840,‡	1,983,790
Total, ...	$4,717,939

This does not include reissues.

* Report of Secretary of the Treasury, November 3, 1838.
† Ibid., 1839.
‡ Supplement to Report of Auditor and Comptroller, December, 1849.

The amount issued subsequently to September, 1839, has been ascer tained by deducting from the total the amounts that appear to have been issued previous to September, 1839.

Probable Amounts in Circulation.

September 30, 1838,*	$684,069 59
November 3, 1838,*	812,454 00
September 30, 1839,†	2,013,762 55
September 30, 1840,‡	3,287,962 42
September 30, 1841,‡	4,381,004 64
January 1, 1850,§	664,593 00
November 12, 1851,§	296,353 00

The scale finally adopted by the auditor and comptroller, for estimating the value the government received in exchange for its treasury notes, was as follows:—

July, 1838, to November, 1838, . . .	80 cents in the dollar.
November, 1838, to March, 1839, . . .	60 " "
March, 1839, to July, 1839, ...	50 " "
July, 1839, to November, 1839, . . .	33⅓ " "
November, 1839, to March, 1840, . . .	25 " "
March, 1840, to June, 1840, ...	20 " "
After June, 1840, ...	16⅔ " "

Up to July, 1838, they appear to have been estimated as of par value with silver. As mentioned in other parts of the volume, they subsequently fell to two cents in the dollar; but then they had ceased to be paid out by the government.

From the Supplement to the Report of the Auditor and Comptroller, December 27, 1849, we gather the following particulars respecting these treasury notes:—

Redeemed at the treasury, and cancelled, ...	$772,439
Invested in ten per cent. stock of 1840, ...	777,080
" in eight per cent. stock of 1840, ...	22,800
Received in collection of revenue, and destroyed, . .	483,074
Due by collectors, and likely to be paid over, . . .	165,000

* Report of Secretary of the Treasury, November 3, 1838.

† Ibid., 1839.

‡ Various public documents. In the total for 1841, treasury bonds are included. In his report of October, 1841, Secretary Chalmers states there had, in that year, been no *new* emission of treasury notes.

§ Reports of Auditor and Comptroller.

Like the audited drafts, not one dollar of these treasury notes was paid in specie. They were paid, or redeemed, at the treasury, after the manner of the Kilkenny banker, by giving new notes for old ones.

C.

REVENUES OF THE REPUBLIC OF TEXAS FROM SEPTEMBER, 1835, TO OCTOBER, 1851.

	Three years, ending Sept. 30, 1838.	One year, ending Sept. 30, 1839.	One year, ending Sept. 30, 1840.
Customs	$133,649 88	$122,169 35	$166,821 12
Direct taxes . . .	100,455 12*		
Lands and land dues	13,920 75†		123,224 66‡
Town lots	7,202 40	5,287 50	168,797 52
Miscellaneous . . .	3,195 00	55,473 43	1,828 56
Total	$258,423 15	$182,930 28	$460,671 86

	One year, ending Sept. 30, 1841.	Three years, 1842–3–4.	Fourteen months, Nov. 1, 1844, to Jan. 1, 1845.
Customs	$151,990 45	$360,177 46	$340,506 40
Direct taxes . . .	179,503 91	80,335 39	27,561 49
Licenses	42,686 37	16,503 50	15,140 16
Lands and land dues	68,025 62		
Miscellaneous . . .	429 32	502 58	1,815 25
Total	$442,635 67	$457,518 93	$385,023 30

	Twenty-two months, Feb. 19, 1845, to Dec. 31, 1847.	Two years, ending Oct. 31, 1849.	Two years, ending Oct. 31, 1851.
Customs	$51,206 13	$8,075 13	$13,446 99
Direct taxes . . .	21,154 87	12,882 20	8,790 34
License-taxes . . .	7,692 29	3,833 53	2,092 09
Lands and land dues			19,708 27
Town lots			475 00
Miscellaneous . . .	29,596 00§	75,363 98	343 00
Total	$109,649 29	$100,154 84	$44,855 69

The whole amount of revenue collected in the two years beginning September 30, 1835, and ending September 30, 1837, appears to have been only $9,607 28, leaving $248,815 87 as the revenue proper to the year ending September 30, 1838.

* Part for land dues and licenses.
† Part for licenses.
‡ Including licenses and land-tax.
§ Including $26,922 57 claims against United States Government.

This table must not be regarded as official, though it has been formed from official documents. It is defective, in one place, in containing no account of the receipts from January 1 to February 19, 1846, and has a surplusage in another, inasmuch as it embraces twice the receipts from October 31, 1847, to December 31, 1847, and, perhaps, those from November 1, 1844, to January 1, 1845. It, however, approximates near enough to correctness for purposes of comparison.

There are discrepancies in some of the documents, owing to changes in modes of keeping accounts, consequent on frequent changes of officers in times of trouble. After the officers of the Treasury Department of Texas shall have got through the arduous duty of paying off the public debt, they may find a revision of the revolutionary accounts of the Republic not unworthy of their attention, provided the Legislature make an appropriation for the necessary expense.

D.

RECAPITULATION OF REVENUE OF THE REPUBLIC OF TEXAS, SHOWING THE TOTAL AMOUNT OF EACH BRANCH.

Customs.		Direct taxes.	
1835–38	$133,649 88	1835–39	$100,455 12*
1838–39	122,169 35	1840–41	179,503 91
1839–40	166,821 12	1842–3–4	80,335 39
1840–41	151,990 45	1844–45	27,561 49
1842–3–4	360,177 46	1846–47	21,154 87
1844–46	340,506 40	1847–49	12,882 20
1846–47	51,206 13	1849–51	8,790 34
1847–49	8,075 13		
1849–51	13,446 99		
Total	$1,348,042 91	Total	$430,683 32

Lands and land dues.		Licenses.	
1835–39	$13,920 75†	1840–41	$42,686 37
1839–40	123,224 66‡	1842–3–4	16,503 50
1840–41	68,025 62	1844–46	15,140 16
1849–51	19,708 27	1846–47	7,692 29
		1847–49	3,833 53
		1849–51	2,092 09
Total	$224,879 30	Total	$87,947 94

* Part land dues and licenses.
† Part for licenses.
‡ Including licenses and land-tax.

Sales of town lots.*		Miscellaneous.	
1835–38	$7,202 40	1835–38	$3,195 00
1838–39	5,287 50	1838–39	55,473 43
1839–40	168,797 52	1839–40	1,828 56
1849–51	475 00	1840–41	429 32
		1842–3–4	502 58
		1844–46	1,815 25
		1846–47	29,596 00
		1847–49	75,363 98
		1849–51	343 00
Total	$181,762 42	Total	$168,547 12

RECAPITULATION.

Customs	$1,348,042 91
Direct taxes	430,683 32
Lands and land dues	224,879 30
Licenses	87,947 94
Miscellaneous	168,547 12
Town lots	181,762 42
Total	$2,441,863 01

SUMMARY OF DIFFERENT PERIODS.

1835–37	$9,607 28
1837–38	248,815 87
1838–39	182,930 28
1839–40	460,671 86
1840–41	442,635 67
1842–3–4	457,518 93
1844–46	385,023 30
1846–47	109,649 29
1847–49	100,154 84
1849–51	44,855 69
Total	$2,441,863 01

A joint committee of the Legislature of the State reported, February 7, 1850, that there were due, by sundry officers of the late Republic of Texas, various sums, amounting in all to $73,601 06 in par funds, and $187,297 19 in Texas promissory note funds, including interest at eight per cent. per annum, and after allowing all the credits claimed by said officers. They further reported the whole amount of unsettled accounts as being $473,394 53 in promissory notes, and $142,612 19 in par funds. Total, $616,006 92.

* These were Galveston and Austin city lots.

E.

KIND OF FUNDS RECEIVED.

According to the best accounts we can gather, the revenue of the Republic of Texas was received in the form following, to wit:—

Audited drafts*	$636,322 66
Treasury notes*	648,074 00
Treasury bonds*	40,100 00
Ten per cent. stock*	10,000 00
Land-script†	7,336 47
Exchequer bills, 1842–46‡	271,351 76
Exchequer bills, specie, &c.‡	70,005 44
Par funds, 1842–46‡	275,420 14
Specie, 1842 to Feb. 19, 1846‡	10,440 49
Special drafts, 1842–46‡	33,855 52
Property taken in payment for taxes‡	8,016 14
Exchequer bills, and special drafts, 1847–49§	1,586 45
Specie, Feb. 20, 1844, to Oct. 31, 1849§	125,292 36
Exchequer bills, and special drafts, 1849–51‖	1,765 42
Specie, 1849–51‖	3,821 01
Audited paper and promissory notes, 1849–51‖	39,270 01
Total revenue of Republic from taxes	$2,182,657 87
From Bank of United States:—‡	
In checks of loan commissioners, payable Sept. 30, 1839	$80,000 00
In post-notes of U. S. Bank, payable Jan. 1, 1840	200,000 00
Acceptances in favor of J. P. Henderson	10,000 00
Government drafts on Hamilton and Burnley, 1840	158,495 98
Funds from same source in fiscal year, 1841	4,776 00
" " " " " balance	4,108 02
Brookfield loan, 1835¶	1,100 00
Triplet loan (1836), specie‡	20,070 00
Erwin loan (1836), specie‡	45,820 00
Total revenue of Republic from taxes and loans	$2,707,027 87

* Supplement to Auditorial Report, Jan. 1, 1850.
† Report of Henry Smith, Secretary of the Treasury.
‡ Manuscript Records of Texas Treasury Department.
§ Treasurer's Report, Nov. 16, 1849.
‖ Comptroller's Report, Nov. 14, 1851.
¶ Journal of Provisional Government.

This includes the amount collected by the State for arrears to the Republic.

With the exception of the one thousand dollar note, referred to in an early part of our history, the post-notes above mentioned were the only bank-notes that appear ever to have come into possession of the Republic of Texas, and they never approached nearer its treasury than the city of New Orleans. There they were sold; some of them at a net discount.

We cannot find from the records that, previous to the adoption of the Exchequer System, the government ever realized one dollar of its taxes in specie. But we learn from undoubted authority that $8 30 were actually paid in for land dues in "hammered" silver. This treasure gave the accounting officers great trouble. They could not pay it out, for that would have been making an improper distinction among the public creditors. They were obliged to keep it, and also to keep a distinct account of it—a separate entry of it being necessary in each general statement.

After the Exchequer System was adopted, the returns were made in such a way that it is impossible to say exactly how much specie was received. So many kinds of "funds" are the *equivalents* of "specie," that the expression "par funds" is very indefinite. Possibly, some government drafts on the depositories, received in payment of public dues, are included in the total. The principle of "set-offs," properly understood and properly applied, is an excellent one; but it is so liable to abuse that, whenever it is used, the treasury records should show how, and to what extent it is applied. A government draft may be the *equivalent* of specie, but yet it is not *the same* as specie. If a public treasurer pays out specie, there is an end of the transaction. But if he gives a draft on a distant depository, it may remain out for months, perhaps for years.

In the year 1842, the Texan Government adopted the practice of drawing drafts on its collecting officers, and making them, by special enactments, receivable for certain public dues. They were known by different names, as "assessors' drafts," "Henderson drafts," &c., according to the name of the person whose claim they were issued to discharge, or the purpose they were intended to serve. We have included them in the table, so far as we could trace them, under the head of "special drafts." Of drafts of this kind, of which special mention is made, from 1842 to Jan. 1, 1846, amounting to $51,402 86, there remained outstanding, on the 1st of Jan. 1846, $17,547 34. The treasurer, on paying them out, credited himself as with so much specie; but that they were not *the same* as specie (though they may have been its equivalent) is sufficiently proved by the fact that some of these drafts were not paid till 1849–51, and some of them may be outstanding yet.

It will, perhaps, be remarked that, while the gross revenues of the Republic amounted to $2,441,863 01, according to Appendix D, the table in Appendix E shows in what kind of funds the amount of only $2,182,657 87 was received. The difference is $259,205 14. A part of this sum, but not probably a large part, was received in exchequer bills between Jan. 1, 1846, and Oct. 31, 1847. But the principal part was probably in treasury notes, which had been received once before in payment of dues, and then reissued. The auditor and comptroller, in their report of Jan. 1850, give only "the amount of treasury notes received in collection of the revenue, and *destroyed*"—not the amount thus received and reissued.

F.

TABULAR VIEW OF THE DEBT OF TEXAS AT DIFFERENT PERIODS.

	Sept. 30, 1838.	Sept. 30, 1839.	Sept. 30, 1840.
Audited drafts . . .	$775,255 73	$284,841 37	$175,209 86
Treasury notes and bonds	684,069 59	2,013,762 45	3,387,962 42
Funded debt	427,200 00	803,479 53	1,617,069 00
Five million loan . . .			305,261 00
	$1,886,525 32*	$3,102,083 35†	$5,485,502 28‡

	Sept. 30, 1841.	Nov. 12, 1851.
Audited drafts	$193,643 53	$116,828 99
Treasury notes and bonds	4,381,004 64	2,967,993 00
Funded debt	1,672,300 00	1,418,777 23
Five million loan	457,380 00	457,380 00
Naval debt	1,000,000 00	475,907 00
	$7,704,328 17¿	$5,436,886 22‖
Interest		$3,150,246 70
Claims filed, but not audited		1,060,120 22
Claims *not* filed		2,789,738 20
		$12,436,991 34‖

This table must, in some of its particulars, be regarded as only an approximation to the truth, for it was not always possible for the officers of

* Treasurer's Report for 1838.

† Treasurer's Report for 1839.

‡ Stock Commissioner's Report and Secretary of Treasury's Report for 1840.

¿ Secretary of Treasury and Treasurer's Report for 1841. Mr. Chalmers estimates the naval debt at $1,000,000, including the bonds forfeited and the interest.

‖ Auditor and Comptroller's Report of November 12, 1851. For particulars, see the report at length in Appendix.

the Republic to ascertain the exact amount due, but it is sufficiently correct to serve the purposes of comparison.

We could find no statements, from which to form a table of the public debt, of a later date than September, 1841, till we came to the auditorial reports of 1850 and 1851. Probably both government and people became tired of thinking about what they could not pay. Very little appears to have been added to the capital of the debt after 1841, for the very good reason that the credit of Texas was by that time so exhausted that she could borrow no more. The increase since that time has been chiefly owing to increments of interest, and to the bringing in of old claims not before presented.

Of the claims not filed, it is probable that only a part will be presented, owing to the death of the parties in some instances, and the loss of vouchers in others.

It may also be expected that, owing to the loss of treasury notes, bonds, and certificates of stock, payment of only part of the certified debt will be demanded.

The following amounts of ascertained claims appear not to have been filed with the auditor and comptroller on the 12th of November, 1851:—

Ten per cent. bonds of 1837	$185,502 77
" " 1840	63,000 00
Eight " " "	2,800 00
Treasury bonds	43,000 00
Treasury notes	296,353 00
Five million loan	280,000 00
	$870,655 77

RECAPITULATION OF PUBLIC DEBT OF TEXAS.

April 11, 1837*	$570,163 44
Nov. 30, 1837*	1,090,986 45
Sept. 30, 1838	1,187,525 32
" 1839	3,102,083 35
" 1840	5,485,502 28
" 1841	7,704,328 17
Nov. 12, 1851	12,436,991 34

* Report of Henry Smith, Secretary of the Treasury. The debt in April and November, 1837, consisted exclusively of audited paper.

G.

IMPORTS AND EXPORTS OF THE REPUBLIC OF TEXAS.

IMPORTS.

From	Year ending July 31, 1843.	Year ending July 31, 1844.	Fifteen months, ending Oct. 31, 1845.
United States	$412,983 03	$593,225 14	$1,151,733 21
Great Britain and Ireland	32,474 57	51,059 89	9,466 73
France	7,425 17	5,524 58	2,048 00
Germany	12,592 73		
Spanish West Indies . .	5,729 82	148 87	11,184 65
British West Indies . . .		3,624 10	3,722 08
Belgium		3,516 48	20,634 01
Hanse Towns		27,494 54	5,113 94
Austrian Adriatic dominions		1,185 86	
Yucatan		663 57	
Sardinia			467 70
Total	$471,205 32	$686,443 03	$1,204,370 32

EXPORTS.

To	Year ending July 31, 1843.	Year ending July 31, 1844.	Fifteen months ending Oct. 31, 1845.
United States	$281,342 64	$249,151 62	$486,327 16
Great Britain and Ireland	76,028 64	205,345 05	103,484 10
France	260 00	15,435 00	8,650 00
Germany	41,710 85		
Spanish West Indies . .	16,426 62	1,031 24	23,262 25
Hanse Towns		112,095 46	85,581 16
Austrian Adriatic dominions		29,013 85	13,468 97
Yucatan		3,047 12	
Belgium			49,434 48
British West Indies . . .			1,455 04
Sardinia			57,551 88
Total	$415,768 75	$615,119 34	$829,215 04

This table is of interest in showing the countries with which Texas traded, and the proportion of her trade with each, during the days of her independence. It is matter of regret that the table does not embrace all the years of the Republic. A summary of the exports and imports of several other years will be found in the adjoining table.

IMPORTS.

From September, 1835, to September 30, 1838 (3 years)	$1,740,376 87
" September, 1838, to September 30, 1839 (1 year)	1,506,897 67
" September, 1839, to December 31, 1840 (15 months)	1,378,568 98
" December, 1840, to December 31, 1841 (1 year)	No returns
" December, 1841, to July 31, 1842 (7 months)	No returns
" July, 1842, to July 31, 1843 (1 year)	471,205 32
" July, 1843, to July 31, 1844 (1 year)	686,503 03
" July, 1844, to October 31, 1845 (15 months)	1,204,370 32

EXPORTS.

From September, 1835, to September 30, 1838 (3 years)	$183,323 00
" September, 1838, to September 30, 1839 (1 year)	274,518 09
" September, 1839, to December 31, 1840 (15 months)	220,401 15
" December, 1840, to December 31, 1841 (1 year)	No returns
" December, 1841, to July 31, 1842 (7 months)	No returns
" July, 1842, to July 31, 1843 (1 year)	415,768 75
" July, 1843, to July 31, 1844 (1 year)	615,119 34
" July, 1844, to October 31, 1845 (15 months)	839,215 00

The returns for the years 1838, 1839, and 1840 (when the treasury notes were in use) illustrate the effect paper-money has in encouraging imports and discouraging exports; while those for 1843, 1844, and 1845 (after the treasury note system had exploded) show the effect hard-money has in discouraging imports and encouraging exports.

H.

RECEIPTS FROM CUSTOMS DURING THE YEAR ENDING JULY 31, 1844.

Districts.	Paid in par funds.	Paid in exchequer bills.	Value of excheq. bills.	Remaining secured in store out of this year's imports.	Total of net revenue at tariff rates.
Galveston	$65,733 17	$86,379 06	$74,427 29	$1,130 50	$141,290 96
Brazos	659 37	1,496 30	1,269 18		1,928 55
Calhoun	5,519 07	10,568 51	9,702 96	4,417 87	19,639 90
Aransaso	513 34			671,38	1,184 72
Sabine	581 33	76 37	48 35		629 68
San Augustine	292 85	6,512 72	5,920 28	863 99	7,077 12
Red River		4,118 55	4,118 55	1,992 37	6,110 92
Total	$73,299 13	$109,151 51	$95,486 61	$9,076 11	$177,861 85

I.

STATEMENT SHOWING THE WHOLE AMOUNT OF EXCHEQUER BILLS ISSUED BY THE TREASURY DEPARTMENT.

Number of bills.	Of what denomination.	Amount issued.
300	$100 00	$30,000
499	50 00	24,950
899	20 00	17,980
2,698	10 00	26,980
7,196	5 00	35,980
1,000	3 00	3,000
1,000	2 00	2,000
2,000	1 00	2,000
3,800	75	2,850
3,800	50	1,900
7,600	25	1,900
7,600	$12\frac{1}{2}$	950

Total amount issued $150,490

From which must be deducted the following amounts, to wit:—

Amount destroyed at different times, under the provisions of the act approved January 29, 1842	$64,865 00
Amount in the treasury at this time	17,600 00
Probable amount in the hands of receiving officers . . .	54,816 71
	$137,281 71

Probable amount in circulation $13,208 29

TREASURY DEPARTMENT, WASHINGTON, } P. B. MILLER,
December 4, 1843. } *Secretary of Treasury.*

RATES OF VALUE OF EXCHEQUER BILLS, JULY 31, 1843, TO JULY 31, 1844.

During quarters ending	Galveston.	Brazos.	Calhoun.	Sabine.	San Augustine.	Red River.
1843, October 31	60		60	60	75	100
1844, January 31	100	$82\frac{1}{2}$	100		75	100
"	80	80			100	
April 30	100		70		75	100
"	80		80			
"	70		100			
"	60					
"	50					
July 31	60		60	80	100	100
"	75		75			
"	80		80			
"			70			

From August 1, 1844, to October 31, 1845 (fifteen months), the value of exchequer bills was as follows :—

At Galveston	80, 90, 80, 90, 95, 100
" Brazos	80, 90
" Calhoun	80, 100, 80, 90, 100
" other places	100

K.

THE PUBLIC LANDS AND LAND-SCRIPT.

Mr. G. W. Smyth, the Commissioner of the General Land-Office, says, in a report dated November 1, 1849 :—

"On the subject of land-script, I have received, through the politeness of James B. Shaw, Esq., Comptroller, a statement of 1,220,387½ acres, the amount sold by the various agents of the government, or unaccounted for by them, and supposed to be sold: to which I have added 108,816, issued by this office, by virtue of an act approved February 5, 1841, making an aggregate of 1,329,203 acres."

The Triplet loan of January 11, 1836, of $20,070, was liquidated by a grant of 153,357 acres; and the Erwin loan of $45,820, with $6,170 44 added for interest, was liquidated by a grant of 121,589 acres of land, and by a payment of about five thousand dollars in money to the heirs of Erwin in February, 1852.

The sales made by the agents abroad, and the liquidation of the Erwin and Triplet loans, appear to have been the chief fiscal aid Texas derived, during her revolutionary struggle, from her immense territorial possessions, except in so far as they enabled her to recruit her armies by land bounties to the soldiers.

An act of February 5, 1841, authorized any holder of promissory notes, bonds, funded debt, or any other liquidated claim against the government, to surrender the same and receive in lieu thereof land-script, at the rate of two dollars an acre. In accordance with this provision, as appears from the report of the Land-Office Commissioner, quoted above, script to the amount of 108,816 acres had been issued up to November, 1849, thus redeeming $217,632 of public liabilities. But, on the other hand, it appears, from the Auditorial Report of January 1, 1850, that $66,400 of ten per cent. stock of 1837 had been issued in exchange for land-script;

thus reducing the net amount of government liabilities, redeemed in this way, to $151,232.

The advantage derived from the 1,220,000 acres sold abroad by agents it is not easy to estimate. Returns were received for part of the same in necessary supplies. Another part, by absorbing some of the treasury notes and bonds thrown into the Mobile and New Orleans market, aided in sustaining the value of Texan securities in the United States.

The following statement in a Texan newspaper, made professedly on the authority of a public document, which appears not to have been printed, embraces the latest information we have met with respecting the public lands of Texas:—

"A report of the late Commissioner of the General Land-Office gives a very lucid and satisfactory exposition of the present condition of Texas land affairs, showing the amount of lands titled by Spain and Mexico; as also the quantity that has been patented by Texas—the amount set apart for universities, colleges, and common schools—and the amount now on hand.

"By the act of 1836, Texas had 379,054 square miles, or 242,594,550 acres. There was ceded to the United States, by the late Compromise Law, 67,000,000 acres—leaving Texas 175,594,560 acres. The whole amount of claims originating under the late Republic and State of Texas is 48,265,663 acres. Making the total amount of every description of claims against the public domain 63,783,054 acres. There will, consequently, remain to Texas, after every legal claim for land officially known to exist against her shall have been satisfied, 111,812,079 acres; this land, estimated at only fifty cents per acre, would be $55,906,039.

"Lands patented for educational purposes:—

"For two State universities .   .   .   . 199,102 acres.
"   denominational colleges   .   .   . 31,106 "
"   schools in each county .   .   .   . 175,945 "

"Total   .   .   .   .   .   . 406,153 acres.

"This includes only the lands surveyed and patented. There are some 300,000 acres more already ordered by law to be surveyed for the primary or common school purposes."—*Marshall Patriot.*

There are great discrepancies in the accounts of the superficial contents of Texas, both before and since the reduction of her limits.

L.

Acts of Texas relating to Duties on Imports and Tonnage.

December 12, 1835. Ordinance imposing twenty per cent. duties on such imports as are entitled to debenture in the ports whence shipped, and ten per cent. on other imports.

December 15, 1835. A tonnage duty of $1 25 a ton imposed, and a duty of twelve and a half cents a gallon on whiskey, American gin, rum, and brandy.

December 27, 1835. The duties on imports increased; those at ten to fifteen per cent., and those at twenty to twenty-five per cent.

[The above were by the Provisional Government.]

December 30, 1836. Act passed imposing duties at various rates, from one per cent. to fifty; and a tonnage duty of twenty-five cents a ton.

June 12, 1837. An act establishing ports of entry, and imposing duties on imports, at various rates, *ad valorem* and specific.

December 18, 1837. An act to admit sugar, coffee, tea, salt, iron, and sundry other articles, free of duty.

May 9, 1838. An act prohibiting giving bonds for duties, and requiring said goods to be held till the duties should be paid. The goods to be sold if the duties were not paid within ten days.

January 15, 1839. An act passed allowing bonds to be given for the payment of duties.

February 5, 1840. An act altering the several acts to raise a public revenue by import duties. This act extends through nineteen sections.

January 4, 1841. An act for the regulation of the coasting trade, and the protection of Texan shipping. Eight sections.

February 5, 1841. An act doubling the specific duties on imports, and increasing the ten and fifteen per cent. *ad valorem* duties to forty-five per cent. Sugar, coffee, salt, iron, and steel were exempted from the operation of this act, and allowed to be imported at the old rates.

January 24, 1842. A supplement passed to the customs act. It extended through twenty-four sections, and imposed duties on articles before exempt: on flour one dollar a barrel; on salt ten cents a bushel; on powder, lead, and firearms of every description, fifteen per cent. *ad valorem*. Nothing was left free of import duty but live stock, Bibles, Testaments, and primary school-books.

Acts of Texas relating to Internal Taxes.

December 21, 1836. The sheriffs made collectors of taxes in their respective counties.

June 12, 1837. An act passed imposing a tax of one and a half per cent. *ad valorem* on all property, real, personal, and mixed; on each wholesale and retail dealer fifty dollars per annum; on each retailer of liquors one hundred dollars; on each billiard-table two hundred dollars; on each nine-pin alley one hundred and fifty dollars; on each tavern in a town one hundred dollars; on horses and cattle, the property of citizens of the United States, one dollar a head; on each white male, from twenty-one to fifty years of age, one dollar a year; on each peddler fifty dollars for each county.

May 24, 1838. An act providing that hereafter direct taxes should be levied only on lands and slaves; horses, over two; mules, over two; neat cattle, over twenty-five in number; clocks, watches, pleasure-carriages, town and city lots, taverns, grogshops, billiard-tables, nine-pin alleys, merchants, and polls.

January 26, 1839. An act passed requiring inventories to be made out and sworn to of all taxable property, and imposing a double tax on all lands held by agents and representatives; also imposing a tax of from one to five dollars on land-certificates.

January 14, 1840. An act passed to raise a revenue by direct taxation. This act extends through forty sections.

January 14, 1841. An act to provide for the better collection of moneys due from delinquent agents and officers of the government. Punishment, fine and imprisonment.

February 5, 1841. An act to amend "an act to raise a revenue by direct taxation." Nine sections.

January 28, 1842. An act prolonging to May, 1842, the period for the payment of taxes for 1841, and abolishing the penalty of double taxes for non-payment of the taxes of 1841.

February 5, 1842. An act to amend "an act to raise a revenue by direct taxation."

January 16, 1843. An act for the more certain collection of the license-tax.

May 13, 1846. An act to provide for the assessment and collection of taxes.

March 20, 1848. An act to provide for the more certain collection of taxes for the years 1846 and 1847.

February 11, 1850. An act passed reducing the taxes on property one-fourth, and the poll-tax one-half.

M.

TENDERS FOR PUBLIC DUES IN TEXAS.

December 30, 1835. Audited drafts made receivable for land dues.

January 10, 1836. McKinney and Williams authorized to raise $100,000 by loan for the use of the government, and the bonds for the same made receivable, six months after date, for all public dues.

January 12, 1836. Authority given to issue treasury notes to the amount of $150,000, and the same made receivable for all public dues.

None of these bonds or treasury notes were issued; but we note the acts as indicative of the principles on which the Government of Texas commenced operations.

October 4, 1836. The notes of any bank making loans to the Republic made receivable to the amount of said loans, for all public dues, so long as the bank should continue specie payments.

December 24, 1836. Audited drafts made receivable for duties on imports.

January 7, 1837. Land-script no longer received in payment of public dues. Up to this date, it appears to have been received without direct authority of law.

January 12, 1837. The islands ordered to be sold for specie, or the notes of current specie-paying banks.

June 9, 1837. The issue of treasury notes authorized, and declaration made that they should be considered as cash and received as cash for all dues to government.

June 12, 1837. It is enacted " that all duties or public dues, of whatever nature or description, shall be collected or paid in gold, silver, or such current bank paper as the authorities may from time to time direct."

June 12, 1837. It is enacted, in another bill, that properly audited drafts should be received in payment of all direct and license-taxes, except those imposed on retailers of liquors, billiard-tables, nine-pin alleys, and games of that kind.

December 14, 1837. Nothing but gold, silver, and treasury notes receivable for customs; and no bank-note to be received in payment of any due to government.

May 6, 1838. A loan of five millions authorized, the bonds to be sold for the notes of any bank whose paper shall be at par with the best bank paper in the cities of New York or Philadelphia. N. B. At this time, the banks of Philadelphia had not resumed specie payments.

May 9, 1838. The prohibition against the receipt of bank-notes for customs renewed.

January 15, 1839. The standard value for gold and silver coin declared to be the same as in the United States.

February 5, 1840. Eight per cent. treasury bonds made receivable for all dues to the government.

June 16, 1840. The receipts of audited drafts restricted to cases in which the public debtor should present to the collector the amount due and no more, if so required by the collector.

February 5, 1841. The public liabilities made receivable in exchange for land-script at two dollars an acre.

January 14, 1842. The auditor required to audit all outstanding just claims against the government, and said audited paper made receivable for all government dues which have *heretofore* accrued, till further ordered.

June 19, 1842. From and after February 1, only gold and silver and exchequer bills receivable for imposts and direct and license-taxes. Land dues (the land-tax excepted) still payable in public liabilities; but the receipt of treasury notes no longer allowed in payment of taxes to be *hereafter* assessed.

January 28, 1842. Those in arrears for taxes allowed to pay them as heretofore in the promissory notes or other liabilities of government, or one-sixth of the amount in gold, silver, or exchequer bills.

February 1, 1842. All postages to be received in gold, silver, or exchequer bills.

June 27, 1842. The collectors of customs, direct and license-taxes, and postages, required to receive exchequer bills at only the current rates at which said bills are selling in the market.

January 17, 1844. Fines and forfeitures payable only in gold, silver, or exchequer bills, and all bonds, obligations, or recognizances to the Republic, made payable in gold or silver only.

February 5, 1844. Auditors' certificates for carrying the mail made receivable in payment of direct taxes. And "Bryan drafts," to the amount of $2,133 62, authorized to bear five per cent. interest per annum, and to be receivable for taxes and customs.

Other special drafts of this kind were authorized under different names.

February 3, 1845. The further issue and reissue of exchequer bills prohibited, and provision made that, from and after the receipt of such public paper as was then˙ receivable by laws, all dues to government should be paid in gold and silver only, except land dues, which might be paid, as heretofore, in audited drafts, treasury notes, or other liabilities of government.

February 3, 1845. County taxes hereafter levied made payable in gold or silver only, or such liabilities of the respective counties as the County Commissioners' Court may direct.

May 13, 1846. All coins made current by the laws of the United States, and the exchequer bills of the Republic of Texas, declared to be receivable in payment of all taxes and revenues. The same re-enacted March 20th, 1848.

March 2, 1848. Government liabilities, when in the hands of *original* holders, made receivable at par rates (*i. e. scaled* rates), as "set-offs" against the claims which government may have on such holders of its liabilities.

January 23, 1850. Arrears of taxes due the late Republic, if originally collectible in government liabilities, made payable in the same, or one-fifth of the amount in gold and silver; if originally collectible in exchequer bills, to be paid in said bills or in gold and silver, or else in government liabilities at the rate of five dollars in such liabilities for one dollar in exchequer bills.

February 11, 1850. All coins made current by the laws of the United States to be received at the rates thereby established.

February 11, 1850. Certificates of audited claims made receivable in exchange for land-script, at the rate of fifty cents an acre.

N.

REVENUE AND EXPENDITURES OF THE STATE OF TEXAS.

RECEIPTS.

	Year ending October 31, 1848.	Year ending October 31, 1849.	Two years, ending October 31, 1851.
Direct and license-taxes . .	$91,905 28	$93,670 38	$200,347 29*
Sales of Austin city lots . .	2,498 00	1,632 20	12,224 73†
Rents of public buildings .	671 73	712 96	·
Sales of custom-houses . .	389 75	942 00	6,068 00
Fees of office	377 29	991 15	3,667 42
Fines and forfeitures . . .	102 22	611 34	923 59
Miscellaneous	189 45		2,249 93‡
Total	$96,133 72	$98,560 03	$225,480 96

* Including land dues and land patents, $4,014 14.
† Including rent of public building.
‡ Including property redeemed for taxes, $1,656 66.

Besides the above, the State appears to have received, between the 20th of February, 1844, and the 31st of October, 1847, the sum of $50,157 85 for direct taxes and licenses. This makes the aggregate revenue, from the foundation of the State government, February 20th, 1846, to the 31st of October, 1851, $470,332 56. The average is $83,000 a year. This is exclusive of county and private trust funds.

In addition to the above, the State has received—

From the Treasurer of the late Republic, in specie	$19,297 51
From arrears of revenue of late Republic, Feb. 1846, to Oct. 1849	125,292 36
" " " " Oct. 1849, to Oct. 1851	3,821 01
	$148,410 88

Making, with the revenue of the State, a total of means, from February 20, 1846, to October 31, 1851, of $618,743 44. Average per annum, $109,190.

EXPENDITURES.

On treasury warrants of late Republic outstanding Feb. 20, 1846	$15,724 29
For appropriations by State Legislature for payment of debts incurred by late Republic	17,998 09
Total on account of late Republic	$33,722 38
On account of the State, from February 20, 1846, to October 31, 1849, three years and eight months	292,349 31
On account of the State, from October 31, 1849, to October 31, 1851, two years	263,427 89
	$589,499 58

In the above, expenditures for county and trust funds to the amount of $3,989 65 are included, leaving for the expenditures of the State, from February 20, 1846, to October 31, 1851, five years and eight months, the sum of $551,787 55. This is at the rate of $97,374 a year, independently of appropriations to the general school fund.

Besides the receipts and expenditures here given, others have been made on account of county and private trust funds.

We have no account in detail of the expenditures for 1846 to 1851; but their character may be judged of from the following estimate, by the comptroller, of the expenses of the State for the year ending October 31, 1852:—

Legislative department	$49,116 00
Executive "	28,000 00
Judicial "	33,500 00
Miscellaneous expenses	16,200 00
Total	$126,816 00

The amount of specie on hand October 31, 1851, was—

General fund	$25,890 68
School fund	12,051 81
County and private trust funds	9,398 84
	$47,341 33

The fiscal concerns of Texas are, so far as regards receipts and payments, now well managed. Its sub-treasury system is more complete than that of the United States, for its payments, as well as its receipts, are in gold and silver.

The whole amount of its receipts and payments is, indeed, but small; but when it is considered that, according to the report of the Commissioner of the Texan Land-Office, the area of the State, within its reduced limits, is 274,366 square miles, it will be obvious that much good management must be requisite to effect receipts and payments in points both numerous and remote.

One of the features of a good treasury system, as well as of a good commercial system, is the prevention of the *unnecessary* carriage of gold and silver from point to point. This is effected by the judicious use of bills of exchange; and hence sound bills of exchange are as necessary as sound money for the perfection of a treasury system. Government drafts are sound public bills of exchange when they are drawn against gold or silver actually in some depository, or in the hands of some public officer. There being in the laws of Texas none of those absurd restrictions on the use of government drafts that are found in the sub-treasury law of the United States, the officers of the Texan Treasury Department make free use of them to prevent the unnecessary carriage of gold and silver from point to point.

The area of Texas being greater than that of all our Atlantic States from the northern limits of Pennsylvania and New Jersey to the southern limits of Georgia, there would be immense expense in bringing all the receipts of the State to Austin, and sending them to the points where they are to be disbursed. This is avoided by giving to the public creditors drafts on the public officers who collect the funds.

In this way, the State not only collects and disburses its own funds, but collects part of the funds due to the counties. A man residing in Brownsville, on the confines of Mexico, may own lands in various counties, some near Arkansas, and some near Louisiana; provision is made that he may pay to the treasurer of the county in which he resides his county taxes on all his lands in all parts of the State. Due report of this is made at Austin, and the officers of the Treasury Department there, by means of government drafts, transfer to each county the balance that is due to it.

These government drafts, being for uncertain amounts of dollars and cents, do not become a common circulating medium, and hence do not drive gold and silver out of circulation. All they do is to prevent the unnecessary carriage of gold and silver from place to place. And in this way they do much good and no evil.

O.

ASSESSMENTS IN TEXAS.

	LAND.		TOWN LOTS.	
	Acres.	Value.	No.	Value.
1848	38,788,439	$24,612,155	31,525	$3,142,900
1849*	40,599,954	23,632,440	24,316	3,121,430
1850†	32,297,199	21,539,810	25,171	3,272,560
1851‡	31,398,609	23,591,230	18,697	3,615,980

	NEGROES.		HORSES.	
	No.	Value.	No.	Value.
1848	40,610	13,398,490	62,384	2,056,575
1849*	38,207	12,773,540	53,470	2,073,395
1850†	48,297	17,492,500	68,507	2,530,375
1851‡	51,064	20,492,250	71,798	2,878,930

	CATTLE.		MONEY-LENDERS.	
	No.	Value.	No.	Amount lent.
1848	518,867	2,117,900	179	101,485
1849*	523,676	2,064,440	255	120,315
1850†	676,545	2,621,895	350	209,415
1851‡	709,396	2,980,485	482	324,675

	STORES.		MISCELLANEOUS PROPERTY.	
				Total value of
	No.	Value.	Value.	property assessed.
1848	403	1,055,065	1,162,730	47,647,300
1849*	480	1,092,755	1,221,625	46,099,940
1850†	581	1,651,340	1,396,720	50,714,615
1851‡	532	1,709,970	1,479,195	57,072,715

			Total of poll	Average value
	Ad valorem tax.§	Total poll-tax.	and ad valorem tax.	of land per acre.
1848	$95,294 60	$21,429 00	$116,723 60	63 cts.
1849*	92,199 88	21,288 00	123,487 60¶	58 "
1850†	76,071 91	11,520 50	89,242 41¶	66 "
1851‡	85,609 07	12,040 00	116,652 07¶	75 "

It will be seen that the value of taxable property increases, though, for some unexplained reason, the number of acres of land returned for assessment decreases.

* No returns from five counties.   † No returns from two counties.
‡ No returns from eight counties.
§ In 1848 and 1849, this tax was 20 cents—in 1850 and 1851, 15 cents—in $100.
|| In 1848 and 1849, $1 00—in 1850 and 1851, 50 cents—a head.
¶ Including estimates for the counties from which returns had not been received.

The following particulars of the assessment of 1845 are given, as that was the year in which Texas was admitted into the Union.

Land 21,885,990 acres		Value $15,830,120	
Town lots, number 18,322		" 1,589,874	
Sales of merchandise		54,484	
Money at interest		9,417	

Negroes	23,262	Saddle horses		800
Pleasure-carriages	218	Stud "		130
Gold watches	508	Work "		12,041
Silver watches	451	Race "		22
Metal clocks	337	Cattle		284,336
Wood "	593			

DIRECT TAXES.

Specific	$21,525 48
Ad valorem	20,372 17
Poll	5,365 00
	$47,262 65

The stores are valued at the amount of merchandise contained in them on the 1st of January.

"Under no system has the entire landed interest of the State been taxed." (Comptroller's Report, Dec. 3, 1849.)

LICENSE-TAXES.

Amount of tax on	1847.	1848.	1849.	1850.
Merchandise	$11,863 01	$7,004 29	$6,367 73	$6,326 64
Spirits by wholesale	3,749 47	2,330 05	} 8,804 04	6,774 90
" " retail	8,109 17	8,279 57		
Peddlers	801 91	489 17	349 32	202 42
Doctors and lawyers	1,393 08	304 18		
Boarding-houses	45 23	11 25		
Taverns	719 34	267 55	20 00	
Billiard-tables	553 32	770 81	1,229 05	1,174 11
Auctioneers	148 13	26 24	329 14	183 83
Restaurants	68 86	98 90	162 00	183 35
Ten-pin alleys	125 29	113 21	229 26	173 32
Brokers	98 95	228 98		
Race-course		7 66	25 00	
Theatre	25 00	33 25		
Exhibitions	38 32		91 65	1 85
Commission merchants			249 98	208 32
Professions			15 00	
Estimate for counties from which no returns were rec'd		1,048 60		1,000 00
	$27,739 08	$21,013 71	$17,872 17	$16,228 24

Note.—Many of the returns for 1850 were for nine months only.

	1848.	1849.	1850.
Direct tax, *ad valorem*	95,294 60	92,199 88	76,071 91
" " poll	21,429 00	21,288 00	11,520 50
Licenses	21,013 51	17,872 17	16,228 24
Total	137,737 11	131,360 05	103,820 65

The decrease in the license-tax is accounted for, in part, "by the change made, at the last session of the Legislature, of the tax on merchants, from a specific tax on that calling, to an *ad valorem* tax of one-fifth of one per cent. on the amount of purchases." (Comptroller's Report, Dec. 29, 1849.)

P.

AGRICULTURAL STATISTICS OF FORTY-ONE COUNTIES IN 1848.

	Quantity.	Value.
Cotton in seed . . .	85,636,513 pounds,	$1,356,617
Sugar	5,816,908 do.	195,934
Molasses	176,446 gallons,	36,850
Corn	3,491,227 bushels,	1,512,731
Wheat	33,039 "	29,052
Rye, oats, &c. . . .	150,515 "	75,650
Potatoes	742,003 "	296,589
Tobacco	92,527 pounds,	7,993
Horses and mules . .	38,182 number,	1,356,79
Cattle	369,901 "	1,895,790
Sheep	39,950 "	61,202
Hogs	223,358 "	315,855
Butter	774,083 pounds,	89,384
Cheese	58,603 "	8,685
Wool	48,856 "	16,586
Total of agricultural products . . .		7,255,712
Total of manufactures		133,436
Total of agricultural products and manufactures .		$7,389,148
Land in cultivation . .	316,153 acres,	$2,684,183

Average value of land in cultivation $8 50 an acre. This table has been abridged from the report of the comptroller, of December 3, 1849. The whole number of counties in the State, in 1848, was seventy-eight, having in them 38,788,439 acres on which taxes had been assessed. The number of acres on which taxes had been assessed, in the forty-one counties from which the above returns were received, was 23,921,357. Supposing the number of acres in cultivation, and the products, to bear the same proportion to the acres taxed in the thirty-seven remaining counties, then the whole number of acres in cultivation in Texas, in 1848, was 512,641, and the total value thereof $4,307 449. On the same principle of calculation, the total value of agricultural products was $11,765,012, and of manufactures $216,362. Aggregate, $11,981,374.

It is evident that all those important branches of industry which are connected with house building are not embraced in these returns; and the probability is that the products of many kinds of handicraft are entirely omitted. From only thirteen counties in forty-one were any returns of manufactures obtained.

Q.

ACT OF ANNEXATION.

In Convention of the people of the Republic of Texas, July 4, 1845.

AN ORDINANCE.

WHEREAS, The Congress of the United States of America has passed resolutions providing for the annexation of Texas to that Union, which resolutions were approved by the President of the United States on the first day of March, one thousand eight hundred and forty-five ; and whereas, the President of the United States has submitted to Texas the first and second sections of the said resolution, as the basis upon which Texas may be admitted as one of the States of the said Union ; and whereas, the existing Government of the Republic of Texas has assented to the proposals thus made, the terms and conditions of which are as follows :—

JOINT RESOLUTION FOR ANNEXING TEXAS TO THE UNITED STATES.

Resolved, by the Senate and House of Representatives of the United States of America in Congress assembled, That Congress doth consent that the territory, properly included within, and rightfully belonging to the Republic of Texas, may be erected into a new State, to be called the " State of Texas," with a republican form of government, to be adopted by the people of said Republic, by deputies in convention assembled, with the consent of the existing government, in order that the same may be admitted as one of the States of this Union.

2. *And be it further resolved,* That the foregoing consent of Congress is

given upon the following conditions, and with the following guarantees, to wit : *First.* Said State to be formed, subject to the adjustment, by this government, of all questions of boundary that may arise with other governments ; and the Constitution thereof, with the proper evidence of its adoption by the people of said Republic of Texas, shall be transmitted to the President of the United States, to be laid before Congress for its final action, on or before the first day of January, one thousand eight hundred and forty-six. *Second.* Said State, when admitted into the Union, after ceding to the United States all public edifices, fortifications, barracks, ports and harbors, navy and navy yards, docks, magazines, arms and armaments, and all other property and means pertaining to the public defence belonging to the said Republic of Texas, shall retain all the public funds, debts, taxes, and dues of every kind, which may belong to, or be due and owing to the said Republic ; and shall also retain all the vacant and unappropriated lands lying within its limits, to be applied to the payment of the debts and liabilities of said Republic of Texas; and the residue of said lands, after discharging said debts and liabilities, to be disposed of as said State may direct; but in no event are said debts and liabilities to become a charge upon the Government of the United States. *Third.* New States of convenient size, not exceeding four in number, in addition to said State of Texas, and having sufficient population, may hereafter, by the consent of said State, be formed out of the territory thereof, which shall be entitled to admission under the provisions of the Federal Constitution. And such States as may be formed out of that portion of said territory lying south of thirty-six degrees thirteen minutes north latitude, commonly known as the " Missouri Compromise Line," shall be admitted into the Union, with or without slavery, as the people of each State asking admission may desire. And in such State, or States, as shall be formed out of said territory, north of said " Missouri Compromise Line," slavery or involuntary servitude (except for crime) shall be prohibited.

Now, in order to manifest the assent of the people of this Republic, as required in the above-recited portions of the said resolutions, we, the deputies of the people of Texas, in convention assembled, in their name, and by their authority, do ordain and declare that we assent to, and accept the proposals, conditions, and guarantees contained in the first and second sections of the resolution of the Congress of the United States aforesaid.

Done at the City of Austin, Republic of Texas, July 4, 1845.

R.

THE BOUNDARY ACT.

An act proposing to the State of Texas the establishment of her northern and western boundaries, the relinquishment by the said State of all territory claimed by her exterior to said boundaries, and of all her claims upon the United States.

Be it enacted, &c., That the following propositions shall be and the same are hereby offered to the State of Texas, which, when agreed to by the said State, in an act passed by the General Assembly, shall be binding and obligatory upon the United States and upon the said State of Texas : *Provided,* That the said agreement by the said General Assembly shall be given on or before the 1st day of December, 1850.

First. The State of Texas will agree that her boundary on the north shall commence at the point at which the meridian of one hundred degrees west from Greenwich is intersected by the parallel of thirty-six degrees and thirty minutes north latitude, and shall run from said point due west to the meridian of one hundred and three degrees west from Greenwich; thence her boundary shall run due south to the thirty-second degree of north latitude; thence on the said parallel of thirty-two degrees of north latitude to the Rio Bravo del Norte; and thence, with the channel of said river, to the Gulf of Mexico.

Second. The State of Texas cedes to the United States all her claim to territory exterior to the limits and boundaries which she agrees to establish by the first article of this agreement.

Third. The State of Texas relinquishes all claim upon the United States for liability for the debts of Texas, and for compensation or indemnity for the surrender to the United States of her ships, forts, arsenals, custom-houses, custom-house revenue, arms and munitions of war, and public buildings, with their sites, which became the property of the United States at the time of annexation.

Fourth. The United States, in consideration of said establishment of boundaries, cession of claim to territory, and relinquishment of claims, will pay to the State of Texas the sum of ten millions of dollars, in a stock bearing five per cent. interest, and redeemable at the end of fourteen years, the interest payable half yearly at the Treasury of the United States.

Fifth. Immediately after the President of the United States shall have been furnished with an authentic copy of the act of the General Assembly of Texas accepting these propositions, he shall cause the stock to be issued in favor of the State of Texas, as provided for in the fourth article of agreement: *Provided*, That not more than five millions of said stock shall be issued until the creditors of the State, holding bonds and other certificates of stock of Texas, for which duties on imports were specially pledged, shall first file at the Treasury of the United States releases of all claim against the United States for or on account of said bonds or certificates, in such form as shall be prescribed by the Secretary of the Treasury, and approved by the President of the United States: *Provided, also,* That nothing herein contained shall be construed to impair or qualify anything contained in the third article of the second section of the joint resolution for annexing Texas to the United States, approved March 1, 1845, either as regards the number of States that may hereafter be formed out of the State of Texas or otherwise.

S.

AN ACT PROVIDING FOR THE LIQUIDATION AND PAYMENT OF THE DEBT OF THE LATE REPUBLIC OF TEXAS, JANUARY 31, 1852.

SEC. 1. *Be it enacted by the Legislature of the State of Texas,* That two millions of dollars of bonds of the indemnity due the State of Texas, and now at her disposal, for the sale to the United States of a portion of her north-western territory, under the provisions of an act of Congress proposing to the State of Texas the establishment of her northern and western boundaries, &c., approved September 9, 1850, are hereby appropriated for the payment of that portion of the debt of the late Republic of Texas embraced in articles third, fourth, ninth, tenth, fourteenth, fifteenth, and sixteenth, and interest which may have accrued thereon included in articles twelfth and thirteenth of this section; which debt has been submitted for adjustment to the auditor and comptroller of the State, under the provisions of an act to provide for ascertaining the debt of the late Republic of Texas, approved March 20, A. D. 1848, and an act supplementary thereto, approved February 8, A. D. 1850, and reported by them to the Legislature in their report of November 12, 1851, as follows:—

First. For ten per cent. consolidated fund, created by act of the 7th of June, 1837, four hundred and forty-two thousand seven hundred and sixty-eight dollars and seventy-six cents.

Second. For ten per cent. consolidated fund created by act of the 7th of June, 1837, issued under an act for the relief of Swartwout and others, seven thousand nine hundred and seventy dollars and forty-three cents.

Third. For ten per cent. funded debt, created by act of 5th of February, 1840, two hundred and twenty-six thousand and two hundred dollars.

Fourth. For eight per cent. funded debt, created by act of 5th of February, 1840, seven thousand two hundred and eighty-four dollars.

Fifth. For eight per cent. treasury bonds, created by act of 5th of February, 1840, one hundred and fifty-three thousand three hundred and sixty dollars.

Sixth. For ten per cent. treasury notes, issued under act of June 9th, 1837, first issue, forty-one thousand six hundred and thirty dollars.

Seventh. For ten per cent. treasury notes, issued under act of June 9, 1837, second issue, one hundred and sixty-five thousand six hundred and eighty-five dollars and fifty cents.

Eighth. For treasury notes without interest, issued under act of 19th of January, 1839, third issue, four hundred and fifty-seven thousand and forty-eight dollars.

Ninth. For audited paper, issued under various enactments, sixty-nine thousand four hundred and fifty-one dollars and fifty-two cents.

Tenth. For miscellaneous liabilities, twenty-six thousand one hundred and twenty-nine dollars and eighty-seven cents.

Eleventh. For ten per cent. bonds, issued by commissioners to negotiate a loan for five millions of dollars, viz.: For loan obtained from Bank of United States, four hundred thousand dollars; for purchase of steamer "Zavalla," ninety thousand and fourteen dollars and eighty-four cents; for purchase of naval vessels under contract with F. Dawson, now owned by James Schott and E. D. Whitney, one hundred and forty thousand dollars.

Twelfth. For interest on the above liabilities, issued subject to interest as stated in the face of the certificates, one million four hundred and sixty-eight thousand one hundred and fifty-five dollars and twenty-six cents.

Thirteenth. For additional interest to July 1, 1850, allowed by act approved February 11, 1850, on claims which had been audited prior to its passage, one hundred and thirteen thousand six hundred and sixty-four dollars and eighty cents.

Fourteenth. For amount filed and receipted for as *second class* debt, six hundred and seventy-nine thousand two hundred and twenty-two dollars and fifty cents.

Fifteenth. For amount filed and receipted for as *third class*, since recognized as second class, sixteen thousand four hundred and sixty-seven dollars and ninety-five cents.

Sixteenth. For amount audited by special act of the Legislature, seventy-two thousand and seventy-seven dollars and twenty-eight cents—less thirty-eight thousand and fifty-three dollars and seventy-three cents, amount acknowledged by joint resolution, approved March 15, 1848.

SEC. 2. That the disbursements herein provided for shall be made in the bonds or stock of indemnity alluded to in the first section of this act, or the proceeds thereof, by the Treasurer of this State upon the certificates of indebtedness, issued by the auditor and comptroller under the provisions of the laws above named; and in all other respects the said Treasurer shall be governed by the laws regulating the payment of money out of the State treasury; and the Comptroller of Public Accounts for the State of Texas is hereby authorized to transfer a sufficient amount of said stock, when the transfer shall be necessary, by simple indorsement, attested by his seal of office, to be countersigned by the Treasurer of the State, which transfer shall divest the State of all interest in such bonds or stock, and invest the same in the holder thereof. Provided, that payment shall be made on any claim against the State included in or forming a part of articles first, second, fifth, sixth, seventh, eighth, and eleventh; or for interest which may have accrued thereon, included in articles twelfth and thirteenth, in the first section of this act. When the Governor of this State shall be notified by the President of the United States that the Secretary of the Treasury of the United States has been required by law to issue to the State of Texas the five millions of dollars of stock withheld under the provisions of said act, approved September 9, 1850, until certain creditors shall have filed releases at the Treasury of the United States, as therein required; or that said Secretary has been required by law to issue to the State of Texas sums of said stock, equal to the sums for which the State may at any time present the required releases from any portion of said creditors, at the Treasury of the United States; after which notice, such claim or claims shall be paid as provided for in other cases; and upon payment of the same, or any portion of said claims, the corresponding amount of bonds of the reserved five millions, which the State may be entitled to receive under the proviso of this section, shall be drawn for by the comptroller, and deposited in the treasury of the State, and shall be regulated and transferred in the same manner as provided for other bonds, and together with the surplus left of the appropriation named in the first section of this act, after payment of the sums to which it is to be applied, appropriated for, and paid out only upon the claims embraced in articles first, second, fifth, sixth, seventh, eighth, eleventh, twelfth, and thirteenth of this act.

SEC. 3. That it shall be the duty of the comptroller, immediately after the passage of this act, to forward to the Secretary of the Treasury of the United States a schedule of the names of the creditors, for the payment of whose claims conditional provision is made by the second section of this act, stating the amount to which each creditor is entitled.

SEC. 4. That before the payment of any of the claims provided for by this act, the claimant shall be required to sign a receipt to the State of Texas, that the amount so received is in full liquidation and payment of the claim or claims so presented; and also a release exonerating the United States from all liability for the same—said release to be in form as prescribed by the Secretary of the Treasury, and approved by the President of the United States, for releases under said act, approved September 9, 1850, and that this act be in force from its passage.

Approved January 31, 1852.

T.

REPORT TO PRESIDENT OF THE UNITED STATES, BY THE SECRETARY OF THE TREASURY, ON THE PUBLIC DEBT OF TEXAS.

In obedience to your order, I proceed to report the condition and amount of the debt of the late Republic of Texas, as reported to me by the authorities of the State, and to present very briefly my construction of the powers and duties of the President, as prescribed by the first section of the act of Congress, approved September 9, 1850.

By the act referred to, in consideration of certain concessions by the State of Texas, it is provided that the United States " shall pay to the State of Texas the sum of ten millions of dollars, in a stock bearing five per cent. interest, and redeemable at the end of fourteen years, the interest payable half yearly at the Treasury of the United States."

In the same section of the law, it is further provided " that no more than five millions of said stock shall be issued until the creditors of the State holding bonds and other certificates of stock of Texas, *for which duties on imports were specially pledged,* shall first file at the Treasury of the United States releases of all claims against the United States for or on account of said bonds or certificates, in such form as shall be prescribed by the Secretary of the Treasury and approved by the President of the United States."

The release thus provided for has been prescribed by the Secretary of the Treasury and approved by the President. It has been published in all the leading newspapers in the commercial cities of the United States, and all persons holding claims of the kind specified in the foregoing proviso were required to file their releases (in the form thus prescribed) in the Treasury of the United States, on or before the 1st day of October, 1851. Although this publication has been continued from the 25th day of March,

1851, yet, up to this time, comparatively few releases have been filed by the creditors of Texas.

By the terms of the law, the President is to cause the stock to be issued, and the restriction which forbids the issuing of five millions of said stock until the releases of claims, as stated in the law, attaches to the stock *in his hands.*

It would seem to result, from the foregoing propositions, that the President should determine what classes and amounts of the Texas debts shall be released to the United States, before he can lawfully deliver the whole of the ten millions of stock to the State of Texas.

To form an opinion on this point, it becomes necessary to ascertain what portion of the public debt of Texas was contracted by her while an independent Republic, with a special pledge of "duties on imports" for its redemption.

I present herewith reports marked A, B, C, D, E, F, G, and H, certified by the auditor of the State, and verified by the signature of Governor Bell and the seal of the State.

These papers show the laws under which the debts of Texas were contracted, and the amount of bonds or other evidences of debt issued under the laws referred to respectively.

The amount of the debt in the aggregate and the character of each class is presented in the paper accompanying this report, submitted to me by the Assistant Secretary of the Treasury, and dated September 10, 1851.

From these papers it is shown that the public debt of Texas, with interest at the rate prescribed by the laws under which it was contracted, computed up to 1st of July, 1850, amounts, in the whole, to the sum of twelve millions four hundred and thirty-five thousand nine hundred and eighty-two dollars and sixty-eight cents ($12,435,982 68).

By the terms of the act of Congress of 9th September, 1850, five of the ten millions of stock provided for are to be issued to Texas at once; the remaining five are to be withheld by the President until all claims against the United States for that portion of the above-stated public debt of Texas, for the payment of which the "duties on imports are specially pledged," shall be released to the United States.

What class or amount of this debt falls within this description is to be ascertained by the laws of Texas, which laws, of course, form the basis of the contract between her and the present holders of these claims.

It is obvious, from the most careless perusal of the law, that Congress considered the United States as liable to pay all that portion of the debt of Texas for the redemption of which "duties on imports" had been pledged by the laws of Texas.

Upon no other hypothesis is there any justifiable motive for requiring releases to the United States to be filed for such claims, before Texas should receive the last five millions of the stock to be paid her. In other words, Congress admitted the liability of the General Government to pay all that portion of the public debt of Texas,. and laid its hand upon five millions of the stock provided for as a security that Texas should pay that portion of her debt, or, in her failure to do so, the five millions thus withheld should be a fund out of which that class of the creditors of both Texas and the United States should be paid in whole or in part, as the relative amount of such debt and the fund reserved should determine.

The history of the debt contracted by Texas while she was yet an independent power, and her subsequent incorporation into the Union as a State of the Republic of the United States, it is believed, makes the United States liable for this portion of the Texas debt.

The laws of nations which govern the subject are well understood, and of easy application to the present question. These laws all proceed upon the idea that the moral obligations of independent States are binding when once they attach to compacts between States, or between States and individuals, and that they never cease except by the voluntary agreement of the parties interested, or by their fulfilment and complete discharge. Hence, where an independent power contracts obligations, and is afterwards, by the act of another power, jointly with herself, incorporated into and subjected to the dominion of the latter, whereby the national responsibility of the former is destroyed, and the means of fulfilling her obligations transferred to the latter, all such obligations, to the extent at least of the means thus transferred, attach with all their force to the nation to whom such means have been so transferred.

It will be found that all writers on public law having any authority are agreed upon this point, from the time of Grotius to the present. Indeed, the proposition thus asserted is so obviously just that it is not possible for a nation in modern times to controvert it, without forfeiting that character for justice and probity which, happily for mankind, has become indispensable for sovereign States. It was this view of the subject which, doubtless, dictated that provision of the law which I am now considering.

It was known to Congress that Texas had contracted debts to a large amount to individuals while she was an independent power. It was equally well known that revenue arising from "duties on imports" was, amongst all nations in modern times, one resource, if not the principal one, for the payment of the debts of nations. It was known, also, by the framers of this act that, by the annexation of Texas to the United States, the power to levy duties on imports within the ports or territories of Texas was taken away from the latter and transferred to the United States. It was therefore assumed that the United States should pay, if Texas did not, all that portion of the debt of Texas for which duties on imports had been pledged ; for the obvious reason that these duties thus pledged were taken from Texas and transferred to the United States; and to that extent the creditors of Texas, by a plain principle of justice, had become the creditors of the United States.

With these facts and principles for the basis of legislation, the question recurs, what class of debts were comprehended in the terms used in the law ?

I entertain no doubt of what was the design of Congress. They evidently intended that Texas should pay out of the ten millions granted all those debts of hers for which they deemed the United States had become liable by the incorporation of Texas into the Union ; and they deemed this government liable for all debts of Texas for the payment of which the duties on imports had been pledged in any form. The words employed are, "for which duties on imports are specially pledged." In all cases, therefore, where duties on imports have, by the laws of Texas, been specially set apart for the payment of any loan, in my judgment it becomes the duty of the President to require the releases specified in the law of Congress before he issues to Texas the remaining five millions of stock.

By the act of 7th June, 1837, the Republic of Texas pledged her public faith for the redemption of every loan under that law, and also " so much of the revenue arising from imports and direct taxation as may be necessary to meet the annual interest of the funded debt." (See Schedule A, and the law there quoted.) Under this act, as appears by Schedule A, a loan was effected, which, with its interest, leaves outstanding on the 1st of July, 1850, $1,651,590 02.

The terms of the law plainly secure, by a pledge of import duties, the payment of the interest, which, in effect, is a *special* pledge of duties on imports for the payment of the interest, which interest, while the fund set apart remains, is perpetually secured. This, then, is one of the loans coming within the proviso referred to, releases of which should be filed in the treasury of the United States, for all interest which has accrued or may accrue before the remaining five millions of stock can be issued to Texas.

The loans designated in Schedule B were made under the acts of the 18th November, 1836; the 16th of May, 1838 ; 22d January, 1839 ; 14th January, 1840; and 5th February, 1840. The amount, with interest computed to 1st July, 1850, under these acts, is $2,582,902 70.

By the 9th section of the act of 1836, the public faith, the proceeds of the sales of public lands, and all the taxes on lands, which may accrue to the State after the year 1838, are set apart for the payment of the interest and principal of the loan therein provided for.

The only provision of the before-mentioned laws which it seems important to consider as bearing on the act of Congress in question, is the 15th section of the act of 14th January, 1840. That section contains the following provision :—

"*Be it further enacted*, That, for the redemption of all loans negotiated by the authority of the Republic of Texas, independently of the reservation of the sinking fund, the proceeds of the sales of the public lands, its *revenues*, and public faith are solemnly pledged."

It seems perfectly clear that a pledge of all the revenue of a government whose organic form admitted the power to raise revenue by "duties on imports" is a special pledge of duties on imports, as well as all the other sources of taxation known to such government. If, instead of a pledge of the "revenues," a term comprehending every item of revenue, another form of expression had been adopted, which had enumerated each item, including duties on imports, then no one would doubt that the law contained a special pledge of the duties on imports.

If, then, the pledge of all "revenue," without enumeration of items or classes, does not include duty on imports, neither does it, for the same reason, include any other species of revenue ; and thus it would follow that nothing was pledged by the act in question—an absurdity too flagrant for consideration. Such a construction would admit the possibility of an intention by the Congress of Texas to hold out to the world a delusive promise seeming to be substantial, and yet, in fact, offering no real security. The section referred to, therefore, must be considered as pledging specially the duties on imports, as well as any other species of revenue possible under the government then existing. If these views are correct, all loans negotiated by Texas prior to the 14th January, 1840, and under that act, are secured by a special pledge of the duties on imports. It follows that the five millions of stock specified in the act of Congress of the 9th September, 1850, should not be issued until releases are filed as prescribed by all owners of that portion of the debt of Texas.

The public debt created under one of the acts of 5th February, 1840, is stated, in Schedule C, to amount, with interest up to 1st July, 1850, to the sum of $1,628,936 26. I do not find any pledge in this act for the payment of either the principal or interest of this portion of the debt.

The debt set out in Schedule D, with interest up to 1st July, 1850, is $1,472,918 80.

This debt was created under another act of the 5th February, 1840. By the 3d section of this act, it is provided that "the bonds before referred to shall be at all times receivable by any collector of revenue, or at the Treasury Department, in payment of any debt to the government, or any duties by imports or direct taxation, for the amount or value of such funds, and the interest which may have accrued thereon."

It will be seen, by inspection of the specimen of the bonds under this act, furnished in Schedule D, that the pledge is stated on its face. The phrase, " receivable for all government dues," is printed on the face of this stock in conspicuous capitals. I cannot suppose that any interpretation can be given to this act which would exclude the idea of a special pledge of duties or " dues" to the government arising from " imports." It would seem that no language could create a special pledge of duties on imports, if a promise to receive the stock in payment for all government dues arising, in the language of the law, " from imports or direct taxation," does not.

I am of opinion, therefore, that the debt set out in Schedule D, amounting to $1,472,918 80, should be released in the form prescribed and approved by the President before the issue to Texas of the last five millions of stock, as provided in the act of Congress of the 9th September, 1850.

The issues set forth in Schedule E are not sufficiently described to enable me to determine whether the whole sum of issues there put down are governed by the same laws. It is quite certain that the sum of $420,000 of principal and $89,000 of interest are due on notes issued and made receivable " for all dues to the government." The $2,586,546 may, or may not fall within any of the laws before mentioned as containing a special pledge. If the latter were issued prior to the law of the 14th January, 1840, then they would be covered by the provisions of the 15th section of that act, which pledges the " *revenues*" of Texas for their redemption; and, in my judgment, all issues of evidence of public debt of Texas prior to that law come within the fair meaning of the proviso in the first section of the act of Congress of the 9th September, 1850. I am also clearly of opinion that any portion of her public debt which, by the laws of Texas, is made receivable in payment of " all dues to the government," are claims for which the revenue arising from duties on imports are specially pledged.

As the report of the authorities of Texas does not enable me to say what amounts are covered by the foregoing principles, it is only necessary for the information of holders of the debt that they should know the classes which the President deems it right should be released before the last five millions of stock can be issued to the Government of Texas.

The amount set out in Schedule F, being $2,117,181 68, is made up of parts of previous issues under the laws of Texas, and it does not appear what portion of this amount falls within any of the laws of Texas authorizing issues or loans.

I repeat, therefore, that, for the information of all concerned, it will suffice to declare that all the public debt of Texas created prior to the act of Congress of that Republic of the 14th January, 1840, and all the debt of said Republic made receivable for all public dues, are, in my judgment, debts of Texas, for which the duties on imports are specially pledged, and that releases of all claim against the United States for or on account of such debts should be filed in the Treasury Department of the United States before the President will be justified in issuing the second five millions of stock to Texas as provided in the act of Congress of the 9th September, 1850.

These views, though hastily sketched at this time, under the pressure of much indispensable current business, are, nevertheless, the result of much previous reflection and examination. I find them to accord with a very elaborate argument on the subject, presented by the late Attorney-General (R. Johnson), and therefore submit them with entire confidence in the legal conclusions stated.

Very respectfully submitted.

THOS. CORWIN,
Secretary of the Treasury.

To the President.

———

EXECUTIVE CHAMBER, WASHINGTON, *Sept.* 13, 1851.

Concurring in the conclusions of the foregoing report, the Secretary of the Treasury is hereby directed to issue the last five millions of stock to Texas, on the condition specified in said report.

MILLARD FILLMORE.

U.

REPORT OF THE AUDITOR AND COMPTROLLER TO THE FOURTH LEGISLATURE ON THE PUBLIC DEBT OF TEXAS.

AUSTIN, *November* 12, 1851.

To the Honorable Legislature of the State of Texas:

In conformity to the requirements of " an act to provide for ascertaining the debt of the late Republic of Texas," approved 20th March, 1848, and the act supplementary thereto, approved February 8th, 1850, we respectfully submit the following report—exhibiting the amount, character, and classification of the claims filed and receipted for by us, under the provisions of said acts:—

FIRST CLASS,

Consisting of audited or ascertained Claims.

Character of liabilities receipted for.	Ostensible.	Rate.	Par value.
Ten per cent. consolidated fund created by act of 7th June, 1837	$632,526 80	at 70 cts.	$442,768 76
Ten per cent. consolidated fund created by act of 7th June, 1837, issued under an act for the relief of Swartwout and others . . .	7,970 43	1 00	7,970 43
Ten per cent. funded debt created by act of 5th February, 1840 .	754,000 00	30	226,200 00
Eight per cent. funded debt created by act of 5th February, 1840	24,280 00	30	7,284 00
Eight per cent. treasury bonds created by act of 5th Feb. 1840	766,800 00	20	153,360 00
Ten per cent. treasury notes issued under act of the 9th June, 1837, first issue	41,630 00	1 00	41,630 00
Ten per cent. treasury notes issued under act of 9th June, 1837, second issue	331,371 00	50	165,685 50
Treasury notes, without interest, issued under act of 19th January, 1839, third issue	1,828,192 00	25	457,048 00
Audited paper issued under various enactments	74,441 26	various.	69,451 52
Miscellaneous liabilities	42,387 73	1 00	42,387 73
Ten per cent. bonds issued by commissioners to negotiate a loan for $5,000,000, viz. :—			
For loan obtained from Bank United States	457,380 00		400,000 00
For purchase of steamer "Zavalla"	195,907 00	50	97,953 50
" " Naval vessels under contract with F. Dawson, now owned by James Schott and E. D. Whitney	280,000 00	50	140,000 00
	$5,436,886 22		$2,251,739 44
Interest on the above liabilities issued subject to interest, as stated in the face of the certificates	2,927,365 50	various.	1,468,185 26
	$8,364,251 72		$3,719,914 70
Additional interest to 1st July, 1850, allowed, by act approved 11th Feb. 1850, on claims which had been audited prior to its passage	239,139 06	various.	113,664 80

Character of liabilities receipted for.	Ostensible.	Rate.	Par value.
Total amount filed of first class, including interest due thereon to 1st July, 1850	$8,603,390 78		$3,833,579 50
Less amount redeemed by issues of land-script	16,257 86	1 00	16,257 86
Total amount first class debt filed, and unredeemed	$8,587,132 92		$3,817,321 64

SECOND CLASS,

Consisting of Claims sufficiently authenticated to admit them to audit under the laws of the late Republic.

	Ostensible amount.	Par value.
Amount filed and receipted for	$755,218 05	$682,672 57
" " " as third class claims since recognized	16,467 95	16,467 95
Amount audited by special acts of Legislature	72,077 28	72,077 28
Estimated amount on file not acted on . .	125,000 00	125,000 00
	$968,763 28	$896,217 80
Less amount redeemed by the issue of land-script and in payment of revenue that accrued under the late Republic	6,318 16	3,450 17
Total amount of second class debts filed	$962,445 12	$892,767 63

THIRD CLASS,

Consisting of Claims not sufficiently authenticated to authorize their being audited under the laws of the late Republic.

	Ostensible amount.	Par value.
Amount filed and receipted for, less $16,467 95, recognized and included in the preceding statement of second class claims	$47,675 10	$47,675 10
Estimated amount on file not acted on .	50,000 00	50,000 00
Total amount third class filed	$97,675 10	$97,675 10

RECAPITULATION.

	Ostensible amount.	Par value.
Amount of first class	$8,587,132 92	$3,817,321 54
" second class	962,445 12	892,767 63
" third class	97,675 10	97,675 10
Totals	$9,647,253 14	$4,807,764 37

From the foregoing statement, it will be perceived that the entire amount of claims filed, including interest on all liabilities stipulated to bear interest, amounts to $9,647,253 14; and, according to the value we have assigned them, they were worth to the government $4,807,764 37.

As nothing has occurred since our report of 27th December, 1849, to induce a change in our opinions respecting the rule which governed us in assigning an equivalent value to each class of liabilities filed, we will repeat the substance of the remarks in said report, as the reasons which guided us in the discharge of that part of our official duty.

TREASURY NOTES.

The first issue of this character of indebtedness is known as the printed interest notes. They were put in circulation during the fall and winter of 1837, for a temporary purpose, and until the engraved notes could be procured; as soon as they were received, the further issue and reissue of the former ceased. This occurred before any perceptible depreciation had taken place, and it was the usage of the department to cancel them as they were received. Hence, the government, for this class of liability, received full consideration, and we have so rated it.

To the engraved interest notes, we have assigned an average value of 50 cents on the dollar. These notes were issued under the provisions of the same act that the printed bills were, and took their place. About the time of the first issue of these notes (the spring of 1838), this species of the government paper commenced depreciating in value, so that, when the act of 19th of January, 1839, prohibiting their further issue, went into operation, they were worth but about 40 cents on the dollar.

To the treasury notes not bearing interest, generally known as "red backs," we have assigned an average value of 25 cents on the dollar. These notes superseded the engraved interest notes above referred to, and the first issue of them was made during the spring of 1839, when they were worth about 37½ cents on the dollar. They continued depreciating, so that in 1841, the government was compelled to pay them out at from 12 to 15 cents on the dollar. The value which we have given them is conceived to be equitable, as an average, both to the government and the holders. It is impossible to ascertain from the date of the issue of these bills, as shown on the face, what they were worth when last paid out. For instance, a bill issued in 1839, at say 37½ cents on the dollar, and after having been returned to the treasury in collection of revenue, may have been reissued the year following at 25 cents on the dollar, and so on; and in 1841, when it may have been last paid out at one-eighth of its ostensible value.

CONSOLIDATED FUNDED DEBT OF 7TH JUNE, 1837.

The stock known by this title was issued under the provisions of an act of Congress approved June 7, 1837, and, could it be analyzed, would be subject to the greatest variety of equivalent rates. We found it impracticable to refer, in each instance, to the original record, to ascertain at what rate each claim had been audited, for which this stock was issued. Even had, or could we have done so, we would have failed to a great extent in acquiring this information, for the reason that the government, for a long time, would not acknowledge any discount on her paper; and the result was that accounts were made out, augmented in amount, so as to make good the deficit in the value of the currency. Hence, the only practicable mode which suggested itself was to make an average of what the stock availed the government; which we accordingly did, and assigned to it a value of seventy cents on the dollar. It is believed that this average is about what the government received in the main, and will, with a few exceptions (which will be alluded to hereafter), fully remunerate the present holders, as it is now generally in the hands of third parties, who, in most instances, acquired it at a much less value from the original *investor* than that now assigned it.

EIGHT AND TEN PER CENT. FUNDED DEBT OF 5TH FEBRUARY, 1840.

We have assigned to this class of securities an average value of thirty cents on the dollar. This stock was issued under the authority of an act of Congress approved February 5, 1840, and was created for the purpose of withdrawing and lessening the amount of revenue currency then in circulation, with a view of enhancing the value of the residue. The inducements held out to the creditors to surrender a revenue currency, and to take one which could not be used in that way, was the promise of the government to pay the stipulated interest semiannually in specie; which, it is well known, she was unable to do. The value attached to this stock may act onerously on some holders, but it will fully remunerate a large majority. It would be much more difficult in this fund than any other to ascertain the exact value the government received for the investments in it, as it is composed of interest notes, " red backs," and audited paper.

EIGHT PER CENT. TREASURY BONDS.

Twenty cents on the dollar is the average equivalent value assigned this class of the government paper. These bonds were issued to supersede, to some extent, and take the place of treasury notes. There is less danger of individual hardship growing out of the assignment of an average equivalent value to these bonds, than that of any other of the government securities : they were seldom ever issued at more than twenty-five cents on the dollar, and rarely less than fifteen cents on the dollar. The value assigned them is deemed equitable.

AUDITED PAPER,

When issued at par, has been allowed accordingly; when less than par, a corresponding deduction has been made; the records and vouchers showing the rate at which it was audited.

In the first class, are included the bonds issued to the Bank of the United States for a loan of $400,000 obtained from that institution in the year 1839; also, the claim of James Holford and associates for the purchase of the steamer "Zavalla." A value corresponding to what the government actually received has been assigned to each.

Since our last report, Messrs. James Schott and E. D. Whitney have filed their claims, composed of one of the bonds issued to Frederick Dawson, of Baltimore, in payment for the navy. These gentlemen, although not known in the contract, are acknowledged by Mr. Dawson to have been equally interested in that transaction; and the readiness manifested in aiding the cause of Texas, by undertaking and carrying out a contract requiring a large pecuniary outlay at a time when the public credit was at an exceeding low stage, procured for the contractors the commendations of the late Republic. In assigning to this claim fifty cents on the dollar, as the value received by the government, we have been governed by the law making the appropriation, and the contract entered into by the agent of the government and Mr. Dawson. This contract, subsequently recognized by legislative enactment (a copy of which accompanies), stipulates the price of the vessels at $280,000; to secure the payment of which, two bonds of the Republic for $280,000 each were deposited with the President of the Girard Bank at Philadelphia, with the understanding that they could be redeemed, at the end of twelve months, by the payment of $280,000 and ten per cent. interest on the two bonds; otherwise, the said bonds to become the property of Mr. Dawson. The government was unable to meet the payment at the time specified; and the president of the bank, according to instructions, delivered the bonds, amounting to $560,000, to Mr. Dawson. We accompany this statement with a communication from Messrs. Schott and Whitney, explanatory of their claim, which is marked "B."

It may be proper to remark that the terms of the contract between the government and James Holford and associates, for the purchase of the steamer "Zavalla," are similar to that entered into with Mr. Dawson.

In the average value assigned to the consolidated fund of 7th June, 1837, there came to our knowledge a few cases of hardship, where the government had received full consideration for the original obligation which had been converted into this fund, and yet owned by the original investor. Had we departed from the rate we had assigned to this or any other character of liability in one instance, no matter how justifiable, others not possessing the same merit would have claimed it; and the consequence would have been, that but few claimants would have been satisfied with any other classification than that of par. For this reason, we determined, in all instances, to adhere to the rate affixed to each class, and report such cases of hardship as might arise, to the Legislature, in order that such relief may be awarded in the premises as appears to be just. We therefore accompany this report with a statement marked " C," of such cases, and hope the same will receive your favorable consideration. In this connection, we refer you to the communication of Dr. John W. King, upon the subject of his claim, which is inclosed in the statement last named.

On the liabilities stipulated to bear interest, we have calculated it from the date of last payment to the 1st of July, 1850, in accordance with an act approved February 11, 1850, except the interest treasury notes, on which we have allowed interest to the 1st of January, 1841; as all holders of this character of notes were required to fund them by that time, and the appropriation for the further payment of interest on said notes was cancelled.

It may be proper to remark that we have attached the same value to the interest which had accrued on the several classes of liabilities that we attached to the liabilities themselves.

THE SECOND CLASS

Is composed of claims against the late Republic of Texas which had not previously been audited, but contracted under the sanction of law. We have assigned to this class of claims, as we did to the first class, an equivalent value proportionate to what each claim availed the government in gold and silver, as far as it was in our power to do. Owing to the large number of claims filed immediately preceding the expiration of the law under which we acted, we have been unable to complete the examination and registration of the second and third classes. We have therefore ascertained, as nearly as practicable, the amount of unexamined claims filed, and report them in bulk.

THE THIRD CLASS.

This class is composed of claims for the auditing of which the existing laws have made no provision, or where the proof is insufficient. In it, however, are many meritorious claims, which will require special legislation to place them on the same footing with valid claims against the government.

A number of claims have been filed for losses sustained during the Revolution and subsequent invasions, being caused by the destruction of property by our own army and that of the enemy. On this character of claims, we have declined taking any action; informing the claimants that the same would be referred to the Legislature, for their consideration and action thereon. These claims, numbered from 1 to 71, amounting to $426,314 03, will be found accompanying, marked "D."

It is necessary that some mode of assignment of the certificates of indebtedness issued should be prescribed by law.

We have audited the claims of those who performed military service, where the needful evidence was on file, regardless of any application of the claimants holding the certificate, subject to his order or that of his legal representative. As many of these parties are now deceased, the proceeds of these claims should inure to the benefit of the heirs of the deceased. We, therefore, respectfully recommend the enactment of the necessary law to protect the rights of the widows and orphans of those who may have fallen in the defence of the country, by prescribing the necessary regulations to prevent persons from administering for the purposes of speculation. A law of this character was enacted by the Congress of the late Republic, for the protection of the estates of deceased soldiers of the Georgia battalion.— [See article 1053, *Hartley's Digest.*]

Statements of several claims that would come under the second class were presented within the term of limitation, but unaccompanied with the needful proof. This the claimants not being able to procure before the expiration of the limit, desire the privilege of producing hereafter. The statements have been filed, but could not be acted on; and it may be a subject worthy of consideration, whether additional time should not be allowed for the presentation of testimony in such cases, if a general extension of the limit be not granted.

Supposing that all the claims against the late government, as shown by the official records, including the amount of supposed unaudited claims outstanding, had been filed as required by law, and assigning each class of those not filed the same equivalent value we have to those filed, the debt would then be as follows:—

	Ostensible.	Par.
Claims filed, of all descriptions, including interest as before stated	$9,647,253 14	$4,807,764 37
Claims not filed, of all descriptions, including interest	2,789,738 20	2,019,514 27
Total debt with interest, including the amount filed and unfiled	$12,436,991 34	$6,827,278 64

All of which will more fully appear by reference to the accompanying statement, marked "A."

Accompanying this report, is a register of the several claims acted on by us, which we respectfully request may be returned when it shall no longer be required by your honorable body.

JOHN M. SWISHER, *Auditor.*
JAMES B. SHAW, *Comptroller.*

V.

MR. PEARCE'S REPORT.

Senate of the United States, August 17, 1852.

The Committee on Finance, to whom were referred sundry memorials from creditors of the late Republic of Texas, report :—

That the object of the memorialists is to obtain directly from the treasury of the United States the payment of their claims against Texas, for which that State had pledged its revenues from customs. They rest their claim upon these grounds :—

First: Because, when one nation is merged in another, " the supereminent power which represents the individual and united sovereignty of both becomes responsible for the debts of the subordinate State."

Second: Because the Government of the United States having appropriated to itself, under the articles of annexation, the revenues of Texas arising from custom-house duties, which were, as the memorialists say, solemnly mortgaged to them for the payment of their respective securities, they have a clear right to ask payment of Congress.

And, third: They consider the obligation of the United States to pay these claims as virtually admitted by the provisions of the act of September, 1850, commonly called the Texas " Boundary Law."

The first of these reasons the committee do not think fairly applicable to the case. It is true that the publicists recognize the doctrine that, when a lawful power contracts, it lays an obligation on the nation itself, and consequently on all the future conductors of the community. So that, when a separate sovereignty or people, being under such obligations, becomes united with and merged in another, the obligations of the government or people so merged fall upon the people or power by whom they are so absorbed ; and that this is a just and proper transfer of obligation must be obvious when it is considered that otherwise the obligations of the community which thus loses its separate existence would be entirely annulled, since there would be no body politic of whom the performance of such obligations could be demanded.

But that is not the case of Texas. Under our peculiar form of government and the articles of annexation, she has indeed parted with her external sovereignty. That, by our constitutional provisions, is vested exclusively in the Union. But her internal sovereignty, though somewhat modified in certain particulars by the Constitution of the United States, still remains in full force and vigor. She is still a separate State, with an independent government; a distinct community, with full power and right to manage her own separate affairs; still liable for her debts, to the payment of which, according to the terms of the contract, she has pledged her faith, her revenues, and her honor; with full capacity to contract new liabilities, with ample resources to pay all her debts, and with every inducement of plighted faith, of public character, of justice and honor, to redeem those obligations which she contracted when her fortunes seemed almost desperate, and which furnished her with the means of securing liberty, independence, and empire.

The second reason, however, has more force.

The publicists maintain that when a province is conquered and the conquest is consummated by cession, it ceases to be a part of the State from which it is wrested, and becomes a stranger to its obligations. "But in that case the conqueror acquires no rights but those of the State with which he is at war, and takes subject to all absolute or qualified alienations previously made." Thus the King of Prussia, when he acquired Silesia by conquest and cession, bound himself by treaty to pay the debts for which that province had been mortgaged to British subjects. But, without such express stipulation, Silesia would still have remained subject to the mortgage, for he could conquer no rights but such as were vested in the enemy.

If this doctrine be true, it will hardly be denied that the peaceful annexation, by legislative compact, of one nation to another, by which the pledged revenues of the one have been transferred to the other, must work a like result, and that the power which takes such pledged revenues must take them *cum onere*. While a separate Republic, Texas had contracted debts by the issue of stock, bonds, and treasury notes, for which she had, in various forms, pledged her revenues from customs. This fact was well known to Congress, as well at the time of annexation as at the period of passing the Texas "Boundary Law." On the former occasion, by the articles of annexation, it was provided that Texas should retain all the vacant and unappropriated lands lying within her limits, to be applied to the payment of her debts and liabilities, which in no event were to become a charge upon the Government of the United States. Under this provision, Texas has bound herself to the United States to pay her liabilities from the proceeds of her public lands, and is estopped from asking the United States to assume these liabilities. But to these articles of annexation, the creditors of Texas were no parties; and while they may well demand of Texas the payment of their securities according to their tenor and form, they are not estopped from saying to the Government of the United States that, as Texas does not pay these securities, and as the United States have possessed themselves of a portion of the resources which were pledged to give value and credit to them, the United States should make them equitable compensation for the diversion of these resources from the purposes to which they were so pledged. This view seems to have been taken by Congress in the passage of the Texas "Boundary Bill." It is provided in that bill that, in consideration of certain concessions of Texas, the United States " shall pay to the State of Texas ten millions of dollars, in a stock bearing five per cent. interest, and redeemable at the end of fourteen years, the interest payable half yearly at the treasury of the United States." But it is also provided that "no more than five millions of said stock shall be issued until the creditors of the State holding bonds and other certificates of stock of Texas, for which duties on imposts were specially pledged, shall first file at the treasury of the United States releases of all claims against the United States for or on account of said bonds or certificates, in such form as shall be prescribed by the Secretary of the Treasury, and approved by the President of the United States." This last provision shows that Congress designed to secure a settlement by Texas with such of her creditors as held evidences of her debt to them, secured by a pledge of the duties on imports, and that the reserved five millions were not to be paid to Texas until she had effected such settlement, and thus relieve the United States from the equitable demand which these creditors might have against the latter government. The proceedings in Congress upon the passage of this act fully confirm this view. It appears, therefore, that the United States have acknowledged a claim by these creditors upon them, and that, at the time of the passage of the said act, the claims of this character were estimated not to exceed five millions of dollars. It has since appeared that, besides the evidences of her debt on the face of which the revenues from customs *eo nomini* were pledged for their payment, there are other evidences of Texan debt, in regard to which the same pledge was given, though not in the same form.

By the act of 7th June, 1837, the Republic of Texas pledged her public faith, and " so much of the *revenues arising from imports*, &c., as may be necessary to meet the annual interest of the funded debt." The loan effected under this act, with interest, was, on the 1st of July, 1850, $1,651,590 02. This class of claims the President of the United States and Secretary of the Treasury consider as coming within the terms of the act of Congress of 1850, since a pledge for the perpetual payment of interest is in effect a pledge for the payment of principal also.

Other loans were made and debts contracted by Texas, to which the same pledge applies by virtue of the fifteenth section of the Texan law of 14th January, 1840. This provides " that for the redemption of all loans negotiated by the authority of Texas, independently of the reservation of the sinking fund, the sales of the public lands, *its revenues*, and public faith are solemnly pledged." This general pledge of "the revenues" of Texas includes a special pledge of the duties on imports. Its effect is precisely the same as if all the sources of revenue were separately designated; since, if this were not the case, the general pledge of its revenues would be a pledge of no single item of revenue, and therefore no pledge of anything at all.

Other debts were created under authority of an act of 5th July, 1840, the third section of which provides that the bonds before referred to shall be at all times *receivable by any collector of revenue,* or at the Treasury Department, in payment of any debt to the government, or any *duties by imports* or direct taxation for the amount and value of such funds, and the interest which may have accrued thereon.

This pledge is evidenced on the face of the issues under this act, the words *receivable* for all government dues being conspicuously printed upon them. This quality of being receivable for all public dues, *duties on imports included,* seems to the committee to be in effect a pledge of duties on imports for their payment. Under this construction, which the President and Secretary of the Treasury have adopted (and as the committee think properly adopted), the amount of Texas debt for which the holders have such an equitable demand, as the committee have before stated, against the United States, considerably exceeds the sum of five millions. The exact amount has not as yet been ascertained by the committee, but it is believed that the whole, principal and interest, exceeds eight millions of dollars.

It is understood that no part of this debt, principal or interest, has been paid by Texas; neither the proceeds of her public lands, according to the articles of annexation, nor the duties from imports, having been in any manner applied to this purpose. Nor has Texas effected any settlement with these creditors whereby the United States have been released from these claims, though nearly two years have elapsed since the passage of the act of Congress of 1850, and more than eighteen months since the acceptance of that act by Texas.

By an act passed on the 31st of January, 1852, the State of Texas has declared its willingness to settle with these creditors, not according to the terms of their contracts, and the tenor of the evidences of debt held by them, except in a few instances, but at certain rates, varying from seventy to twenty per centum.

The second section of this act provides that payment at these reduced rates shall not be made until " the Governor of this State shall be notified by the President of the United States that the Secretary of the Treasury of the United States has been required by law to issue to the State of Texas the five millions of dollars of stock withheld under the provisions of said act, approved 9th September, 1850, until certain creditors shall have filed releases at the Treasury of the United States as therein required, or that said Secretary has been required by law to issue to the said State of Texas sums of said stock equal to the sums for which the State may at any time present the required releases from any portion of said creditors at the Treasury of the United States, after which notice, such claim or claims shall be paid, as provided for in other cases," &c.

This provision is wholly unsatisfactory to the most of the creditors holding these debts, though it would doubtless be accepted by the comparatively few whose claims are scaled at the rate of seventy per cent.

The committee do not think that it would become the United States, by the passage of such a law as is contemplated in the above cited act, to unite with Texas in the effort to compel her creditors to submit to the arbitrary reduction of these claims which Texas proposes. And inasmuch as no portion of these claims has been paid by Texas since the date of annexation, nor any satisfactory arrangement made or proposed for their liquidation and the release of the United States since the passage of the " Boundary Bill," the committee think that the Government of the United States should protect itself from these demands, increasing as they are, for the most part, at the rate of ten per cent. per annum, and relieve the necessities of these creditors, to many of whom longer delay must prove entirely ruinous, by the passage of some act which shall at the same time satisfy the creditors, relieve the United States from further demands by them, and meet the claim of Texas for the reserved five millions.

This they think may be effected by issuing to the said creditors stock of the United States to the amount of $8,555,000, bearing an interest of five per cent. per annum, redeemable at the pleasure of the Government of the United States after —— years, and taking from the creditors their receipts in full and assignments of their evidences of debts, which may be held by the United States as a set-off to the claim of Texas to the five millions reserved under the act of September —, 1850.

This arrangement, it is believed, would be perfectly satisfactory to the creditors of Texas, entirely equitable on the part of the United States, and defensible as regards the State of Texas, while at the same time such provisions may be adopted as in the end will make this arrangement no more burdensome to the National Treasury than if the reserved five millions were applied to these claims or paid to Texas.

W.

DEBTS OF THE REPUBLIC AND DEBTS OF THE STATE.

After the note to Chapter XXX. was in the hands of the printer, we, for the first time, saw a communication on this subject in the Washington Union of March 13, 1852, so much of which as our typographical arrangements will admit of, we shall now give to the reader.

Adverting to the assumption made by some, that "the final decree of Texas, as to the amount and character of the Texas debt, is binding upon the United States Government," the writer says—

"If this be the legal and constitutional construction of the law of the 9th of September, 1850, in which the Federal Government requires certain holders of the debt to release her, as a condition precedent to her paying Texas a given sum of money, the State has a right to certify that there is *no debt*, or that she *owes nothing*, and the United States would be bound by it. The release from the creditors required by the law would be full and complete in a law of the State declaring that there was *no debt*, and this sovereign declaration of a sovereign State to another power equally sovereign would exonerate both from all responsibility for the debt in question.

"The creditors of Texas have the right, *nay*, *have been required*, to present their claims at the treasury in Washington, and in so doing have notified the Federal Government of the amount and character of them. Furthermore, the Secretary of the Treasury, previous to the passage of the late law enacted by the Texas Legislature, had received officially from the authorities of the State, all the laws of the late Republic, creating and authorizing the various classes of debt, as well as the amount and character of it. These laws, passed from 1836 to 1840, 'form,' in the language of the Secretary, ' the basis of the contract between the present holders and the State,' and from them it is ascertained that the amount of the debt is much larger than that *certified* by the recent law of Texas. Now, in adjusting this discrepancy, by which law is Congress to be governed? by that *creating* the debt, or by that *reducing* or *denying* it?

"The cardinal error of those who reason in this way lies in the *unqualified* assumption that, as Texas is a sovereign State, her acts, although subversive of her own constitution, cannot be questioned or set aside by any judicial proceeding. This doctrine is admissible and true as between her and a private citizen, but untenable where the Federal Government or another State is the party litigant. The Constitution of the United States points out the method of adjusting difficulties of this character. The question under discussion involves a case in point. The *Republic* of Texas, by various laws obtained various loans, and issued the evidence of such indebtedness in bonds and treasury notes. When she ceased to exist as a political body, and was merged into the present *State*, the latter bound herself to the United States, in the treaty of annexation, to pay the debt of the former out of the proceeds of the public lands. The State also, in her constitution, secured to the holders of the obligations of the late Republic 'all the rights' which they had against her during her political existence. In other words, the State of Texas, when erected into a member of the Union, declared, in her organic law, that the debt of the Republic should be determined by the laws creating it."

The case appears to us to be briefly this :—

A sovereign State has, by virtue of her sovereignty, the right, *i. e.*, the political power, to repudiate her debts, either wholly or in part, and that with or without reason.

But the legislature of a State is not *The State*. It is a body of limited powers, defined by the constitution of the State, and, in a certain sense, by the Constitution of the United States. As such, the *legislature* of a State has no right to repudiate contract debts ; such an act being subversive of the organic law to which it owes its existence, and by which its powers are defined. If the contract debts of a State are repudiated, it can be only by *The State*, that is, by the people of the State in convention assembled.

The Republic of Texas incurred certain debts for which she pledged her revenue.

The State of Texas, that is, the people of Texas, in convention assembled, in the articles of annexation which they adopted as part of their constitution, assumed these debts as defined by the Republic.

The *Legislature* of Texas has no authority to set aside or define "by municipal regulations," the debts thus assumed by *the State* of Texas.

Texas having failed to discharge these debts according to her compact with the United States, the Federal Government becomes liable for them, both according to the principles of equity and the laws of nations.

The Federal Government is liable for these debts, as defined by the Republic of Texas, and as assumed by the State of Texas, that is, by the people in convention assembled. The Legislature of Texas, a body of limited powers, has no authority to set aside the decisions of the Republic of Texas and of the State of Texas.

The doctrine of State rights cannot, therefore, be invoked in defence of the course the Legislature of Texas has pursued ; and, even if it could, it ought not to be. When State legislatures violate the obligations of contracts, State-Rights men ought to be foremost in denouncing such iniquity.

INDEX.

CATALOGUE

OF

VALUABLE BOOKS,

PUBLISHED BY

LIPPINCOTT, GRAMBO & CO.,

(SUCCESSORS TO GRIGG, ELLIOT & CO.)

NO. 14 NORTH FOURTH STREET, PHILADELPHIA;

CONSISTING OF A LARGE ASSORTMENT OF

Bibles, Prayer-Books, Commentaries, Standard Poets,

MEDICAL, THEOLOGICAL AND MISCELLANEOUS WORKS, ETC.,

PARTICULARLY SUITABLE FOR

PUBLIC AND PRIVATE LIBRARIES.

FOR SALE BY BOOKSELLERS AND COUNTRY MERCHANTS GENERALLY THROUGH-
OUT THE UNITED STATES.

THE BEST & MOST COMPLETE FAMILY COMMENTARY.

The Comprehensive Commentary on the Holy Bible;

CONTAINING

THE TEXT ACCORDING TO THE AUTHORIZED VERSION,

SCOTT'S MARGINAL REFERENCES; MATTHEW HENRY'S COMMENTARY,
CONDENSED, BUT RETAINING EVERY USEFUL THOUGHT; THE
PRACTICAL OBSERVATIONS OF REV. THOMAS SCOTT, D. D.;

WITH EXTENSIVE

EXPLANATORY, CRITICAL AND PHILOLOGICAL NOTES,

Selected from Scott, Doddridge, Gill, Adam Clarke, Patrick, Poole, Lowth,
Burder, Harmer, Calmet, Rosenmueller, Bloomfield, Stuart, Bush, Dwight,
and many other writers on the Scriptures.

The whole designed to be a digest and combination of the advantages of
the best Bible Commentaries, and embracing nearly all that is valuable in

HENRY, SCOTT, AND DODDRIDGE.

Conveniently arranged for family and private reading, and, at the same time,
particularly adapted to the wants of Sabbath-School Teachers and Bible
Classes; with numerous useful tables, and a neatly engraved Family Record.

Edited by Rev. WILLIAM JENKS, D. D.,

PASTOR OF GREEN STREET CHURCH, BOSTON.

Embellished with five portraits, and other elegant engravings, from steel
plates; with several maps and many wood-cuts, illustrative of Scripture
Manners, Customs, Antiquities, &c. In 6 vols. super-royal 8vo.
Including Supplement, bound in cloth, sheep, calf, &c., varying in
Price from $10 to $15.
The whole forming the most valuable as well as the cheapest Commentary
published in the world.

NOTICES AND RECOMMENDATIONS
OF THE
COMPREHENSIVE COMMENTARY.

The Publishers select the following from the testimonials they have received as to the value of the work:

We, the subscribers, having examined the *Comprehensive Commentary*, issued from the press of Messrs. L., G. & Co., and highly approving its character, would cheerfully and confidently recommend it as containing more matter and more advantages than any other with which we are acquainted; and considering the expense incurred, and the excellent manner of its mechanical execution, we believe it to be one of the *cheapest* works ever issued from the press. We hope the publishers will be sustained by a liberal patronage, in their expensive and useful undertaking. We should be pleased to learn that every family in the United States had procured a copy.

B. B. WISNER, D. D., Secretary of Am. Board of Com. for For. Missions.
WM. COGSWELL, D. D., "   " Education Society.
JOHN CODMAN, D. D., Pastor of Congregational Church, Dorchester.
Rev. HUBBARD WINSLOW,   "   " Bowdoin street, Dorchester.
Rev. SEWALL HARDING, Pastor of T. C. Church, Waltham.
Rev. J. H. FAIRCHILD, Pastor of Congregational Church, South Boston.
GARDINER SPRING, D. D., Pastor of Presbyterian Church, New York city.
CYRUS MASON, D. D.,   "   "   "   "   "
THOS. M'AULEY, D. D.,   "   "   "   "   "
JOHN WOODBRIDGE, D. D., "   "   "   "   "
THOS. DEWITT, D. D.,   "   Dutch Ref.   "   "   "
E. W. BALDWIN, D. D.,   "   "   "   "   "
Rev. J. M. M'KREBS,   "   Presbyterian "   "   "
Rev. ERSKINE MASON,   "   "   "   "   "
Rev. J. S. SPENCER,   "   "   "   Brooklyn.
EZRA STILES ELY, D. D., Stated Clerk of Gen. Assem. of Presbyterian Church.
JOHN M'DOWELL, D. D., Permanent "   "   "   "
JOHN BRECKENRIDGE, Corresponding Secretary of Assembly's Board of Education.
SAMUEL B. WYLIE, D. D., Pastor of the Reformed Presbyterian Church.
N. LORD, D. D., President of Dartmouth College.
JOSHUA BATES, D. D., President of Middlebury College.
H. HUMPHREY, D. D.,   "   Amherst College.
E. D. GRIFFIN, D. D.,   "   Williamstown College.
J. WHEELER, D. D.,   "   University of Vermont, at Burlington.
J. M. MATTHEWS, D. D., "   New York City University.
GEORGE E. PIERCE, D. D., "   Western Reserve College, Ohio.
Rev. Dr. BROWN,   "   Jefferson College, Penn.
LEONARD WOODS, D. D., Professor of Theology, Andover Seminary.
THOS. H. SKINNER, D. D., "   Sac. Rhet.   "   "
Rev. RALPH EMERSON,   "   Eccl. Hist.   "   "
Rev. JOEL PARKER, Pastor of Presbyterian Church, New Orleans.
JOEL HAWES, D. D., "   Congregational Church, Hartford, Conn.
N. S. S. BEAMAN, D. D., "   Presbyterian Church, Troy, N. Y.
MARK TUCKER, D. D., "   "   "   "   "
Rev. E. N. KIRK,   "   "   "   Albany, N. Y.
Rev. E. B. EDWARDS, Editor of Quarterly Observer.
Rev. STEPHEN MASON, Pastor First Congregational Church, Nantucket.
Rev. ORIN FOWLER,   "   "   "   "   Fall River.
GEORGE W. BETHUNE, D. D., Pastor of the First Reformed Dutch Church, Philada.
Rev. LYMAN BEECHER, D. D., Cincinnati, Ohio.
Rev. C. D. MALLORY, Pastor Baptist Church, Augusta, Ga.
Rev. S. M. NOEL,   "   "   "   Frankfort, Ky.

From the Professors at Princeton Theological Seminary.

The Comprehensive Commentary contains the whole of Henry's Exposition in a condensed form, Scott's Practical Observations and Marginal References, and a large number of very valuable philological and critical notes, selected from various authors. The work appears to be executed with judgment, fidelity, and care; and will furnish a rich treasure of scriptural knowledge to the Biblical student, and to the teachers of Sabbath-Schools and Bible Classes.

A. ALEXANDER, D. D.
SAMUEL MILLER, D. D.
CHARLES HODGE, D. D.

2

The Companion to the Bible.

In one super-royal volume.

DESIGNED TO ACCOMPANY

THE FAMILY BIBLE,

OR HENRY'S, SCOTT'S, CLARKE'S, GILL'S, OR OTHER COMMENTARIES:

CONTAINING

1. A new, full, and complete Concordance;

Illustrated with monumental, traditional, and oriental engravings, founded on Butterworth's, with Cruden's definitions; forming, it is believed, on many accounts, a more valuable work than either Butterworth, Cruden, or any other similar book in the language.

The value of a Concordance is now generally understood; and those who have used one, consider it indispensable in connection with the Bible.

2. A Guide to the Reading and Study of the Bible;

being Carpenter's valuable Biblical Companion, lately published in London, containing a complete history of the Bible, and forming a most excellent introduction to its study. It embraces the evidences of Christianity, Jewish antiquities, manners, customs, arts, natural history, &c., of the Bible, with notes and engravings added.

3. Complete Biographies of Henry, by Williams; Scott, by his son; Doddridge, by Orton;

with sketches of the lives and characters, and notices of the works, of the writers on the Scriptures who are quoted in the Commentary, living and dead, American and foreign.

This part of the volume not only affords a large quantity of interesting and useful reading for pious families, but will also be a source of gratification to all those who are in the habit of consulting the Commentary; every one naturally feeling a desire to know some particulars of the lives and characters of those whose opinions he seeks. Appended to this part, will be a

BIBLIOTHECA BIBLICA,

or list of the best works on the Bible, of all kinds, arranged under their appropriate heads.

4. A complete Index of the Matter contained in the Bible Text.

5. A Symbolical Dictionary.

A very comprehensive and valuable Dictionary of Scripture Symbols, (occupying about *fifty-nx* closely printed pages,) by Thomas Wemyss, (author of "Biblical Gleanings," &c.) Comprising Daubuz, Lancaster, Hutcheson, &c.

6. The Work contains several other Articles,

Indexes, Tables, &c. &c., and is,

7. Illustrated by a large Plan of Jerusalem,

identifying, as far as tradition, &c., go, the original sites, drawn on the spot by F. Catherwood, of London, architect. Also, two steel engravings of portraits of seven foreign and eight American theological writers, and numerous wood engravings.

The whole forms a desirable and necessary fund of instruction for the use not only of clergymen and Sabbath-school teachers, but also for families. When the great amount of matter it must contain is considered, it will be deemed exceedingly cheap.

"I have examined 'The Companion to the Bible,' and have been surprised to find so much information introduced into a volume of so moderate a size. It contains a library of sacred knowledge and criticism. It will be useful to ministers who own large libraries, and cannot fail to be an invaluable help to every reader of the Bible."
HENRY MORRIS,
Pastor of Congregational Church, Vermont.

The above work can be had in several styles of binding. Price varying from $1 75 to $5 00.

LIPPINCOTT'S EDITION OF
BAGSTER'S COMPREHENSIVE BIBLE.

In order to develope the peculiar nature of the Comprehensive Bible, it will only be necessary to embrace its more prominent features.

1st. The SACRED TEXT is that of the Authorized Version, and is printed from the edition corrected and improved by Dr. Blaney, which, from its accuracy, is considered the standard edition.

2d. The VARIOUS READINGS are faithfully printed from the edition of Dr. Blaney, inclusive of the translation of the proper names, without the addition or diminution of one.

3d. In the CHRONOLOGY, great care has been taken to fix the date of the particular transactions, which has seldom been done with any degree of exactness in any former edition of the Bible.

4th. The NOTES are exclusively philological and explanatory, and are not tinctured with sentiments of any sect or party. They are selected from the most eminent Biblical critics and commentators.

It is hoped that this edition of the Holy Bible will be found to contain the essence of Biblical research and criticism, that lies dispersed through an immense number of volumes.

Such is the nature and design of this edition of the Sacred Volume, which, from the various objects it embraces. the freedom of its pages from all sectarian peculiarities, and the beauty, plainness, and correctness of the typography, that it cannot fail of proving acceptable and useful to Christians of every denomination.

In addition to the usual references to parallel passages, which are quite full and numerous, the student has all the marginal readings, together with a rich selection of *Philological, Critical, Historical, Geographical,* and other valuable notes and remarks, which explain and illustrate the sacred text. Besides the general introduction, containing valuable essays on the genuineness, authenticity, and inspiration of the Holy Scriptures, and other topics of interest, there are introductory and concluding remarks to each book—a table of the contents of the Bible, by which the different portions are so arranged as to read in an historical order.

Arranged at the top of each page is the period in which the prominent events of sacred history took place. The calculations are made for the year of the world before and after Christ, Julian Period, the year of the Olympiad, the year of the building of Rome, and other notations of time. At the close is inserted a Chronological Index of the Bible, according to the computation of Archbishop Ussher. Also, a full and valuable index of the *subjects* contained in the Old and New Testaments, with a careful analysis and arrangement of texts under their appropriate subjects.

Mr. Greenfield, the editor of this work, and for some time previous to his death the superintendent of the editorial department of the British and Foreign Bible Society, was a most extraordinary man. In editing the Comprehensive Bible, his varied and extensive learning was called into successful exercise, and appears in happy combination with sincere piety and a sound judgment. The Editor of the Christian Observer, alluding to this work, in an obituary notice of its author, speaks of it as a work of "prodigious labour and research, at once exhibiting his varied talents and profound erudition."

LIPPINCOTT'S EDITION OF
THE OXFORD QUARTO BIBLE.

The Publishers have spared neither care nor expense in their edition of the Bible; it is printed on the finest white vellum paper, with large and beautiful type, and bound in the most substantial and splendid manner, in the following styles: Velvet, with richly gilt ornaments; Turkey super extra, with gilt clasps; and in numerous others, to suit the taste of the most fastidious.

OPINIONS OF THE PRESS.

"In our opinion, the Christian public generally will feel under great obligations to the publishers of this work for the beautiful taste, arrangement, and delicate neatness with which they have got it out. The intrinsic merit of the Bible recommends itself; it needs no tinsel ornament to adorn its sacred pages. In this edition every superfluous ornament has been avoided, and we have presented us a perfectly chaste specimen of the Bible, without note or comment. It appears to be just what is needed in every family—'the *unsophisticated* word of God.'

"The size is quarto, printed with beautiful type, on white, sized vellum paper, of the finest texture and most beautiful surface. The publishers seem to have been solicitous to make a perfectly unique book, and they have accomplished the object very successfully. We trust that a liberal community will afford them ample remuneration for all the expense and outlay they have necessarily incurred in its publication. It is a standard Bible.

"The publishers are Messrs. Lippincott, Grambo & Co., No. 14 North Fourth street, Philadelphia." — *Baptist Record.*

"A beautiful quarto edition of the Bible. by L., G. & Co. Nothing can exceed the type in clearness and beauty; the paper is of the finest texture, and the whole execution is exceedingly neat. No illustrations or ornamental type are used. Those who prefer a Bible executed in perfect simplicity, yet elegance of style, without adornment, will probably never find one more to their taste." — *M. Magazine.*

LIPPINCOTT'S EDITIONS OF

THE HOLY BIBLE.

SIX DIFFERENT SIZES,

Printed in the best manner, with beautiful type, on the finest sized paper, and bound in the most splendid and substantial styles. Warranted to be correct, and equal to the best English editions, at much less price. To be had with or without plates; the publishers having supplied themselves with over fifty steel engravings, by the first artists.

Baxter's Comprehensive Bible,

Royal quarto, containing the various readings and marginal notes; disquisitions on the genuineness, authenticity, and inspiration of the Holy Scriptures; introductory and concluding remarks to each book; philological and explanatory notes; table of contents, arranged in historical order; a chronological index, and various other matter; forming a suitable book for the study of clergymen, Sabbath-school teachers, and students.

In neat plain binding, from $4 00 to $5 00. — In Turkey morocco, extra, gilt edges, from $8 00 to $12 00. — In do., with splendid plates, $10 00 to $15 00. — In do., bevelled side, gilt clasps and illuminations, $15 00 to $25 00.

The Oxford Quarto Bible,

Without note or comment, universally admitted to be the most beautiful Bible extant.

In neat plain binding, from $4 00 to $5 00. — In Turkey morocco, extra, gilt edges, $8 00 to $12 00. — In do., with steel engravings, $10 00 to $15 00. — In do., clasps, &c., with plates and illuminations, $15 00 to $25 00. — In rich velvet, with gilt ornaments, $25 00 to $50 00.

Crown Octavo Bible,

Printed with large clear type, making a most convenient hand Bible for family use.

In neat plain binding, from 75 cents to $1 50. — In English Turkey morocco, gilt edges, $1 00 to $2 00. — In do., imitation, &c., $1 50 to $3 00. — In do., clasps, &c., $2 50 to $5 00. — In rich velvet, with gilt ornaments, $5 00 to $10 00.

The Sunday-School Teacher's Polyglot Bible, with Maps, &c.,

In neat plain binding, from 60 cents to $1 00. — In imitation gilt edge, $1 00 to $1 50. — In Turkey, super extra, $1 75 to $2 25. — In do. do., with clasps, $2 50 to $3 75. — In velvet, rich gilt ornaments, $3 50 to $8 00.

The Oxford 18mo., or Pew Bible,

In neat plain binding, from 50 cents to $1 00. — In imitation gilt edge, $1 00 to $1 50. — In Turkey, super extra, $1 75 to $2 25. — In do. do., with clasps, $2 50 to $3 75. — In velvet, rich gilt ornaments, $3 50 to $8 00.

Agate 32mo. Bible,

Printed with larger type than any other small or pocket edition extant.

In neat plain binding, from 50 cents to $1 00. — In tucks, or pocket-book style, 75 cents to $1 00. — In roan, imitation gilt edge, $1 00 to $1 50. — In Turkey, super extra, $1 00 to $2 00. — In do. do., gilt clasps, $2 50 to $3 50. — In velvet, with rich gilt ornaments, $3 00 to $7 00.

32mo. Diamond Pocket Bible;

The neatest, smallest, and cheapest edition of the Bible published.

In neat plain binding, from 30 to 50 cents. — In tucks, or pocket-book style, 60 cents to $1 00. — In roan, imitation gilt edge, 75 cents to $1 25. — In Turkey, super extra, $1 00 to $1 50. — In do. do., gilt clasps, $1 50 to $2 00. — In velvet, with richly gilt ornaments, $2 50 to $6 00.

CONSTANTLY ON HAND,

A large assortment of BIBLES, bound in the most splendid and costly styles, with gold and silver ornaments, suitable for presentation; ranging in price from $10 00 to $100 00.

A liberal discount made to Booksellers and Agents by the Publishers.

ENCYCLOPÆDIA OF RELIGIOUS KNOWLEDGE;

OR, DICTIONARY OF THE BIBLE, THEOLOGY, RELIGIOUS BIOGRAPHY, ALL RELIGIONS, ECCLESIASTICAL HISTORY, AND MISSIONS.

Designed as a complete Book of Reference on all Religious Subjects, and Companion to the Bible; forming a cheap and compact Library of Religious Knowledge. Edited by Rev. J. Newton Brown. Illustrated by wood-cuts, maps, and engravings on copper and steel. In one volume, royal 8vo. Price, $4 00.

Lippincott's Standard Editions of
THE BOOK OF COMMON PRAYER.
IN SIX DIFFERENT SIZES,
ILLUSTRATED WITH A NUMBER OF STEEL PLATES AND ILLUMINATIONS.
COMPREHENDING THE MOST VARIED AND SPLENDID ASSORTMENT IN THE
UNITED STATES.

THE ILLUMINATED OCTAVO PRAYER-BOOK,

Printed in seventeen different colours of ink, and illustrated with a number of Steel Plates and Illuminations; making one of the most splendid books published. To be had in any variety of the most superb binding, ranging in prices.

In Turkey, super extra, from $5 00 to $8 00. — In do. do., with clasps, $6 00 to $10 00. — In do. do., bevelled and panelled edges, $8 00 to $15 00. — In velvet, richly ornamented, $12 00 to $20 00.

8vo.

In neat plain binding, from $1 50 to $2 00. — In imitation gilt edge, $2 00 to $3 00. — In Turkey, super extra, $2 50 to $4 50. — In do. do., with clasps, $3 00 to $5 00. — In velvet, richly gilt ornaments, $5 00 to $12 00.

16mo.
Printed throughout with large and elegant type.

In neat plain binding, from 75 cents to $1 50. — In Turkey morocco, extra, with plates, $1 75 to $3 00. — In do. do., with plates, clasps, &c., $2 50 to $5 00. — In velvet, with richly gilt ornaments, $4 00 to $9 00.

18mo.

In neat plain binding, from 25 to 75 cents. — In Turkey morocco, with plates, $1 25 to $2 00. — In velvet, with richly gilt ornaments, $3 00 to $8 00.

32mo.
A beautiful Pocket Edition, with large type.

In neat plain binding, from 50 cents to $1 00. — In roan, imitation gilt edge, 75 cents to $1 50. — In Turkey, super extra, $1 25 to $2 00. — In do. do., gilt clasps, $2 00 to $3 00. — In velvet, with richly gilt ornaments, $3 00 to $7 00.

32mo., Pearl type.

In plain binding, from 25 to 37 1-2 cents. — Roan, 37 1-2 to 50 cents. — Imitation Turkey, 50 cents to $1 00. — Turkey, super extra, with gilt edge, $1 00 to $1 50. — Pocket-book style, 60 to 75 cents.

PROPER LESSONS.
18mo.
A BEAUTIFUL EDITION, WITH LARGE TYPE.

In neat plain binding, from 50 cents to $1 00. — In roan, imitation gilt edge, 75 cents to $1 50. — In Turkey, super extra, $1 50 to $2 00. — In do. do., gilt clasps, $2 50 to $3 00. — In velvet, with richly gilt ornaments, $3 00 to $7 00.

THE BIBLE AND PRAYER-BOOK,
In one neat and portable volume.

32mo., in neat plain binding, from 75 cents to $1 00. — In imitation Turkey, $1 00 to $1 50. — In Turkey, super extra, $1 50 to $2 50.

18mo, in large type, plain, $1 75 to $2 50. — In imitation, $1 00 to $1 75. — In Turkey, super extra, $1 75 to $3 00. Also, with clasps, velvet, &c. &c.

The Errors of Modern Infidelity Illustrated and Refuted.
BY S. M. SCHMUCKER, A. M.
In one volume, 12mo.; cloth. Just published.

We cannot but regard this work, in whatever light we view it in reference to its design, as one of the most masterly productions of the age, and fitted to uproot one of the most fondly cherished and dangerous of all ancient or modern errors. God must bless such a work, armed with his own truth, and doing fierce and successful battle against black infidelity, which would bring His Majesty and Word down to the tribunal of human reason, for condemnation and annihilation.—*Alb. Spectator.*

The Clergy of America:

CONSISTING OF

ANECDOTES ILLUSTRATIVE OF THE CHARACTER OF MINISTERS OF RELIGION IN THE UNITED STATES,

BY JOSEPH BELCHER, D. D.,

Editor of "The Complete Works of Andrew Fuller," "Robert Hall," &c.

" This very interesting and instructive collection of pleasing and solemn remembrances of many pious men, illustrates the character of the day in which they lived, and defines the men more clearly than very elaborate essays." — *Baltimore American.*

" We regard the collection as highly interesting, and judiciously made." — *Presbyterian.*

JOSEPHUS'S (FLAVIUS) WORKS,

FAMILY EDITION.

BY THE LATE WILLIAM WHISTON, A. M.

FROM THE LAST LONDON EDITION, COMPLETE.

One volume, beautifully illustrated with Steel Plates, and the only readable edition published in this country.

As a matter of course, every family in our country has a copy of the Holy Bible; and as the presumption is that the greater portion often consult its pages, we take the liberty of saying to all those that do, that the perusal of the writings of Josephus will be found very interesting and instructive.

All those who wish to possess a beautiful and correct copy of this valuable work, would do well to purchase this edition. It is for sale at all the principal bookstores in the United States, and by country merchants generally in the Southern and Western States.

Also, the above work in two volumes.

BURDER'S VILLAGE SERMONS;

Or, 101 Plain and Short Discourses on the Principal Doctrines of the Gospel.

INTENDED FOR THE USE OF FAMILIES, SUNDAY-SCHOOLS, OR COMPANIES ASSEMBLED FOR RELIGIOUS INSTRUCTION IN COUNTRY VILLAGES.

BY GEORGE BURDER.

To which is added to each Sermon, a Short Prayer, with some General Prayers for Families, Schools, &c., at the end of the work.

COMPLETE IN ONE VOLUME, OCTAVO.

These sermons, which are characterized by a beautiful simplicity, the entire absence of controversy, and a true evangelical spirit, have gone through many and large editions, and been translated into several of the continental languages. " They have also been the honoured means not only of converting many individuals, but also of introducing the Gospel into districts, and even into parish churches, where before it was comparatively unknown."

" This work fully deserves the immortality it has attained."

This is a fine library edition of this invaluable work; and when we say that it should be found in the possession of every family, we only reiterate the sentiments and sincere wishes of all who take a deep interest in the eternal welfare of mankind.

FAMILY PRAYERS AND HYMNS,

ADAPTED TO FAMILY WORSHIP,

AND

TABLES FOR THE REGULAR READING OF THE SCRIPTURES.

By Rev. S. C. WINCHESTER, A. M.,

Late Pastor of the Sixth Presbyterian Church, Philadelphia; and the Presbyterian Church at Natchez, Miss.

One volume, 12mo.

SPLENDID LIBRARY EDITIONS.

ILLUSTRATED STANDARD POETS.

ELEGANTLY PRINTED, ON FINE PAPER, AND UNIFORM IN SIZE AND STYLE.

The following Editions of Standard British Poets are illustrated with numerous Steel Engravings, and may be had in all varieties of binding.

BYRON'S WORKS.

COMPLETE IN ONE VOLUME, OCTAVO.

INCLUDING ALL HIS SUPPRESSED AND ATTRIBUTED POEMS; WITH SIX BEAUTIFUL ENGRAVINGS.

This edition has been carefully compared with the recent London edition of Mr. Murray, and made complete by the addition of more than fifty pages of poems heretofore unpublished in England. Among these there are a number that have never appeared in any American edition; and the publishers believe they are warranted in saying that this is *the most complete edition of Lord Byron's Poetical Works* ever published in the United States.

The Poetical Works of Mrs. Hemans.

Complete in one volume, octavo; with seven beautiful Engravings.

This is a new and complete edition, with a splendid engraved likeness of Mrs. Hemans, on steel, and contains all the Poems in the last London and American editions. With a Critical Preface by Mr. Thatcher, of Boston.

"As no work in the English language can be commended with more confidence, it will argue bad taste in a female in this country to be without a complete edition of the writings of one who was an honour to her sex and to humanity, and whose productions, from first to last, contain no syllable calculated to call a blush to the cheek of modesty and virtue. There is, moreover, in Mrs. Hemans's poetry, a moral purity and a religious feeling which commend it, in an especial manner, to the discriminating reader. No parent or guardian will be under the necessity of imposing restrictions with regard to the free perusal of every production emanating from this gifted woman. There breathes throughout the whole a most eminent exemption from impropriety of thought or diction; and there is at times a pensiveness of tone, a winning sadness in her more serious compositions, which tells of a soul which has been lifted from the contemplation of terrestrial things, to divine communings with beings of a purer world."

MILTON, YOUNG, GRAY, BEATTIE, AND COLLINS'S POETICAL WORKS.

COMPLETE IN ONE VOLUME, OCTAVO.
WITH SIX BEAUTIFUL ENGRAVINGS.

Cowper and Thomson's Prose and Poetical Works.

COMPLETE IN ONE VOLUME, OCTAVO.

Including two hundred and fifty Letters, and sundry Poems of Cowper, never before published in this country; and of Thomson a new and interesting Memoir, and upwards of twenty new Poems, for the first time printed from his own Manuscripts, taken from a late Edition of the Aldine Poets, now publishing in London.

WITH SEVEN BEAUTIFUL ENGRAVINGS.

The distinguished Professor Silliman, speaking of this edition, observes: "I am as much gratified by the elegance and fine taste of your edition, as by the noble tribute of genius and moral excellence which these delightful authors have left for all future generations; and Cowper, especially, is not less conspicuous as a true Christian, moralist and teacher, than as a poet of great power and exquisite taste."

THE POETICAL WORKS OF ROGERS, CAMPBELL, MONTGOMERY, LAMB, AND KIRKE WHITE.

COMPLETE IN ONE VOLUME, OCTAVO.

WITH SIX BEAUTIFUL ENGRAVINGS.

The beauty, correctness, and convenience of this favourite edition of these standard authors are so well known, that it is scarcely necessary to add a word in its favour. It is only necessary to say, that the publishers have now issued an illustrated edition, which greatly enhances its former value. The engravings are excellent and well selected. It is the best library edition extant.

CRABBE, HEBER, AND POLLOK'S POETICAL WORKS.

COMPLETE IN ONE VOLUME, OCTAVO.

WITH SIX BEAUTIFUL ENGRAVINGS.

A writer in the Boston Traveller holds the following language with reference to these valuable editions:—

"Mr. Editor: — I wish, without any idea of puffing, to say a word or two upon the 'Library of English Poets' that is now published at Philadelphia, by Lippincott, Grambo & Co. It is certainly, taking into consideration the elegant manner in which it is printed, and the reasonable price at which it is afforded to purchasers, the best edition of the modern British Poets that has ever been published in this country. Each volume is an octavo of about 500 pages, double columns, stereo-typed, and accompanied with fine engravings and biographical sketches; and most of them are reprinted from Galignani's French edition. As to its value, we need only mention that it contains the entire works of Montgomery, Gray, Beattie, Collins, Byron, Cowper, Thomson, Milton, Young, Rogers, Campbell, Lamb, Hemans, Heber, Kirke White, Crabbe, the Miscellaneous Works of Gold smith, and other masters of the lyre. The publishers are doing a great service by their publication, and their volumes are almost in as great demand as the fashionable novels of the day; and they deserve to be so: for they are certainly printed in a style superior to that in which we have before had the works of the English Poets."

No library can be considered complete without a copy of the above beautiful and cheap editions of the English Poets; and persons ordering all or any of them, will please say Lippincott, Grambo & Co.'s illustrated editions.

A COMPLETE

Dictionary of Poetical Quotations:

COMPRISING THE MOST EXCELLENT AND APPROPRIATE PASSAGES IN THE OLD BRITISH POETS; WITH CHOICE AND COPIOUS SELECTIONS FROM THE BEST MODERN BRITISH AND AMERICAN POETS.

EDITED BY SARAH JOSEPHA HALE.

As nightingales do upon glow-worms feed,
So poets live upon the living light
Of Nature and of Beauty.
Bailey's Festus.

Beautifully illustrated with Engravings. In one super-royal octavo volume, in various bindings.

The publishers extract, from the many highly complimentary notices of the above valuable and beautiful work, the following:

"We have at last a volume of Poetical Quotations worthy of the name. It contains nearly six hundred octavo pages, carefully and tastefully selected from all the home and foreign authors of celebrity. It is invaluable to a writer, while to the ordinary reader it presents every subject at a glance." — *Godey's Lady's Book.*

"The plan or idea of Mrs. Hale's work is felicitous. It is one for which her fine taste, her orderly habits of mind, and her long occupation with literature, has given her peculiar facilities; and thoroughly has she accomplished her task in the work before us." — *Sartain's Magazine.*

"It is a choice collection of poetical extracts from every English and American author worth perusing, from the days of Chaucer to the present time." — *Washington Union.*

"There is nothing negative about this work; it is *positively* good." — *Evening Bulletin.*

THE DIAMOND EDITION OF BYRON.

THE POETICAL WORKS OF LORD BYRON,

WITH A SKETCH OF HIS LIFE.

COMPLETE IN ONE NEAT DUODECIMO VOLUME, WITH STEEL PLATES.

The type of this edition is so perfect, and it is printed with so much care, on fine white paper, that it can be read with as much ease as most of the larger editions. This work is to be had in plain and superb binding, making a beautiful volume for a gift.

" *The Poetical Works of Lord Byron*, complete in one volume ; published by L., G. & Co'., Philadelphia. We hazard nothing in saying that, take it altogether, this is the most elegant work ever issued from the American press.

" 'In a single volume, not larger than an ordinary duodecimo, the publishers have embraced the whole of Lord Byron's Poems, usually printed in ten or twelve volumes ; and, what is more remarkable, have done it with a type so clear and distinct, that, notwithstanding its necessarily small size, it may be read with the utmost facility, even by failing eyes. The book is stereotyped ; and never have we seen a finer specimen of that art. Everything about it is perfect — the paper, the printing, the binding, all correspond with each other ; and it is embellished with two fine engravings, well worthy the companionship in which they are placed.

" 'This will make a beautiful Christmas present.'

" We extract the above from Godey's Lady's Book. The notice itself, we are given to understand, is written by Mrs. Hale.

" We have to add our commendation in favour of this beautiful volume, a copy of which has been sent us by the publishers. The admirers of the noble bard will feel obliged to the enterprise which has prompted the publishers to dare a competition with the numerous editions of his works already in circulation ; and we shall be surprised if this convenient travelling edition does not in a great degree supersede the use of the large octavo works, which have little advantage in size and openness of type, and are much inferior in the qualities of portability and lightness." — *Intelligencer.*

THE DIAMOND EDITION OF MOORE.

(CORRESPONDING WITH BYRON.)

THE POETICAL WORKS OF THOMAS MOORE,

COLLECTED BY HIMSELF.

COMPLETE IN ONE VOLUME.

This work is published uniform with Byron, from the last London edition, and is the most complete printed in the country.

THE DIAMOND EDITION OF SHAKSPEARE,

(COMPLETE IN ONE VOLUME,)

INCLUDING A SKETCH OF HIS LIFE.

UNIFORM WITH BYRON AND MOORE.

THE ABOVE WORKS CAN BE HAD IN SEVERAL VARIETIES OF BINDING.

GOLDSMITH'S ANIMATED NATURE.

IN TWO VOLUMES, OCTAVO.

BEAUTIFULLY ILLUSTRATED WITH 385 PLATES.

CONTAINING A HISTORY OF THE EARTH, ANIMALS, BIRDS, AND FISHES; FORMING THE MOST COMPLETE NATURAL HISTORY EVER PUBLISHED.

This is a work that should be in the library of every family, having been written by one of the most talented authors in the English language.

" Goldsmith can never be made obsolete while delicate genius, exquisite feeling, fine invention, the most harmonious metre, and the happiest diction, are at all valued."

BIGLAND'S NATURAL HISTORY

Of Animals, Birds, Fishes, Reptiles, and Insects. Illustrated with numerous and beautiful Engravings. By JOHN BIGLAND, author of a " View of the World," " Letters on Universal History," &c. Complete in 1 vol., 12mo.

THE FARMER'S AND PLANTER'S ENCYCLOPÆDIA.

The Farmer's and Planter's Encyclopædia of Rural Affairs.
BY CUTHBERT W. JOHNSON.
ADAPTED TO THE UNITED STATES BY GOUVERNEUR EMERSON.

Illustrated by seventeen beautiful Engravings of Cattle, Horses, Sheep, the varieties of Wheat, Barley, Oats, Grasses, the Weeds of Agriculture, &c. ; besides numerous Engravings on wood of the most important implements of Agriculture, &c.

This standard work contains the latest and best information upon all subjects connected with farming, and appertaining to the country ; treating of the great crops of grain, hay, cotton, hemp, tobacco, rice, sugar, &c. &c. ; of horses and mules ; of cattle, with minute particulars relating to cheese and butter-making ; of fowls, including a description of capon-making, with drawings of the instruments employed ; of bees, and the Russian and other systems of managing bees and constructing hives. Long articles on the uses and preparation of bones, lime, guano, and all sorts of animal, mineral, and vegetable substances employed as manures. Descriptions of the most approved ploughs, harrows, threshers, and every other agricultural machine and implement ; of fruit and shade trees, forest trees, and shrubs ; of weeds, and all kinds of flies, and destructive worms and insects, and the best means of getting rid of them ; together with a thousand other matters relating to rural life, about which information is so constantly desired by all residents of the country.

IN ONE LARGE OCTAVO VOLUME.

MASON'S FARRIER—FARMERS' EDITION.
Price, 62 cents.

THE PRACTICAL FARRIER, FOR FARMERS:
COMPRISING A GENERAL DESCRIPTION OF THE NOBLE AND USEFUL ANIMAL,
THE HORSE;
WITH MODES OF MANAGEMENT IN ALL CASES, AND TREATMENT IN DISEASE.
TO WHICH IS ADDED,
A PRIZE ESSAY ON MULES: AND AN APPENDIX,
Containing Recipes for Diseases of Horses, Oxen, Cows, Calves, Sheep, Dogs, Swine, &c. &c.
BY RICHARD MASON, M. D.,
Formerly of Surry County, Virginia.
In one volume, 12mo.; bound in cloth, gilt.

MASON'S FARRIER AND STUD-BOOK—NEW EDITION.

THE GENTLEMAN'S NEW POCKET FARRIER:
COMPRISING A GENERAL DESCRIPTION OF THE NOBLE AND USEFUL ANIMAL,
THE HORSE;
WITH MODES OF MANAGEMENT IN ALL CASES, AND TREATMENT IN DISEASE.
BY RICHARD MASON, M. D.,
Formerly of Surry County, Virginia.
To which is added, A PRIZE ESSAY ON MULES; and AN APPENDIX, containing Recipes for Diseases of Horses, Oxen, Cows, Calves, Sheep, Dogs, Swine, &c. &c. ; with Annals of the Turf, American Stud-Book, Rules for Training, Racing, &c.

WITH A SUPPLEMENT,
Comprising an Essay on Domestic Animals, especially the Horse ; with Remarks on Treatment and Breeding ; together with Trotting and Racing Tables, showing the best time on record at one, two, three and four mile heats ; Pedigrees of Winning Horses, since 1839, and of the most celebrated Stallions and Mares ; with useful Calving and Lambing Tables. By J. S. SKINNER, Editor now of the Farmer's Library, New York, &c. &c.

HINDS'S FARRIERY AND STUD-BOOK—NEW EDITION.

FARRIERY,

TAUGHT ON A NEW AND EASY PLAN:

BEING

A Treatise on the Diseases and Accidents of the Horse;

With Instructions to the Shoeing Smith, Farrier, and Groom; preceded by a Popular Description of the Animal Functions in Health, and how these are to be restored when disordered.

BY JOHN HINDS, VETERINARY SURGEON.

With considerable Additions and Improvements, particularly adapted to this country,

BY THOMAS M. SMITH,

Veterinary Surgeon, and Member of the London Veterinary Medical Society.

WITH A SUPPLEMENT, BY J. S. SKINNER.

The publishers have received numerous flattering notices of the great practical value of these works. The distinguished editor of the American Farmer, speaking of them, observes:—"We cannot too highly recommend these books, and therefore advise every owner of a horse to obtain them."

"There are receipts in those books that show how *Founder* may be cured, and the traveller pursue his journey the next day, by giving a *tablespoonful of alum*. This was got from Dr. P. Thornton, of Montpelier, Rappahannock county, Virginia, as founded on his own observation in several cases."

"The constant demand for Mason's and Hinds's Farrier has induced the publishers, Messrs. Lippincott, Grambo & Co., to put forth new editions, with a 'Supplement' of 100 pages, by J. S. Skinner, Esq. We should have sought to render an acceptable service to our agricultural readers, by giving a chapter from the Supplement, 'On the Relations between Man and the Domestic Animals. especially the Horse, and the Obligations they impose;' or the one on 'The Form of Animals;' but that either one of them would overrun the space here allotted to such subjects."

"Lists of Medicines, and other articles which ought to be at hand about every training and livery stable, and every Farmer's and Breeder's establishment, will be found in these valuable works."

TO CARPENTERS AND MECHANICS.
Just Published.

A NEW AND IMPROVED EDITION OF

THE CARPENTER'S NEW GUIDE,

BEING A COMPLETE BOOK OF LINES FOR

CARPENTRY AND JOINERY;

Treating fully on Practical Geometry, Saffit's Brick and Plaster Groins, Niches of every description, Sky-lights, Lines for Roofs and Domes; with a great variety of Designs for Roofs, Trussed Girders, Floors, Domes, Bridges, &c., Angle Bars for Shop Fronts, &c., and Raking Mouldings.

ALSO,

Additional Plans for various Stair-Cases, with the Lines for producing the Face and Falling Moulds, never before published, and greatly superior to those given in a former edition of this work.

BY WILLIAM JOHNSON, ARCHITECT,
OF PHILADELPHIA.

The whole founded on true Geometrical Principles; the Theory and Practice well explained and fully exemplified, on eighty-three copper plates, including some Observations and Calculations on the Strength of Timber.

BY PETER NICHOLSON,

Author of "The Carpenter and Joiner's Assistant," "The Student's Instructor to the Five Orders," &c.

Thirteenth Edition. One volume, 4to., well bound.

A DICTIONARY OF SELECT AND POPULAR QUOTATIONS,

WHICH ARE IN DAILY USE.

TAKEN FROM THE LATIN, FRENCH, GREEK, SPANISH AND ITALIAN LANGUAGES.

Together with a copious Collection of Law Maxims and Law Terms, translated into English, with Illustrations, Historical and Idiomatic.

NEW AMERICAN EDITION, CORRECTED, WITH ADDITIONS.

One volume, 12mo.

This volume comprises a copious collection of legal and other terms which are in common use, with English translations and historical illustrations; and we should judge its author had surely been to a great "Feast of Languages," and stole all the scraps. A work of this character should have an extensive sale, as it entirely obviates a serious difficulty in which most readers are involved by the frequent occurrence of Latin, Greek, and French passages, which we suppose are introduced by authors for a mere show of learning—a difficulty very perplexing to readers in general. This "Dictionary of Quotations," concerning which too much cannot be said in its favour, effectually removes the difficulty, and gives the reader an advantage over the author; for we believe a majority are themselves ignorant of the meaning of the terms they employ. Very few truly learned authors will insult their readers by introducing Latin or French quotations in their writings, when "plain English" will do as well; but we will not enlarge on this point.

If the book is useful to those unacquainted with other languages, it is no less valuable to the classically educated as a book of reference, and answers all the purposes of a Lexicon — indeed, on many accounts, it is better. It saves the trouble of tumbling over the larger volumes, to which every one, and especially those engaged in the legal profession, are very often subjected. It should have a place in every library in the country.

RUSCHENBERGER'S NATURAL HISTORY,

COMPLETE, WITH NEW GLOSSARY.

The Elements of Natural History,

EMBRACING ZOOLOGY, BOTANY AND GEOLOGY:

FOR SCHOOLS, COLLEGES AND FAMILIES.

BY W. S. W. RUSCHENBERGER, M.D.

IN TWO VOLUMES.

WITH NEARLY ONE THOUSAND ILLUSTRATIONS, AND A COPIOUS GLOSSARY.

Vol. I. contains *Vertebrate Animals.* Vol. II. contains *Invertebrate Animals, Botany, and Geology.*

A Beautiful and Valuable Presentation Book.

THE POET'S OFFERING.

EDITED BY MRS. HALE.

With a Portrait of the Editress, a Splendid Illuminated Title-Page, and Twelve Beautiful Engravings by Sartain. Bound in rich Turkey Morocco, and Extra Cloth, Gilt Edge.

To those who wish to make a present that will never lose its value, this will be found the most desirable Gift-Book ever published.

"We commend it to all who desire to present a friend with a volume not only very beautiful, but of solid intrinsic value." — *Washington Union.*

"A perfect treasury of the thoughts and fancies of the best English and American Poets. The paper and printing are beautiful, and the binding rich, elegant, and substantial; the most sensible and attractive of all the elegant gift-books we have seen." — *Evening Bulletin.*

"The publishers deserve the thanks of the public for so happy a thought, so well executed. The engravings are by the best artists, and the other portions of the work correspond in elegance." — *Public Ledger.*

"There is no book of selections so diversified and appropriate within our knowledge." — *Pennsylv'n.*

"It is one of the most valuable as well as elegant books ever published in this country." — *Godey's Lady's Book.*

"It is the most beautiful and the most useful offering ever bestowed on the public. No individual of literary taste will venture to be without it." — *The City Item.*

15

NEW AND COMPLETE COOK-BOOK.

THE PRACTICAL COOK-BOOK,

CONTAINING UPWARDS OF

ONE THOUSAND RECEIPTS,

Consisting of Directions for Selecting, Preparing, and Cooking all kinds of Meats, Fish, Poultry, and Game; Soups, Broths, Vegetables, and Salads. Also, for making all kinds of Plain and Fancy Breads, Pastes, Puddings, Cakes, Creams, Ices, Jellies, Preserves, Marmalades, &c. &c. &c. Together with various Miscellaneous Recipes, and numerous Preparations for Invalids.

BY MRS. BLISS.

In one volume, 12mo.

The City Merchant; or, The Mysterious Failure.

BY J. B. JONES,

AUTHOR OF "WILD WESTERN SCENES," "THE WESTERN MERCHANT," &c.

ILLUSTRATED WITH TEN ENGRAVINGS.

In one volume, 12mo.

EL PUCHERO; or, A Mixed Dish from Mexico.

EMBRACING GENERAL SCOTT'S CAMPAIGN, WITH SKETCHES OF MILITARY LIFE IN FIELD AND CAMP; OF THE CHARACTER OF THE COUNTRY, MANNERS AND WAYS OF THE PEOPLE, &c.

BY RICHARD M'SHERRY, M. D., U. S. N.,

LATE ACTING SURGEON OF REGIMENT OF MARINES.

In one volume, 12mo.

WITH NUMEROUS ILLUSTRATIONS.

MONEY-BAGS AND TITLES:

A HIT AT THE FOLLIES OF THE AGE.

TRANSLATED FROM THE FRENCH OF JULES SANDEAU.

BY LEONARD MYERS.

One volume, 12mo.

"'*Money-Bags and Titles*' is quite a remarkable work, amounts to a kindly exposure of the folly of human pride, and also presents at once the evil and the remedy. If good-natured ridicule of the impostures practised by a set of self-styled reformers, who have nothing to lose, and to whom change must be gain — if, in short, a delineation of the mistaken ideas which prevent, and the means which conduce to happiness, be traits deserving of commendation, — the reader will find much to enlist his attention and win his approbation in the pages of this unpretending, but truly meritorious publication."

WHAT IS CHURCH HISTORY?

A VINDICATION OF THE IDEA OF HISTORICAL DEVELOPMENTS,

BY PHILIP SCHAF.

TRANSLATED FROM THE GERMAN.

In one volume, 12mo.

17

DODD'S LECTURES.

DISCOURSES TO YOUNG MEN.

ILLUSTRATED BY NUMEROUS HIGHLY INTERESTING ANECDOTES.

BY WILLIAM DODD, LL. D.,

CHAPLAIN IN ORDINARY TO HIS MAJESTY GEORGE THE THIRD.

FIRST AMERICAN EDITION, WITH ENGRAVINGS.

One volume, 18mo.

THE IRIS:

AN ORIGINAL SOUVENIR.

With Contributions from the First Writers in the Country.

EDITED BY PROF. JOHN S. HART.

With Splendid Illuminations and Steel Engravings. Bound in Turkey Morocco and rich Papier Mache Binding.

IN ONE VOLUME, OCTAVO.

Its contents are entirely original. Among the contributors are names well known in the republic of letters; such as Mr. Boker, Mr. Stoddard, Prof. Moffat, Edith May, Mrs. Sigourney, Caroline May, Mrs. Kinney, Mrs. Butler, Mrs. Pease, Mrs. Swift, Mr. Van Bibber, Rev. Charles T. Brooks, Mrs. Dorr, Erastus W. Ellsworth, Miss E. W. Barnes, Mrs. Williams, Mary Young, Dr. Gardette, Alice Carey, Phebe Carey, Augusta Browne, Hamilton Browne, Caroline Eustis, Margaret Junkin, Maria J. B. Browne, Miss Starr, Mrs. Brotherson, Kate Campbell, &c.

Gems from the Sacred Mine;

OR, HOLY THOUGHTS UPON SACRED SUBJECTS.

BY CLERGYMEN OF THE EPISCOPAL CHURCH.

EDITED BY THOMAS WYATT, A. M.

In one volume, 12mo.

WITH SEVEN BEAUTIFUL STEEL ENGRAVINGS.

The contents of this work are chiefly by clergymen of the Episcopal Church. Among the contributors will be found the names of the Right Rev. Bishop Potter, Bishop Hopkins, Bishop Smith, Bishop Johns, and Bishop Doane; and the Rev. Drs. H. V. D. Johns, Coleman, and Butler; Rev. G. T. Bedell, M'Cabe, Ogilsby, &c. The illustrations are rich and exquisitely wrought engravings upon the following subjects: — "Samuel before Eli," "Peter and John healing the Lame Man," "The Resurrection of Christ," "Joseph sold by his Brethren," "The Tables of the Law," "Christ's Agony in the Garden," and "The Flight into Egypt." These subjects, with many others in prose and verse, are ably treated throughout the work.

HAW-HO-NOO:

OR, THE RECORDS OF A TOURIST.

BY CHARLES LANMAN,

Author of "A Summer in the Wilderness," &c. In one volume, 12mo.

"In the present book, 'Haw-ho-noo.' (an Indian name, by the way, for America,) the author has gathered up some of the relics of his former tours, and added to them other interesting matter. It contains a number of carefully written and instructive articles upon the various kinds of fish in our country, whose capture affords sport for anglers; reminiscences of unique incidents, manners, and customs in different parts of the country; and other articles, narrative, descriptive, and sentimental. In a supplement are gathered many curious Indian legends. They are related with great simplicity and clearness, and will be of service hereafter to the poem-makers of America. Many of them are quite beautiful." — *National Intelligencer.*

LIPPINCOTT, GRAMBO & CO.'S PUBLICATIONS.

LONZ POWERS; Or, The Regulators.
A ROMANCE OF KENTUCKY.
FOUNDED ON FACTS.
BY JAMES WEIR, ESQ.
IN TWO VOLUMES.

The scenes, characters, and incidents in these volumes have been copied from nature, and from real life. They are represented as taking place at that period in the history of Kentucky, when the Indian, driven, after many a hard-fought field, from his favourite hunting-ground, was succeeded by a rude and unlettered population, interspersed with organized bands of desperadoes, scarcely less savage than the red men they had displaced. The author possesses a vigorous and graphic pen, and has produced a very interesting romance, which gives us a striking portrait of the times he describes.

THE WESTERN MERCHANT.
A NARRATIVE,
Containing useful Instruction for the Western Man of Business, who makes his Purchases in the East. Also, Information for the Eastern Man, whose Customers are in the West. Likewise, Hints for those who design emigrating to the West. Deduced from actual experience.

BY LUKE SHORTFIELD, A WESTERN MERCHANT.
One volume, 12mo.

This is a new work, and will be found very interesting to the Country Merchant, &c. &c. A sprightly, pleasant book, with a vast amount of information in a very agreeable shape. Business, Love, and Religion are all discussed, and many proper sentiments expressed in regard to each. The "moral" of the work is summed up in the following concluding sentences: "Adhere steadfastly to your business; adhere steadfastly to your first love; adhere steadfastly to the church."

A MANUAL OF POLITENESS,
COMPRISING THE
PRINCIPLES OF ETIQUETTE AND RULES OF BEHAVIOUR
IN GENTEEL SOCIETY, FOR PERSONS OF BOTH SEXES.
18mo., with Plates.

Book of Politeness.
THE GENTLEMAN AND LADY'S
BOOK OF POLITENESS AND PROPRIETY OF DEPORTMENT.
DEDICATED TO THE YOUTH OF BOTH SEXES.
BY MADAME CELNART.
Translated from the Sixth Paris Edition, Enlarged and Improved.
Fifth American Edition.
One volume, 18mo.

THE ANTEDILUVIANS; Or, The World Destroyed.
A NARRATIVE POEM, IN TEN BOOKS.
BY JAMES M'HENRY, M.D.
One volume, 18mo.

19

MECHANICS FOR THE MILLWRIGHT, ENGINEER AND MACHINIST, CIVIL ENGINEER, AND ARCHITECT:

CONTAINING

THE PRINCIPLES OF MECHANICS APPLIED TO MACHINERY

Of American models, Steam-Engines, Water-Works, Navigation, Bridge-building, &c. &c. By

FREDERICK OVERMAN,

Author of "The Manufacture of Iron," and other scientific treatises.

Illustrated by 150 Engravings. In one large 12mo. volume.

WILLIAMS'S TRAVELLER'S AND TOURIST'S GUIDE
Through the United States, Canada, &c.

This book will be found replete with information, not only to the traveller, but likewise to the man of business. In its preparation, an entirely new plan has been adopted, which, we are convinced, needs only a trial to be fully appreciated.

Among its many valuable features, are tables showing at a glance the *distance, fare,* and *time* occupied in travelling from the principal cities to the most important places in the Union; so that the question frequently asked, without obtaining a satisfactory reply, is here answered in full. Other tables show the distances from New York, &c., to domestic and foreign ports, by sea; and also, by way of comparison, from New York and Liverpool to the principal ports beyond and around Cape Horn, &c., as well as *via* the Isthmus of Panama. Accompanied by a large and accurate Map of the United States, including a separate Map of California, Oregon, New Mexico and Utah. Also, a Map of the Island of Cuba, and Plan of the City and Harbor of Havana; and a Map of Niagara River and Falls.

THE LEGISLATIVE GUIDE:

Containing directions for conducting business in the House of Representatives; the Senate of the United States; the Joint Rules of both Houses; a Synopsis of Jefferson's Manual, and copious Indices; together with a concise system of Rules of Order, based on the regulations of the U. S. Congress. Designed to economise time, secure uniformity and despatch in conducting business in all secular meetings, and also in all religious, political, and Legislative Assemblies.

BY JOSEPH BARTLETT BURLEIGH, LL. D.
In one volume, 12mo.

This is considered by our Judges and Congressmen as decidedly the best work of the kind extant. Every young man in the country should have a copy of this book.

THE INITIALS; A Story of Modern Life.
THREE VOLUMES OF THE LONDON EDITION COMPLETE IN ONE VOLUME 12MO.
A new novel, equal to "Jane Eyre."

WILD WESTERN SCENES:
A NARRATIVE OF ADVENTURES IN THE WESTERN WILDERNESS,

Wherein the Exploits of Daniel Boone, the Great American Pioneer, are particularly described. Also, Minute Accounts of Bear, Deer, and Buffalo Hunts — Desperate Conflicts with the Savages — Fishing and Fowling Adventures — Encounters with Serpents, &c.

By LUKE SHORTFIELD, Author of "The Western Merchant."
BEAUTIFULLY ILLUSTRATED. One volume, 12mo.

POEMS OF THE PLEASURES:

Consisting of the PLEASURES OF IMAGINATION, by Akenside; the PLEASURES OF MEMORY, by Samuel Rogers; the PLEASURES OF HOPE, by Campbell; and the PLEASURES OF FRIENDSHIP, by M'Henry. With a Memoir of each Author, prepared expressly for this work. 18mo.

23

BALDWIN'S PRONOUNCING GAZETTEER.

A PRONOUNCING GAZETTEER:

CONTAINING

TOPOGRAPHICAL, STATISTICAL, AND OTHER INFORMATION, OF ALL THE MORE IM-
PORTANT PLACES IN THE KNOWN WORLD, FROM THE MOST
RECENT AND AUTHENTIC SOURCES.

BY THOMAS BALDWIN.

Assisted by several other Gentlemen.

To which is added an APPENDIX, containing more than TEN THOUSAND ADDITIONAL NAMES,
chiefly of the small Towns and Villages, &c., of the United States and of Mexico.

NINTH EDITION, WITH A SUPPLEMENT,

Giving the Pronunciation of near two thousand names, besides those pronounced in the Original
Work : Forming in itself a Complete Vocabulary of Geographical Pronunciation.

ONE VOLUME 12MO.—PRICE, $1.50.

Arthur's Library for the Household.

Complete in Twelve handsome 18mo. Volumes, bound in Scarlet Cloth.

1. WOMAN'S TRIALS; OR, TALES AND SKETCHES FROM THE LIFE AROUND US.
2. MARRIED LIFE; ITS SHADOWS AND SUNSHINE.
3. THE TWO WIVES; OR LOST AND WON.
4. THE WAYS OF PROVIDENCE; OR, "HE DOETH ALL THINGS WELL."
5. HOME SCENES AND HOME INFLUENCES.
6. STORIES FOR YOUNG HOUSEKEEPERS.
7. LESSONS IN LIFE, FOR ALL WHO WILL READ THEM.
8. SEED-TIME AND HARVEST; OR, WHATSOEVER A MAN SOWETH THAT SHALL HE
ALSO REAP.
9. STORIES FOR PARENTS.
10. OFF-HAND SKETCHES, A LITTLE DASHED WITH HUMOR.
11. WORDS FOR THE WISE.
12. THE TRIED AND THE TEMPTED.

The above Series are sold together or separate, as each work is complete in itself. No Family should
be without a copy of this interesting and instructive Series. Price Thirty-seven and a Half Cents per
Volume.

FIELD'S SCRAP BOOK.—New Edition.

Literary and Miscellaneous Scrap Book.

Consisting of Tales and Anecdotes — Biographical, Historical, Patriotic, Moral, Religious, and Sentimental Pieces, in Prose and Poetry.

COMPILED BY WILLIAM FIELDS.

SECOND EDITION, REVISED AND IMPROVED.

In one handsome 8vo. Volume. Price, $2.00.

THE ARKANSAW DOCTOR.

THE LIFE AND ADVENTURES OF AN ARKANSAW DOCTOR.

BY DAVID RATTLEHEAD, M. D.

"*The Man of Scrapes.*"

WITH NUMEROUS ILLUSTRATIONS. PRICE FIFTY CENTS.

THE HUMAN BODY AND ITS CONNEXION WITH MAN.

ILLUSTRATED BY THE PRINCIPAL ORGANS.

BY JAMES JOHN GARTH WILKINSON,

Member of the Royal College of Surgeons of England.

IN ONE VOLUME, 12MO—PRICE $1 25.

BOARDMAN'S BIBLE IN THE FAMILY.

𝕮𝖍𝖊 𝕭𝖎𝖇𝖑𝖊 𝖎𝖓 𝖙𝖍𝖊 𝕱𝖆𝖒𝖎𝖑𝖞:

OR,

HINTS ON DOMESTIC HAPPINESS.

BY H. A. BOARDMAN,

PASTOR OF THE TENTH PRESBYTERIAN CHURCH, PHILADELPHIA.

One Volume 12mo.—Price, One Dollar.

WHEELER'S HISTORY OF NORTH CAROLINA.

𝕳𝖎𝖘𝖙𝖔𝖗𝖎𝖈𝖆𝖑 𝕾𝖐𝖊𝖙𝖈𝖍𝖊𝖘

OF

NORTH CAROLINA,

From 1584 to 1851.

Compiled from Original Records, Official Documents, and Traditional Statements ; with Biographical Sketches of her Distinguished Statesmen, Jurists, Lawyers, Soldiers, Divines, &c.

BY JOHN H. WHEELER,

Late Treasurer of the State.

IN ONE VOLUME OCTAVO.—PRICE, $2.00.

THE NORTH CAROLINA READER:

CONTAINING

A HISTORY AND DESCRIPTION OF NORTH CAROLINA, SELECTIONS IN PROSE AND VERSE, (MANY OF THEM BY EMINENT CITIZENS OF THE STATE), HISTORICAL AND CHRONOLOGICAL TABLES,

𝕬𝖓𝖉 𝖆 𝖁𝖆𝖗𝖎𝖊𝖙𝖞 𝖔𝖋 𝕸𝖎𝖘𝖈𝖊𝖑𝖑𝖆𝖓𝖊𝖔𝖚𝖘 𝕴𝖓𝖋𝖔𝖗𝖒𝖆𝖙𝖎𝖔𝖓 𝖆𝖓𝖉 𝕾𝖙𝖆𝖙𝖎𝖘𝖙𝖎𝖈𝖘.

BY C. H. WILEY.

"My own green land for ever!
Land of the beautiful and brave—
The freeman's home—the martyr's grave."

Illustrated with Engravings, and designed for Families and Schools.

ONE VOLUME 12MO. PRICE $1.00.

THIRTY YEARS WITH THE INDIAN TRIBES.

PERSONAL MEMOIRS

OF A

𝕽𝖊𝖘𝖎𝖉𝖊𝖓𝖈𝖊 𝖔𝖋 𝕮𝖍𝖎𝖗𝖙𝖞 𝖄𝖊𝖆𝖗𝖘 𝖜𝖎𝖙𝖍 𝖙𝖍𝖊 𝕴𝖓𝖉𝖎𝖆𝖓 𝕿𝖗𝖎𝖇𝖊𝖘

ON THE AMERICAN FRONTIERS:

With brief Notices of passing Events, Facts, and Opinions,

A. D. 1812 TO A. D. 1842.

BY HENRY R. SCHOOLCRAFT.

ONE LARGE OCTAVO VOLUME. PRICE THREE DOLLARS.

THE SCALP HUNTERS:

OR,

ROMANTIC ADVENTURES IN NORTHERN MEXICO.

BY CAPTAIN MAYNE REID,

AUTHOR OF THE "RIFLE RANGERS."

Complete in One Volume. Price Fifty Cents.

FROST'S JUVENILE SERIES.

TWELVE VOLUMES, 16mo., WITH FIVE HUNDRED ENGRAVINGS.

WALTER O'NEILL, OR THE PLEASURE OF DOING GOOD. 25 Engrav'gs.
JUNKER SCHOTT, and other Stories. 6 Engravings.
THE LADY OF THE LURLEI, and other Stories. 12 Engravings.
ELLEN'S BIRTHDAY, and other Stories. 20 Engravings.
HERMAN, and other Stories. 9 Engravings.
KING TREGEWALL'S DAUGHTER, and other Stories. 16 Engravings.
THE DROWNED BOY, and other Stories. 6 Engravings.
THE PICTORIAL RHYME-BOOK. 122 Engravings.
THE PICTORIAL NURSERY BOOK. 117 Engravings.
THE GOOD CHILD'S REWARD. 115 Engravings.
ALPHABET OF QUADRUPEDS. 26 Engravings.
ALPHABET OF BIRDS. 26 Engravings.

PRICE, TWENTY-FIVE CENTS EACH.

The above popular and attractive series of New Juveniles for the Young, are sold together or separately.

THE MILLINER AND THE MILLIONAIRE.

BY MRS. REBECCA HICKS,

(Of Virginia,) Author of "The Lady Killer," &c. One volume, 12mo.

Price, 37½ cents.

STANSBURY'S
EXPEDITION TO THE GREAT SALT LAKE.

AN EXPLORATION
OF THE VALLEY OF THE GREAT SALT LAKE
OF UTAH,

CONTAINING ITS GEOGRAPHY, NATURAL HISTORY, MINERALOGICAL RE-
SOURCES, ANALYSIS OF ITS WATERS, AND AN AUTHENTIC ACCOUNT OF

THE MORMON SETTLEMENT.

ALSO,

A RECONNOISSANCE OF A NEW ROUTE THROUGH THE ROCKY MOUNTAINS.

WITH SEVENTY BEAUTIFUL ILLUSTRATIONS,

FROM DRAWINGS TAKEN ON THE SPOT,

AND TWO LARGE AND ACCURATE MAPS OF THAT REGION.

BY HOWARD STANSBURY,

CAPTAIN TOPOGRAPHICAL ENGINEERS.

One volume, royal octavo.

ARTHUR'S
𝕹𝖊𝖜 𝕵𝖚𝖛𝖊𝖓𝖎𝖑𝖊 𝕷𝖎𝖇𝖗𝖆𝖗𝖞.

BEAUTIFULLY ILLUSTRATED,

1. WHO IS GREATEST? and other Stories.
2. WHO ARE HAPPIEST? and other Stories.
3. THE POOR WOOD-CUTTER, and other Stories.
4. MAGGY'S BABY, and other Stories.
5. MR. HAVEN'T-GOT-TIME AND MR. DON'T-BE-IN-A-HURRY.
6. THE PEACEMAKERS.
7. UNCLE BEN'S NEW-YEAR'S GIFT, and other Stories.
8. THE WOUNDED BOY, and other Stories.
9. THE LOST CHILDREN, and other Stories.
10. OUR HARRY, and other Poems and Stories.
11.
12.

EACH VOLUME IS ILLUSTRATED WITH
ENGRAVINGS FROM ORIGINAL DESIGNS BY CROOME,
And are sold together or separately.

BYRNE ON FOOD AND HEALTH.

A TREATISE

ON THE

ADULTERATION OF FOOD AND DRINK,

AND

PLAIN AND SIMPLE DIRECTIONS FOR DETECTING THEM,

WITH

ONE HUNDRED RECIPES

FOR **TOOTH-POWDERS, HAIR DYES, SKIN POWDERS, PERFUMES, &c.**

BY M. P. BYRNE, M. D.

One Volume, 12mo., Cloth Gilt. Price, Fifty Cents.

THE THIRD AND CONCLUDING VOLUME OF

HISTORICAL SKETCH

OF THE

SECOND WAR BETWEEN THE U. STATES AND GREAT BRITAIN.

IN THREE VOLUMES, OCTAVO.